DOING BUSINESS IN THE
KNOWLEDGE-BASED ECONOMY
Facts and Policy Challenges

DOING BUSINESS IN THE KNOWLEDGE-BASED ECONOMY
Facts and Policy Challenges

edited by

Louis A. Lefebvre

Elisabeth Lefebvre

Pierre Mohnen

Published in association with

 Industrie Canada   Industry Canada

KLUWER ACADEMIC PUBLISHERS
Boston / Dordrecht / London

Distributors for North, Central and South America:
Kluwer Academic Publishers
101 Philip Drive
Assinippi Park
Norwell, Massachusetts 02061 USA
Telephone (781) 871-6600
Fax (781) 871-6528
E-Mail <kluwer@wkap.com>

Distributors for all other countries:
Kluwer Academic Publishers Group
Distribution Centre
Post Office Box 322
3300 AH Dordrecht, THE NETHERLANDS
Telephone 31 78 6392 392
Fax 31 78 6546 474
E-Mail <services@wkap.nl>

 Electronic Services <http://www.wkap.nl>

Library of Congress Cataloging-in-Publication Data

Doing business in the knowledge-based economy : facts and policy challenges / edited
by Louis A. Lefebvre, Élisabeth Lefebvre and Pierre Mohnen.
    p. cm.
  Includes bibliographical references and index.
  ISBN 0-7923-7244-1 (alk. paper)
   1. Knowledge management--Congresses. 2. Management information
systems--Congresses. 3. Management--Data processing--Congresses. 4. Business--Data
processing--Congresses. 5. Electronic commerce--Congresses. 6. International
trade--Congresses. 7. Information technology--Economic aspects--Congresses. 8.
Information technology--Government policy--Congresses. I. Lefebvre, L.A. II.
Lefebvre Élisabeth. III. Mohnen, Pierre A.

HD30.2 .D64 2000
658.4'038--dc21   00-051988

Printed on acid-free paper. Printed in the United States of America

TABLE OF CONTENTS

CONTRIBUTORS

John R. Baldwin
Statistics Canada
Ottawa, Ontario

Frederick Betz
University of Maryland
College Park, MD

Marcel Boyer
École Polytechnique de Montréal,
Université de Montréal & CIRANO
Montréal, Québec

Cécile Carpentier
Université Laval
Québec, Québec

Paul Chwelos
University of British Columbia,
Vancouver, B.C.

Iain M. Cockburn
NBER and Boston University
Boston, MA

Patrick Cohendet
Université Louis-Pasteur
Strasbourg, France

John E. Ettlie
Rochester Institute of Technology
Rochester, NY

Dominique Foray
Université Paris-Dauphiné
Paris, France

Guy Gellatly
Statistics Canada
Ottawa, Ontario

Surendra Gera
Industry Canada
Ottawa, Ontario

Dominique Guellec
OECD
Paris, France

Jean-François L'Her
École des Hautes Écoles Commerciales de
Montréal & CIRANO
Montréal, Québec

Clifton Lee-Sing
Industry Canada
Ottawa, Ontario

Louis A. Lefebvre
École Polytechnique de Montréal &
CIRANO
Montréal, Québec

Élisabeth Lefebvre
École Polytechnique de Montréal &
CIRANO
Montréal, Québec

Sunder Magun
Applied International Economics Inc.
Ottawa, Ontario

Jacques Mairesse
CREST & NBER
Paris, France

Pierre Mohnen
Université du Québec à Montréal &
CIRANO
Montréal, Québec

Randall Morck
University of Alberta
Edmonton, Alberta

Keith Newton
Carleton University
Ottawa, Ontario

Maria-Angels Oliva
MIT Sloan School of Management
Cambridge, MA

Luis A. Rivera-Batiz
McGill University, Montréal, Québec
Universitat Pompeu Fabra
Inter-American Development Bank

Jacques Robert
Université de Montréal & CIRANO
Montréal, Québec

Hugues Santerre
CIRANO
Montréal, Québec

Luc Soete
University of Maastricht & MERIT
Maastricht, Netherlands

Jean-Marc Suret
Université Laval & CIRANO
Québec, Québec

Bernard Yeung
University of Michigan
Ann Arbor, MI

ACKNOWLEDGMENTS

The contributions to this book are the result of a conference sponsored by Industry Canada and CIRANO on the theme of "Doing business in the KBE." We are indebted to our colleagues who agreed to share their ideas and experiences with us and make this a truly international exchange of views on a very important issue facing many countries and societies. The papers remain the sole responsibility of the authors and do not necessarily reflect the policies or opinions of Industry Canada or the Government of Canada.

FOREWORD

On September 17 and 18, 1998, a conference took place at Mont Tremblant on the theme "Doing Business in a Knowledge-Based Economy." This conference brought together some hundred participants from government, business and academia, with backgrounds in business administration, engineering, public administration and economics, to provide a multidisciplinary analysis of what has come to be known as the "Knowledge-Based Economy" (KBE). The aim was to come up with suggestions and recommendations about how to do business in a knowledge-based economy, both at the firm level and at the government level. All presenters were explicitly asked to conclude with policy recommendations. The conference was sponsored by Industry Canada and organized by the Centre of Interuniversity Research on the Analysis of Organizations (CIRANO). The conference papers offered U.S., Canadian and European perspectives on the management of a knowledge-based economy.

This volume is divided into three parts. The papers in part I set the stage by describing the salient features of the KBE. What is so special about it? What are its economic underpinnings? What are its technological characteristics? Knowledge plays a crucial role in a KBE, hence its name. Whereas, in the past, growth was determined primarily by the availability of land, natural resources, labour and capital successively, at the end of the twentieth century, knowledge has become a (if not the) major factor of economic growth. Humanity has always searched for ways to alleviate the struggle to produce basic necessities and has usually, at the height of great civilizations, devoted specific resources towards the development of science and technology. What makes knowledge so important today is the progress of information and communication technologies (ICT), the increased level and widespread availability of public education, the increase in wealth, and the mobility of resources (capital, labour, enterpreneurship and even, to some extent, natural resources). Progress in the means of transportation, lowering of barriers to trade, and technological advances in ICT have transformed the world into a global village. In this new setting, we have reached a stage where competition has become fiercer and is increasingly dictated by innovativeness, access to networks, and proficiency in the use of ICT, all of which increase the demand for qualified and highly skilled labour.

Surendra Gera, Clifton Lee-Sing and Keith Newton illustrate, with convincing statistics, the above state of affairs and some of its ramifications: increased trade, foreign direct investment, the shift of economic activity towards services, and the rising importance of intangibles (R&D, patents, networks). They assess where Canada stands along all these yardsticks characterizing a KBE. Randall Morck and Bernard Yeung, in their first contribution to this volume, explain the inner workings of a KBE, its economic and political underpinnings, and its social and economic consequences. Knowledge is the prime weapon of competition and comes in various forms: knowledge of technologies, yes, but also of marketing and distribution. It is essential to know what the customer wants, what suppliers and competitors can produce, and how it can be delivered to the customer at the right time and at the best price. Appropriability, empowerment, flexibility, and incentives, but also risk, the need to learn and adapt, and unequal distribution of income are part of the game. Louis-André Lefebvre, Élisabeth Lefebvre and Pierre Mohnen focus on the characteristics of virtual enterprises and their extension to the notion of a virtual economy. Virtual enterprises operate in virtuality, integrating numerous stages of production along the product value chain in order to maximize the value delivered to the consumer. E-commerce is the most visible form of the virtual economy, but it is only the tip of the iceberg. The virtual economy rests on four pillars: economic integration, global information infrastructures, virtual enterprises and networks, and technologies evolving towards a common platform. The movement of a KBE towards a virtual economy has many consequences and raises a number of policy challenges which are analyzed in the paper.

The papers in part II of the volume analyze in greater detail a selected number of management issues and economic phenomena typical of a KBE. Three papers deal with organizational issues. Keith Newton and Sunder Magun emphasize the need to adopt strategies of organizational learning and intellectual capital management in order to prosper in a KBE. They review the literature for definitions and metrics of organizational learning and intellectual capital and present empirical evidence supporting the link between organizational learning and economic performance. On the basis of case studies, they show the important factors underlying corporate success in a KBE. What makes new technology adoption and implementation successful? What can government do to make it more successful? Those are the questions that John Ettlie examines in light of U.S. manufacturing companies' experience with knowledge management. He shows that it is not so much the number of new technologies adopted that matters as the particular mix and the concomitant organizational changes. The more radical the technological departure, the more radical the required organizational change. Enterprise integration (ERP) and E-commerce are two of the most vivid examples. Ettlie then goes over a number of policy actions taken by the U.S. government and examines their success in improving firms' performance. Frederick Betz stresses how essential it is to build strategic partnerships between government, industry and universities to combine science and technology. The cultures, values and reward systems are different in these three types of institutions. Betz lists a number of conditions for successful cooperation between the three partners, having to do with focus, scope, completeness and timing.

The next three papers touch upon policy issues specific to knowledge-based firms: how to distinguish high-tech from low-tech, how to evaluate knowledge-intensive firms, and how much leeway to grant knowledge-based firms in forming strategic alliances to internalize their knowledge spillovers. John Baldwin and Guy Gellatly criticize the usual classification of firms into high-tech, medium-tech and low-tech categories according to their R&D intensity. Instead, they propose a multidimensional, firm-based classification. They distinguish three dimensions of innovation – introduction of new products or processes, purchase and adoption of new technologies, and development of human capital – and demonstrate, with data on new small technology-based firms, that firms need not be innovative in all dimensions and that industries traditionally regarded as low-tech are not devoid of high-tech firms. Jean-Marc Suret, Cécile Carpentier and Jean-François L'Her compare various methods of evaluating knowledge-based start-up firms. Their econometric analysis shows that Canadian R&D-based firms listed on the stock exchange have a lower rate of return, and hence cost of capital, than non-R&D-based firms. At least for these firms, there does not seem to be any problem accessing financing. Another manifestation of a KBE is the search for synergies and diversification across R&D projects. Maria-Angels Oliva and Luis Rivera-Batiz examine the wave of mergers and acquisitions involving R&D-intensive firms in the pharmaceutical and biotechnology industries. Under pressure to introduce new products, reduce costs due to the rise of generics, and cope with delays in patent approvals, many pharmaceutical firms acquired biotech firms in the 1990s; there was a predominance of European acquisitions of U.S.-based biotech firms. The authors also note that the most regulated countries are the least innovative in those two fields.

The last set of papers, forming part III, is directly oriented towards questions of political economy and economic policy considerations. Luc

Soete analyses a set of policy issues related to electronic commerce. They can be technical i (e.g., questions of security, privacy, consumer protection), economic (e.g., open standards, compatibility, interconnectivity) or societal (new possibilities for data-mining, communication, increased financial services and government services). Patrick Cohendet, Dominique Foray, Dominique Guellec and Jacques Mairesse revisit the issue of the public management of R&D externalities. They articulate and qualify the classical tradeoff between knowledge diffusion and invention protection. Iain Cockburn and Paul Chwelos review the challenges in the area of international property rights in a KBE, in particular regarding biotechnology, software and digital intellectual property. Marcel Boyer, Jacques Robert and Hugues Santerre address some of the reasons for success or failure to implement organizational and technological changes. They explain, and illustrate with case studies, a set of principles of organizational change. Randall Morck and Bernard Yeung, in their policy paper, argue forcefully for embarking on a whole range of public policy directions. The basic thrust of their recommendations is that an innovative, empowering and competitive government must be in charge of public policy.

Élisabeth Lefebvre, Pierre Mohnen and Louis-André Lefebvre wrap up the volume by summarizing what we have learned in this conference about how firms and government ought to do business in a knowledge-based economy.

Louis A. Lefebvre
École Polytechnique, CIRANO

Élisabeth Lefebvre
École Polytechnique, CIRANO

Pierre Mohnen
Université du Québec à Montréal, CIRANO

CIRANO, January 2001

1. THE EMERGING GLOBAL KNOWLEDGE-BASED ECONOMY: TRENDS AND FORCES

Surendra Gera
Industry Canada

Clifton Lee-Sing
Industry Canada

Keith Newton
Carleton University

This paper was prepared for the *Doing Business in the Knowledge-Based Economy: Facts and Policy Challenges* Conference sponsored by CIRANO and Industry Canada, September 21-22, 1998. The views expressed in this paper are those of the authors and do not necessarily reflect those of Industry Canada. We are most grateful to Denis Gauthier and Ron Hirshhorn for their valuable insights throughout various stages of the project.

1. INTRODUCTION

The dramatic changes that are under way in the global economy provide the backdrop to this conference. It is widely recognized that the "rules of the game" for economies and for firms are changing, and that a central feature of this change in the global economic environment is an increase in the role and importance of knowledge. In the new economic order, the fortunes of firms, workers and economies have all come to depend largely on the development, acquisition and use of knowledge.

This paper explores these and related shifts taking place within individual economies and internationally. Our examination of broad macro trends and forces underlying the emergence of a global knowledge-based economy complements the other micro-based studies prepared for this conference.

With an appreciation of the transformation under way in the global economy and the major changes occurring in the pattern of Canadian economic activity, we can better understand the challenges confronting individual Canadian firms. We can also gain a useful "top-down" perspective on the research needed to understand the prospects of Canadian firms and industries in the new global economic order.

The term "knowledge-based economy" was coined by the OECD to give recognition to the crucial role knowledge, in all its forms, plays in economic processes: "Intangible investment is growing more rapidly than physical investment. Individuals with more knowledge get better paid jobs, firms with more knowledge are winners on markets and nations endowed with more knowledge are more productive" (OECD, 1996a). In this paper, we argue that the emergence of the knowledge-based economy, which is linked to the information revolution and also to the increasing internationalization of business, represents a paradigm shift. It involves a deep structural change that differs in size and pervasiveness from the incremental changes to which the economy is constantly subject. Industrialized economies are being transformed by the increasing emphasis on cognitive skills, the development of ideas, the assimilation of technologies and participation in international networks for the exchange of products, capital and knowledge. The emergence of the knowledge-based economy is being accompanied by changes in economic activities and organizational processes that require major adjustments by economies, firms and individuals.

Various strands of economic literature can help us understand the significance and implications of the changes that are taking place within industrialized economies. In particular, new growth theory, with its emphasis on the critical role of knowledge creation and human capital accumulation, provides a useful framework within which to examine the emergence of knowledge-based economic systems.

The rest of the paper is organized as follows. We begin by highlighting a number of key features of the new global economy in Section 2. This is followed by an examination of the major forces propelling change and shaping the transformation of world economies in Section 3. Section 4 draws on the economic literature, including new growth theory and studies of historical experience, to identify the defining features of a knowledge-based economy (KBE). The main focus is on the macro-economic characteristics of a KBE, but consideration is also given to the changes that must occur within individual firms as countries evolve into knowledge-based economies. In Section 5, we review various pieces of evidence to assess how well Canada conforms to the model of a knowledge-based economy. The general features of the Canadian economy are examined against the background of the discussion that was set out in Section 3; the structural changes taking place in the economy are reviewed; and some areas where the Canadian economy seems to lag behind the requirements for knowledge-based growth are identified. The final section draws together the paper's conclusions and identifies some key issues for further research.

2. KEY FEATURES OF THE NEW GLOBAL ECONOMY

Suppose the main economic developments over the past few decades could be represented on a world map, much as changes in day-to-day weather patterns are indicated on climate maps. What are the major patterns that would strike an observer? From among the various shifts in economic activity, we believe five broad developments would stand out.

The first is the increased openness of the world economy. Economic boundary lines have declined in importance because of a number of developments, including the implementation of the World Trade Organization (WTO) multilateral trade agreement along with regional trade agreements such as the European Union and NAFTA; a substantial reduction in foreign investment restrictions; and internal market reforms (mainly deregulation and privatization) that have expanded opportunities for international competition. From 1985 to 1997, world exports increased from US$1,970 to US$5,475 billion. At the same time, major multinational enterprises (MNEs), some with revenues approximating the GDPs of small countries (i.e., General Motors, Ford, Toyota, Exxon, Royal Dutch/Shell, IBM), have become a more important factor in the global economy. Largely stateless MNEs, with operations dispersed to take advantage of capabilities and opportunities around the world, now account for a major share of the world's production, investment and trade.

A second and related development is the increased global importance of a number of emerging economies. While recent economic turmoil has removed some of the shine from the economic performance of the so-called Dynamic Asian Economies, Singapore, Hong Kong, South Korea, and Taiwan – along with other countries including India, China and Brazil – have become major centres of industrial activity with strong trade and investment linkages with the G-7 countries. The improvement in living standards achieved by a number of these emerging economies contrasts with the sluggish performance of most African and many Eastern European countries and the slowdown in economic growth in major industrialized economies over the past few decades.

A third development that would stand out on our map is the changing composition of production in more advanced economies. As firms in major OECD countries have responded to economic pressures and opportunities, there has been a shift from goods to service production and, within services themselves, from lower to higher value-added activities. The growth in the importance of service production can be clearly seen in Figure 1.

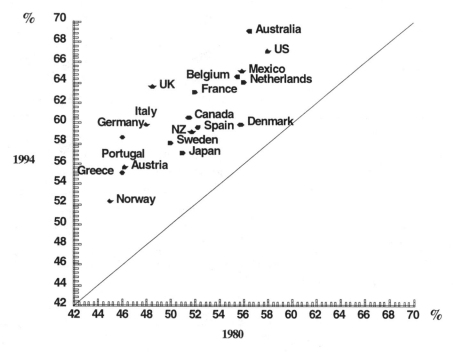

Figure 1: Evolution of the share services in value-added in the business sector

Knowledge-based activities, which include high-technology manufacturing along with finance, insurance and business services, and communications services, accounted for a third or more of business growth over 1985-1994 in Canada, the U.K., France, and the U.S. The changing composition of production has been accompanied by a growth in the demand for high-skilled workers. Figure 2 shows the shift towards employment of high-skilled white-collar and away from low-skilled blue-collar workers that has occurred between 1980-1994 in a number of major OECD countries.

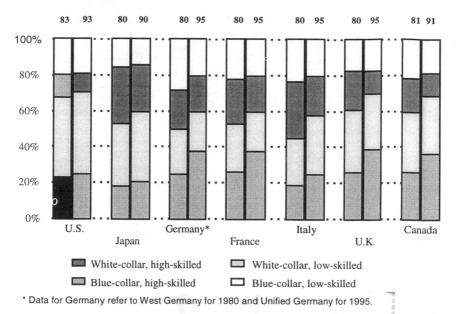

* Data for Germany refer to West Germany for 1980 and Unified Germany for 1995.

Figure 2: Trends in the distribution of skills in total employment

The fourth development that would strike an observer is the revolutionary change in information and communications technology (ICT). Increasingly powerful computer and communications products have changed the nature of goods and service production, and have impacted on international transactions and pervaded the lives of individuals in industrialized economies, touching them in their roles as workers, consumers, patients, students, and members of various communities of interest. Between 1990 and 1995, ICT sales rose 60% faster than world GDP. At close to $US1.4 trillion, 1995 worldwide ICT sales were equivalent to more than 5% of world GDP. Traditional communications networks have expanded rapidly – with, for example, the global base of main telephone lines increasing from 388 million in 1984 to almost 700 million in 1995 – but the most dramatic growth has occurred in new systems that are a product of recent technological advances. Over the past decade, annual growth in the number of cellular telephone subscribers has exceeded 60%, while the rate of growth of the worldwide Internet has exceeded 100% per year.

A fifth and related development has been the emergence of new arrangements of work, production, shopping and education, based on the application of ICTs. "Virtual firms" and "virtual factories" have come into being as entrepreneurs take advantage of the new opportunities for reducing transaction costs.[1] Firms such as Amazon.com, the Internet bookseller listed on the New York Stock Exchange, are carving out a market by relying exclusively on electronic commerce. In other cases, virtual enterprises have been formed by distinct business entities that have used electronic systems to link and coordinate their production. Electronic modes of business activity that change the nature of markets and market competition are increasing in popularity. Global estimates of 1997 e-commerce range from US$10.4 to $27 billion. Over the next five years, global e-commerce is projected to explode, reaching a level in 2002 that is 30 to 45 times the 1997 estimates. At the same time, the application of ICTs is presenting individuals with new options in other areas. Teleworking has become an attractive alternative for some workers. Telelearning and telehealth have become important vehicles for ensuring service availability to residents in distant locations. An observer of our economic map would be struck by the significant and growing role of these and other forms of electronic interchange and interaction.

The major structural shifts that are under way have not impacted to the same extent on all economies. Within industrial economies, not all industries, firms and individuals have significantly participated in developments affecting production, markets and competition. Moreover, some structural changes that have occurred over the past few decades are evolutionary in nature – an extension of secular trends that have existed for a long period. But some of what we are observing is the result of powerful new forces that are fundamentally reshaping the economic landscape. We now turn to an examination of these forces.

3.   THE NEW GLOBAL ECONOMY: FORCES DRIVING THE TRANSFORMATION

While a number of factors underlie the developments described above, we would argue that there are two forces that have been central to these events and to the emergence of the new economic order: the increasing internationalization of production and the increased drive for new knowledge. Through their interaction, these factors are exerting a major influence on the course and direction of global economic activity.

The increasing internationalization of production is partly a result of the growth in world trade. More significant, however, has been the growth in foreign direct investment (FDI) along with other transactions that support international production, including subcontracting, licensing, franchising and alliances.

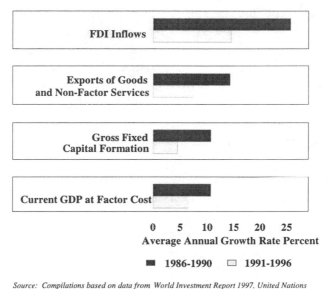

Source: *Compilations based on data from World Investment Report 1997, United Nations*

Figure 3:   Growth of world FDI, exports, grass fixed capital
formation and GDP

While exports of goods and services have grown more rapidly than world output over the past decade, FDI flows have outpaced the growth of world trade (Figure 3). The growth of FDI has been particularly rapid over the 1990s. Through this foreign investment, the world's 45,000 MNEs have established approximately 280,000 affiliates and created jobs for about 75 million workers. The sales of goods and services by foreign affiliates are estimated to be one and a half times the value of world exports.

Globalization itself is not a new phenomenon. In the decades before 1914, foreign trade and international financial transactions also represented a very high share of global economic activity. But in this earlier period we did not witness the internationalization of business. The period before 1914 was, to use Bradford De Long's (1997) apt phrase, a "low bandwidth" international environment, which was quite different from the "high bandwidth" global economy we have today. In this earlier period, it was not possible to exercise corporate control across national boundaries, to coordinate operations being performed in different countries, and to establish the strong communication links needed to closely monitor the activities of foreign suppliers and the demands of foreign consumers (Bradford De Long, 1997). A main feature of the present-day globalization is the growing interdependence between FDI, trade, transfer of technology and capital transfers. FDI flows generate exports from the countries making the investments. In turn, these exports are accompanied by transfer of technology and know-how, and capital movements.

Highly mobile investment and footloose MNEs that shift discrete segments of the value-added chain among countries to reduce costs, improve sales or reduce risks are hallmarks of the new age of internationalized business. As MNEs scan the globe in search of new synergies, we are witnessing a process of deepening global economic integration. The increased flows of goods, services and technology among dispersed units of MNEs account for the growing importance of intrafirm trade, and also, to some extent, the increase in interindustry trade. It is estimated that about one-third of world trade now occurs within firms. Between 1982 and 1994, intrafirm exports increased from 44% to 55% of the total exports by foreign firms in developed countries. The growth in foreign direct investment has been accompanied by an increase in interfirm collaboration. Firms have turned to international agreements, including joint ventures, non-equity agreements and minority participation, to gain access to new markets, to acquire new technologies or new resources, to reduce project costs and risks, and to overcome regulatory impediments. As Globerman and Wolf (1994) discuss, joint ventures are often used by firms that lack product or geographic market knowledge as an early entry strategy into international markets undergoing rapid structural change. The number of collaboration agreements doubled during the 1980s and has subsequently remained at a high level (Table 1). The highest proportion of agreements has involved large firms in Europe, the U.S. and Japan in sectors such as automobiles, electronics, aerospace, telecommunications and computers.

Table 1: Collaboration agreements 1980-1992

		Average Number Per Year					
		1980-84	1985-89	1990-92			
		120	240	220			
Main Regions*	%	Main Industries*		%	Main Purpose		%
Within Europe	30	Automotive		21	Development		31
Europe – North America	23	Electronics		17	Production		25
Europe – Japan	15	Aerospace		15	Marketing		13
North America – Japan	11	Telecommunications		14	Mixed		30
Within North America	10	Computers		13			
Other	10	Other		20			

* Includes collaboration agreements before 1980

The second major force, the increased drive for new knowledge, is inextricably linked with the first; the much heightened emphasis on knowledge acquisition is both a cause and a consequence of the increasing internationalization of production. The highly sophisticated information and communications products that have come about through innovation and the emphasis on knowledge acquisition have played a key role in the growth of MNEs. The ability of MNEs to exercise control over foreign affiliates and integrate activities performed in widely dispersed units has been gradually enhanced by the introduction of more powerful and less costly computing and communications products and services. The left-hand panel of Figure 4 illustrates the dramatic declines in computer processing costs and transmission costs that have been important contributors to the growing internationalization of business. Using e-mail, firms can transmit documents to several overseas offices at a fraction of the cost and in a fraction of the time formerly required to send the information to a single overseas recipient (right-hand panel of Figure 4).

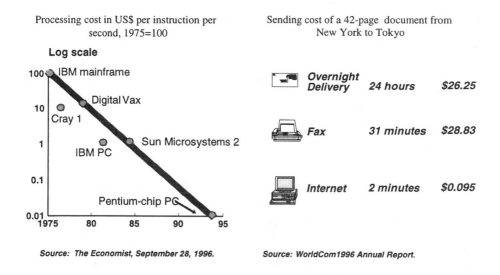

Figure 4 : Computer processing costs and transmission costs

At the same time, the new technologies have themselves been an important focus of global trade and investment. The role of technology in the expansion of international trade is illustrated in Figure 5, which highlights the growing importance of high technology[2] exports in OECD countries. The ICT products have experienced particularly strong international market growth and now account for more than a tenth of international merchandise trade. A substantial portion of overseas investment has also been directed towards high-technology products such as computers, semiconductors, drugs and pharmaceuticals, telecommunications products, aerospace and scientific instruments. Firms often prefer to invest abroad rather than to sell or license new leading-edge technologies because markets for new technology tend to be highly imperfect and licensing can create competitive risks.

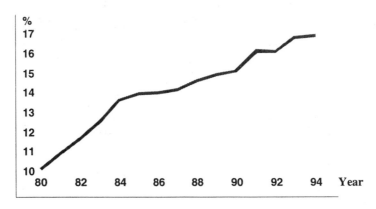

Source: OECD, Technology, Productivity and Job Creation - Best Policy Practices, 1998a

Figure 5: High-technology exports as a share of total OECD manufacturing exports

As noted above, causation also works in the other direction: the increasing importance of new knowledge is, as well, a consequence of global economic integration. There are a number of channels through which the growth of global business contributes to the emphasis on knowledge acquisition. First, global markets increase the potential return from innovation. Firms can devote increased resources to research and development when the resulting product and process innovations can be marketed internationally. And global markets can justify R&D that would be uneconomic for firms serving only domestic markets.

Second, the internationalization of production, and the accompanying intensification of international competition, have increased the pressure on firms to acquire new knowledge. While, in globally integrated markets, firms can realize higher profits from successful innovation, they also face an increased risk of failure if they do not invest in the development of new products and processes. This may arise through product obsolescence – a danger which applies particularly, but not solely, to firms in the high-technology sectors. Less innovative firms also face the risk that their productivity will lag behind that of more innovation-oriented firms and their cost structure will become uncompetitive. While firms may be able to perform at a high level by acquiring modern technology rather than investing in development of new equipment and processes, firms that invest significantly in R&D have tended to achieve higher productivity than firms undertaking little or no R&D (Figure 6).

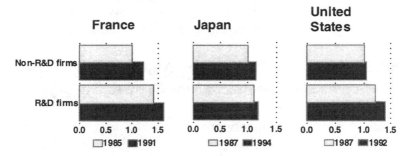

* Labour productivity levels expressed relative to non-R&D firms in initial period (=1).

Figure 6: Comparative productivity for R&D and non R&D firms*

The increased importance attached to the acquisition of new knowledge is reflected in the increased commitment to R&D. Among OECD countries, R&D expenditures increased from 1.2% of GDP in 1981 to 1.5% in 1995. In some newly industrializing economies, the increases over this period were more dramatic - with, for example, R&D expenditures as a share of GDP doubling to 1.8% of GDP in Chinese Taipei and quadrupling to 2.8% of GDP in Korea. Another indicator of the increasing pressure to innovate is the strong upward trend in the number of patents granted in the U.S., the patent country of choice for many innovators worldwide.[3]

The importance of knowledge acquisition has long been recognized, but it has acquired a new urgency in the increasingly integrated global economy. The internationalization of production is creating new incentives and opportunities and generating new pressures for knowledge acquisition. It is the interaction of the mutually reinforcing pressures from the internationalization of business and the drive for new knowledge that makes the emerging business environment quite different from anything experienced in the past.

4.   TOWARDS A KNOWLEDGE-BASED ECONOMY

While all countries are being confronted by the forces described above, some economies are better positioned than others to benefit from the transformation in the structure of the global economy. What are the characteristics of those economies that are well advanced in their evolution towards "knowledge-based economies"? This is a huge question that incorporates many of the specific issues addressed in other papers prepared for this conference; in more general terms, it can be partly answered from existing literature. In this section, we selectively review a number of important strands of theoretical and empirical research that help point towards the defining features of a knowledge-based economy.

4.1   Understanding the Unique Nature and Role of Knowledge: The Insights of New Growth Theory

The insights of new growth theory provide a useful starting point in this exercise. While the role of knowledge is central in new growth theory, the crucial importance of knowledge had, of course, been recognized long before recent theoretical developments using general equilibrium models. Classical economists such as Schumpeter and Marx were well aware of the important contribution of knowledge accumulation, in the form of technological progress, to long-term growth. Similarly, neoclassical growth models developed by Solow and Swan and, subsequently, others demonstrated how technological progress was necessary for sustained long-run growth. In an environment of diminishing returns on capital, the savings generated by new investment will ultimately only be able to support the replacement of worn-out machines and the equipping of new workers; advances in technology are necessary to offset the downward trend in the marginal product of capital and to overcome the tendency towards stagnating per capita incomes. In one exercise in which he inserted U.S. data for the 40-year period up to 1949 into his model, Solow (1957) found that technological progress accounted for more than four-fifths of the measured growth in output per worker. This and other early work, such as the growth-accounting studies of Denison (1962), highlighted the important role of technological change. But it did not provide insights into the *process* of technological change and the actions needed to augment technological progress.

The new growth theories take us, to some extent, inside the "black box" of technological change. The new models start with the neoclassical production function and add to it a theory about how technological progress occurs.

Increases in output can be sustained in the long run through knowledge-related investments which are not subject to diminishing returns at the aggregate level. Such investments give rise to beneficial external effects which offset the limiting consequences of increasing capital per worker within a given firm; hence, while investments by individual firms remain subject to diminishing returns, there is no decline in the overall marginal product of capital.

Central to the new theories is the unique "non-rivalrous" character of knowledge. The consumption of a non-rivalrous good by one individual does not impair the ability of others to enjoy the same good. Moreover, knowledge can be passed from user to user at close to zero cost. Based on the special characteristics of knowledge, it has been demonstrated how externalities arise from, *inter alia*, investment in capital embodying new technology (Romer, 1986), the development of human capital (Lucas, 1988), and investment in R&D (Romer, 1990).

The new growth theories highlight a number of other considerations that must be well understood within economies that aspire to be KBEs. First, unlike the neoclassical models, which treated new technology as a fortuitous outcome of scientific breakthroughs, the new growth theories recognize that knowledge is not free; economies have to forego current consumption to pay for the development of knowledge. Second, there is recognition that valuable additions to the stock of knowledge can come in many forms; while some innovations will lead to advances in "hard" technologies, others will create value through the development of more "synergistic" forms of organization or more imaginative processes for managing, training and rewarding workers.

Third, the theories show that the characteristics that make knowledge a highly valuable and productive commodity also make it difficult to establish an efficient knowledge market – that is, a market that provides incentives for both the production of knowledge and its distribution to all those who can benefit from it. In the endogenous models, to help create the needed incentives for firms to invest in knowledge development, markets are assumed to be imperfectly competitive. In the current context, this issue has implications for a wide range of government policies, including those pertaining to the protection of intellectual property, the treatment of R&D, expenditures in support of university research, and public investment in education. While innovations with direct commercial application can be partially protected through patents, more general discoveries with potential widespread benefits cannot and should not be protected. Difficult questions are involved in designing an overall policy framework that provides appropriate protection for proprietary technologies and, at the same time, creates appropriate incentives for the development of more general knowledge, including both basic science and generic technologies. KBEs are beginning to grapple with these issues and will need to devote serious efforts to designing policies that address basic deficiencies within the knowledge market.

4.2   Taking Account of the Influence of Market Size and Openness

In a KBE, large markets and openness to foreign trade and investment contribute to knowledge development and knowledge acquisition. The importance of these factors is illustrated by some of the literature that falls under the heading of what Nelson and Winter (1982) term "appreciative theorizing," economic reasoning that is closely based on empirical findings but lacks the logical rigour of formal theorizing.

One interesting group of such studies has focused on explaining the United States' important early technology lead that dates to before the turn of the century. Researchers such as Rosenberg (1982) and Wright (1990) have pointed to the advantages the U.S. acquired over the 19th century because of both its ample natural resources and its large markets. A large population of relatively homogeneous consumers and relatively well-developed transport links encouraged firms to invest in the technology to produce long production runs of standardized goods. This, in turn, led to the production of specialized machines and encouraged inventive activity aimed at producing both improved capital and consumer goods. At a time when international trade was limited, the U.S. was in a highly favourable position compared with other countries because of its large domestic market. The central message that large markets are important in creating incentives for knowledge production remains relevant and important.

Additional insights can be gathered from research exploring the nature of the U.S. technological lead over Japan and Europe. The U.S. successfully maintained its lead in the interwar years, but after World War II, Europe and Japan achieved considerable progress in closing the technological gap. Postwar developments are consistent with a convergence process; over this period, European and Japanese firms took advantage of the major opportunities to increase productivity and profits by adopting American technology and practices. The puzzle as to why a similar process did not occur in the interwar years has been examined by Nelson and Wright (1992).

They attribute the difference to the greater trade and increased flow of financial and physical capital in the postwar era. As compared to the interwar years, the postwar environment was more conducive to the international flow of technology and to the adoption of capital-intensive processes that required access to large markets. This piece of historical evidence underlines the role of openness along with well-developed trade and investment links in both facilitating access to knowledge and creating the necessary conditions for adoption of the new technology.

More recent evidence further documents the important role of trade and investment as mechanisms of knowledge acquisition. In their study of OECD economies, for example, Coe and Helpman (1995) found that total productivity growth in smaller economies was more responsive to changes in the R&D of their main trading partners than to changes in domestic R&D. There is a large literature, some of which is reviewed in Blomström (1991), documenting the benefits host countries derive from technology transfers to MNE subsidiaries and spillovers to other host-country firms. MNEs account for an estimated 75% to 80% of all global, civilian R&D,[4] and foreign affiliates have privileged access to the resulting innovations. Moreover, along with new technology, MNEs often transfer specific skills and on-the-job know-how that is needed to effectively utilize new technology but is difficult to acquire separately. Bernstein (1994) looks more generally at the R&D spillovers between Canada and the U.S. arising from trade, investment and other formal and informal mechanisms. He finds that R&D spillovers from the U.S. exert a greater influence on Canadian industries than domestic spillovers and are a major contributor to total factor productivity growth rates in Canada.

4.3   Building a Supportive Infrastructure

In a KBE, domestic institutions support knowledge development and acquisition. Here again, the convergence literature is instructive. Most recent studies examining the experience of developing economies have found that economies in which productivity or per capita incomes have most significantly converged towards U.S. levels are characterized not only by a high degree of openness but also by the presence of certain conditioning factors.[5] An economy's ability to take advantage of international knowledge transfers has been found to depend particularly on its level of human capital development and rate of capital formation.

A broad range of other institutional factors affect an economy's capacity to take advantage of new technology, although their influence has generally been more difficult to isolate quantitatively.[6] Factors identified include: a stable political environment; efficient financial institutions; modern physical infrastructure; high-quality management training; a strong base of civic institutions; and well-developed economic adjustment mechanisms.

Institutional factors are of importance partly because of their influence on foreign and domestic investment. There is increasing recognition that economies that wish to enjoy the knowledge transfers from foreign direct investment (as discussed above) must establish a fiscal and regulatory environment that compares favourably from a business perspective with that in competing jurisdictions. At the same time, domestic investment is important because much new knowledge is embodied in investment capital; investment is a major vehicle through which new technology enters into the productive process. In knowledge-based economies, therefore, attention is devoted to encouraging investment, and strengthening institutional factors, such as the efficiency of capital markets and the state of the country's physical infrastructure, that may affect the investment process. In KBEs, there is a recognition that, where inadequacies in infrastructure or the structure of capital markets constrain or distort investment, technological change could in turn be significantly impaired.

Special importance attaches to information infrastructure, which has become the main focus of interest in industrial economies, drawing at least as much attention as was devoted in earlier decades to transportation facilities, local utilities and public buildings. KBEs recognize the important contribution of advanced information systems in facilitating access to knowledge and promoting the spread of ideas. Accordingly, they are committed to establishing advanced communications networks, ensuring the development of accompanying applications for manipulating and transmitting information, and building a policy and regulatory framework that supports the development and use of information hardware and applications.

In the term "infrastructure" we would also include those intangible factors that influence an economy's ability to take advantage of new knowledge. The education and training of the labour force is one key factor, as has been documented in the convergence literature. Recent studies suggest that investment in human capital has become more important within industrialized economies.[7] Within OECD economies, technological change is raising the relative demand for skilled workers and correspondingly reducing the requirement for unskilled workers (Berman, Bound and Machin, 1997). There is growing recognition that, along with enhancing educational opportunities and devising more effective teaching approaches, KBEs must invest in retraining and in facilitating the movement towards lifelong learning.[8]

The capabilities of an economy depend, as well, on the level of management training and those diverse factors that influence management culture and the way firms organize (Newton, 1997). Management and organizational practices will help determine how receptive firms are to new information. They will also determine how successfully firms implement complex new technologies that may involve major changes in work procedures and significant on-the-job learning.

In this area, as well, some of the most significant contributions have come from historical studies. In his account of the rise of large-scale industry in the U.S., for example, Chandler (1962) describes the important contribution of professional management and the evolution of new organizational structures. As operations became more complex, firms needed to restructure their operations so they had a capacity to respond to both short-term market demands and long-term market trends. The success of U.S. firms such as DuPont was due partly to their capacity to implement new organizational arrangements that addressed the inadequacies in the traditional centralized management structure. Now, as then, one of the characteristics of more successful economies is likely to be the presence of dynamic organizations that can transform themselves so they are well positioned to respond to new opportunities.

4.4   Incorporating   New   Understandings   About   the Innovation Process

From recent research on the innovative process, it is possible to add some additional details to our sketch of the institutional characteristics of KBEs. New research challenges the traditional linear model which compartmentalized innovation into separate phases of basic research, applied research, and development and commercialization. Innovation is now seen to be more of a cumulative, interactive and continuous process involving researchers, engineers and technicians, and users of technology.

As one aspect of this new understanding, there is now an increased appreciation of the role of tacit or uncodified knowledge. This knowledge, which comes from doing and using rather than formal instruction and plays an important role in the implementation of new technologies, is now recognized to also be an important factor in the innovation process. Studies by Rosenberg (1982) and others have found that users of technologies have made an important contribution by identifying problems and stimulating the stream of improvements needed to make new technologies operationally useful.

There is, as well, a better understanding of how innovation is often a result of insights gained from marrying knowledge in different disciplines, different activities and different industries. There can be important benefits, therefore, from arrangements that promote cooperation and cross-fertilization both within and between organizations. This suggests that in KBEs, efforts would be directed towards encouraging the sorts of interactions among organizations, researchers and technicians that can lead to new findings.

Another significant change has involved the development of closer links between science and technology. In fields such as biotechnology, computers and telecommunications, much new technological development involves efforts to build on new scientific insights. At the same time, scientific discoveries tend to find their way into commercial applications more quickly than in the past.

For firms, these findings raise questions about how to structure their operations to allow opportunities for fruitful interaction among workers with different expertise. They also suggest the need to open channels of communication with users and to explore possibilities for cooperative research and development ventures with other organizations, including firms developing complementary technologies in other industries.

For governments, traditional policies aimed at supporting research in which social returns exceed private returns would be supplemented by measures that take account of the broad nature of spillovers in innovative activities. Hence, governments may attempt to use their research support to promote potentially beneficial linkages between scientific and engineering workers in different industries and in government and academia. New understandings about the innovation process are also likely to reinforce the importance of building an information and communications infrastructure that supports information-sharing and cooperation among scientific researchers and between scientists and others involved in the innovative process.

4.5   A Sum-Up

What emerges from all this is not a precise definition of a KBE, but an indication of some important developments impacting on industrialized economies (see inset), along with a rough representation of an idealized KBE and the organizations within this economy. While countries are evolving as KBEs along somewhat different paths, successful economies are likely to rank high in a number of the characteristics highlighted in our literature review. Moreover, the firms in successful economies are likely to have certain distinguishing features.

In terms of the economy itself, a first major feature would be the commitment to the development of new knowledge, broadly defined. Large markets and an open trade environment help create an incentive for innovation and allow for the implementation of technologies involving significant scale economies. At the same time, support is available to encourage research into more general areas of knowledge development where intellectual property rights cannot reasonably be established and enforced. The policy and institutional environment also promotes the beneficial spillovers from encouraging interaction and cooperation among researchers in different institutions, disciplines and industries.

Towards a definition of a KBE

- Precise definitions are elusive but most would stress the global nature of the new economy and the importance of continuous innovation, and of information and communications technologies:
  - many would agree that knowledge is now the critical factor in the production process and the principal source of competitive advantage; and
  - many maintain that it is the ability to harness "tacit" (as well as "codified") knowledge that is the key to continuous innovation
- What is new about the knowledge economy is that the very nature of the production function has undergone radical and irreversible change:
  - the concept of *land* has changed; telecommunications have rendered location increasingly meaningless; more and more offices are becoming virtual;
  - *labour* has changed ("brains, not brawn"); the very notion of a "job" is questioned;
  - *capital* used to be machinery and equipment and money in the bank; now we must distinguish among physical, financial, human, structural, organizational, social and intellectual capital – to name just a few types;
  - *raw materials* carry diminishing weight; think of the amount of sand that goes into a microchip versus the amount of brainpower; and
  - the *management* function in the production process is also changing profoundly: hierarchies are giving way to teamwork and participative decision-making.

Second, KBEs are characterized by well-developed mechanisms to enhance access to knowledge developed in other countries. In particular, efforts are directed to developing the two major formal mechanisms of knowledge transfer – trade and foreign direct investment. Government policies in a KBE give recognition to the importance of creating a business environment which is attractive to foreign direct investment.

Third, attention is given to the significant role of capital investment as a vehicle through which new knowledge is incorporated into the production process. KBEs promote productive investment and also ensure that the investment process is not impaired or distorted by significant institutional problems, such as bottlenecks in physical infrastructure or financial market inefficiencies.

Fourth, KBEs devote considerable effort to developing those intangible aspects of infrastructure that influence an economy's capacity to both develop and use new knowledge. The workforce is highly educated and well trained, and programs are available to encourage and facilitate lifelong learning. There is an emphasis on management training. KBEs also give attention to the difficult-to-define factors that determine the management culture and influence firms' responsiveness to new information and their receptiveness to new ideas.

Fifth, KBEs recognize the important role of a well-developed information infrastructure which can facilitate the diffusion of knowledge and the spread of ideas. Special importance is given to establishing the required physical and information service components of information networks and developing an appropriate policy framework.

Within organizations, there is an understanding that, in an environment characterized by intense competition and rapid change, success depends on the ability to innovate. In successful firms, there is a systematic husbanding of intellectual capital. Know-how and creativity are nurtured by managers who recognize that these are critical elements in the production process and key sources of competitive advantage. Workers are encouraged to pursue further training and offered incentives for experimentation and the development of ideas. The focus on innovation extends beyond the search for new products and production technologies to include the development of improved organizational arrangements and human resource practices that encourage innovation and build the firm's knowledge capital.

The most successful firms in KBEs will have systematically transformed themselves into "learning organizations." They will have put in place structures that not only effectively gather and process codified information, but also tap the tacit knowledge, including the insights and intuitions, of workers. In keeping with new understandings about the innovative process, successful organizations will have established teams and developed other interactive mechanisms that promote knowledge transfers among workers, cross-fertilization, and joint efforts to improve the firms' products and processes.

5.   THE EMERGING KNOWLEDGE ECONOMY IN CANADA

What can the evidence tell about Canada's evolution as a knowledge economy? Since knowledge production and use cannot be directly measured, Canada's development as a knowledge economy can only be assessed using a variety of observable indicators. Moreover, there is a need to rely largely on aggregate data; very little information is available on the changes under way within firms – although, as we will see from later papers in this volume, some progress is being made. From available information, we have a picture of an economy that is acquiring a number of significant features of a KBE, but that remains subject to some significant challenges in terms of ability to develop and access knowledge. The economy's evolution can be seen by examining indicators of knowledge production and access identified in Section 4 and also by looking at transformation under way in the structure of the Canadian economy. Following the discussion of these two issues, we consider the challenges that must be addressed to further Canada's development as a KBE.

5.1   Relevant Characteristics of the Canadian Economy

5.1.1   International Trade and FDI

One of the most notable developments over the past decade has been the substantial increase in the importance of foreign trade and investment. As discussed above, trade and investment are significant for a number of reasons, but especially because they are the two most important mechanisms for acquiring knowledge developed abroad. The growth in exports and imports relative to GDP is shown in Figure 7. It can also be seen that Canada's trade orientation is high by comparison to other industrialized countries; in 1997, the proportion of Canada's economic output involved in international trade was close to twice the average for all G-7 countries.

Trade orientation has increased across all provinces and all manufacturing industries. Much of the growth has occurred in Canada's trade with the U.S., and partly reflects increasing product specialization as firms, including multinational enterprises (MNEs), restructure and otherwise adjust to the increased economic integration arising from implementation of the FTA and NAFTA.

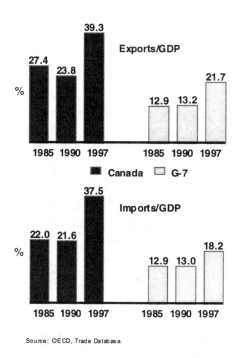

Source: OECD, Trade Database.

Figure 7: Share of exports and imports in GDP- Canada and the G-7

One of the immediate and more readily observable consequences of trade is that it enhances a country's access to new knowledge that is incorporated in intermediate and capital goods developed abroad. The share of technology obtained through imports has increased over time in most OECD countries. For Canada, a recent study by Gera, Gu and Lee (1999a) shows that more than 65% of acquired technology comes from abroad, with the proportion rising to more than 75% in the manufacturing sector (Figure 8). The research shows productivity growth in Canada owes more to R&D spillovers from abroad than to domestic influences.

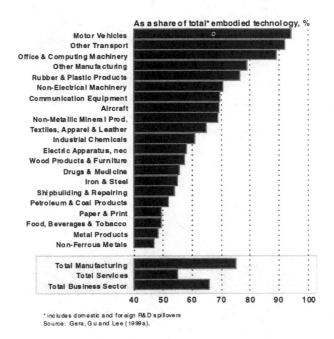

Figure 8: Technology acquired from abroad as a share of total embodied technology

The growth of direct investment by foreigners in Canada and Canadian foreign direct investment (FDI) abroad is shown in Figure 9. While both Canada's inward and outward FDI stocks have increased in importance over the last decade, Canada's outward investment has grown at a particularly rapid pace. MNEs have long been recognized as bearers of innovation and ideas (Romer, 1993). A number of studies indicate that, consistent with the theory of direct investment, MNE subsidiaries in Canada have provided significant learning opportunities for domestic firms.[9] The evidence also suggests that, by improving market access, outward FDI has improved incentives for Canadian firms to undertake R&D and to install equipment involving the latest technological innovations. Rao, Legault and Ahmad (1994), for example, find that the growth, productivity and profit performance of outward-oriented Canadian firms, on average, has been superior to that of domestically oriented firms.

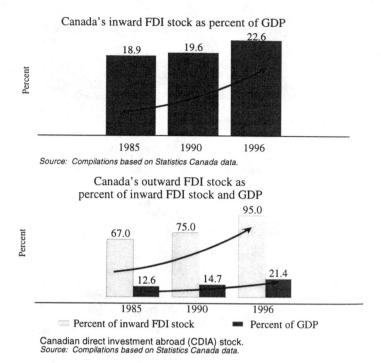

Figure 9: Canada's inward and outward FDI stock

5.1.2   Human Capital Infrastructure

Another characteristic that distinguishes the Canadian economy is the comparatively high educational attainment of its workforce. In 1996, more than half of the Canadian labour force aged 25 to 64 had a post-secondary degree or diploma. This was more than 10 percentage points higher than the tertiary educational rate in the U.S. and close to 20 points above that of most other OECD nations (see Figure 10).[10]

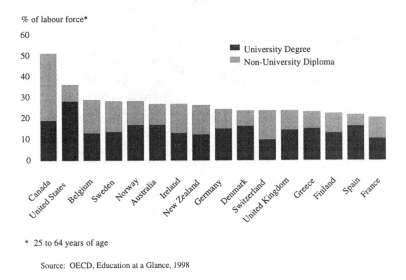

% of labour force*

* 25 to 64 years of age

Source: OECD, Education at a Glance, 1998

Figure 10: Share of labour force with a post-secondary degree/diploma, 1996

Canadian firms and individuals are investing significantly in skills upgrading and retraining. Here, however, there is significant room for improvement. While lifelong learning is becoming more important in Canada, according to 1994-1995 OECD data,[11] the proportion of 36-55-year-old Canadians participating in educational and training courses was somewhat below that in the U.S. and well below the proportion in many European countries, including the U.K., Switzerland and Sweden. Moreover, Canada's incidence of employer-provided training is low by international standards. The 1995 Working With Technology Survey reported that 63% of Canadian establishments undertake formal training,[12] well below the incidence reported in U.S. surveys.[13] Manufacturing and service firms that are "innovative," based on a number of criteria, were almost twice as likely to engage in training as non-innovative firms.[14] Work-training opportunities tend to be especially poor for certain groups of workers, including part-time employees, less-educated workers and those working in small firms, new firms and industries that are subject to high rates of turnover.[15]

5.1.3   Information and Communications Infrastructure

Along with human capital, information and communications networks and related services constitute a key component of the infrastructure of a knowledge economy. With respect to this latter form of capital, the Canadian economy is also well served. Canadian telecommunications firms have made major investments in digitalization, advanced switching systems and high-capacity intercity fibre-optic links, all of which have contributed to a significant improvement in the quality of transmission, and reduction in its cost. Telecommunications access, as indicated by residential telephone mainlines per 100 inhabitants, is higher in Canada than in most other G-7 countries. At the same time, annual telephone charges in Canada for residential, business and mobile telephone service are among the lowest in the G-7.

Canadian usage rates for other forms of information and communications technology are also relatively high. This country ranks close to the top globally in terms of computer penetration rates – at 297 per 1,000 people in 1996. Internet penetration in Canada is below that of leading countries, including Finland and the U.S., but it is high by international standards. Recent surveys indicate that the Internet is accessed by about 13% of Canadian households and 31% of small and medium-sized enterprises.

Over the last two decades, an increased share of industrial investment in Canada has gone towards information technology (Figure 11).

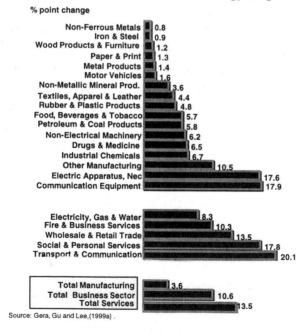

Source: Gera, Gu and Lee,(1999a) .

Figure 11: Share of real IT investment in total investment: 1971-1990

The increase has been particularly marked in the service sector, where the information technology share rose by 13.5 percentage points between 1971 and 1990. The evidence also indicates that information and communications technology (ICT) goods and services have come to account for an increased share of all purchases by Canadian firms. According to the Conference Board (1996), this latter measure of ICT intensity stood at 5.2% in 1992, almost double what it was in 1986.

While it takes time for organizations to effectively integrate information technology into their operations and some industries are still at an early stage in this process, evidence of the economic benefits of information technology is beginning to appear. A number of recent studies show that investment in information technology stimulates productivity growth across industries.[16] Gera, Gu and Lee (1999a) specifically document the gains to Canadian firms from investment in information technology. The rate of return on IT investment is estimated to be between 27% and 36%.

Canada's progress in developing the basic foundations of a knowledge economy is also noted in a recent report by the World Economic Forum. In the Forum's 1997 *Global Competitiveness Report*, Canada is ranked first among the G-7 for "technology potential," an index based on a number of information technology and human capital characteristics.

5.1.4   A Shift Towards Knowledge-Intensive Industries

Canada's evolution towards a knowledge-based economy is reflected not only in the development of certain important capabilities, but also in the major structural changes that are occurring as firms and workers adjust to the challenges and opportunities of a rapidly changing economic environment. The increasing importance of knowledge-based activities is giving rise to significant changes in the industrial structure and employment composition of the Canadian economy (Gera and Mang, 1998; Gera and Massé, 1996).

The shift from goods to service production, which has been an important longer-term trend in all industrialized economies, has been reinforced by globalization and advances in information and communications technology. In the recent period, global forces have strengthened pressures to relocate manufacturing activity to developing countries. At the same time, knowledge-intensive service activities have become increasingly important in the production (including the development, marketing and distribution) of goods. Within Canada, the growing demand for services by both producers and final consumers has been met by a continuing reallocation of resources from goods to service production. Since 1945, private sector services have grown from approximately 35% to over 60% of GDP, while manufacturing has declined from 27% to about 17% of Canada's GDP.

Canada's transition to a knowledge-based economy is more directly reflected in a second important trend: the movement towards the greater use of knowledge workers. In the top half of Figure 12, non-information workers are distinguished from two categories of knowledge-based workers: those in "knowledge occupations," such as pure or applied scientific research, engineering, or professional activities in the social sciences or humanities, which involve the manipulation of concepts and generation of ideas or expert opinions; and those including clerical workers in "data occupations" which involve the use, transmission or manipulation of knowledge. As can be seen from the figure (top half), since 1981, both knowledge workers and data workers have come to account for a significantly higher share of employment at the expense of non-information workers (Gera, Gu and Lin, 1999). There has been a particularly strong growth in the relative importance of knowledge occupations, and this shift has become evident in both manufacturing and service industries (as shown in the lower half of Figure 13).

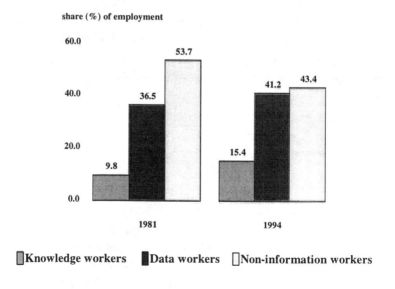

Figure 12: Skill composition in Canadian industries, 1981-1994

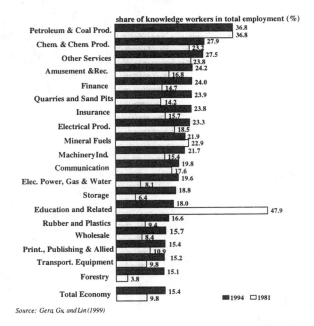

share of knowledge workers in total employment (%)

Industry	1994	1981
Petroleum & Coal Prod.	36.8	36.8
Chem. & Chem. Prod.	27.9	23.2
Other Services	27.5	23.8
Amusement &Rec.	24.2	16.8
Finance	24.0	14.7
Quarries and Sand Pits	23.9	14.2
Insurance	23.8	15.7
Electrical Prod.	23.3	18.5
Mineral Fuels	21.9	22.9
Machinery Ind.	21.7	15.4
Communication	19.8	17.6
Elec. Power, Gas & Water	19.6	8.1
Storage	18.8	6.4
Education and Related	18.0	47.9
Rubber and Plastics	16.6	9.4
Wholesale	15.7	8.4
Print., Publishing & Allied	15.4	10.9
Transport. Equipment	15.2	9.8
Forestry	15.1	3.8
Total Economy	15.4	9.8

■1994 □1981

Source: Gera, Gu, and Lin (1999)

Figure 13: Share of knowledge workers in total employment
in Canadian industries 1981-1994

The growing importance of knowledge workers is partly a result of the increased educational attainment of Canada's labour force, which was discussed in the previous section. It also, however, reflects important changes under way on the demand-side. In particular, with the implementation of advanced information and communication systems, firms are increasing their requirement for "symbolic analysts," workers who have acquired the knowledge and skills needed for gathering, manipulating and organizing information at varying levels of complexity. Both Canadian and U.S. evidence indicates that workers who use computers earn significantly more than other workers, with the Canadian differential averaging 15%.[17] Moreover, the likelihood of using a computer increases with education.[18] In a recent study, Gera, Gu and Lin (1999) find that biased technological change has played a dominant role in skill upgrading across Canadian industries since the beginning of the 1980s.

The increased importance of knowledge workers is also due to the rapid growth of those Canadian industries that tend to be relatively knowledge-intensive. Figure 14 highlights this latter development. Here, industries have been classified into high-, medium- and low-knowledge, based on a combination of indicators of R&D activity and human capital requirements. Over the first half of the 1990s, the growth of high-knowledge industries significantly exceeded that of medium- and low-knowledge industries (Gera and Mang, 1998). Although low-knowledge industries were an important source of new jobs over the period, high-knowledge industries gained

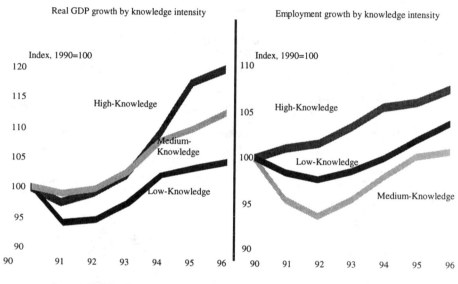

Source: Industry Canada compilations based on Gera and Mang (1998) and Gera and Massé (1998).

Figure 14: Real GDP and employment growth by knowledge intensity

employment share at the expense of industries in both the low- and medium-knowledge categories (Gera and Massé, 1996).

Employment has grown rapidly in a number of knowledge-intensive service industries. This partly reflects the trend towards increased complexity and greater specialization in service functions, developments that have led organizations to become dependent on outside experts for activities once conducted in-house. Over 1986 to 1996, the management consulting industry experienced the most rapid rate of employment growth, at close to 12% per year. Employment in "other business services," another high-knowledge industry, also grew strongly (i.e., at about 5% per year) over this period. Besides the expansion in high-knowledge service jobs, more highly educated workers have benefited from the growth in some of Canada's high-technology goods-producing industries.

One of the most dynamic segments of the Canadian economy, accounting for a significant share of increased resources devoted to knowledge-intensive activities, is information and communications technologies (ICTs). The ICT sector – which includes telecommunications equipment and services, broadcasting services, computer equipment and services, and consumer electronics – accounted for 7.2% of GDP and 3.1% of total employment in 1996. Over the 1990 to 1996 period, the real growth rate of the ICT sector was 7.6%, which is more than five times the growth rate (1.5%) achieved by

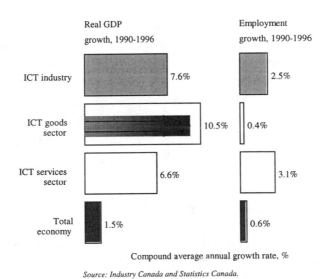

Source: Industry Canada and Statistics Canada.

Figure 15: Real GDP and employment growth in the ICT sector, 1990-1996

the overall economy (see Figure 15). ICT goods production grew at the extraordinarily rapid rate of 10.5% per year. The greatest employment growth has occurred in software and computer services, where employment rose by 90% between 1990 and 1996.

The ICT sector is of interest in a number of respects: as the sector that is responsible for building Canada's information infrastructure; as an important and growing source of employment opportunities for highly skilled and well-educated Canadian workers; and as a major source of R&D with important spillover benefits for other Canadian industries. In 1996, the ICT sector invested $3 billion in R&D. This represented 37% of total R&D spending by Canada's private sector. Telecommunications equipment firms were responsible for about half of the sector's R&D investment. Significantly, in the first half of the 1990s, labour productivity growth in the ICT sector increased at an annual average rate of over 5%, many times faster than the 1% growth rate of the total economy. In ICT manufacturing, productivity increased at an annual average rate of over 12%. Moreover, Bernstein (1996) shows that spillovers from R&D in communications equipment also contribute significantly to productivity gains in Canadian manufacturing as a whole. His estimates show that, over the period 1966-1991, the social rate of return on R&D investment by Canadian communication equipment firms was 55%, which was over three times the private rate of return (17%).[19]

In Section 2, we noted the changes in the composition of production occurring within advanced economies generally. This section indicates that the process of structural change induced by globalization and rapid technological change is well advanced in Canada. Consistent with the move towards a knowledge-based economy, there has been an increase in the demand for more highly educated and skilled workers and a growth in importance of services, especially information-intensive service activities, along with some dynamic, high-technology goods-producing industries whose R&D generates important spillover benefits for other Canadian industries.

5.2   The Payoff Is Beginning

The above discussion suggests that Canada has made progress in important aspects of its development as a KBE. And the signs suggest that the payoff is beginning. Canada moved from twentieth place in 1994 to fifth place in

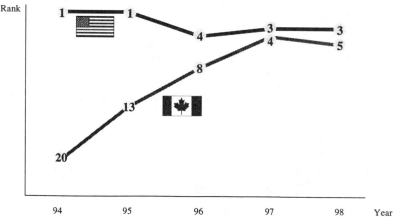

Source: WEF, Global Competitiveness Report for 1996, 1997, 1998 and IMD, World Competitiveness Yearbook for 1994 and 1995.

Figure 16: World Economic Forum competitiveness ranking, Canada and U.S.

1998 in the global competitiveness ranking of the World Economic Forum (see Figure 16).Canada's labour productivity performance in the business sector has improved in the 1990s, averaging about 1.4% per year during the 1990-1997 period, more than 50% greater than the pace from 1980 to 1990 (Figure 16). The U.S. economy has also experienced a bounce-back in productivity growth during this period, averaging about 2% in the last three years, roughly double the pace from 1973 to 1995. The question posed by economists is whether the higher productivity growth is the long-awaited confirmation that the economy's steadily rising investment in computers and communications is finally paying off. The evidence is starting to point in that direction (see, for example, Gera, Gu and Lee, 1999a; and Sichel, 1999)[20]

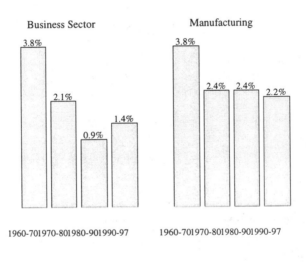

Source: Statistics Canada

Figure 17: Canadian Labour productivity growth

5.3   Remaining Challenges

However, challenges remain. Canada's productivity performance has been, and continues to be, weak. Growth in productivity has been trending downward for decades. In particular, manufacturing has had lacklustre productivity growth over the past 30 years (see Figure 17). For the overall economy, the level of Canadian productivity is about 15% below that of the U.S. (at a PPP rate of US$0.85 per C$). This level gap has remained not only significant but relatively constant for the past two decades. For the manufacturing sector, the level gap reached 25% in the 1990s[21] (see Figure 18).

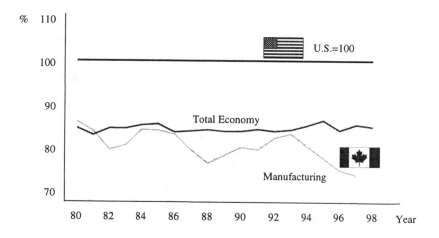

Source: Statistics Canada, U.S. Bureau of Labor Statistics

Figure 18: Canadian Labour productivity gap with the United Stated

One reason for Canada's poor productivity performance has been our low investment rate in Machinery and Equipment (M&E) - especially vis-à-vis the U.S. For example, in 1998, our investment rate in M&E was about 35% below that of the U.S. Studies by the OECD point out that Canada has an "innovation gap" and that this is part of the reason that the post-1993 drop in productivity was sharper in this country than in the U.S. and most other advanced economies. The main elements of this innovation gap are: weak knowledge generation and diffusion; weak technology diffusion and adoption; and poor entrepreneurial drive (see, for example, OECD, 1995).

R&D is a major source of knowledge generation, and it has long been recognized that Canada trails behind most other major industrialized countries in terms of its relative commitment to R&D (Figure 18). Private-sector firms devote a relatively low proportion of GDP to R&D in Canada, notwithstanding the existence of R&D tax incentives that are generous by international standards.[22] The right-hand panel of Figure 19 shows that, when the focus shifts from an input measure, R&D expenditures, to an output indicator, patents, Canada still ranks poorly in terms of knowledge generation. In 1995, both patent applications at home and patents secured abroad, relative to population, were lower for Canada than for all other G-7 countries.

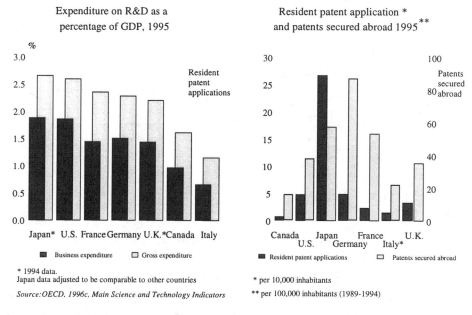

Figure 19: Canadian R&D expenditures and patent intensities

Over the past few decades, many Canadian industries have significantly increased their commitment to R&D. Figure 20 shows that, while R&D intensity is especially high in a small number of Canadian industries (i.e., computers, communications equipment, aircraft, and drugs and medicine), R&D expenditures as a share of value added have grown significantly in manufacturing as a whole and in services such as Finance, Insurance and Real Estate, and Transportation and Communications. These increases have helped narrow the gap in R&D between Canada and other countries, but only very partially. While, in 1981, for example, Canada's R&D spending as a percentage of GDP was just over half that of the U.S., by 1995 this ratio had improved to just over 60%.[23]

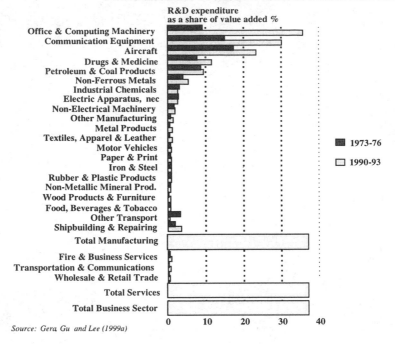

Figure 20: R&D intensity across Canadian industries

Canadian firms' limited commitment to R&D is, in part, a result of their relatively favourable access to new technology developed in the U.S. and elsewhere. This applies particularly to Canadian-based firms that are affiliates of MNEs. Since they are able to tap into the R&D their parent undertakes around the globe, foreign affiliates tend to perform less research in Canada than domestic firms. While large domestic firms in the manufacturing sector spent 2.6% of sales on R&D in 1995, the R&D intensity of large foreign-controlled manufacturing firms was only 1.0%. For small and medium-sized enterprises in manufacturing, the R&D intensity of foreign affiliates was about 15% below the 3.4% spending rate of domestic firms (Whewell, 1999). Canada's foreign-owned auto assembly industry, for example, uses state-of-the-art technology, most of which is a product of research and engineering activities performed in Detroit or Tokyo or at satellite research centres in other major markets.

Domestic firms obtain new technology embodied in intermediate and capital goods imports, as noted above (see Figure 8), and also derive significant spillover benefits from the technology foreign investors transfer to their affiliates in Canada. However, these transfers do not fully compensate for inadequate levels of domestic R&D. In a highly competitive global environment in which success is closely tied to the generation of new products and processes, Canada is seriously disadvantaged by the private sector's low investment in R&D. Inadequate innovation is one probable reason why Canada's average rate of labour productivity growth in manufacturing started to lag behind that of the U.S. in 1986 – labour productivity grew on average 1.6% per year in Canada and 2.6% in the U.S. – trailing the U.S. growth rate by almost 40%.

In addition, Canadian firms are slow to adopt advanced technologies. As can be seen in Table 2, the gap between Canada and the U.S. has narrowed since 1989, but Canada continues to lag significantly behind the U.S. in its use of technologies such as computer-aided design and engineering systems, numerically controlled machines, robots, automated material handling systems, and automatic inspection equipment. The disparity is most pronounced among small and medium-sized manufacturing establishments, with Canadian SMEs falling significantly behind their U.S. counterparts in the adoption of one or more technologies. While, for example, 53% of U.S. manufacturing establishments in the 100-to-499-employee range had adopted five or more technologies in 1993, the comparable incidence of use in Canada was only 33%. For small establishments with 20 to 99 employees, the incidence of adoption for five or more technologies was 14% in Canada and 20% in the U.S. (Baldwin and Sabourin, 1996).

Table 2: Use of at least one technology by plant size[*] (percentage of establishments)

No. of employees	1989		1993	
	Canada	U.S.	Canada	U.S.
20-99	50	67	70	75
100-499	81	89	85	94
500 or more	98	98	94	97
All sizes	58	74	73	81

Percentage of establishments
* Based on a comparison for the five industries
Source: Baldwin and Sabourin (1996).

Large establishments, which have been by far the most responsive to new technological innovations, account for a major share of Canadian manufacturing shipments. Therefore, notwithstanding the relatively slow adoption rate of SMEs, by 1993, over 90% of all manufacturing shipments came from establishments using at least one advanced technology. Establishments using 10 or more advanced technologies accounted for almost 40% of manufacturing shipments[24] (Baldwin and Sabourin, 1995).

Baldwin, Sabourin and Rafiquzzaman (1996) find that more advanced technology users in Canada reap greater benefits than other firms from using particular technologies. Among other things, a higher proportion of more advanced users reported increases in productivity.

Recent studies have singled out a fourth and related problem affecting Canada's development as a KBE – namely, the failure of Canadian firms to introduce the organizational and human resource innovations needed to realize the full potential of advanced technologies. While new digital technologies expand information flows and opportunities for information sharing within organizations, corporate incentives often reward individual achievement and do not encourage sharing. Skilled workers with advanced technology are in a position to assume increased responsibilities, but managers may not delegate adequate decision-making authority or instill workers with the needed commitment to the achievement of corporate objectives. There is an increasing appreciation that in more successful firms the introduction of advanced technologies tends to be accompanied by complementary innovations in management systems and incentive arrangements.[25] The literature also indicates that, overall, Canadian companies have not given adequate attention to these workplace innovations.

One aspect of this problem is highlighted by a recent survey of the human resource practices of Canadian firms. It was found that most Canadian establishments use very few innovative human resource practices; 70% of the respondents were judged to be "traditional" in their approach (Figure 21, top half). Of the 30% that had introduced innovative approaches, 18% had emphasized intrinsic rewards based on increasing employee involvement and identification with the enterprise and 12% had emphasized extrinsic rewards such as performance-based compensation systems.

The graph in the bottom half of Figure 21 is similar to findings in other studies that indicate that Canadian firms' investment in soft technologies is not keeping pace with their investment in hard technologies. Companies have been slow to change their organizational structures and work patterns so that they can fully realize the opportunities created by new information and communications technologies. While, as we noted above, there is evidence of the productivity gains from investment in new technology, we might expect that these gains would have been much more substantial if Canadian firms had given greater attention to the workplace changes needed to exploit the potential of advanced technologies.[26]

Innovations in HR practices

Participation-based
18.0%

Compensation-based
12.0%

Traditional
70.0%

Traditional — using very few innovative HR practices

Participation-based — focusing on employee involvement, job design,
quality and intrinsic rewards

Compensation-based — relying on extrinsic rewards and incentives
such as variable pay, internal promotion and generous wage and
benefit packages

The new innovation gap: between "hard" and "soft" technologies

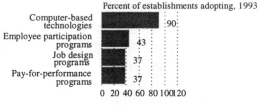

Percent of establishments adopting, 1993

Computer-based technologies : 90:
Employee participation programs 43
Job design programs 37
Pay-for-performance programs 37

0 20 40 60 80 100 120

Source: Betcherman et al. (1998)

Figure 21: Innovations and technology adoptions

6.   CONCLUSIONS AND ISSUES FOR FURTHER RESEARCH

Economies and firms are being forced to adapt to a global economic environment that is being transformed by the mutually reinforcing pressures associated with the increasing internationalization of business and the drive for new knowledge.   These forces are leading to a paradigm shift that involves fundamental changes in the nature of production and the role of the factors of production.   Within firms and within economies, intellectual capital is increasingly being recognized as the critical asset.   There is a growing appreciation that successful performance by countries and by organizations is linked to development of mechanisms that foster the development of intellectual capital, provide incentives for the development of ideas, and facilitate and promote knowledge acquisition.

Much of the responsibility for adaptation to the new economic imperatives falls on individual firms.   However, by establishing an appropriate policy framework, governments can help an economy evolve into a KBE. The economic literature highlights the importance of policies directed towards: promoting foreign trade and investment; facilitating productive investment by domestic firms; building a solid infrastructure and, especially, developing the nation's human capital and its information infrastructure; and encouraging investment in the development of general knowledge that cannot be protected through intellectual property rights.

Canada ranks well on many of the general characteristics of a KBE, but there is significant scope for improvement in many areas. Significant attributes of the Canadian economy include its high and growing foreign trade and investment orientation; the comparatively high educational attainment of its workforce; and its well-developed information and communications infrastructure. The industrial structure of the Canadian economy and the skill mix of Canadian workers are evolving in a direction that is consistent with the progress of the economy as a KBE. At the same time, however, Canada lags behind other major industrial economies in the extent of employer-provided formal training; in the commitment to R&D and the development of patentable innovations; in the adoption of advanced technologies; and in the introduction of the human resource and organizational innovations needed to fully exploit advanced technologies.

These broad findings give rise to a number of more specific questions about the firm strategies and government policies that are likely to contribute to success in a knowledge-based economic environment. Many of these issues are taken up in other conference papers.

First, there are those questions that relate to the successful adoption of modern technologies. There is evidence, as we noted earlier, that investment in information technologies provides firms with productivity benefits – contrary to what is alleged under the so-called "productivity paradox." But there is reason to doubt that possibilities in this area have been fully exploited. There are lags in the adoption of advanced technologies – a problem that may be due, in part, to strategic considerations relating to managers' perceptions about the reaction of other firms in the industry. As well, there have been problems in successfully implementing new process innovations involving significant investments in new computer hardware and software technology. This may reflect problems in firms' investment planning process. It may also be due to the failure to implement needed organizational and human resource changes.

Some progress has been made in identifying the characteristics of more successful enterprises. One recent study finds that organizations that are successfully adapting new information and communications technologies are experimenting with organizational innovations intended to enhance flexibility

(Betcherman and McMullen, 1998). By contrast, those organizations that have had difficulty generating increases in productivity from new technology have been reluctant to let go of traditional structures and practices. One important area of innovation is in human resource strategies. Newton (1997) examines a number of new human-resource-based management strategies aimed at fostering an environment of creativity and flexibility that gives recognition to the importance of tacit knowledge and takes account of new understandings about the innovative process. Evidence suggests that new strategies emphasizing the central role of the human factor and encouraging organizational learning have had a positive impact on corporate performance. This perspective is further developed in the paper by Newton and Magun in this volume.

A second set of issues pertains to the challenges particular types of enterprises confront in the KBE. The poor performance of small firms, in particular, needs further investigation. Small Canadian firms perform poorly in the generation and adoption of new knowledge. Less than 1% of all Canadian firms engage in R&D. Moreover, small firms are slow to adopt advanced technologies and they tend to be poor at implementing the organizational and human resource practices needed to realize the gains from new innovations. While the performance of outwardly oriented small and medium-sized enterprises is superior to that of domestically oriented SMEs, Canadian SMEs have largely ignored opportunities in export markets (Rao and Ahmad, 1996). Is the limited export activity of SMEs a reflection or a cause of their lack of competitiveness? What factors are impeding the adoption of advanced technologies by SMEs? The innovation survey discussed by John Baldwin, as well as other conference papers, may shed light on these questions.

The so-called "virtual enterprise" also merits special attention, but for different reasons. It is important to understand the factors underlying the emergence of this new organizational arrangement and the implications of the growth in electronic commerce for the operation of domestic and international markets. A number of papers in this volume address these issues. They explore the unique features and the dynamics of the virtual organization; address the special valuation and financing problems posed by virtual enterprises; and provide a broad overview of the issues associated with the growth of electronic commerce.

A third category of issues pertains to the appropriate government policies for a knowledge-based economy. As we discussed above, the economic literature can provide some general guidance in this area. The policy lessons arising from the economic literature are further explored in a number of papers in this volume. In addition to examining what economics can teach us in general terms, however, it is important to look at the efforts of different governments to design policies that foster knowledge development and acquisition. These include the design of programs to support basic research; the creation of mechanisms to enhance the social benefits from cooperation among researchers in different institutional environments; and the development of an intellectual property regime that creates an appropriate mix of incentives for both innovation and technology diffusion.

NOTES

[1] The virtual economy refers to an era of business without borders (temporal, geographical, functional or organizational) and to entities called virtual enterprises which operate in high-performance networks. By definition, "a virtual enterprise involves people or companies in different geographical locations, whether several states away or halfway around the globe. It requires mastering specific technological skills so that a company can strike deals quickly then move on the next deal with a different cast of players." For a detailed discussion on this issue, see Lefebvre, Lefebvre and Mohnen's paper in this volume.

[2] For a discussion of the high-technology list of manufacturing industries, see OECD (1994). These industries include aerospace, computers, electronics, electrical machinery, pharmaceuticals and scientific instruments.

[3] In a recent paper, Rafiquzzaman and Whewell (1998) find that the propensity for domestic patents has grown in Canada at a faster rate than in many industrialized countries between 1978-1984 and 1985-1992. The pace of growth has increased since the mid-1980s. Although the U.S. experienced the highest growth in the propensity for domestic patenting, Canada followed closely behind. The propensity declined in other countries with the exception of France.

[4] UNCTAD, *World Investment Report, 1995*, p. 149.

[5] For example, Gould and Ruffin (1992), Dollar and Wolff (1993), and Baumol, Nelson and Wolff (1994).

[6] See, for example, Levine and Renelt (1992).

[7] See, for example, Barro (1992) and Benhabib and Speigel (1992).

[8] See, for example, Betcherman, McMullen and Davidman (1998).

[9] In a recent paper, Gera, Gu and Lee (1999b) find that inward FDI generated production cost advantages and contributed to productivity growth across Canadian industries over the 1973-1992 period. For a review of the recent research on these issues, see Hirshhorn (1997).

[10] As compared to many Asian (e.g., Japan, Korea, Chinese Taipei) and European countries (e.g., U.K., Germany, Sweden, Italy), Canada has a higher share of university graduates in the humanities and a lower share in mathematics, science and engineering – the latter group being fields of study that are in increasing demand. Moreover, in a recent international study comparing eighth grade students in mathematics and science achievement, Canada's results were unimpressive: Canada ranked thirteenth among the 26 participating countries in mathematics and fifteenth in science (see the Third International Mathematics and Science Study, OECD, 1996a).

[11] For the report of the International Adult Literacy Survey, 1994-1995, see OECD (1996b).

[12] While this is only one of a number of estimates of employer-provided training in Canada, other studies point towards similar conclusions. A recent survey by Betcherman, Leckie and McMullen (1997), for example, indicates that 70% of establishments undertake some training, while only 40% provide formal or structured training.

[13] See, for example, Lynch and Black (1995).

[14] Baldwin and Johnson (1996).

[15] See Betcherman (1992) and Hum, Simpson and Holmes (1996).

[16] See Gera, Gu and Lee (1999a), Siegel and Griliches (1991), and Brynjolfsson and Hitt (1995).

[17] The Canadian evidence is based on Statistics Canada's 1994 General Social Science Survey. See Morrissette and Drolet (1997). For U.S. evidence, see Krueger (1993).

[18] Morissette and Drolet (1997).

[19] In a recent study, Gera, Gu and Lee (1999a) report that the R&D spillovers in Canada are primarily international in scope. They find that international R&D spillovers from both ICT and non-ICT sectors contribute significantly to productivity growth across Canadian industries. However, the spillovers from the ICT sector are greater than those from the non-ICT sector.

[20] Recently, U.S. Federal Reserve chairman Alan Greenspan expressed his enthusiasm about IT's contribution to economic growth and productivity improvements: "The rapid acceleration of computer and telecommunications technologies is a major reason for the appreciable increase in our productivity in this expansion, and is likely to continue to be a significant force in expanding standards of living into the twenty-first century" (Alan Greenspan, "The Implications of Technological Changes," remarks at the Charlotte Chamber of Commerce, Charlotte, North Carolina, July 10, 1998).

[21] Sharpe (1999) points out that the widening of the productivity gap in the manufacturing sector is concentrated in the two fastest growing industries: Electronic and Other Electronic Equipment and Industrial Machinery and Equipment.

[22] See Mohnen, Dagenais and Viennot (1997).

[23] A recent study by Mohnen, Dagenais and Viennot (1997) using the universe of Canadian R&D expenditures over a 30-year span (1963-1992) at the level of two-and three-digit industries concludes that R&D increases by at least 20% above the costs incurred by governments to support the R&D incentives.

[24] Similarly, an Industry Canada survey of the use of ICTs in service industries has found that there are significant differences between large and small firms. Larger firms (with over 200 employees) were found to be much more likely to have taken advantage of technologies such as computerized financial systems, wireless communications, e-mail, desktop publishing, the Internet, and electronic funds transfer.

[25] See, for example, Conference Board (1997).

[26] Newton (1997) argues that individual human resource/organizational change practices do not generate desirable outcomes - what is needed is synergistic "bundles."

REFERENCES

Baldwin, J. and J. Johnson, "Human Capital Development and Innovation: A Sectoral Analysis." in Howitt (ed.) *The Implications of Knowledge-Based Growth for Micro-Economic Policies*. The Industry Canada Research Series. Calgary: University of Calgary Press, 1996.

Baldwin, J. and D. Sabourin, *Technology Adoption in Canadian Manufacturing*. Ottawa: Statistics Canada, 1995.

Baldwin J. and D. Sabourin, "Technology and Competitiveness in Canadian Manufacturing Establishments." *Canadian Economic Observer*, May 1996, 3.1-3.15.

Baldwin, J., D. Sabourin and M. Rafiquzzaman, *Benefits and Problems Associated with Technology Adoption in Canadian Manufacturing: Survey of Innovation and Advanced Technology 1993*. Ottawa: Statistics Canada, 1996.

Barro, R., "Human Capital and Economic Growth." Working Paper, Harvard University, July 1992.

Baumol, W.J., R.R. Nelson and E.N. Wolff, *Convergence of Productivity: Cross-National Studies and Historical Evidence*. New York: Oxford University Press, 1994.

Benhabib, J. and M.M. Speigel, "The Role of Human Capital in Economic Development: Evidence from Aggregate Cross-Country and Regional U.S. Data." Department of Economics, New York University, 1992.

Berman, E., J. Bound and S. Machin, "Implications of Skill-Biased Technological Change: International Evidence." NBER Working Paper No. 6166, 1997.

Bernstein, J., "International R&D Spillovers Between Industries in Canada and the U.S." Industry Canada Working Paper No. 3, 1994.

Bernstein, J., "R&D Productivity Growth in Canadian Communications Equipment and Manufacturing." Industry Canada Working Paper No. 10, 1996.

Betcherman, G., "Are Canadian Firms Underinvesting in Training?" *Canadian Business Economics*, 1(1), 1992, 25-33.

Betcherman, G., N. Leckie and K. McMullen, *Developing Skills in the Canadian Workplace – The Results of the Ekos Workplace Training Survey*. Study No. W/02. Ottawa: CPRN, 1997.

Betcherman, G. and K. McMullen, "Impact of Information and Communication Technologies on Work and Employment in Canada." CPRN Discussion Paper No. W/01, 1998.

Betcherman, G., K. McMullen and K. Davidman, *Training for the New Economy - A Synthesis Report*. Ottawa: CPRN, 1998.

Betcherman, G., K. McMullen, N. Leckie and C. Caron, *The Canadian Workplace in Transition*. Kingston: Industiral Relations Centers, Queen's University, 1999.

Blomström, M., "Host Country Benefits of Foreign Investment," in D. McFetridge (ed.), *Foreign Investment, Technology and Economic Growth*. The Investment Canada Research Series. Calgary: The University of Calgary Press, 1991.

Bradford De Long, J., "Global Trends: 1980-2015 and Beyond." Paper prepared for Industry Canada, April 1997.

Brynjolfsson, E. and L. Hitt, "Information Technology as a Factor of Production: The Role of Differences Among Firms." *Economics of Innovation and New Technology*, 3, 1995, 183-199.

Chandler, A.D., Jr., *Strategy and Structure: Chapters in the History of the Industrial Enterprise*. Cambridge, MA: MIT Press, 1962.

Coe, D.T. and E. Helpman, "International R&D Spillovers." *European Economic Review*, 39, 1995, 859-887.

Conference Board, *Jobs in the Knowledge-Based Economy: Information, Technology and the Impact on Employment*. Ottawa: Conference Board of Canada, 1996.

Conference Board, *Micro Level Investigation of the Process of Innovation*. Ottawa: Conference Board of Canada, 1997.

Denison, E., *The Sources of Economic Growth in the United States and the Alternatives Before Us*. Washington, DC: Committee for Economic Development, 1962.

Dollar, D. and E.N. Wolff, *Competitiveness, Convergence and International Specialization*. Cambridge, MA: MIT Press, 1993.

Gera, S., W. Gu and F.C. Lee, "Information Technology and Productivity Growth: An Empirical Analysis for Canada and the United States." *Canadian Journal of Economics*, 32(2), April 1999a, 384-407.

Gera, S., W. Gu and F.C. Lee, "Foreign Direct Investment and Productivity Growth: The Canadian Host-Country Experience." Industry Canada Working Paper No. 30, 1999b.

Gera, S., W. Gu and Z. Lin, "Technology and the Demand For Skills: An Industry-Level Analysis." Industry Canada Working Paper No. 28, 1999.

Gera, S. and K. Mang, "The Knowledge-based Economy: Shifts in Industrial Output." *Canadian Public Policy*, XXIV(2), 1998, 149-184.

Gera, S. and P. Massé, "Employment Performance in the Knowledge-based Economy." Industry Canada Working Paper No. 14, 1996.

Globerman, S. and B.M. Wolf, "Joint Ventures and Canadian Outward Direct Investment," in S. Globerman (ed.), *Canadian-Based Multinationals*. Calgary: University of Calgary Press, 1994.

Gould, D. and R. Ruffin, "Human Capital Externalities, Trade and Economic Growth." Mimeo, Federal Reserve Bank of Dallas and the University of Houston, September 1992.

Hirshhorn, R., "Industry Canada's Foreign Investment Research: Messages and Policy Implications," Industry Canada Discussion Paper No. 5, October 1997.

Hum, D., W. Simpson and R. Holmes, *Maintaining a Competitive Workforce: Employer-Based Training in the Canadian Economy.* Montreal: IRPP, 1996.

Krueger, A.B., "How Computers Have Changed Wage Structure? Evidence From Micro Data." *Quarterly Journal of Economics*, 108(1), 1993, 33-60.

Levine, R. and D. Renelt, "A Sensitivity Analysis of Cross-Country Growth Regressions." *American Economic Review*, 82, 1992.

Lucas, R.E., "On the Mechanisms of Economic Development." *Journal of Monetary Economics*, 22(1), 1988, 3-42.

Lynch, L. and S. Black, "Beyond the Incidence of Training: Evidence from a National Employers Survey." National Bureau of Economic Research Working Paper No. 5231, 1995.

Mohnen, P., M. Dagenais and N. Viennot, "The Effectiveness of R&D Tax Incentives in Canada." Industry Canada mimeo, June 1997.

Morissette, R. and M. Drolet, "Computers, Fax Machines and Wages in Canada: What Really Matters?" Statistics Canada Working Paper, 1997.

Nelson, R.R. and S.G. Winter, *An Evolutionary Theory of Economic Change.* Cambridge, MA: Harvard University Press, 1982.

Nelson, R.R. and G. Wright, "The Rise and Fall of American Technology Leadership: The Postwar Era in Historical Perspective." *Journal of Economic Literature*, 30, 1992.

Newton, K., "Management Strategies in the Knowledge-Based Economy." Industry Canada Occasional Paper No. 14, 1997.

OECD, *Jobs Study: Evidence and Explanations.* Paris: OECD, 1994.

OECD, *OECD Economic Surveys: Canada.* Paris: OECD, 1995.

OECD, *Technology, Productivity and Job Creation.* Paris: OECD, 1996a.

OECD, *Literacy Skills for the Knowledge Society.* Paris: OECD, 1996b.

OECD, *Main Science and Technology Indicators.* Paris: OECD, 1996c.

OECD, *Technology, Productivity and Job Creation - Best Policy Practices.* Paris: OECD, 1998a.

OECD, *Education at a* Glance. Paris: OECD, 1998b.

Rafiquzzaman, M. and L. Whewell, "Recent Jumps in Patenting Activities: Comparative Innovative Performance of Major Industrial Countries, Patterns and Explanations." Industry Canada Working Paper No. 27, December 1998.

Rao, S. and A. Ahmad, "Canadian Small and Medium-Sized Enterprises: Opportunities and Challenges in the Asia Pacific Region," in R. Harris (ed.), *The Asia Pacific Region in the Global Economy: A Canadian Perspective.* Calgary: University of Calgary Press, 1996.

Rao, S., M. Legault and A. Ahmad, "Canadian-Based Multinationals: An Analysis of Activities and Performance." in S. Globerman (ed.), *Canadian-Based Multinationals.* The Industry Canada Research Series. Calgary: The University of Calgary Press, 1994.

Romer, P.M., "Increasing Returns and Long-Run Growth." *Journal of Political Economy,* 94(5), 1986, 1002-1037.

Romer, P.M., "Endogenous Technical Change." *Journal of Political Economy*, 98(5), part 2, 1990, S71-S102.

Romer, P.M., "Idea Gaps and Object Gaps in Economic Development" *Journal of Monetary Economics,* 32, 1993, 543-573.

Rosenberg, N., *Inside the Black Box: Technology and Economics* Cambridge: Cambridge University Press, 1982.

Sharpe, A., "New Estimates of Manufacturing Productivity Growth for Canada and the United States." Paper prepared for the meeting of the Research Advisory Committee on the Centre for the Study of Living Standards Project on the Canada-U.S. Manufacturing Productivity Gap, March 25, 1999, Chateau Laurier, Ottawa.

Sichel, D., "Computers and Aggregate Economic Growth." *Business Economics*, XXXIV(2), 1999, 18-24.

Siegel, D., and Z. Griliches, "Purchased Services, Outsourcing, Computers and Productivity in Manufacturing." NBER Working Paper No. 3678, 1991.

Solow, R.M, "Technical Change and the Aggregate Production Function," *Review of Economics and Statistics*, 39, 1957, 312-320.

UNCTAD, *World Investment Report 1995: Transnational Corporations and Competitiveness,* New York and Geneva: United Nations, 1995.

Whewell, L., "The Importance of Firm Size, Sectoral Patterns of R&D, Industrial Structure, and Foreign Ownership for Canada's R&D Performance Relative to the U.S." Industry Canada Staff Paper, April 1999.

Wright, G., "The Origins of American Industrial Success, 1879-1940." *The American Economic Review*, 80(4), 1990, 651-668.

2. THE ECONOMIC UNDERPINNINGS OF A KNOWLEDGE-BASED ECONOMY

Randall Morck
University of Alberta

Bernard Yeung
University of Michigan

Acknowledgment: We are most grateful to Marina Whitman for many stimulating comments.

1. WHAT IS A KNOWLEDGE-BASED ECONOMY?

1.1 The Knowledge Content of Goods and Services

As the 20th century draws to a close, the knowledge content of everyday goods and services is rising as never before. Accompanying this is an equally amazing explosion in the amount of information available to ordinary people.

Consider the letters on these pages. Only a couple of generations ago, a quill and a dark fluid were all a writer needed. Anyone of normal intelligence could pluck a bird's tail-feathers and set verse to paper. A generation ago, people used pens and pencils. Although virtually no one, on his or her own, could have manufactured a ballpoint pen, or even a pencil, from metal ores, coal tar, or tree branches, the workings of these writing instruments were comprehensible to most of humanity. Now, to write these unworthy pages, we are using a PC vastly more powerful than the room-sized computer that guided men to the moon in 1969. We print hard copies with a laser printer – yet lasers were props of science fiction only a few years ago.

Each advance in writing tools was built on humanity's accumulating hoard of knowledge. Aeons ago, someone discovered how a quill feather could spread a coloured liquid across a flat surface. Others, watching, copied her. Over the ages, certain observant people found that some feathers and some liquids worked better than others. A store of knowledge grew, and new scribes had to learn it before they could practise their art. Yet until the industrial age, every scribe could, on his own, build the tools of his trade from scratch.

By the renaissance, this was no longer true. Johannes Gutenberg, who built the first printing press, was a metal-smith, and knew nothing of smelting or mining. Yet knowledge of these trades was embedded in his printing press. The metal from which he built his press was produced by a smelter with knowledge of metallurgy and furnaces. He, in turn, used ore that was mined by a miner, whose knowledge of ores and earths led him to dig his mine. Both relied on equipment produced by other craftsmen from materials produced by yet others. The knowledge embedded in the Gutenberg press in 1436 was already beyond the capacity of a single mind.

Today, the accumulated knowledge embedded in everyday goods and services is extraordinary. PCs are ultimately made of common things: sand (silicon), metal ores (circuits), coal tar residuals (plastics), and the like. Certainly, no human being could, alone, build a PC, or even a printer, from nature's providence. Humanity's collective knowledge of metallurgy, electronics, petrochemicals, and other specialized fields is embedded in these common appliances that a free market economy provides to an average worker for a few dozen hours of his wages.

1.2   The Knowledge-Based Economy

The knowledge content of today's goods and services is vastly more important than it was even a few decades ago. To deal with this, successful companies must make the gathering, filtering, and processing of new information to produce useful knowledge a routine part of doing business.

The sharply rising knowledge intensity in 21st century production means that successful managers and employees need "information handling" skills. The need for these skills is clearly not restricted to companies' upper echelons. Modern cars contain advanced technology like computer chips that control fuel delivery and power distribution, that record gas mileage, and so on. Mechanics trained in the 1970s and even the 1980s are unable to service today's reliable and fuel-efficient cars unless they have "upgraded" their car knowledge.

Knowledge is much more than technical training. Much of the knowledge intensity in today's goods and services is on the "soft" side. An individual who can, from scratch, optimally organize and manage production and marketing in today's world is about as rare as one who can build a PC from coal tar and sand. Generations of experience, ideas, failed experiments, and unexpected successes underlie the organization of large business enterprises.

Moreover, technical knowledge and "soft" knowledge must be linked. Car manufacturers like Chrysler regularly link engineers, material scientists, service mechanics, advertising agents, car dealers, market analysts, and accountants together in designing new car models. The launch of a new model draws on much wider and deeper knowledge than that of engineers and computer scientists alone. Consumers and services groups play increasingly critical roles. The result is more appealing new cars that are easier to service when they (increasingly rarely) require it. These successes are due to more than new technology, though that is certainly important. They depend on the automaker's ability to coordinate the work of related and unrelated teams of specialists. Information sharing and simultaneous information processing are stages in the production of the knowledge that gets embedded in each new car model.

Even in the manufacturing of simple commodities like clothing, the process has fundamentally changed. Computers feed consumer purchase patterns (e.g., style, colour, material) directly to distributors, who use this knowledge to choose designs and place direct orders to manufacturers. They then deliver the clothes to stores "just in time." The consequence is much more rapid style cycles (twelve per year instead of only four), more satisfied customers, lower purchase prices, and yet higher profits. The cornerstone of this process is distributors' continuously updated information about consumers' demands, manufacturers' capabilities, raw material supplies, and their own delivery systems, and their use of this information to produce knowledge about what style of jeans should be shipped to each clothing store in Kitchener or Red Deer this afternoon.

Marketing techniques are also changing to reflect better knowledge of consumers' tastes. The selling of Saturns is based on a marketing concept previously used only for specialty items like Harley Motorcycles. GM created a Saturn Club that provides Saturn owners with activities ranging from get-togethers for swapping their experiences to reunion parties. A few Japanese Saturn users have apparently actually shipped their Saturns from Japan to Texas to join reunion parties. The marketing technique that builds up such "consumption capital" and customer loyalty relies on "knowing consumers" and continuously updating this knowledge.

Such sophisticated knowledge-based marketing techniques have spread even to the marketing of toys. Any parent, grandparent, uncle or aunt to a pre-school or elementary school child is aware of the Beanie Baby phenomenon. Beanie Babies are modestly priced animal-shaped bags stuffed with plastic beads. The Beanie Baby is not just a toy, however. It is part of a series of "issues" of different animal shapes, some of which become collector items valued hundreds of times higher than the original store price. There is a Beanie Baby handbook, a Beanie Baby website, electronically connected user clubs, and so on. An active black market exists for rarer "issues" and for Beanie Babies from foreign countries. In 1998, the U.S. Customs Service was ordered to confiscate Beanie Babies crossing the border from Canada, presumably to raise the black market prices of issues that were rare in the U.S., but relatively common in Canada. The manufacturers sell not Beanie Babies, but some abstract consumption capital stemming from the Beanie Baby series.

Distribution in a knowledge-based economy is much more complicated than ordering, stocking, and selling. The success of distributors like Wal-Mart and Toys'R'Us is based on sophisticated logistic management systems. These firms collect detailed information about changes in their inventories, customers' purchase patterns, suppliers' prices and capabilities, and their own transportation capabilities. They use this to know what stocks are "just right" to satisfy customers. They precisely coordinate their transportation system. Trucks are linked to docks and stores electronically, so loading and unloading time is economized, routes and movements of empty vehicles are minimized, and so on. The result is convenient shopping and lower prices for consumers, leading to a massive customer base and thus the distributor's bargaining power to bid manufacturers' prices yet further down. The system translates spending power into lower merchandise prices (thus higher consumer value), and higher distributors' profit. These companies have revolutionized the distribution process through their "knowledge" of customer needs, manufacturing supplies, transportation systems, and general logistic capabilities.

Financial services businesses like investment, consulting, and accounting firms are serving their customers using the knowledge they build company-wide and globally. Firms that are leaders in these areas, like the Bank of Montreal with its Mbanx computer banking system and the Toronto-Dominion Bank with its computerized discount brokerage business, are industry leaders. The gains they can make by making these knowledge-intensive products available to more customers are cited as justification for their mergers with the Royal Bank and CIBC respectively.

The successes of such knowledgeable firms have left their former competitors with declining customer bases, unattractive merger proposals, and even bankruptcy rulings. As traditional department stores' toy floors lost out to Toys'R'Us, their other floors simultaneously lost customers to "big box" specialty stores that used these same knowledge-intensive distribution methods. Established department store chains like Woodward's and Eaton's filed for bankruptcy. Automakers like Jaguar, American Motors, and others that failed to keep pace with technology became subsidiaries or divisions of more successful companies.

These changes have certainly increased potential productivity throughout the economy. In recent years, much has been made in some quarters of a so-called "productivity puzzle." The basic allegation is that, all else equal, high investment in information technology is not clearly associated with increased productivity. These arguments have been shown to be faulty – mainly because the "all else equal" assumption is usually inappropriate. The first problem is the way the "productivity puzzle" economists tried to measure "productivity," as sales minus costs. Sales is price times units of output. Increased information content is reflected both in better-quality units of output and in lower output prices, like Henry Ford's Model T cars and the various generations of powerful PCs. Consequently, sales minus cost figures can be grossly misleading if interpreted casually as measures of productivity. The second problem is that whole new markets and professions have been created around information flow and information processing. These are entirely missing from studies that find evidence of a "productivity puzzle."[1] In short, the world has changed so much that many of these studies are founded on fundamentally flawed assumptions about what has remained constant.[2]

The world certainly has changed. The inevitable conclusion from these illustrations is that a vast amount of knowledge is embedded in everyday goods and services. This embedded knowledge raises their value to consumers. It is a crucial input in virtually every business. Knowledge has become the primary weapon in competition for profits and corporate survival. It is this central role of knowledge in competition that distinguishes our modern economy as a "knowledge-based economy."

2.   HOW A KNOWLEDGE-BASED ECONOMY WORKS

2.1   Human Beings Strive for Knowledge and Its Value

Human nature encapsulates both innate curiosity and the desire for consumer goods. Sociobiological studies of human behaviour find clear and consistent evidence of spontaneous curiosity and hoarding, characteristics we share with most primate species.[3] Philosophers and ethicists may question these aspects of human nature, but their arguments are unlikely to overturn traits that arise from deep within the human genome. The genius of a knowledge-based economy is that it lets us satisfy one of these primeval compulsions (wealth accumulation) by satisfying the other (curiosity).

Humans are fundamentally resourceful, and crave improvements in their lives. We value ideas that improve our well-being and that help us overcome environment constraints and other adversaries. Since our own bodies are relatively weak, some eight millennia ago we acquired knowledge about training oxen, and later horses, as beasts of burden. We supplemented this source of energy with water power, steam, and other steadily more knowledge-intensive sources of energy. We developed ways to use energy to give us light, heat, and so on.

Markets underlay the development and spread of all of these innovations. Even the first use of beasts of burden in the ancient Near East was contemporaneous with the first organized trade.[4] Markets reward people who commercialize ideas and inventions that others value. They give others incentives to copy these ideas in other places, and to improve them if they can.

Thomas Edison's laboratory in New Jersey produced innovations ranging from the light bulb to motion pictures. The same technology Edison used was known elsewhere in the world, including in Canada. The dynamic free market economy of the United States at the beginning of the 20th century meant that innovators there stood to make and keep more money than innovators elsewhere could. Edison argued that his work was "for the betterment of mankind," but he was always careful to safeguard his patent rights. Indeed, the loss of his motion picture patents deeply embittered him in his later life, despite the fact that his loss created a whole new industry. Alexander Graham Bell actually invented the telephone in Canada, but famously took his invention to the United States when no financial backing was forthcoming for such an odd device in this land of woods and water.

Inventors themselves may not see the commercialization possibilities, but the profit incentive makes sure someone does. The hydraulic piston motor had been used, with water power, in China since c. 530 AD. Joseph Cugnot built a steam-powered horseless carriage in 1769; but his funding disappeared with the disgrace of his patron, the Duke de Choiseul, foreign minister to Louis XV. Fuel oil predates recorded history in the ancient Near East, but the first gasoline-powered piston engine was not built until 1876, when Nikolaus Otto put two and two together. Entrepreneurs, like Gottlieb Daimler, Karl Benz, Eli Olds and the Packard brothers, used old technology when they built the first, very expensive, commercial automobiles in the late 19th century. Henry Ford revolutionized auto making by introducing assembly line production in the 1920s, bringing affordable automobiles to the masses.

Ultimately, human beings have collectively overcome adversaries and constraints. The awareness of what needs improvement, the ability to find solutions, and the ability to appropriate commercial value from these solutions, together give rise to the continuous introduction of ever more knowledge into goods and services. The result is the improvement of living standards, and huge fortunes to the successful innovators!

2.2   Commercialization

Commercializing knowledge means putting knowledge into a business. It means acquiring and assimilating information, creating new knowledge from that information, identifying the commercial opportunities that make the knowledge valuable, and having the ability to act on the new knowledge.

Again, notice here that advanced technology is just one ingredient leading to commercial success. It is neither necessary nor sufficient. When desktop copiers were introduced, Xerox probably had patents on virtually every aspect of copying technology. It had the rights, and the ability, to produce personal desk copiers. Yet, it took Canon, a little "David" with far less technological capability, to give consumers desktop copiers. Canon's managers saw the need for inexpensive, reliable, small-volume copiers that can fit into any corner of an office; and Canon delivered exactly that. Canon's critical knowledge was not the technology of making small copiers, for that belonged to Xerox. Its "edge" was its knowledge of what buyers wanted. The moral of Xerox's forfeit of this whole line of business is that technology is useful, but knowledge of consumer needs and production possibilities is essential to profitably commercializing that technology. It takes the full spectrum of knowledge to give the supplier and customers a win-win outcome.

Knowledge comes wrapped in people. People collect, store, and sort information, and their thoughts process this raw information into useful knowledge. Acquiring knowledge is an economic activity like any other, in that it has an economically meaningful cost. An individual must exert effort, first to acquire information and then to gain useful knowledge from it. We can attest, by personal experience earlier in our lives, that staring at a book, even for many hours, yields no information. You have to read, analyze, and ponder it. Then you have to repackage the book's contents in your own words, and relate it to other information you possess. This "decoding" and "recoding" process requires labour (the time spent reading and thinking), capital (the book, a place to read it, and the background knowledge to understand it), and energy (the light to read by and the food to sustain the reader). Intense thought is every bit as draining as hard labour. But without going through this process, you gain no knowledge from your book.

Innate curiosity leads us to collect information, but acquiring valuable knowledge can be a hard job, and people need motivation to undertake it. We acquire knowledge of operas not just because we ourselves find them entertaining. Rather, knowing such things conveys insinuations about social status, wealth, intelligence, and other qualities that attract attention and praise – a real, albeit intangible, value.

People work hard to develop knowledge with commercial value if they can appropriate a considerable part of that commercial value. The Chinese inventor who built the world's first piston engine lived in an economy where only the feudal aristocracy was entitled to an income above subsistence levels. Any wealth he accumulated would have rightfully belonged to his local warlord. The same conditions prevailed in most pre-industrial societies. Property rights were such that average people earned nothing from innovations – indeed, their value often accrued to hated overlords. Unsurprisingly, economically important innovations were few and far between. It is no coincidence that the pace of innovation only picked up in the last few centuries as modern concepts of property rights evolved. A large and increasingly influential school of economic historians argues that legal reform, especially the extension of effective property rights protection beyond the aristocracy, is the crucial difference between our age and earlier ones.[5]   By protecting the return from commercialized innovation, these reforms set the stage for the rapidly rising knowledge intensity of our contemporary economy.

In an organization, individuals work as a team. This makes economic sense because different individuals can distill different knowledge from the same information.   In a team, employees independently and jointly acquire, process, and generate knowledge and then act to capture its commercial value.   Creating successful knowledge-intensive products requires firms to have effective coordination mechanisms for fostering such interactions. That means management must understand employees' vantage points so as to create effective incentives to cooperate in these ways. When this is done well, the firm has vastly more knowledge capability than the sum of the individuals it employs. But, when its employees' incentives are in disarray, an organization's knowledge capability quickly falls to match the minimum competence level among its managers and employees.

The importance of the soft "institutional" side for inducing the creation and utilization of knowledge cannot be under-emphasized. Intensive thought is work, but it is hard to meter such work.   This often makes standard hierarchical management structures liabilities rather than assets. As the Dilbert comic strip illustrates every day, it is harder to manage people paid to think than to manage people paid to work assembly lines or dig for ore. Employees in today's economy are about as willing to devise innovations that enrich only their employers as serfs were to devise innovations that enriched only their feudal lords.

The only proven way to get people to create knowledge, work that is both hard and difficult to measure, is to give them clear monetary incentives based on results rather than effort. They must be empowered with both freedom from standard managerial oversight and at least partial property rights over the proceeds of their knowledge.   For a company to be knowledge-based, it has to give employees these incentives to create knowledge with commercial value.

It also has to encourage coordination and cooperation in work processes. The importance of information sharing and teamwork in knowledge creation seems self-evident, and no self-respecting company is without access to powerful communication technology. But few companies burst at the seams with knowledge creation. A consulting company instructs its consultants to share insights and knowledge in a company-wide e-mail network. But there is no return for the extra work. The result: no one uses the system other than for appearance's sake. Each individual employee still acts based on his/her own knowledge because that course is the most financially sensible. As a consequence, from an outsider's perspective, the company is at best as knowledgeable as the individual employee the outsider is dealing with.

Company politics can impose further constraints, so that the individual employee displays less intelligence than he actually has. A junior executive's idea threatens a senior executive's power and remuneration if the idea reduces the company's dependence on the senior executive's knowledge, or if the senior executive should have thought of the idea herself. To protect their power bases, senior executives have been known to use their discretionary power to retard the development of knowledge that substitutes for their past ideas and to reward the development of knowledge and ideas that complement their own.[6] Competing employees have also been known to feed one another misleading or deceptive information and to deny one another access to information the company possesses.

Fortunately, examples of how to successfully manage coordination and cooperation exist. The analysts, consultants, and bank representatives of Citibank regularly write onto and read from "citimail," its bank-wide information network system. The reason: if an idea is used, its originator receives a real cash bonus. Citibank acts as if it has the sum of its employees' information, and can use this store to create knowledge. The result is a highly competitive market position and a good bottom line.

This discussion highlights three basic principles that govern the utilization of information and thus the creation and commercialization of knowledge within an organization – empowerment, incentives, and the appropriability of returns. The use of these principles to make an organization knowledge-based is a central concern in the fields of organizational economics, sociology, and management.[7]

2.3   Free Enterprise and Entrepreneurship

In five millennia of recorded history, humans have experimented with every conceivable approach to organizing their societies. Divine pharaohs, tribal chieftains, social idealists and cynical dictators have all had their turns. Feudalism, mercantilism, socialism and theocracy have all been tried in different combinations and permutations. One and only one mode of organizing society has proved amicable to the rapid creation and application of valuable knowledge. That mode of organization is free market capitalism. The market mechanism allows individuals or firms to capture the commercial value of the knowledge they create; thus it links effort to reward.

Capitalism, and only capitalism, has propelled the creation and commercialization of knowledge that has made modern society possible. Socialist, social democratic, communist, and Islamic economies have proven barely able to incorporate new knowledge developed in their capitalist neighbours, and totally inept at creating knowledge on their own.

The state-owned factories of post-socialist countries in Eastern Europe and the former Soviet Union are living museums to the technology that was current when those countries became socialist. Czech factories preserved the technology of the late 1940s and Russian factories preserved that of 1917. The only real exception to this was Soviet military technology, which was considered too important to be centrally planned. Instead a generous system of perks and privileges rewarded successful managers of military projects and top Soviet scientists in fields with military uses. In contrast, fields with no perceived military purpose, such as the biological sciences, were infused with Marxist theory. Soviet genetics lagged the West by decades because acknowledging that science meant disavowing the Party Line that human nature was infinitely malleable to Marxist indoctrination. Even the liberal social democracies of Northern Europe are increasingly faced with the technological obsolescence of their key industries and with stagnant real standards of living.

The reason for this general absence of innovation is easy to see. Why should a firm adopt a new production process that reduces its labour needs in a country with labour laws that ban dismissals without cause? Why should a firm implement cost-cutting technology if most of its increased profit is absorbed by higher tax bills? In such an environment, innovation is a pointless nuisance. In 1945, the United Kingdom's Enigma project had given it a commanding lead over the rest of the world in computing technology. But the project's leader, Alan Turing, did nothing to commercialize his inventions. Nor did anyone else in Labour-ruled postwar Britain. Rather, Turing's ideas were developed and commercialized in the United States, where these enterprises could generate profits for the entrepreneurs who led them.

No one can deny the difficult ethical and human questions that free market economics stirs up. Capitalism is clearly an unsatisfactory way to run an economy in a host of dimensions. But arguments of this sort tend to obscure the fact that all the alternatives tried so far are worse. This is most blindingly apparent when we consider knowledge production and commercialization. First-class minds are rare, and their owners understandably want to live in economies that give them the freest access to information and the most generous rewards for valuable knowledge. In this light, it is no surprise that the vast majority of Nobel laureates in the sciences have been American-born or naturalized Americans, and that almost all the important R&D in many key industries is done in that country.

If other parts of the world are to compete meaningfully in the 21st century's growth industries, they must find ways to attract and keep creative thinkers (other than imprisoning them, as the Soviets did). The United States is justly and unjustly criticized on many fronts, but the rest of the world has no other model of such a thoroughgoing knowledge-based economy at this time. Other countries may have little to learn from the United States about gun control, wars on drugs, interracial harmony, convicting murderous football stars, or electing monogamous politicians. We do, however, clearly have much to learn from the Americans about how to organize a knowledge-based economy. The rest of us should not let misplaced nationalist sentiments blind us to this solid and indisputable fact.

2.4   The Austrian School of Economics

The textbook view of a free market economy sees many firms competing for each other's customers by cutting prices, for each other's workers by offering better salaries, and for each other's investors by offering higher returns. This competition discourages inefficiency by keeping prices as low as possible and wages and investment returns as high as possible. But this competition is, at the margin, a zero-sum game. Ultimately, prices get as low as they can while wages and returns to investors rise as high as they can. Profits disappear altogether and a competitive economy of this sort theoretically settles into a stable state where no one can be made better off without making someone else worse off. In the long run, textbook microeconomics theoretically must lead to a stagnant zero-sum game where my gain is your loss.

How does this square with the irrepressible dynamism of free market economies like the United States? The missing piece to this puzzle is the economics of knowledge. The first serious study of knowledge accumulation was undertaken by a group of economists in late 19th and early 20th century Vienna called the Austrian School.[8] This was at a time of accelerating technological change, as radical new high-tech industries like precision steel casting, railroads, and electricity found large-scale commercial application. The Austrian School sought to explain these phenomena, along with the wave of corporate mergers, opaque new financing techniques, and vast wealth creation they engendered. The school was neglected in the postwar era, mainly because it meshed poorly with the mathematical restatement of economics that was then the central project of academic economists. The recent integration of Austrian economics into the superstructure of economic theory, an undertaking called "endogenous growth theory," has revived the intuitive arguments of the Austrians. This intuition forms our basic understanding of a knowledge-based economy.

The principles that govern the creation of a knowledge-based organization also govern the creation of a knowledge-based economy. A knowledge-based economy is one that grants its prospective entrepreneurs the right to capture a large portion of the profits their enterprises produce. A free enterprise economy that safeguards intellectual property rights is the only known form of economic organization that does this. The knowledge real-world free enterprise economies create is the engine of their dynamism. It is the reason actual free market economies are positive-sum games, rather than zero-sum games.

In a knowledge-based economy, the primary competition between companies is not competition to cut prices, but competition to innovate first. Firms collect and digest information to create new knowledge, based on which they offer innovations. To be profitable, innovations must raise "consumer value"; that is, they must satisfy consumers' desires that previously were unmet, or that could formerly be satisfied only at greater expense. A company with an innovation that no one else has can cut its prices, pay its employees more, give its investors a better return, and yet avoid an unhealthy fixation on simple cost cutting. The essence of innovation is getting more valuable outputs from the same old inputs. The consequence is the creation of genuinely new wealth – a positive-sum economy.

This does not mean textbook economic competition is irrelevant. Competition to innovate does not replace more traditional sorts of competition. Instead, successful innovation makes it easier for firms to be competitive in the traditional arenas of prices, wages and investment returns. Because successful innovators have an "edge" that lets them push their rivals aside in these traditional arenas, the return to innovation can be vastly higher than the return to other economic activities.

The theme in a knowledge-based economy, like that in a knowledge-based company, is the empowerment of people. People must have access to information and markets, so that the chances of their generating valuable knowledge are as high as possible; and people who develop valuable knowledge must earn a substantial enough profit from their ideas to justify the enterprise in the first place. Their ability to appropriate these returns is the economically important meaning of "empowerment."

This version of empowerment must extend not just to entrepreneurs, but to everyone. Consumers must be able to buy the new product if it better meets their needs. They must be unhindered by trade barriers, discriminatory taxes, or other distortions that artificially separate the entrepreneur from her customers. Workers must move freely from old firms to new, more knowledge-intensive firms. This migration must not be impeded by migration restrictions, subsidies to old firms, taxes on new firms, or rigid labour laws. Savers must be able to invest their money in knowledge-based firms. Their investment choices must not be curtailed or distorted by discriminatory tax rules, bureaucratic interference, or other artificial impediments. Finally, losers must be free to fail. Bankruptcy wrests control over productive assets from slow or unsuccessful innovators, as their creditors seize assets for sale to the highest bidder – who is often a successful innovator in the same industry able to more profitably use the same assets. Protection from failure leaves poor innovators in charge, and thus impedes knowledge creation and use. Anything short of full empowerment in all of these ways suppresses the returns to innovation, and consequently constricts knowledge creation.

Economies that deny their citizens these sorts of empowerment are less able, or in many cases unable, to create new, more knowledge-intensive products. Again, extreme examples are the communist economies whose institutions discouraged information accumulation (by private citizens) and made knowledge creation for private gain a felony. The Soviet economy famously produced more low-quality steel pipe than any other country. Unfortunately, nobody wanted it. The Chinese Red Flag automobile, which was still produced in the early 1980s, used 1949 engine technology. It is tempting to laugh at such arrested development until we recall that, in the

high returns as the brains (headquarters) of globe-spanning operations that utilize resources in non-knowledge-based economies. Since their knowledge is the indispensable input, while traditional inputs like low-skill labour and raw materials can be found in many places, knowledge-based companies can dictate the terms of this game, and capture the lion's share of the profit produced.

This happens despite the fact that a knowledge-based economy is essentially a service economy. It provides knowledge to serve the global economy and collects a hefty return. A knowledge-based economy's wealth increases if it generates more ideas and applies them on a wider scale and scope. Its people can earn more without putting in more hours or saving more. On the other hand, non-knowledge-based economies collect only basic returns for commodities sold, hours worked and money saved away.[15]

2.7   Creative Destruction and the "Winner Take All" Economy

Economists of the Austrian School call economic growth through knowledge creation "creative destruction." This is because knowledge-based companies are fundamentally creative enterprises, and because of the sure and certain destruction of firms that fail to innovate. Because of this stark distinction between winners and losers, and because of the immense bargaining power a successful innovator has, a knowledge-based economy is rightly described as a "winner take all" economy. Winners at innovation can totally displace less innovative firms, disrupting entire industries. The personal computer essentially destroyed the typewriter industry, battering venerable names like Smith-Corona and Remington. Innovations are often hard for older firms to imitate, certainly at short notice. The result is sudden death for losers and immense profits for winners – at least until other innovators come along and displace them.

A successful knowledge-based economy thus has a high bankruptcy rate and many corporate takeovers. Bankruptcy is a disruptive and high-cost way to transfer productive assets from the hands of losers to the hands of winners. Corporate takeovers are less disruptive ways of making the same transfer.[16] In a corporate takeover, the owners of the old firms get a competitive price for their assets and walk away to retirement. They are only ruined if they insist on continuing to fail until bankruptcy is inevitable. Indeed, sometimes the mere threat of a corporate takeover is enough to limber up ossified management.[17]   Regardless, flexibility in allowing the ready transfer of control over corporate assets is an important policy objective for a knowledge-based economy.

Note that the "winner take all" phenomenon absolutely does not mean that everyone else is impoverished. The winner takes all the profits away from other firms, but it still has to pay competitive prices for what it buys. However, without unique knowledge, other parties in the economy are often "price-takers." That is, competition means they get only an ordinary return for their ordinary capabilities. In contrast, the winner's unique knowledge gives his strong bargaining power and therefore extraordinary returns – at least until he, in turn, is displaced.

This logic applies to wages too. Imagine a restaurant chain with unique marketing and management knowledge that captures consumers *en masse*. Because of competition for jobs, the meat suppliers, food preparers, and so on, earn ordinary returns, the same money they would get for the same work anywhere else. The owners, however, take all the surplus because of the unique knowledge and skills they own.   That is the McDonald's phenomenon.

Simply put, knowledge-based firms earn extraordinary income while ordinary firms earn only ordinary income.   Individuals with valuable knowledge earn extraordinary salaries while others earn only basic wages.

Moreover, as knowledge-based firms internationalize, their earnings further increase, and so does the pay their knowledge creators draw. This happens for two reasons. First, their knowledge is now applied to a larger scale of operations. Second, they become less dependent on ordinary inputs from any specific location. This increases the return to knowledge and thus encourages more investment in knowledge creation.

The social consequence of this is an uneven income distribution. Its political consequence is lobbying by non-innovators to capture innovators' gains through redistributive taxes or other mechanisms. Some of them are motivated by genuine concern for the displaced, others are exhibiting another primal human trait: envy. In dealing with this lobbying, the government of a knowledge-based economy must recognize that lowering the return to innovation reduces the amount of innovation in the economy. Radical redistribution can look good for a while, but ultimately it impoverishes the whole economy relative to other, more knowledge-based, economies.

2.8 A High Return Usually Means a High Risk

The essence of competition in a knowledge-based economy is creative destruction. New knowledge is often disruptive. And today's winner can be next week's loser. The fortunes of individuals and firms with specific knowledge can fluctuate wildly. Many modern high-paying jobs in computers, finance, and other knowledge-intensive fields are high-return, high-risk propositions.[18]

PCs and networking systems, today's innovators, destroyed mainframe computer making, yesterday's innovator. Digital image presentation is threatening the old-fashioned film and image development business. Advances in computing capability have virtually wiped out old-fashioned book-keeping jobs and have forced accounting firms to radically upscale their services. The possible development of room temperature superconductors would lay waste to firms and people in industries ranging from energy production to auto parts.

Just as globalization increases the return to people with unique knowledge, it also increases the risks they face. Because knowledgeable people are highly mobile within multinational firms, new substituting skills can arrive suddenly from the least expected corners. Even skilled workers can lose their jobs with little advance notice. Few would have expected Asian chip-makers to devastate DRAM chip production in almost all the advanced countries. But they did.

Because of these looming risks, firms and individuals look for insurance. Some are keen on developing deep and generally applicable knowledge. Sony has focused on miniaturization and is always searching for new applications of its skill in that area. Its latest project is a "knee-top" computer – a powerful laptop weighing less than three pounds, not much larger than a legal pad, and selling for less than C$2,400. Other firms are keen on becoming big or diversified. Canada's banks have adopted this strategy. Yet others aim for continuous knowledge creation capability. To move in this direction, many firms pin their hopes on "chief information officers" while their senior managers and management researchers busy themselves studying how to become a "learning organization." Despite the unfortunate prevalence of buzzwords and bizarre acronyms, these are real issues.

It makes sense for individuals to follow the same sorts of strategies. The analogous buzzwords are "continuous learning," "learning to learn," and so on. This has created a booming business in executive training courses. However, the younger generation seems more prepared for high job turnover, not expecting to work for one company only. New knowledge-based businesses, like headhunting, are emerging to make greater job mobility easier, to find better job matches, and to accumulate knowledge about labour markets.

In this context, unions should change too. Their focus on protecting jobs must be a losing concern in a knowledge-based economy because it is ultimately a fight against innovation. Their concerns should be how to increase union members' productivity and mobility, and how to provide job and income insurance for their members. That is a more sustainable and socially constructive way to attract new members and address genuine social problems.

While such volatility in individuals' and firms' fortunes can be disconcerting, especially to those directly affected, the aggregate fortune of a knowledge-based economy can be relatively unaffected. This is because the basis of the micro-level volatility is creative destruction. The destruction of each $1-million firm is offset by the creation of another firm worth more than that and the destruction of each $40,000 job appears to be offset by the creation of a new one that pays more (albeit often for an employee with very different qualifications). The aggregate macroeconomic performance of a knowledge-based economy can be a smooth, upward climb, punctuated only by the same sorts of economic disturbances that afflict any economy.

Finally, it makes sense for governments to follow the same sorts of strategies firms and individuals follow. From an international perspective, economies are competing with each other pretty much as firms are competing with each other. A knowledge-based economy will win out against traditional economies because its innovative firms will continuously win out against those of other countries. Though each winning innovator firm's victory may be short-lived, a succession of such winners from knowledge-based economies will steadily add to those economies' wealth. Firms and individuals in other economies will continue collecting their ordinary wages and returns.

Government policies that reduce the return to knowledge creation and application can disrupt the positive feedback process that fuels knowledge creation. In the 18th and 19th centuries, Britain's success was due to its innovators. Britain's industries were the envy of the world and at the forefront of virtually every field. At the same time, the social injustice of Dickensian fame raised genuine questions about British capitalism. In the mid-20th century, Britain chose a socialist path to right such wrongs. Within a couple of decades, British industry had fallen far behind its chief foreign competitors, British innovators and academics had moved abroad in droves, and the British economy was stagnating. Once knowledge-based growth is disrupted, an economy quickly drifts back to providing ordinary returns for ordinary labour, and overall standards of living quickly fall behind those of more knowledge-intensive economies.

3. WHY IS THE KNOWLEDGE-BASED ECONOMY A MORE RELEVANT CONCEPT NOW THAN IN THE PAST?

Britain's economic success in previous centuries was due to its knowledge-based manufacturing industries. The basic principles of knowledge-based growth were worked out by economists in Vienna a century ago. Clearly, the concept of a knowledge-based economy is nothing new. Why is the topic gaining so much attention now? The answer is that all economies, even primitive hunter-gatherer cultures that use bird feathers for drawing, are knowledge-based. The differences are of degree, not of kind.

Knowledge has always been the driving force for social and economic progress. The difference between a knowledge-based economy and an ordinary one is that, in the former, the main competition between individuals, firms, and countries is competition to innovate. Other forms of competition, like price-cutting, become secondary. The result is increasingly knowledge-intensive goods and services and disproportionately rapid economic growth in knowledge-intensive sectors and economies. Why is knowledge-based commercial activity more prevalent now than in the past? We believe that there are several reasons.

First, radical developments have changed the technology for handling information itself. Information processing power has followed an exponential growth path. This has lowered the cost of gathering information and thus made knowledge production easier.

Second, public education and relatively equal access to university education have greatly increased the number of people qualified for knowledge-intensive jobs. In a normal industry, an abundance of employees depresses wages, but knowledge-based activities are different because they are subject to positive feedback. Any depression in the return to knowledge due to an abundance of knowledge workers is likely to be temporary. The self-reinforcing growth of a knowledge-based economy creates a revised version of the venerable Saye's Law: the supply of knowledge creates its own demand.

Third, capital mobility has increased substantially in recent years, due to new technologies, better developed capital markets, and liberalization in cross-border investment. Higher capital mobility leads to more competitive capital costs. Sound knowledge-based commercial activities can find financing from anywhere in the world, driving down capital costs in formerly closed economies. Knowledge-based economies attract capital while other economies export their savings.

Fourth, foreign goods and services themselves and foreign direct investment can be the origin of domestic creative destruction. Globalization thus makes it harder for entrenched, established firms to maintain the *status quo*. In the past, they could do this by starving innovative domestic firms of financing and by erecting other market entry barriers. In the era of more liberalized cross-border trade and investment, their grip is challenged by strong foreign firms' exports and by foreign direct investment. Foreign competition weakens large, entrenched domestic firms financially and politically. This opens the door to local innovators. Foreign direct investment can provide financial backing to these local innovators.[19]

Fifth, our world has become richer. As people get richer, they seek more sophisticated goods and services – even if these are more costly. To satisfy these more sophisticated demands, suppliers need knowledge. We prefer more sophisticated cars and household appliances; and we search and compare models on the Internet before we visit showrooms. We demand more comprehensive banking that goes beyond savings accounts with minimal interest rates. We are informed book buyers and want bookstores that can instantaneously locate our choices, offer user-friendly information services, and give us a cultural experience with each visit. The owners of dingy bookstores in strip malls face disaster without state intervention to save them.

Finally, the world has become more like economics textbooks always made it out to be. Globalization means that cosy local monopolies have been broken up, sweetheart deals between local bigwigs and corrupt politicians are harder to pull off, and people in one country no longer meekly accept paying more for groceries, books, or automobiles than people in other countries pay. This heightened "ordinary" competition has paved the way for heightened competition to innovate by giving entrepreneurs more secure access to wider markets and more secure property rights over the returns from their innovations.

4. SOME HARD QUESTIONS

4.1 Do Advanced Economies Like Canada's Have Any Alternative Other Than Shifting Towards a More Knowledge-Based Economy?

The options are limited and unattractive. Canadian firms are competing with U.S. firms and other countries' firms for both domestic customers and foreign customers. Knowledge-based firms will win because they are successful innovators producing goods or services that consumers want, at lower prices than their competitors. At the same time, innovators can attract the best employees by paying higher wages than their competitors. Finally, innovators can attract new capital to finance their expansion by offering investors higher and more certain returns. These competitive "edges" let innovators quickly gain large market shares through higher capital spending or acquisitions, and equally quickly push their less innovative competitors out to the fringes of the economy or into bankruptcy.

Canadian firms that survive this competition will also have to be knowledge-based firms with continuous learning and innovative capabilities. Skilled Canadians will work for knowledge-based firms, Canadian-owned or foreign-owned. Clearly, the cause for concern is Canadian firms that cannot compete and Canadian individuals who lack the skills to join knowledge-based firms.

It would be dangerously misguided to artificially halt Canada's transformation towards a more knowledge-based economy on this account. There are, however, real concerns that some Canadian firms will not survive and that some Canadians will suffer permanent declines in their living standards. This is the standard trade-off we face when discussing trade liberalization. Is some level of protection acceptable?

We need to be very sensitive to the extremely high costs of even some mitigated form of protection in a knowledge-based world. First, as we pointed out earlier, knowledge creation, and thus innovation, is subject to positive feedback - it breeds itself. Detriments to knowledge creation that disrupt this self-sustaining economic growth are extraordinarily costly. Second, as we pointed out in the previous section, protection, or subsidies for entrenched Canadian firms, hurts potential Canadian entrepreneurs. When the behemoths eventually fail, as fail they must, the only buyers for their assets will be foreigners. Finally, we must accept the logic of international trade economics: paying employment insurance to displaced workers is far cheaper than artificially protecting their jobs.

The United States, largely by accidents of history, demography, and politics, has developed laws, regulations, and customs that make innovation relatively easy and rewarding there. This means successful (i.e., innovative) American businesses are increasingly out-competing their rivals in other countries. Unless other countries find ways to accelerate innovation in their economies, they are likely to experience steadily worsening terms of trade with the United States, steadily stronger competition from the United States in third-country markets, and steadily eroding living standards. We can choose not to become a knowledge-based economy, but our children are unlikely to forgive us.

4.2   Do We Have to Abandon Social Fairness in a Knowledge-Based Economy?

A knowledge-based society is a society with legal, regulatory and informal codes of behaviour that support a knowledge-based economy by encouraging innovation and discouraging an unhealthy fixation on the *status quo*. In this very basic sense, a knowledge-based society is a "liberal" society. It is resolved to overcome the vested interests that defend old capital, old jobs, and other dimensions of the *status quo*. In this most basic sense, the interests that oppose the growth of a knowledge-based society are "conservative," even though many of these interests regard themselves as leftist or progressive.

In a knowledge-based economy, uneven and volatile income distribution is expected. This violates our usual sense of equity. Creative destruction inevitably hits some Canadians with substantial losses in their earnings, and this happens periodically. That is a serious concern!

To deal with it, we first need to develop a concept of fairness that makes sense in a knowledge-based economy. Fairness has traditionally meant income equality. Certainly, the ease with which innovators can dislodge, and even impoverish, old money in a knowledge-based economy must count as another sort of fairness. The philosophical basis of this concept of fairness is that every individual, even an innovator, should be able to improve her lot in life as much as possible.

Second, the high returns to knowledge-based activities come with high risks. Egalitarian judgements should not focus on the returns and ignore the risks. Their high earnings compensate innovators for the risks they have undertaken.

Third, not all change is bad. The sharp contrasts in income should not lead us to overlook the fact that innovators' high earnings are due to their abilities to fuel creative destruction. This raises the overall wealth level of the economy, and improves the lives of workers, customers and investors across the economy. In contrast, the wealth of the rich in a non-knowledge-intensive economy is usually inherited. This is harder to justify on egalitarian grounds.

Fourth, individuals and firms can conduct their own hedging of earning risks in a knowledge-based economy. Government-provided security can cause a moral hazard problem – certain individuals and firms will always try to scam the system. This can be expensive to the system and expensive to detect, and can undermine support for other government redistribution programs. In contrast, private insurance, for example, learning new skills, is free of such problems.

Social fairness remains in a knowledge-based economy, but we do need to think more carefully about what we really mean by the term. Socio-economic mobility and "risk management" have to become more important, and income equality less important.

4.3   Is Government Less Relevant in a Knowledge-Based Economy?

Absolutely not. Good government is critical in a knowledge-based economy. There are several tasks before it that call for deep thought. First, government needs to provide the institutional structure that lets knowledge-based activities take place. It must remove artificial entry barriers and prevent new ones from rising. It must provide the laws that let markets function well. It must provide public goods, like public health, information and education. It must protect property rights, especially those of innovators.

Second, government must promote economic openness. Though it is among the largest in the world, Canada's economy is small relative to that of the world's most important knowledge-based economy, that of the United States. If Canadian innovators are to generate knowledge as intensively as their U.S. counterparts, they must be able to make returns just as high. That means they must have clear access to markets at least as large as those their U.S. rivals can reach.

Finally, government should explicitly recognize that social programs should promote socio-economic mobility and "income risk management," not provide long-term "income support." Government can open doors for young people from low-income families with good public education and university scholarships. The current federal scholarship initiative is a commendable step in this direction. Government can also aid Canadians in managing their earning risks while undermining neither people's own efforts at risk management nor overall knowledge production and application. Examples of how to do this include risk-based unemployment insurance, tax-smoothing arrangements, and many other things. Examples of what not to do include ubiquitous universal transfer programs funded by high income taxes on innovators' profits, knowledge workers' pay, and so on.

Canadians accept that government must look after those who are truly desperate. They also recognize that their taxes support many worthwhile public goods – universal health care and quality public education, to name but the two most popular. But many other government expenditures have questionable returns. Runaway taxes to cover pointless government programs can quash creative destruction, killing the Canada goose that lays the golden eggs.

5. CONCLUSION

Curiosity and the desire for a better life are two of the most basic human instincts. A knowledge-based economy uses the satisfaction of one of these primal instincts, curiosity, to satisfy the other, longing for a better material life. So far, one and only one economic system, free enterprise, has proven able to combine these basic human motivations in a self-sustaining way.

Unlike most other economic inputs, knowledge is not destroyed when it is used. This means it can be used simultaneously in many places. One piece of knowledge can improve productivity all over the economy. This increased productivity can fund more knowledge creation. This effect, called positive feedback or increasing returns to scale for knowledge, appears to underlie the rapid growth of the Western World over the past three centuries.

The work of commercializing an idea is often hard and expensive. All our experience so far shows that only a free-market economy that gives innovators high returns for their work can become and remain a knowledge-based economy. Under all other economic systems, from feudalism to communism, those in power are able to wrest all or most of the return to innovation away from the innovators. Even social democracy tends to impose the views of "wise men" on the rest of us, often in ways that render innovation economically pointless for innovators. Without a clear link between creativity and economic reward, nothing in any of these systems steered innovation towards satisfying common people's wants and needs. Consequently, technological innovations that improved living standards in such economies were rare.

In a very profound sense, a knowledge-based economy is a marvellous manifestation of human transcendence. By harnessing instincts from deep in our evolutionary past, we can build an economic order based on both knowledge and satisfying people's wants and needs. In the democratic world, the business of government is also to serve the people. The care and feeding of our knowledge-based economy is therefore the government's duty.

The most important thing government can do to nourish a knowledge-based economy is to let successful innovators become very wealthy. Egalitarian leanings to tax inherited wealth, lottery winnings, land holdings, consumption goods, and the like may or may not be more beneficial than harmful. But government must take great care not to tax overly hard the returns to knowledge. Discouraging knowledge creation and use by taxing it too heavily undermines the growth through increasing returns to scale that makes a knowledge-based economy so attractive in the first place.

In the global economy, countries are "clubs," whose members are their citizens. When a club is not well run, its members begin to explore other clubs. People move their savings abroad or buy goods made elsewhere. A declining club loses its most important members first, for they are the ones the other clubs most gladly take in. Whether an economy is attracting or losing skilled people, their savings, and their consumption is therefore a direct measure of how well a government manages its "club." The winning "club" these days is unquestionably a knowledge-based economy that empowers people to become wealthy by creating knowledge that improves people's lives. Social programs and other traditional public goods must be popular not only with those who benefit from them but also with those who might most easily leave the "club." This means we need Peter's OK before we can tax him to pay Paul. Democratic governments therefore confront a binding constraint on the power of political majorities to redistribute wealth and income.

Because of this, we need some serious rethinking of the meaning of good economic governance. Part of our government's current burden is to reverse well-meaning past policies that now hinder knowledge creation and application. High income taxes unquestionably cause people with economically useful knowledge to flee this country in droves. Others arrive from Hong Kong, India and elsewhere to take their places, but Canada would be much better off if we could attract skilled immigrants *and* hold onto our own best and brightest. Our government must empower its people. It must provide the educational opportunities that its people need to participate in a knowledge-based economy, and then it must protect their rights to keep most of the fruits of their knowledge. If it does not, some other government surely will - and it can probably provide a better climate too.

NOTES

[1] There are other problems. Measuring investment in knowledge is usually quite difficult. For example, R&D spending is very fungible so that it is hard to specify R&D spending by industry. The problem applies in measuring other inputs too. Another problem is that the timing of the benefits of investment in knowledge may be quite volatile; some come more immediately and some only after a long delay.

[2] In any case, studies based on macro data are quite supportive of the importance of technological progress. For examples, see Lau (1997) and Lucas (1997). Both papers were presented at the Far Eastern Meeting of the Econometric Society, Hong Kong, 1997.

[3] See Wilson (1978, 1998).

[4] See Messadié (1988).

[5] See Rosenberg and Birdzell (1986).

[6] Exactly this behaviour by IBM's top management led to that company's largely missing out on the PC market in the 1980s; see Betz (1993). IBM's top researchers and managers had careers that were built around mainframe computers. Shifting to PCs meant running a nontrivial risk of marginalizing themselves.

[7] See, e.g. Jensen and Meckling (1995).

[8] See Schumpeter (1954).

[9] Lucas (1997) says, "On this general view of economic growth, then, what began in England in the eighteenth century and is continuing to diffuse throughout the world up to the present day was something like this. Technological advances occurred that increased the wages of those with the skills needed to make economic use of these changes. These wage effects stimulated others to accumulate skills, and stimulated many families to decide against having a large number of unskilled children and in favour of fewer children, with more time and resources invested in each. The presence of a higher skilled workforce increased still further the return to acquiring skills, keeping the process going." Lucas later mentions that countries that have been kept out of this process are those suffering from socialist planning or simply corruption and lawlessness. The ingredient of growth we emphasized is the empowerment of individuals and firms to establish and take advantage of the linkage between knowledge creation and reward.

[10] See Morck and Yeung (1997).

[11] See Morck and Yeung (1992).

[12] See Morck and Yeung (1990).

[13] See Mitchell, Morck, Shaver and Yeung (forthcoming).

[14] See Acs, Morck, Shaver and Yeung (1997).

[15] See Oxley and Yeung (1998).

[16] See Morck, Shleifer and Vishny (1989).

[17] See Morck, Shleifer and Vishny (1988).

[18] See Mandel (1996).

[19] See Morck, Stangeland and Yeung (1998).

REFERENCES

Acs, Z., R. Morck, M. Shaver and B. Yeung, "The Internationalization of Small and Medium Size Firms: A Policy Perspective." *Small Business Economics*, 9(1), 1997, 7-20.

Betz, F., *Strategic Technology Management*. New York: McGraw Hill, 1993.

Jensen, M.C. and W.H. Meckling, "Specific and General Knowledge, and Organizational Structure." *Journal of Applied Corporate Finance*, 8, 1995, pp. 4-18.

Lau, L., "The Sources of and Prospects for East Asian Economic Growth." Paper presented at the Far Eastern Meeting of the Econometric Society, Hong Kong, 1997.

Lucas, R.E., Jr., "The Industrial Revolution: Past and Future." Paper presented at the Far Eastern Meeting of the Econometric Society, Hong Kong, 1997.

Mandel, M., *The High Risk Society*. Times Business. New York: Random House, 1996.

Messadié, G., *Great Inventions Through History*. Toronto: Chambers, 1988.

Mitchell, W., R. Morck, M. Shaver and B. Yeung, "Causality Between International Expansion and Investment in Intangibles, with Implications for Financial Performance and Firm Survival," in J.-F. Hennert (Ed.) *Global Competition and Market Entry Strategies*. The Hague: Elsevier, North-Holland, forthcoming.

Morck, R., A. Shleifer and R. Vishny, "Managerial Ownership and Corporate Performance: An Empirical Analysis." *Journal of Financial Economics*, 20 (1/2), 1988, 293-315.

Morck, R., A. Shleifer and R. Vishny, "Alternative Mechanisms for Corporate Control." *American Economic Review*, 79 (4), 1989, 842-852.

Morck, R., D. Stangeland and B. Yeung, "Inherited Wealth, Corporate Control, and Economic Growth, the Canadian Disease." NBER Working Paper # 6814 nov. 98.

Morck, R. and B. Yeung, "Why Investors Value Multinationality." *Journal of Business*, 64 (2), 1990, 165-187.

Morck, R. and B. Yeung, "Internalization, An Event Study Test." *Journal of International Economics*, 33, 1992, 41-56.

Morck, R. and B. Yeung, "Why Investors Sometimes Value Diversification: Internalization vs. Agency Behavior." University of Alberta Working Paper. May 1997.

Oxley, J. and B. Yeung. "Industry Location, Growth, and Government Activism: The Changing Economic Landscape," in J. Oxley and B.Yeung (Eds.) *Structural Change, Industrial Location and Competitiveness*. Cheltenham, U.K. and Northampton, MA: Edward Elgar Co., 1998.

Rosenberg, N. and L.E. Birdzell, Jr., *How the West Grew Rich*. New York: Basic Books, 1986.

Schumpeter, J., *A History of Economic Thought*. Oxford: Oxford University Press, 1954.

Wilson, E.O., *On Human Nature*. Cambridge, MA: Harvard University Press, 1978.

Wilson, E.O. *Consilience*. New York: Alfred A. Knopf, 1998.

3. THE GLOBAL INFORMATION INFRASTRUCTURE: FROM THE VIRTUAL ENTERPRISE TO THE VIRTUAL ECONOMY

Louis A. Lefebvre
École Polytechnique & CIRANO

Élisabeth Lefebvre
École Polytechnique & CIRANO

Pierre Mohnen
Université du Québec à Montréal & CIRANO

Innovation is of importance... It enables the whole quality of life to be changed for better or for worse. It can mean not merely more of the same goods but a pattern of goods and services which has not previously existed, except in the imagination. (Freeman, 1982, p. 3)

1. INTRODUCTION

Today's economic landscape is characterized in the popular press by the metaphors "globalization", "knowledge-based economy", and "information society." Globalization refers to the worldwide scale of production, distribution and ownership. Transnational corporations organize their production from facilities in several countries. Financial markets are integrated and R&D is spread around the globe. "Knowledge-based society" refers to the recognition of knowledge as a proxy for technological change and as a key factor in economic growth. Competition in new products and improved product quality replaces the traditional price competition. "Information society" refers to the information and communication technologies (ICT) as a new techno-economic paradigm, revolutionizing how we do business and affecting many aspects of our daily life. These three facets are, of course, interrelated and mutually reinforcing. One feature of the new economic order, which also relates to the other three, and which we want to bring to the forefront in this paper, is the growing importance of virtual enterprises and their impact on the emergence of a virtual or digital economy. The "virtual" or "digital" economy refers to an era of business without borders (temporal, geographical, functional or organizational) fueled by the activities of entities called "virtual enterprises" which operate in high-performance networks of suppliers, competitors and consumers.

Technological change, international trade, and international capital flows have always existed, as far back as history goes. What distinguishes nowadays from yesterday is the possibility of quasi-instantaneous information exchange and real-time interactions between customers, producers and scientists. Progress in the means of transportation, lowering of tariff barriers, improvements in private property protection and especially advances in ICT have made this world a global village and a global marketplace. The purpose of this paper is to examine the consequences of the global information infrastructure on firm behavior, industrial structures and government policies. We shall argue that we are heading towards a new paradigm characterized by virtual enterprises and virtual economies, where opportunities are infinite but where the current ground rules will need to be redefined.

Urban communities, states, provinces and countries continue to exist and serve as a basis to organize social life. But more and more new entities come to dominate the traditional geographically defined economies. Multinational corporations (MNCs) and producer networks constitute economies of their own, often larger in value-added, capital endowment, population, and wealth than some of the official countries in the world. Members of those networks are tied by explicit contracts (ownerships, partnerships, collaborations, trade agreements, licences, subcontracts, etc.), almost as countries are unified by a constitution. These multinational economies are being shaped and reshaped under the pressure of competition and the evolution of technologies and markets. A new governance structure is in the making. New laws and regulations have to be set up to protect the consumer, the inventor, the Internet surfer, the worker, the investor, the citizen so that the new technology of the global information infrastructure will allow our well-being to reach new heights instead of threatening the social order in which we live.

2. THE MAIN DRIVERS OF THE VIRTUAL ECONOMY

The virtual economy is based on four drivers which are mutually interacting: the socio-political-economic zones of integration, the national and global information infrastructure, the rise of the virtual enterprise and the emergence of new technological platforms (Figure 1).

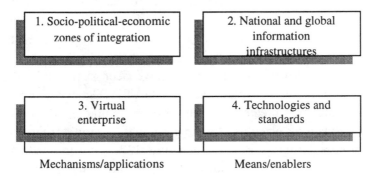

Figure 1: The virtual economy and its four drivers

2.1 Socio-Political-Economic Zones of Integration

The first building block of the virtual economy is the social, political and economic zones of integration that have slowly brought the world closer together. As a result of progress in the means of transportation (railways, steam engines, automobiles, airplanes) and in the means of communication (television, satellites, faxes, Internet), people from various parts of the world are in constant touch and ideas circulate quickly and freely. International institutions (like the United Nations, the International Monetary Fund, the OECD, the World Bank, the International Court of Justice) have been created to monitor the economic, social and political changes around the globe, to avoid major economic, financial, political and social crises, and to provide a forum for the exchange of ideas and the settlement of conflicts. Even if success on all these fronts has not been overwhelming, the fact remains that nations are linked, communicate with each other, and can hardly hide from world attention.

At the same time, transportation costs have substantially dropped, allowing production to take place far away from consumption locations. Proximity to natural resources is still essential in some sectors like aluminum. Proximity to the consumer, however, has become of secondary importance. For instance, when choosing where to invest in plants or R&D labs, MNCs are sensitive to differences in tax rates across countries, not just to transportation costs. Altshuler et al. (1998) estimate that a 1% increase in after tax returns led to a 3% increase in real capital stock of overseas manufacturers of U.S. MNCs in 1992. Hines (1994) estimates that U.S. multinational parent firms respond to higher tax rates on royalties to their affiliates by paying fewer royalties and performing more R&D at home. Hines (1996) finds that local taxes influence if not the location of capital flows at least their ownership structure. He evaluates that FDI stocks respond by 9% to 11% to a 1% increase in local tax rates on corporate earnings.

Since the end of World War II, efforts have been spent on bilateral and multilateral talks to remove trade barriers. GATT (General Agreement on Tariffs and Trade) was created as an institution. Inside GATT a number of trade negotiations took place, leading to a gradual lowering of tariff barriers. In particular, the Uruguay Round, including 122 countries, led to further tariff reductions in the trade of goods, the extension of free trade to services, and the TRIPS agreement (trade related intellectual property rights). The World Trade Organization (WTO) was created with the power to enforce negotiated agreements through a dispute settlement procedure.

In parallel to these multilateral talks, regional trade groupings were formed in various parts of the world. In 1959, the EEC (European Economic Community) was created in Europe and initially had six member countries. It developed to become the EU (Economic Union) with 15 member countries. In North America, the Free Trade Agreement between the United States and Canada came into effect in 1989. In 1994, NAFTA (the North American Free Trade Agreement) was signed between the U.S., Canada and Mexico. Similar regional trade groupings of the customs union (no tariffs within the union and common external tariffs) or the free trade agreement type (no tariffs for internal trade and separate external tariffs) exist in other parts of the world (APEC, Mercosur, ASEAN, etc.).

Hence, although in the 1970s and 1980s there was some resurgence of protectionism (Bhagwati, 1988), it remains true that the trend towards free trade and economic integration is outstanding. The increase in economic integration has three effects. First, firms are more exposed to competitive pressure. To retain their domestic and foreign market shares, firms must deliver quality at low prices. Competition thus stimulates firms to do research and to be efficient. Second, trade is a vehicle for the transmission of ideas.

International R&D spillovers and outright technology transfers speed up the diffusion of inventions and stimulate innovations. Third, the suppression of barriers to free trade in effect increases the market size and allows the exploitation of economies of scale.

Restrictions on international capital movements have also decreased. The creation of monetary unions like the upcoming Euro-system in Europe and the effort on the part of many governments to contain fluctuations in the exchange rates have, in effect, deepened the integration of international financial markets. As a result, investments in a country are freed from the constraint of the availability of domestic savings and inflationary pressures are contained by the provision of goods from all over the world. The drawback of the increased mobility of capital is the sensitivity of exchange rates and the vulnerability of exporters to speculative movements across currencies.

Finally, foreign direct investments are on the rise, not so much to avoid trade restrictions as to exploit cost advantages. Joint ventures, R&D collaborations, and interlocking directorates bring managers closer together and occasionally turn fierce competitors into temporary partners.

Other industry-led initiatives for creating zones of economic collaboration are now being set. An example of this is the ANX network in the automobile industry. This network, which constitutes a private network over the Internet, will bring together hundreds of thousands of industrial partners from the U.S., Europe, and Asia. It will be used for the exchange of commercial and technical information. When in full operation it will allow for savings of US $70 per car produced, amounting to billions in savings per year for the industry.

The integration across many dimensions of the world economy is a background structure facilitating the virtual economy. The most immediate determinant of the virtual economy, however, is the revolution in information and communication technologies (ICT), and, even more than that, it is the integrative and interactive power of the technologies grouped together under the generic name of "Information Infrastructure."

2.2 National and Global Information Infrastructures

Information technologies (IT) have experienced very strong growth in the 24 OECD member countries: the IT market segment of US $220 billion in 1985 jumped to US $460 billion in 1995 (a 109% increase over 8 years), with an even sharper increase for packaged software (a 183% increase over the same period). As a percentage of world merchandise trade, information and communication technologies also experienced strong and healthy growth, reaching almost 12% of world merchandise trade in 1994.[1] According to the U.S. Bureau of Economic Analysis, the IT industry accounted, as early as 1996 for a "stunning 33% of GNP growth propelled by Internet" (*Business Week*, March 31, 1997).

Advances in ICT have lowered the cost of transmitting information, increased the potential for information storage and intelligent organization, and facilitated the quick retrieval of information. The codification of knowledge has made it easier to transmit knowledge and possibly also increased productivity in research and development.

These upward trends are expected to continue with the increased development and improvement of national information infrastructures (NII). These include initiatives such as connection of schools, public libraries, and households to the information superhighway, development of open networking technologies (products, applications, software and services), e-filing of tax returns, information on government contracts and open bidding through the Internet, national electronic bulletin boards for job applications and job openings, etc. According to several observators, the US have upgraded facilities for NII, with annual investments reaching between US $50 billion and US $100 billion, and similar orders of magnitude hold for other countries.

NII programs have become a matter of national priority but, since information infrastructures cannot be limited to national boundaries, a worldwide strategy under the name of "Global Information Infrastructure" (GII) is also currently under way. Such a strategy requires extensive cooperation among individual countries, governments, industry and international organizations such as the OECD, WTO, ISO, ITU or WIPO.[2] Although there is no doubt that the GII represents a much more complex undertaking than the NII, as the latter reflect the historical, cultural, economic, social, regulatory and political characteristics of each nation, progress towards the GII was made in 1995 since the initial G-7 Ministerial Conference on the Global Information Society (Brussels, February 25-26, 1995). The G-7 countries have not only agreed on eight main principles but have also launched several joint pilot projects, whose main objective is to stimulate the development of GII by demonstrating its potential. For example, (i) expand the CommerceNet/NIST (National Institute of Standards and Technology) Smart Procurement demonstration into a full-fledged global project pilot; (ii) develop a pilot implementation to demonstrate a manufacturing environment for product development and supply chain management using the STEP standard for exchange of product data, IGES, CAD systems, etc.; (iii) develop directory services for resources on the GII (see Adam and Yesha, 1996).

The NII/GII has two main characteristics. First, by its very nature it is integrative, either with respect to technology (broadband communication, telecommunications, and information technologies) or with respect to the convergence of content (business documents, product designs, pictures, music or books being converted into digital information). Key components of existing NII and GII allow the resulting digital information to be accessed, processed, analyzed and enhanced in various ways. Ultimately, NII/GII could bring together ideas, knowledge and data from anywhere to anyone. This is truly a network of networks, able to expand exponentially. Secondly, the NII/GII consists of several interactive innovations (for instance, EDI and the Internet) and interactive innovations tend to diffuse more rapidly in earlier stages than non-interactive ones. Furthermore, an interactive innovation is of little interest to an individual (or a firm) unless another individual (or firm) also adopts the innovation in question. As such, the utility (real or perceived) of an interactive innovation increases for all adopters with each additional individual or firm that adopts it (Rogers, 1995). An interactive innovation leads to the well-known positive network externalities and therefore promotes what Markus (1990) terms reciprocal interdependence (as opposed to sequential interdependence), a concept whereby "benefits flow backward in time to previous adopters as well as forward in time to future adopters" (Rogers, 1995, p. 315). Finally, the diffusion becomes self-sustaining once a critical mass is reached, as evidenced by the rapid rise in Internet connections around the world.

All facets of network connections displayed substantial growth in recent years. For instance, Intranets (electronic networks linking employees inside a corporation or linking the subsidiaries of a multinational corporation) have experienced a sharp increase. The Intranet market is expected to grow at an annual rate of 49% for the next five years according to the recent study carried out by Kellen and Associates. EDI, which relies mainly on private networks and is still expensive to set up, is also on the rise with almost 95% of Fortune 1000 companies using EDI for some aspect of their businesses as early as in 1997 (*The Economist*, May 10, 1997). The growth in the number of Internet users is the most spectacular and the best publicized: their number has almost doubled every year for the last two years: in 1996 some 23.4 million households (or 35 million users) had access to the Internet and 550 million users are projected in the early 2000 according to some estimates. The U.S. Japan, Germany, Canada and the U.K. led the way in 1996. As a direct consequence of these increased levels of electronic interactions, electronic commerce is booming and is forecasted to account for 7.5% of total worldwide sales of goods and services by the year 2000 (equivalent to US \$600 billion). However, electronic commerce is only one dimension, albeit an important one, of the virtual economy.

2.3   The Virtual Enterprise

The virtual enterprise is defined by the National Industrial Information Infrastructure Protocols (NIIIP, 1996) as "a temporary consortium of independent member companies which come together to quickly exploit fast-changing worldwide product manufacturing opportunities. Virtual enterprises assemble themselves based on cost effectiveness and product uniqueness without regard for organization, size, geographic location, computing environments, technologies deployed, or processes implemented. Virtual enterprise companies share costs, skills, and core competencies which collectively enable them to access global markets with world class solutions that could not be provided individually."

Virtual enterprises can operate in any sector or in multiple sectors of economic activity. Although the above definition seems to be directed at the manufacturing sector, the service industry, for instance financial services, is obviously well suited to become virtual. In fact, if an organization does not turn out a physical product, it can be totally virtual: it can deliver its services completely by electronic means and no longer needs to maintain physical facilities as it can perform most business functions with little physical platforms; in short, it relies on the exploitation of its electronic capabilities and networks.

At the heart of the model are the product integrators (Figure 2), which may be TNCs, SMEs or governments which, through a common information base and common international norms and standards, will integrate suppliers, subcontractors, vendors and bankers along a product's value chain to maximize the value between the different components of the chain and to provide the best possible product for all customers worldwide. This is done by ensuring that the network of firms involved is composed of a very effective and efficient cast of players operating in what we have referred to as a "high-performance network."

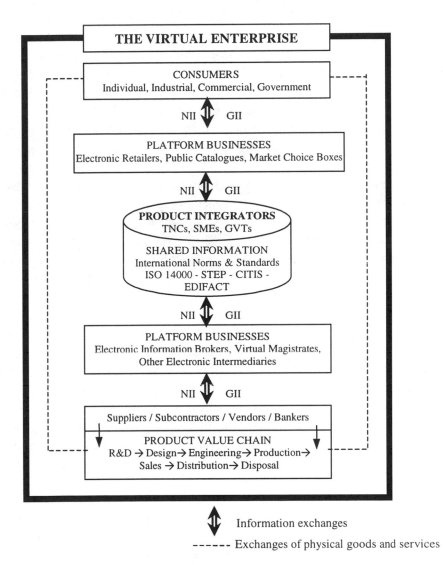

Figure 2: The virtual enterprise model

This model also relies on a new set of players, referred to as "platform businesses," who play an intermediary role between trade partners that are likely to be far apart and never to have traded with each other in the past. In that context, platform businesses provide the functions essential to trade on an open computer network, namely provision of partner search functions, creation of trust among trading partners, evaluation of economic value, provision of standardized interface, and integration of functions (see Kokuryo and Takeda, 1997). The platform businesses also act as intermediaries between customers and product integrators, for example, in electronic retailing and market choice boxes. Of course, in this new model, countries and borders become blurred. For instance, an automobile manufacturer may order prefabricated chunks and parts and assemble them just-in-time to meet the customer's demand. General Motors Corp. has sold its Delphi Automotive Systems components unit to specialize in marketing and leave the production to subcontractors, which manufacture parts for automobiles of different brands.

As a deliberate strategic move, a growing number of firms have chosen to manage some of their internal core functions in a virtual way and some have rapidly decided to integrate their activities into a virtual value chain. Virtual design is one of the earlier moves made by firms to fully exploit the benefits derived from the existing electronic methodologies and the digitalization of products and processes. Thus, firms achieve significant benefits by (i) substantially improved efficiency in data re-entry (minimizing errors); (ii) working on a 24-hour basis through the exploitation of different time zones (e.g., Eastern U.S.A., Japan and Europe); (iii) ongoing and real-time input from geographically dispersed customers. The design of Boeing's 777 is a prime example of virtual design. Boeing's paperless design of the 777 Aircraft was set up by more than 200 "design building teams." Each of the 234 teams included engineers from major carriers (including those from American Airlines, which placed the first order for 34 planes, estimated to reach $3 billion) in order to better capture customer needs. Virtual design leads to virtual products that "mostly exist even before they are produced" (Davidow and Malone, 1992, p. 4).

Electronic commerce represents the most visible component of the virtual economy. Activities formerly performed by hand, in person, by fax or by mail can now be executed automatically and electronically, regardless of location, by all parties involved in a given business venture (customers, manufacturers, suppliers, distributors, financial institutions, etc.). Some firms have taken full advantage of at least one aspect of electronic commerce. On-line selling is booming: for instance, Cisco Systems sells goods from its Web site at the annual rate of US $5 billion (*Business Week*, August 24, 1998); on-line sales of PCs on the web represent close to 10% of business for Gateway 2000 and Dell Computer; Chrysler, whose Internet sales for its first year on line reached 1.5% of its total sales, expects them to climb to 25% in four years' time (*The Economist*, May 10, 1997). On-line procurement activities are also moving at a fast pace. General Electric purchased $1 billion worth of components on-line from its suppliers in 1996 and this was predicted to reach $5 billion, that is, almost the totality of GE's purchases, by the year 2000. Through electronic commerce, inventories are kept down to a minimum. Dell Computer Corporation does not order components from suppliers until an order is booked. In an industry where prices tend to decrease, this policy yields a 6% profit advantage. The average time to convert a sale into cash is less than 24 hours for Dell against 35 days for Compaq Computer Corporation (*Business Week*, April, 7, 1997; *The Economist*, May 10, 1997).

2.4 Technologies and Standards

NII/GII, as mentioned previously, constitutes the backbone of the virtual economy but is in a rudimentary form. Continuous improvements are being made and will continue to be made as a result of many technological advances in fiber-optic systems, digital compression, storage capacity of computer systems, digital wireless systems and software. Any forecast concerning technology evolution is plagued by the considerable complexity raised by the technological convergence required by NII/GII. Further, technology evolution is linked to the development and deployment of business and non-business applications which are still largely deficient but improving at an incredible pace. For instance, when the U.S. Department of Defense formed the ARPA (Advanced Research Projects Agency), it was impossible to envision the applications currently found on the Internet.

According to the notion of technology cycles, technological discontinuities or breakthroughs lead to an "era of ferment" where substitution processes and design competition among rival technologies occur, resulting in a period of high uncertainty. The selection of a dominant design is "community-driven": Dominant designs "emerge not from a technical logic but from a negotiated logic enlivened by actors with interests in competing technical systems" and are "shaped by a process of compromise and accommodation between suppliers, vendors, customers and governments" (Tushman and Rosenkopf, 1997, p. 194). Once a dominant design is settled on, numerous incremental innovations elaborate, extend and reinforce the dominant design, and "normal science" (Kuhn, 1970) goes on until the next "scientific revolution," making a complete cycle.

With respect to many aspects of NII/GII, we are in the era of ferment prior to the selection of dominant designs. For instance, CALS ("Continuous Acquisition and Life-Cycle Support," also known as "Commerce At Light Speed") could turn out to be the dominant design for future business platforms on NII/GII. CALS is a global strategy to further enterprise integration through the streamlining of business processes and the application of standards and technologies for the development, management, exchange and use of business and technical information. The CALS technology relies on several data, functional and technical interchange standards (see Exhibit 1).

Exhibit 1
CALS Technologies

- STEP (Standard for the Exchange of Product Model Data), which has been used by Boeing and Rolls-Royce (for the Boeing 777), McDonnell Douglas (for the C17 aircraft) and the U.S. Army (for RAMP – Rapid Acquisition of Manufactured Parts). STEP is the cornerstone of concurrent engineering. The improvement and implementation of STEP in the automobile industry are done by powerful associations such as VCALS for the JAMA (Japanese Automobile Manufacturers Association), VDA-proSTEP in Germany, GALIA in France or Odette in Sweden.
- CITIS (Contractor Integrated Technical Information Services), which will manage both the bidding side (suppliers) and the demand side.
- EDI (Electronic Data Interchange) and ISO 14000 (more specifically, ISO 14040). This last standard is particularly useful for the life-cycle assessment of a product/service.

Projects involving CALS technology are under way in several countries including the U.S., Japan, the U.K., Sweden, Finland, Australia and Korea and, although CALS originated in the defence sector, projects are now directed towards the aerospace, automobile, construction, software, energy, chemical products, pharmaceutical products and health-care sectors (Lefebvre et al., 1997). Multinationals (such as Lockheed Martin or IBM), governments (such as the MITI in Japan), small businesses (e.g., the group called Technology 2020) and international agencies (such as NATO) are heavily involved in pilot projects. This strongly suggests that CALS technology could be one dominant design[3] in the next century, since there is ample evidence at this stage of the willingness of many countries to fulfill its development and promote its applications in different industrial sectors.

One other major concern in the virtual economy is the development of a fully integrated platform for all applications of electronic commerce. One particular area which will have significant repercussions is electronic payment technology. On-line credit-card-based systems constitute a case in point. As of February 1996, Visa and MasterCard announced that SET (Secure Electronic Transactions) is the single technical standard (based on a public key encryption and authentication technology from RSA Data Security) for on-line credit-card systems (on the Internet or any other open network). The SET consortium includes leading participants such as Microsoft, Netscape, IBM, GTE, SAIC and Terisa Systems. Multos, which was launched on March 15, 1997, goes one step further. Multos is a "lifestyle card" using the most advanced open technology platform.[4]

Other technological developments deal with the emerging interactive electronic vehicles such as VOD (video on demand) or multimedia kiosks. The list of promising technologies for NII/GII goes on and on. The few technologies presented here exemplify the diversity and complexity of applications (most being software-driven) that will be found on NII/GII. It has been demonstrated that rival technologies and powerful actors struggle and compete while making the transition from the old to the new regime. The uncertainty in the present era of ferment depends on three underlying factors: first, the difficulty of integrating all aspects related to complex technologies where pilot projects and experiments can provide only partial answers; second, an unclear appreciation of the behavior of consumers, firms, institutions and governments and their willingness to change; third, a misunderstanding or a biased appreciation of the intrinsic merits of the new regime, as future applications of NII/GII are difficult to foresee and their relative benefits hard to assess.[5]

3. THE VIRTUAL ECONOMY: AN EMERGING PARADIGM

The virtual economy will have profound repercussions on management, industry structures, and economic policy. This section describes the economy in action: its major players and their strategies, the new governance environment in the virtual economy, the predictable changes in industry structures and in firm behaviors.

3.1   The Lead Agents in the Virtual Economy

The transition to the virtual economy is being accelerated by three types of lead users: MNCs, national governments, and supranational agencies.

MNCs can collectively exert an enormous influence: their total revenues exceed US $15.5 trillion; they account for 40% of the world's manufacturing output, almost a quarter of world trade and about a quarter of the world's output (Bartlett and Ghoshal, 1995, p. 4-5, Lipsey et al., 1995). The total revenues of General Motors exceed the GDP of Turkey, those of Royal Dutch Shell the GDP of Norway.[6] Most MNCs have already managed one or more of their internal key functions virtually and are now in the process of extending this process to take full advantage of the potential of NII/GII. In the aeronautics industry, Lockheed Martin is deploying its full spectrum electronic commerce. Over the period 1995-2005, it should move its network-enabled business practices from a simple EDI platform to outsourcing over GII and eventually to virtual enterprise operations. The program involves all of Lockheed Martin's suppliers worldwide including a significant number of SMEs. Lockheed Martin has recently extended the reach of this program by involving McDonnell Douglas and Dassault Systems. IBM is using its CATIA System to bridge the gap by allowing different suppliers from different parts of the world to operate in a virtual manner on product development cycles. In the automobile industry, JAMA (Japanese Automobile Manufacturers Association), which is composed of most of the major actors in the industry, i.e., Honda, Nissan, Mazda, Mitsubishi and Toyota, is actively developing its electronic commerce model based on the CALS platform.

As for governments, their role has been and will continue to be instrumental. Government-driven consumption of goods and services represents between 5% and 15% of total GDP expenditures for OECD countries, with Japan being at the lower end of the scale and Canada, the U.S. and the U.K. at the higher. Actions such as that taken by the American Department of Defense (DOD) have had drastic impacts on numerous firms: as early as 2000, suppliers to DOD have to integrate the underlying standards for CALS. The CALS technology will thus become a prequalifier for firms wanting to do business with DOD. Further, governments play an active role by ensuring the adequate diffusion of technologies, norms and standards. CommerceNet in the U.S., SWEDCALS in Sweden (a government-industry group which, among other activities, is extensively developing the new international norms and standards with the ISO Group) and CIRPLS (Computer Integration for Requirements, Procurement and Logistic Support) in the U.K. are all good examples of government initiatives aimed at ensuring adequate adoption and diffusion of international norms and standards that will be required to operate on international business platforms.

At the supranational level, many organizations are preparing the transition to the virtual economy. NATO has been working since 1993 on the definition of the new business platform including the international norms and business practices required to operate on the GII. This effort is fueled by the understanding that one of the cornerstones of the new emerging economy is the need to rely on the best competencies, irrespective of their location, and to form the best performing supplier chain. Also, it wants to exploit to its full potential the information exchange between customers, prime contractors, subcontractors and suppliers. In Japan, MITI supports the MATIC project (manufacturing technology supported by advanced and integrated information system) initiated in 1994 by Japan, China, Indonesia, Malaysia, Singapore and Thailand.

3.2　Restructuring to Compete

As firms turn virtual, industries are reorganizing and redefining themselves. This trend disrupts, although unevenly, firms in many traditional sectors. Some sectors are already heavy users of the information superhighway (banks and financial institutions deliver some of their core services on line) while others are just starting to envision the possibilities. Business in the financial sector with discount on-line brokers such as Schwab or in the retail sector with Auto-by-Tel (an Internet car-buying service) is booming. Virtual shopping malls are on the horizon. The health sector is particularly well suited to adapt to the virtual economy. The creation of "virtual health-care enterprises," loosely coupled and geographically dispersed health-care groups, will allow managers to effectively integrate and coordinate via open-systems-based networks the complex processes associated with health care such as procurement, clinical information, administrative information, insurance claims, and monitoring.

While some traditional sectors are being restructured in depth, new ones are created. This is the case of the fast-growing multimedia sector fueled by the anticipated convergence of audio, video and computing technologies. The multimedia industry will probably generate a multitude of activities related to content either for entertainment (interactive video games, for instance), education, or business applications. New electronic marketplaces are being created. For instance, Freemarkets Online Inc. in Pittsburgh runs auctions for such products as steel parts and printed circuit boards. It identifies suppliers, finds buyers and runs auctions which provide real-time prices (*Business Week*, August 24, 1998).

3.2.1   The Disappearance of Low-Value-Added Traditional Intermediaries

The industry value chain is also evolving as a consequence of NII/GII's potential. Firms redefine their upstream and downstream relationships by the extensive use of NII/GII. For instance, the reduction of transaction costs represents one of the strong incentives for firms to electronically coordinate their activities along the industry value chain. In some cases, a manufacturer can leap over many intermediaries and substantially reduce the final cost of a particular product or service, as illustrated in the example of a high-quality shirt manufacturer in Figure 3.

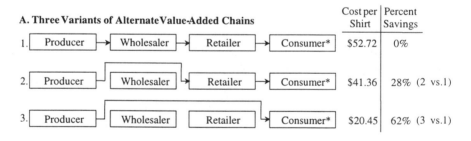

A. Three Variants of Alternate Value-Added Chains

				Cost per Shirt	Percent Savings
1. Producer → Wholesaler → Retailer → Consumer*				$52.72	0%
2. Producer — Wholesaler → Retailer → Consumer*				$41.36	28% (2 vs.1)
3. Producer — Wholesaler — Retailer → Consumer*				$20.45	62% (3 vs.1)

B. Growth in Value Added and Selling Prices

	Producer	Wholesaler	Retailer	Consumer*
Value Added	$20.45	$11.36	$20.91	
Selling Price	$20.45	$31.81	$52.72	$52.72

*Consumer transaction costs are not considered

Source: Kalakota and Whinston (1996)

Figure 3: Reconfiguration of an industry value chain

As illustrated in Figure 3, low-value-added traditional intermediaries can be bypassed or replaced by electronic intermediaries. The use of intelligent search agents allows the final customer (whether an individual, an industrial firm or a governmental agency) to find the best product at the lowest price with customized characteristics from any place in the world. Market imperfections (inadequate or partial information, prohibitive costs to obtain exhaustive information) are therefore disappearing but so are actual intermediaries who thrive on these imperfections. Travel agents, retailers, insurance brokers or car dealers are among the traditional intermediaries whose future might be at stake.

Furthermore, for smaller firms, the GII/NII constitutes a rather inexpensive way to communicate, at least when compared to the more traditional means of communicating (like long-distance calls, faxes or travel). From that perspective, the world is opening up to the small companies[7] as long as they agree to bear the initial costs of implementing the required norms and standards. This obviously causes a polarization of strong and weak performers and eventually the elimination of the inefficient firms.

3.2.2 Reorganizing around the Product or the Service

Not only is the vertical structure of the different sectors of economic activity modified as a result of increased use of electronic interactions among key actors, but firms or institutions reorganize themselves around *the* product or *the* service which becomes the central focus of all strategic attention. This is obviously in line with the customer-driven approach prevalent in all sectors of economic activity in developed countries.

In order to deliver a product or render a service, a number of activities have to be performed. This is best represented by a product/service value chain. In the case of a manufactured good, the product value chain consists of a collection of activities from inbound logistics to applied research, process and product design, plant engineering, warehousing, manufacturing, quality control, market research, marketing, advertising, sales, distribution, repair, and customer service, all of which add value to the products. With a closer look at these activities, it is possible to observe that service activities (compared to production activities) are now crucial value-added activities in the value chain. In fact, "even in manufacturing companies, typically only 10-35 percent of all activities are involved in direct production" and "most of the value added in manufacturing is created by knowledge-based service activities" (Quinn, 1992, p. 41).

The product value chain appears in the right-hand side of Figure 4 and the left-hand side of the same figure illustrates how firms and other key actors reconfigurate themselves in a new organizational form called the "virtual enterprise". The complex links between the product value chain and the virtual enterprise are also shown in Figure 4.

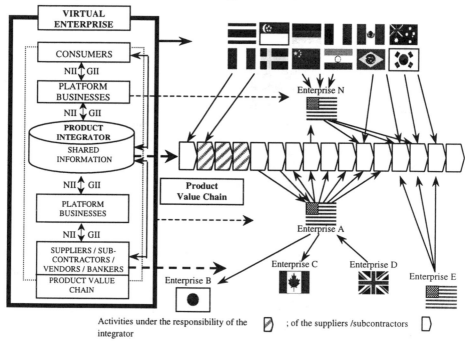

Figure 4: Product value chain integration

Let us first observe that the virtual value chain transcends national borders since firms tend to mobilize the best resources and form temporary alliances with the best firms already connected in high-performance networks. For example, in Figure 4, One firm integrates the various operations of the product value chain, contracting out market research, marketing and advertising to a Canadian firm, logistics, plant engineering, warehousing, manufacturing and quality control to a Japanese firm, sales, distribution, repair and after-sales service to another U.S. firm, and itself performing only the activities of applied research, process design and product design. This seriously challenges the relationships between prime contractors and the different levels of suppliers/subcontractors (first-tier, second-tier, etc.). The pyramidal structure of an industry sector may thus be modified. Even well-established structures such as the Japanese keiretsus are being called into question (Kokuryo and Takeda, 1997).

Second, in the restructuring required to build the virtual enterprise, innovation strategies will also have to take into account a new kind of business called "platforms businesses," which we described earlier as an intermediary between customers and product integrators and between product integrators and value chain suppliers. The concept of product integrator also departs from the more traditional concept of the firm since it implies that any one firm can act as a product integrator for numerous products and as a supplier to numerous other product integrators. This new multiweb structure will provide opportunities for firms, large or small, inasmuch as they can offer distinct value-adding competencies. Numerous examples of this organizational form exist, starting with the well-known case of the textile industry in the Prato region of Italy where over 15,000 small textile firms act by working in networks for brokers (*impannatori*) who provide the interface with the customers.

We observe an increase in intra-industry trade between countries. Specialization occurs not just between broadly defined industries but at a much finer level of detail. In fact, countries tend to specialize in specific activities in the value chain of a particular good. According to Hummels, Rapoport, and Yi (1998), the so-called vertical specialization trade accounts for 20% to 25% of world trade. It increased by 20% from the late 1960s and early 1970s to the beginning of the 1990s in ten OECD countries.

MNCs move their production and R&D operations to wherever profit opportunities are highest given differences in wages, taxes, regulations of any kinds (labour, environmental, investment, etc.), general business conditions, government policies and attitude towards business, endowments of human capital, infrastructure, and natural resources, proximity to input providers and output buyers, to name just a few. The value added of foreign affiliates accounted for 6% of world GDP in 1991, three times more than in 1982 (Hummels et al., 1998). Management of these corporations is internationalized, capital is footloose (Hirst and Thompson, 1996) and they are, in Ohmae's words, "stateless" (Ohmae, 1995) and, in some cases, as powerful as certain countries.

The following extract from Enright et al. (1997, p. 54) illustrates the new business philosophy: "A Hong Kong company might help a United States apparel company design its fall collection and then organize purchasing, manufacturing, and logistics to get the product on the retail shelves on time, meeting the right quality and product standards, and on budget. Design and prototyping might be done in Hong Kong. Then for the long production run, fabric might be sourced in Malaysia, zippers in Japan, buttons in Taiwan, and thread in South Korea. The fabric might be cut in Hong Kong and the garment assembled on the Chinese mainland. The customer never knows what a complex network was involved in creating the end product. In fact, the Hong Kong company managed the entire process, with a large proportion of the high value-added located in the territory."

3.3   New Business Conduct

Firms are restructuring to offer better quality, better prices and more customization to increasingly demanding and geographically dispersed customers. The pressures are significant and potential cost savings are huge, as may be witnessed from the estimates provided by the American group CommerceNet on the impacts of CALS technology utilization for companies: 80% reduction in purchasing cycle, 5%-10% reduction in inventories, 90% reduction in engineering changes.[8] In fact, the potential for an increase in operating efficiency by firms is so significant that opting out of the upcoming ways of doing business could be suicidal.

However, the virtual economy is a double-edged phenomenon: operating costs are being drastically reduced while profit margins are cut by 10% to 15%, based on the trend observed in electronic commerce. Lower profit margins are occurring because individual consumers are shopping electronically to find the best deal, leading us to believe that patterns of consumption are also changing radically. Virtual consumption in the "global general store" is at our doorstep and is being driven by a proliferation in the use of electronic commerce by consumers today in North America and Europe and tomorrow in the Asia-Pacific region. New patterns of consumption are thus both the direct consequence of the virtual economy and at the same time the most powerful driving force behind it.

In the virtual economy, the rapid spread of technologies, the acceleration of technological change as evidenced by ever shorter product cycles, the shortening of the appropriation time and the need to introduce new products at the right time, to be present on many markets, and to master a multiplicity of technologies will make it necessary, now more than ever, to engage in

R&D, establish research joint ventures and be integrated in a research and communication network, thereby reinforcing the very principles of the virtual economy.

We are witnessing a change in attitude and management style dictated by economic integration but also by accelerating technological change. Product cycles have dwindled to a few years or even months. As a result, a snowball effect is set in motion: firms must do R&D to keep up with the accelerating technological trend, and thereby they add fuel to the speed of discovery.

This will drastically shorten the various stages of an innovation. It will take less time to invent new products because information will spread faster, as knowledge is more codified and research more cooperative. The virtual economy will enhance and accelerate global learning. Growing evidence is found at the level of MNCs. A multinational corporation has the initial stock of internal knowledge on which it can build the strength to go abroad. However, it is not to its advantage to continue to exploit its own internalized capabilities as it can (and should) tap into special skills and knowledge from distinct foreign environments.[9] Further, global learning arises not only from pooling technical knowledge specific to foreign environments, but also from experiencing societal differences in managerial/organizational processes or systems.

The pressure for innovation will increase. As the world becomes more integrated, firms will find themselves forced to innovate in order to survive. Competition will rise with the increase in information but most of the known determinants of innovation will continue to be effective if properly focused. Firms innovate when they find it profitable or when they are forced to. They find it profitable if the expected rewards are huge (because of big market shares, an anticipated demand for the innovative products, a low degree of competition, a diversified portfolio of activities and integrated research projects, or a high degree of appropriability of research benefits) and/or if the expected costs are low (because of the possession of complementary assets, economies of scale, easy access to financing, a sound knowledge base or technological opportunity). In the global information infrastructure, rewards are likely to be higher as producers will be able to reach a larger market. Yet, at the same time, returns are likely to be more difficult to appropriate as information will disseminate faster and the returns will have to be shared among the members of the virtual economy.

3.4   Labour Market

The new organizational forms will tend to rely on a smaller number of full-time employees with uniquely valuable skills. These skills correspond to the core competencies of firms and/or to abilities to develop and use the tools, applications or content required to operate in the virtual economy. New skills will include, for example, continuous bidding on different platforms of virtual enterprises, product and know-how marketing in cyberspace, and electronic consumer interface including billing. All key service activities of the value chain can be managed virtually, thus deeply affecting the functioning of firms and the tasks of the different employee groups. Both ends of the value chain require highly strategic competencies, stressing the importance of being able to communicate in a virtual manner with both the demand and the supply side of the virtual economy.

From the above discussion, it becomes obvious that the transition to the virtual economy requires envisioned innovative strategies at the firm level to create new organizational forms, new skills and new core competencies. Labour insecurity will remain high. In a static world with routine work, job security seems appropriate but, when competition becomes a "war of movement," continuous and dynamic adaptation is necessary. Job redistribution within and among sectors of economic activity is also very likely and job redistribution among different countries is an even more disturbing possibility. The number of non-permanent jobs is likely to increase. Some of these trends are already observable today. The proportion of part-time and self-employed workers has increased. Jobs are redistributed from manufacturing to services and, within industry, from low- to high-knowledge-intensive sectors (Lee and Has, 1996). At the firm level, high-performance firms not only display employment growth but also have a more skilled workforce (OECD, 1996a). For example, in America, recent estimates indicate that 16% of all factory operations staff and labourers have a college education, and among production and craft workers the figure rises to 32%.[10] There is a growing cliff observable in the industrial countries between the demand for and the wages earned by qualified and unqualified workers. The main explanations for it are liberalized trade and technological change, but most of the empirical evidence points to the latter.

The virtual economy relies heavily on information technology and so far, although information technology is predominant in all sectors, there is no strong evidence that IT is a "job-killer" (OECD, 1996a; Conference Board of

Canada, 1996). It may very well create more jobs than it destroys. For instance, Canada will be short of at least 20,000 jobs in the software sector by the year 2000 while today there are at least 190,000 vacant positions in the IT industry (ITAA, 1997). Will the virtual economy have no more impact on the labour market than IT had? We believe that the virtual economy will be much more disruptive than can be anticipated. Firms will have productivity gains but will lower profit margins and will experience vast reductions in costs (mainly from the disappearance of workers with no unique skills).

The transition to the virtual economy will not occur without painful adjustments. Two widely discussed phenomena could be explained by this transition. The first is the productivity slowdown despite the revolution in IT. It takes time to switch to the new IT-based system of production and to learn to make efficient use of computerized equipment. The second is the observed widening wage gap between qualified and less-qualified labour. The new IT equipment and production system requires new skills. Unqualified workers are no longer in high demand and hence their relative wage has taken, and will continue to take, a plunge.

4.   NEW ISSUES IN THE VIRTUAL ECONOMY

National governments still have an active role to play in the virtual economy. Besides being a catalyst for the development of NII/GII and a lead user (and large consumer) of virtual services and products, government, as a policy-maker, can play a very important role in the difficult challenge of creating an appropriate national framework for such an economy and choosing an appropriate technological platform.

4.1   Laws and Regulations in Cyberspace

National economies are subsumed into the global system through the dynamics generated by the conduct of business activities which have become increasingly transnational. In fact, most MNCs are already TNCs. To the interdependencies between TNCs and national governments one must add the roles of international regulatory agencies (such as the World Trade Organization), international trade agreements (such as NAFTA), international norms and standards (such as ISO 14000) and transnational laws and regulations. As a result, most of the dominant problems of economic governance lie in the international domain.

The absence of territorial borders raises the problematic issue of the power of local governments to assert control over global behaviour, to formulate rules applicable in cyberspace and to enforce rules applicable to global phenomena. In other words, are territorial rules still legitimate and effective in a world without borders? Pioneering work is being carried out by the Harvard Information Infrastructure Project on issues of regulation and law in cyberspace. The project group is coming to grasp with the basic parameters of moving from a legal system largely anchored on territorial borders in a "real world" to a system characterized by the absence of territorial borders and functioning in a "virtual world." The absence of territorial borders also challenges the ability of sovereign states to continue to protect their economic well-being.

The trend towards a virtual economy calls for a more cooperative and coordinated approach to regulation. National governments will function less as "sovereign" entities and more as partners in an international commercial and trade policy. For instance, in a world with footloose capital there is no point in embarking on a war of tax incentives to attract high-tech enterprises. It is like the prisoner's dilemma. No government would win in that process, and the taxpayer would end up subsidizing firms. Likewise, MNCs have the ability to circumvent national regulations, if they are considered inimical to profit, by moving their production elsewhere. Thus, regulations must be more uniform across countries and based upon commonly agreed-upon objectives that go beyond the national interest. It is therefore likely that regulations will be more of the incentive-driven type: for example, price-caps rather than constraints on the rates of return for public utilities, use of pollution permits rather than pollution quotas. Efficiency-obstructive regulations must be based on sound agreed-upon non-economic objectives such as national content rules in broadcasting, offensive material on the Internet, environmental protection, and health and safety standards.

4.2   Inertia and Momentum in Developing Standards

The obstacles on the way to the establishment of NII/GII must not be underestimated. Reaching a consensus on a common set of technical standards in order to obtain compatibility and interoperability of systems, ensuring that the skills and ability of potential users are adequate, and addressing the complex privacy and security issues, all requires time. It is also not clear whether interactive innovations can accelerate indefinitely before negative externalities kick in, such as congestion on the Internet.

Adopters of NII/GII innovations are not all equally well informed about their potential. This proposition holds true among different countries and, within any given country, among firms or individuals. It has been shown that incomplete information can lead either to excess momentum or excess inertia (Farell and Saloner, 1986). When the benefits of adoption are perceived to exceed the costs of non-adoption, excess momentum or a "bandwagon effect" is created, with each potential adopter rushing to be the first to adopt out of fear of being temporarily stranded. On the other hand, the first adopter may very well fear that he will be left out if other users do not switch to the new technology. Excess inertia is then created with no potential adopter willing to take the plunge and everyone applying a "wait and see" strategy.

Whether momentum or inertia will build up for or against NII/GII is difficult to predict and, therefore, so is an exact timeframe for developing these networks. Public policy can definitely play a major role here. Most of the G-7 countries have set the pace by providing a concrete agenda for actions with clear deadlines. A number of proactive smaller countries such as Korea and Singapore (Kahin and Wilson, 1997), Finland and Norway will also go ahead, while others such as Brazil and India have launched a variety of initiatives (McKnight and Botelho, 1997; Petrazzini and Harindranath, 1997). Obviously, the international agencies (such as the WTO, WIPO, ISO, ITU and OECD) will be instrumental in defining norms and standards and resolving trade issues over the next few years.

Government can make firms aware of changing conditions in international competition, the new rules of the game, so to speak, e.g., the rise of CALS standards and the need for small and large firms to adapt and learn if they want to be part of the global information infrastructure. In particular with regard to the adoption of production and communication standards, government has a vital role to play in ensuring that firms adopt common norms and standards through which they can join international consortia and tender for domestic and foreign government procurement contracts or private subcontracting jobs. Without the guiding role of government, firms might invest in different norms and standards and not in those that are most likely to be adopted worldwide. The government can perform this task through its involvement in international negotiations on the adoption of standards, speaking with one voice to defend its country's best interests. In that respect, it can act as a coordinator, saving on transaction costs. It also has a very useful role to play as a technological gatekeeper.

4.3   New Challenges for Public Policy

In the virtual economy, governments are faced with a set of new challenges:

• **Competition policy**. At whatever level of governance (community, local, regional, national or international), governments have to make sure competition is on a level playing field. Access to electronic networks, to communication infrastructures, to research consortia, and to public procurement contracts must be safeguarded without excess interference in private decision-making. Markets must remain contestable.

• **Fiscal policy**. As firms can circumvent state taxes by selling their products and services in states where taxes are lower or nonexistent, it becomes more difficult for governments to raise locally based consumption taxes. Corporations can also transfer the high-value-added components of the value chain to low-tax locations. Various possibilities can be envisaged. Countries or states (provinces) could coordinate their tax rates, a central authority (like a supergovernment) could tax the virtual enterprises, or other tax revenues could be imagined (like the debatable bit tax). Public provision of local goods could be financed locally by the residents benefiting from these local goods. Some services which extend beyond the confines of a local community could be provided and financed jointly. In any case, unnecessary taxes should be eliminated and some public goods and services (e.g., health care) could be provided by sufficiently large private companies.

• **Protection of privacy and intellectual property**. The emergence of a surveillance society, which could alienate the freedom of certain persons, represents another disturbing possibility. "The medium of electronic interaction is increasingly used as a pervasive surveillance instrument." Second, the increasing number of data mining applications[11] such as "consumer profiling" raises new issues of privacy: these applications allow users to infer important details concerning a person's life even though these details could not be legally obtained from direct questions. Third, the issue of privacy is international in scope since "countries that are willing to address privacy concerns may nevertheless be unable to offer their own citizens assurances that personal information in an international networked environment will be fairly used in accordance with information practice standards" (Gellman, 1997, p. 277). As a result, the government's role regarding the protection of its citizens is getting more and more complex and requires increased attention.

• **Modernize labour standards legislation**. There is mounting evidence of the inflexibility of the labour market, partly due to the present system of benefits to the unemployed and the rigidity of labour laws and regulations.[12] This will increasingly constitute a major handicap as we move into the virtual economy.

• **International trade**. Tariff reductions and investment liberalization are essential to the realization of virtual economies. International specialization by production stages becomes too costly if companies cannot locate production where it is cheapest and if tariffs have to be paid severe times along the value chain.

• **A chance for all**. From the structural changes described in the previous sections, there is a potential threat of excluding people from productive and social participation in society because of their inability to work, live and socially interact in electronically mediated environments. The transition to the virtual economy may exacerbate knowledge and skill gaps between and within countries. Less developed countries should obviously gain access to NII/GII: this is already a prime concern for the OECD and the World Bank. However, even in industrialized countries, there is the possibility of a two-tier society in the form of "information rich" and "information poor" or "haves" and "have nots." This is a rather disturbing possibility but empirical evidence points to a polarization in the use by individuals of electronic interconnections and computers. It is biased towards high income (Frank, 1995) and younger generations (Sciadias, 1996). The same phenomenon is observed with Internet and Web users in the U.S.: 42% of Internet and Web users have annual household incomes of more than US$ 50,000 (*Business Week*, May 5, 1997). Since income seems the most significant determinant, one of the highest priorities is to give universal access to the NII/GII. Any citizen should be able to tap into the opportunities created by these infrastructures from libraries, schools and other public institutions.

• **Education**. In addition, public education systems will have to be aligned with the new required skills of the virtual economy and, therefore, will need to be upgraded and enhanced. Lifelong learning is a possibility to be considered. Higher education could be largely self-financed by repayable government loans or by grants issued by private companies for the acquisition of particular skills that are badly needed. In this way, the brain drain is no longer an issue of public finance. In fact, it is important to enhance a variety of skills in order to avoid what has been termed a "lock-in phenomenon." Too much focus on one particular technological discipline may become a competence trap which prevents the needed flexibility in a changing environment. The virtual economy leads to true globalization and Canadians will have to become increasingly aware and knowledgeable of other cultures and languages. Mastering the elements of international law, finance or management in addition to "cultural literacy" will represent crucial assets in the workplace.

• **Social cohesion**. The next century could be high-tech with high social content. The impersonality of the electronic medium could drive the need for social contacts and closer face-to-face relationships. Let us take an example. "If banking is essential, banks are not" (McElhatton, President of Master-Card's Global Technology and Operations).[13] Each banking service can be provided in a virtual manner and banks could close all of their branches, at the same time displacing or laying off all bank tellers. However, specialized advisors could, in the comfort of customers' homes, give information on mortgages, financial planning or retirement investments. This would be a high-tech (on line traditional banking services), high-social-contact (face-to-face advice on specialized services) industry. The health sector and many other sectors could display the same duality. This would leave much room for workers with strong abilities for social interactions but no particular inclination toward "digital literacy."

• **Access to business platforms**. While a great deal needs to be said about the technological platforms, organizational requirements and skills to do business in a KBE, another important aspect is the presence of business platforms or information brokers. These market intermediaries will become increasingly influential agents in electronic commerce. These platforms can be industry-driven, as is the case for the TPN Register, or government-induced, as is the case for UK Trade. Industry-driven platforms are created and supported by the large multinational corporations present in Canada only through subsidiaries. One important challenge will be to ensure access for Canadian companies to these platforms by making them aware first of their existence and second of their requirements. This is particularly true for subcontracting SMEs in numerous sectors of economic activity.

• **Industry value chain analysis**. Value chain analysis is a powerful analytical tool for eliminating all non-value-added activities along product/service supply chains and for identifying those activities that companies within an industry should be concentrating on. Introducing this kind of analysis in regional economic development could prove useful in the allocation of the scarce resources governments have to ensure and promote development. It forces choices along industry value chains by taking into consideration the particular mix of competencies developed in the different regions of Canada. In Hong Kong, for example, a thorough industry value chain study was conducted among members of the influential business community to identify which value-added activities they expected to retain within the region. Results from the study indicate a strong tendency to concentrate on those activities which can be performed in a virtual mode and which by definition constitute in today's market high-value-added activities such as headquarter operations, trade finance, R&D, design or marketing. These activities correspond to what the knowledge-based economy is all about, that is, brainpower activities.

5.   CONCLUSION

Change is under way and we are entering a largely misunderstood realm of business. The technological revolutions, in particular in transportation, communication and information technologies, the social, political and economic forces tending towards an integrated world economy, the development of national and global information infrastructures, the appearance of so-called virtual enterprises, and the creation of new technological platforms constitute the basic structure on which the virtual economy rests. This new concept refers to an economy without well-defined borders, with intercontinental markets of all sorts, highly specialized division of labour, ever-changing production networks, and electronic real-time exchange of information, research, production, distribution and after-sales services.

The major players are multinational and transnational enterprises, networks, national governments and international agencies. The emergence of the virtual economy challenges governments, firms and individuals. Competition is intense, innovation is a must, technology evolution is in an era of ferment, characterized by uncertainty. Industry restructures to compete. New industries are created as well as new agents in the value chain, namely the product integrators and platforms businesses. Value added is mainly derived from services at both ends of the value chain. Brainpower dominates.

New skills are required. Governments face new challenges: how to raise taxes from stateless corporations? How to protect privacy and intellectual capital? How to reorganize education to meet the demands for new skills? How to regulate without raising self-inflicted obstacles? How to coordinate technology choices and public policies with foreign governments? How to ensure social cohesion? The consumer must be able to master the electronic means of communication. The worker must be ready to adapt to new technologies, new jobs and new working habits, and to mingle with different cultures.

NII/GII will be the enabling technology for the virtual economy. The transition to the virtual economy will radically modify the ground rules of competition and call for a new governance. Either we agree to operate with these new rules or our economic well-being will decrease. Any process of change (technology-driven or not) unevenly affects people, firms, sectors and industries. So will the transition to the virtual economy. Major structural and social changes will occur. The challenges are tremendous, the trend is irreversible.

NOTES

[1] Source: OECD (1997).

[2] WTO: World Trade Organization, WIPO: World Intellectual Property Organization, ISO: International Organization For Standardization, ITU: International Telecommunication Union.

[3] Harmonization of standards is difficult. In 1991, 29 different forms of EDI existed. Today, EDIFACT is the chosen norm for Europe and ANSI X12 for North America. EDIFACT and ANSI X12 are now being integrated.

[4] "What a Multos-based card becomes to the cardholder is a lifestyle card, allowing the consumer to include the standard applications of debit and credit along with other selected applications such as Mondex electronic cash, an airline loyalty program and a transit pass, and the ability to meet the cardholders' changing needs by adding or deleting applications through the telephone, or an ATM." (Release from MasterCard's New York headquarters on March 15, 1997).

[5] This occurs frequently. When faced with the early introduction of CT scanners, doctors were at odds with the benefits of "seeing with sound" as Yoxen (1987) puts it and "were not clear about the relative priorities of scan time versus resolution" (Tushman and Rosenkopf, 1997, p. 171).

[6] Source: Human Development Report, 1997.

[7] Small firms can indeed perform very well in the virtual economy. Amazon.com is already a classic example: it is a virtual store (with no physical retail site) which grew to be the largest book retailer in the U.S. with an inventory of 2.5 million titles (most large retailers have around 175,000 titles).

[8] The five stage transition model from the traditional firm to the virtual enterprise using a CALS platform proposed by Lefebvre et al. (1997) also indicate potentially substantial cost reductions as well as profound organizational impacts (mostly on the workforce). Past experience also confirms these trends: after introducing CALS, the U.S. Navy saved 90% in design and data maintenance costs, 80% of production problem costs and 30% of training costs.

[9] Earlier examples of this genuine global learning such as the case of Procter and Gamble are well documented. The 150-year-old company Procter and Gamble (P&G) fully exploits its access to worldwide information and expertise through its foreign subsidiaries. One of its products, known as Liquid Tide in the U.S., Liquid Arid in Europe and Liquid Cheer in Japan, is a direct consequence of truly global learning. The new ingredient that helps to suspend dirt came from its American research centre and corresponds to the American desire for improved cleansing capability. The formula for the surfactants was developed by P&G scientists in Japan because Japanese consumers wash their clothes in colder water than European or American consumers. The ingredients that fight the mineral salts present in hard water came from its scientists in Brussels, as water in Europe contains more than twice the mineral content of water in the U.S. By levering the company's intelligence and expertise worldwide, P&G developed a very successful and superior product that incorporated several technological breakthroughs.

[10] See Thurow (1998).

[11] Data mining techniques can identify, create and test thousands of relationships from very large databases (OECD, 1997).

[12] These issues are raised in the Economic Freedom of the World report (1997) and the World Competitiveness Report (1997).

[13] Quote from a speech delivered at the Conference on Bank Structure, May 1, 1997.

REFERENCES

Adam, N.R. and Y. Yesha (Eds.), *Electronic Commerce: Current Issues and Applications.* Berlin : Springer, 1996.

Altshuler, R., H. Grubert and T. Scott Newlon, "Has U.S. Investment Abroad Become More Sensitive to Tax Rates?" NBER Working Paper 6383, 1998.

Bartlett, C.A. and S. Ghoshal, *Transnational Management*, Second Edition. Chicago: Irwin, 1995.

Bhagwati, J., *Protectionism*. Cambridge, MA : MIT Press, 1988.

Business Week, "The New Business Cycle," March 31, 1997, 58-68.

Business Week, "Whirlwind on the Web," April 7, 1997, 132-136.

Business Week, "A Census in Cyberspace," May 5, 1997, 5.

Business Week, "The 21st Century Economy," August 24-31, 1998.

Conference Board of Canada, *Jobs in the Knowledge-Based Economy* ✎ *Information Technology and the Impact on Employment*, 1996.

Davidow, W.H. and M.S. Malone, *The Virtual Corporation*. New York : Harper Collins Publishers, 1992.

Enright, M.J., E.E. Scott and D. Dodwell, *The Hong Kong Advantage*. Oxford : Oxford University Press, 1997.

European Commission, *Building the European Information Society for Us All. Final Policy Report of the High-Level Expert Group*. Luxembourg : Office for Official Publications of the European Communities, 1997.

Farrell, J. and G. Saloner, "Installed Base and Compatibility: Innovation, Product Preannouncements, and Predation," American Economic Review, 26, 940-955, 1986.

Freeman, C., *"The Economics of Industrials Relations*, Pinter, London, 1982.

Frank, J., "Preparing for the Information Highway : Information Technology in Canadian Households", in *Canadian Social Trends*. Statistics Canada, cat. 11-008^E, Autumn, 1995.

Gellman, R., "Conflict and Overlap in Privacy Regulation: National, International, and Private" in B. Kahin and C. Nerson (eds.), *Borders in Cyberspace*. Cambridge, Ma : MIT Press, 1997.

Gwartney, James D., *Economic Freedom of the World: 1997 Annual Report*. Vancouver: Fraser Institute, 1997.

Hines, J.R., Jr., "Taxes, Technology Transfer, and the R&D Activities of Multinational Firms." NBER Working Paper 4932, 1994.

Hines, J.R., Jr., "Taxes and the Location of Foreign Direct Investment in America." *American Economic Review*, 86(5), 1996, 1076-1094.

Hirst, P. and G. Thompson, *Globalization in Question*. Cambridge: Polity Press, 1996.

Human Development Report. New York: Oxford University Press, 1997.

Hummels, D., D. Rapoport and K.-M. Yi, "Vertical Specialization and the Changing Nature of World Trade." *Economic Policy Review*, 4(2), 1998, 79-99.

ITAA (Information Technology Association of America*), Help Wanted: The Information Workforce Gap at the Dawn of a New Century*. February 1997.

Kahin, B. and E. Wilson (Eds.), *National Information Infrastructure Initiatives: Vision and Policy Design*. A Publication of the Harvard Information Infrastructure Project in collaboration with the GII Commission.Cambridge, MA : MIT Press, 1997.

Kalakota, R. and A.B. Whinston, *Electronic Commerce*, Addison-Wesley, Reading, Mass., 1996.

Kokuryo, J. and Y. Takeda, *"The Role of Platform Businesses in Electronic Commerce."* Working paper, Keio University, Japan, 1997.

Kuhn, T., *The Structure of Scientific Revolutions*, Second Edition. Chicago : University of Chicago Press, 1970.

Lee, F.C. and H. Has, "Évaluation quantitative des industries à forte concentration de savoir par rapport aux industries à faible concentration de savoir" in P. Hovitt (ed.), *La croissance fondée sur le savoir et son incidence sur les politiques microéconomiques*. Industry Canada Research Series. Calgary : University of Calgary Press, 1996.

Lefebvre L.A., E. Lefebvre, L. Cassivi and C. Lebrun, *L'entreprise virtuelle et CALS: la nouvelle dynamique commerciale mondiale*, EPM/RT-97-15, CDT. Montréal : Centre de veille concurrentielle, École Polytechnique, 1997.

Lipsey, R., M. Blomström and E. Ramstetter, "Internationalized Production in World Output." NBER Working Paper 5385, 1995.

Markus, M.L., "Toward a Critical Mass Theory of Interactive Media." in J. Fulk and C. Steinfield (eds.), *Organizations and Communication Technology*. Newbury Park, CA : Sage, 1990.

McKnight, L. and A.J.J. Botelho, "Brazil: Is the World Ready for When Information Highways Cross the Amazon?" in B. Kahin, and E. Wilson (eds.) *National Information Infrastructure Initiatives: Vision and Policy Design*. Cambridge, MA : MIT Press, 1997.

OECD, *Technologies, Productivity and Job Creation*. March 1996a.

OECD, *Information Infrastructure Policies in OED Countries*. OEDE, May 1996b.

OECD, *Information Technology Outlook 1997*, 1997.

Ohmae, K., "Putting Global Logic First." *Harvard Business Review*, Jan.-Feb., 1995, 119-125.

Petrazzini, B.A. and G. Harindranath, "Information Infrastructure Initiatives in Emerging Economies: The Case of India," in B. Kahin, and E. Wilson (eds.) *National Information Infrastructure Initiatives: Vision and Policy Design.* Cambridge, MA : MIT Press, 1997.

Quinn, J.B., *Intelligent Enterprise.* The New York : Free Press, 1992.

Rogers, E.M., *Diffusion of Innovations*, Fourth Edition. New York : The Free Press, 1995.

Sciadias, G., *Linking Information Highway Infrastructures with Transactions.* Services, Science and Technology Division, Statistics Canada, 1996.

The Economist, "Electronic Commerce − In Search of : the Perfect Market.", May 10, 1997, pp. 3-18.

Thurow, L.C., "An Era of Man-Made Brainpower Industries," in D. Neel (ed.), *The Knowledge Economy.* Boston : Butterworth-Heineman, 1998.

Tushman, M.L. and L. Rosenkopf, "Organizational Determinants of Technological Change: Toward a Sociology of Technological Evolution," in B. Kahin and E. Wilson (eds.) *National Information Infrastructures Initiatives: Vision and Policy Design.* Cambridge, MA : MIT Press, 1997.

World Competitiveness Report. Genève: EMF Foundation, 1997.

Yoxen, E., "Seeing with Sound: A Study of the Development of Medical Imaging," in W. Bijker, T. Hughes and T. Punch (eds.), *Social Construction of Technological Systems, Cambridge:* MIT Press, 1987.

4. ORGANIZATIONAL LEARNING AND INTELLECTUAL CAPITAL

Keith Newton
Carleton University ou (Carleton Research Unit on Innovation, Science & Environment)

Sunder Magun
Applied International Economic Inc.

1. INTRODUCTION AND OUTLINE

The logic of this paper is straightforward. It starts from the premise that there is now general consensus that, as the millennium approaches, the global economy is increasingly "knowledge-based." The evidence on this is now voluminous and the arguments are so familiar as to amount almost to dogma. Briefly stated, in the new global economy, the headlong pace and sheer pervasiveness of technological advance are accompanied by increased turbulence, uncertainty and discontinuity. The very basis of competition has not only intensified but has changed fundamentally in its nature: continuous innovation is now the principal way to survive and prosper. Innovation, in turn, implies a need for knowledge and knowledge creation, new ideas, know-how, knack, and creativity. Physical and financial capital, material resources, even advanced technologies, therefore, are necessary but not sufficient conditions for success. Superior performance derives from another kind of asset – intangible, intellectual. As a recent OECD (1996) report puts it, "knowledge plays today in all its forms a crucial role in economic processes. Intangible investment is growing more rapidly than physical investment. Individuals with more knowledge get better paid jobs, firms with more knowledge are winners on markets, and nations endowed with more knowledge are more productive."

Such fundamental re-alignment of the entire process of production (and consumption) calls for radical responses by individuals, firms, institutions, and society at large. The present paper focuses on the second of these – adjustments by firms. It builds on earlier work (Newton, 1996) that examined the importance of the human factor in management strategies to address performance objectives in the knowledge-based economy (KBE). That study demonstrated how a nexus of innovative HR-based management strategies (organizational innovation, TQM and the "new" human resource management) could build high-performance work systems. Two promising new directions in human resource management were identified and are the particular concern of the present study – namely, the concepts of organizational learning and intellectual capital.

Thus the underlying theme of the paper is that in order to survive and prosper – in order to successfully do business (in the words of the theme of this volume) – firms must adopt strategies of organizational learning and develop and manage intellectual capital.

Accordingly, the paper is structured as follows. The next section briefly describes some of the characteristics of the KBE which are of principal concern – namely, the increasing knowledge- and skill-intensity of the economy. The third section sets out the basic conceptual elements of the learning organization and summarizes key elements of the literature. Section four does the same for the concept of intellectual capital: what is the theory and how is the concept measured? The fifth section reviews empirical literature and the sixth reports new information from Canadian case studies. Conclusions and policy implications follow.

2. THE CONTEXT: RISING SKILL AND KNOWLEDGE REQUIREMENTS

Certainly, the evolution of the KBE is reflected in the growing skill- and knowledge-intensity of occupations and industries. Numerous recent empirical studies indicate these trends. Gera and Massé (1996), for example, show how in both manufacturing and services, for the period 1971-1993, the employment share of higher-skilled occupations (managerial, professional, technical, fore(wo)men, and skilled crafts and trades) grew at the expense of the lower-skilled (clerical, sales and service workers, and low- and semiskilled manual workers). Next, using occupational trait data such as general educational development, specific vocational preparation, cognitive complexity and task diversity, Leckie (1996) shows that the employment shares of jobs requiring the highest skill levels, in all categories of skill, have risen monotonically between 1971 and 1991.

Two other pieces of empirical evidence lend support to the message of the rising importance of knowledge and skills presented above. The first, based on the work of Lee and Has (1996) and subsequently of Gera and Massé (1996), focuses on the knowledge-intensity of Canadian industries. Industries are partitioned into high, medium and low categories of knowledge-intensity based on a combination of several indicators of R&D activity and human capital content. The three R&D measures are: R&D expenditures; the proportion of R&D personnel in the workforce; the proportion of university-level R&D personnel. For human capital content, the measures are: the proportion of workers with post-secondary education; the proportion of "knowledge workers,"[1] the proportion of scientists and engineers. To be "high-knowledge" an industry has to have two of its R&D indicators in the top one third *and* two of its human capital indicators in the top one third. To be "low" the reverse rule applies. All other industries are classified as "medium." Using these definitions, Gera and Massé show that, with an employment share of only 15.4%, the high-knowledge industries nevertheless contributed 41.2% of the *growth* in employment in the period 1986-1991. Low-knowledge industries, with nearly 45% of total employment, contributed only one-fifth of the job growth in the same period.

The most recent empirical evidence for Canada (Gera, Gu and Lin, 1998) uses two skill classification schemes: one developed by the new National Occupational Classification (NOC) and the other following the criteria used in the classic work by Wolff and Baumol (1989). The novelty of this new research is that, in addition to addressing the question of trends in skill intensity in Canadian industry, it also investigates the issue of skill-biased technological change. Three major findings emerge. First, the relative demand for more-skilled workers rose over the period 1981-1994, and this rise in skill intensity was pervasive across all (29) industries. Second, the shift in demand for more-skilled workers was entirely driven by "within-industry" skill utilization rather than "between-industry" employment shifts – a result that is consistent with the hypothesis of skill-biased technological change. Third, various technology indicators, including R&D capital, the stock of patents used by industry, the vintage of the capital stock, and total factor productivity, are strongly correlated with skill intensity. From this the authors infer that skill-biased technological change has been a key factor in within-industry skill upgrading across Canadian industries.

Taken together, these various pieces of evidence show a clear trend of rising skill and knowledge intensity in the Canadian labour market. This is the learning challenge for individuals, parents, teachers, employers, learning institutions both public and private, and governments at various levels. Clearly, education must be a key priority to survive and flourish in the KBE.

In addition, however, the *culture* of learning must adapt to the new realities. Simply because of the speed of change and, therefore, the rapid rate of obsolescence of knowledge and skills, learning must be continuous or "lifelong." The next section looks at how firms are meeting the challenge of continuous learning and knowledge generation for "innovation competition."

3. THE LEARNING ORGANIZATION: THEORY AND APPLICATION

This section is divided into four main parts. In the first we look at various approaches to the definition of the learning organization. Next, some elements of learning theory are discussed. Then we briefly review some of the ways in which the theoretical concepts have been applied – some "models" of the learning organization. Finally, certain measurement questions are considered.

3.1 Definitional Issues

The first point that should be noted is that some writers distinguish between "organizational learning" (OL) and the "learning organization" (LO). The former is used to describe learning by individuals or groups *within* an organization, while the latter describes a particular kind of organization. The distinction is, we would argue, a little forced. After all, as Tsang (1997) suggests, perhaps a learning organization could simply be defined as one that is particularly good at organizational learning! In any event, as Table 1 shows, there are many definitions of OL and LO that reflect different perspectives and analytical approaches.

Table 1. Definitions of organizational learning

Definition	Perspective	Nature of Study
"Organizational learning refers to the process by which the organizational knowledge base is developed and shaped" (Shrivastava, 1981).	Cognitive	Descriptive
"An entity learns if, through its processing of information, the range of its potential behaviours is changed" (Huber, 1991).	Cognitive and behavioural (potential)	Review
"By the term 'organizational learning' we mean the changing of organizational behaviour" (Swieringa and Wierdsma, 1992).	Behavioural (actual)	Prescriptive
"Where people continually expand their capacity to create the results they truly desire, where new and expansive patterns of thinking are nurtured, where collective aspiration is set free, and where people are continually learning how to learn together" (Senge, 1990).	Cultural	Prescriptive
"A learning organization is an organization skilled at creating, acquiring and transferring knowledge, and at modifying its behaviour to reflect new knowledge and insights" (Garvin, 1993).	Cognitive and behavioural (actual)	Prescriptive
"We define organizational learning as the capacity or processes within an organization to maintain or improve performance based on experience" (Nevis et al., 1995).	Behavioural (potential)	Prescriptive

Source: Tsang (1997)

Following Tsang (1997), therefore, it is useful to note that most definitions involve aspects of both cognitive and behavioural changes. The former is concerned with knowledge, understanding and insights. But as for the latter, there is disagreement as to whether the learning process results in a *potential* or an *actual* change in behaviour. Moreover, among the many studies of OL/LO a distinction can be made between two streams of research: the *descriptive* stream which asks "how *does* an organization learn?" and the *prescriptive* stream which asks "how *should* an organization learn?" In prescriptive studies, definitions tend to incorporate actual behavioural change since, after all, their readership is mainly made up of action-oriented practitioners. In descriptive studies, the objective is to determine empirically whether learning has actually occurred and whether it has resulted in changes in potential or actual behaviour. The descriptive/prescriptive rubric is a useful sorting device to characterize studies and the definitions they proffer. The other major element of Tsang's approach to definition is captured in his deceptively simple but heuristically powerful model of how the learning process takes place and is applied within organizations (Figure 1).

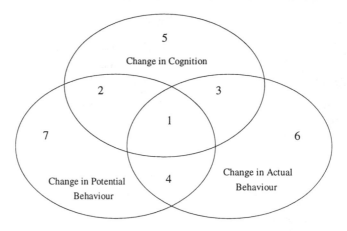

Figure 1: Key conditions of organizational learning definitions

The figure incorporates basic elements common to most definitions of OL/LO. First, for learning to take place, knowledge, insight and/or understanding are gained (cognition); second, this is acted upon in such a way that improved methods, procedures, processes, policies or practices are introduced (change in actual behaviour); or, third, the learning process provides the basis, the launch-pad, for the introduction of the *new* policies, procedures and practices to meet *future* needs (change in potential behaviour). Thus the area of intersection labelled "1" represents an organizational learning process in which a gain in knowledge, understanding and/or insight leads to an immediate behavioural application within the firm but also provides the basis for meeting the exigencies of future development. In terms of the definitions we have set out, the key intersections are clearly the areas 1, 2 and 3. An interesting case, however, is area 4, where one might posit that changes in potential and actual behaviour in the firm are *imposed*, without the benefit of a change in cognition. In other words, the new rules and practices are not the outcome of enhanced knowledge and understanding – indeed, people do not know why they have been introduced.

A couple of additional defining characteristics of OL/LO should be noted. First, OL can take place at a number of levels. Clearly much OL is done by individuals "learning by doing" or acquiring skills and knowledge in more intentional, systematic or formal ways. Next, learning can be a group undertaking, with participants interacting with and learning from each other. A third level is learning of and by the organization as it consciously puts in place the procedures, practices, routines and incentives that create a climate and culture conducive to the acquisition and application of knowledge. Next, interfirm relationships of various kinds yield learning opportunities, as do firm-client relationships and joint research partnerships with universities. At a fifth, "meta-learning" level, an economy's learning infrastructure or national system of innovation facilitates the identification and acquisition of knowledge by firms, individuals and institutions. Marquardt and Reynolds (1994) suggest a sixth level in their concept of "global learning." That is, in the global KBE, the firm's learning process must increasingly encompass an international perspective that takes account of other languages, cultures, tastes and production methods.

A final defining concept of OL/LO is that of organizational memory. Some of this memory is embodied in policies, practices and routines. Some is in the memories of individuals. And some may be stored in information systems from which the lessons of past projects can be retrieved. On the other hand, the ability of the organization to "forget" or "unlearn" old rules or routines may be necessary if new methods are to be learned and new knowledge acquired.

3.2   Some Elements of Theory, Application and Measurement

The theoretical and applied literature on OL/LO is voluminous and even a synthetic discussion is beyond the scope of this paper. The following paragraphs are intended to give the reader unfamiliar with this field a brief taste of some key points. The reference section points to the wider literature. The first crucial concept for OL/LO lies in the distinction between codified and tacit knowledge (Soete, 1997; Lundvall and Johnson, 1992; Nonaka, 1991). The distinction is critical because, in the KBE, the winners in the competitive wars are those who can best marshal their knowledge forces. And the main point here is that the power of information and communication technologies (ICTs) is revolutionizing the pace and extent to which formerly tacit knowledge can be codified and rendered explicit. So competitive edge depends on the ability to effect this transformation and then to exploit the potential of the newly created explicit knowledge.

Second, any account of the basic theoretical building blocks of OL/LO must include a word on the now-classic contribution of Argyris (1977) – namely the concept of *double loop learning*. For Argyris, learning occurs in two ways. First, it occurs when an organization achieves what is intended –

i.e., when there is a match between its strategic actions and actual outcomes. Second, learning occurs when there is a mismatch between intentions and outcomes and this is identified and corrected so that the mismatch is turned into a match. If a mismatch occurs and an error is detected and corrected without questioning or modifying the basic, underlying values and assumptions of the organization, its corporate philosophy and strategy, learning is said to be "single loop." Double loop learning occurs when mismatches are addressed by first examining and changing the "governing variables" – the organization's fundamental strategy and underlying assumptions. To take an illustration from electrical engineering, a thermostat could be called a single loop learner: it is programmed to identify states of "too hot" and "too cold," and to correct the situation accordingly. If it questioned fundamental principles, such as "why am I programmed this way?" or "why am I placed in this location?", it would be a double loop learner.

Models of OL/LO are numerous and varied and run the gamut of the descriptive-prescriptive spectrum (see, e.g., Levitt and March, 1988; Huber, 1991; Nevis, diBella and Gould, 1995). A recent article (Garvin, 1993) argues that some of the more prominent contributions to the literature have been "far too abstract" and that "we need clearer guidelines for practice, filled with operational advice rather than high aspirations." He identifies as practical building blocks five main activities.

- *Systematic problem-solving.* This derives in large measure from the principles and methods of the quality movement and includes a reliance on scientific method, data as opposed to assumptions, and statistical tools for measurement and analysis.

- *Experimentation.* This involves a systematic search for new knowledge and takes two main forms. The first is ongoing programs of experimentation to reap incremental knowledge gains. These are the basis for the continuous improvement programs that are central to TQM, for example. Second are the rather larger and more complex demonstration projects that involve systemwide changes to organizational structure, strategy or style. They are often more a transition than an endpoint inasmuch as they are pilots for a more widespread application at a later date. As such, they involve a very large component of learning by doing.

- *Learning from experience.* This means systematic review and assessment of successes and failures – what has been called the

"Santayana review" after the philosopher who averred, "Those who cannot remember the past are condemned to repeat it."

- *Learning from others.* This is the process of environmental scanning, benchmarking and identification and adoption of best practices described above. It involves learning not only from suppliers and competitors but from customers, too.
- *Transferring knowledge.* The means of dissemination and communication of knowledge are critical. They include information systems and technologies, documentation, data storage, reports, meetings, site visits and tours, conferences, etc. But passive learning is not as powerful as actively experiencing something. Hence learning by doing through personnel rotation programs is very effective.

As far as measurement is concerned, the concepts of the *"learning curve"* and *"manufacturing progress functions"* date back to the 1920s and 1930s when it was observed that the costs of airframe manufacture fell *pari passu* with cumulative production volume. This piece of empirical evidence, more than any other, underlines the theory of learning by doing and exemplifies the importance of this phenomenon in OL/LO. The extension of the early studies to subsequent analyses of shipbuilding, oil refining and consumer electronics turned up learning rates of incredible magnitude: with a doubling of cumulative production, costs fell 80%-85%. Precise mathematical functions were modelled for various processes in several industries. The results of these empirical studies, powerful evidence of economies of scale, still have practical application today. Such measures have limited use, however. For one thing, they focus on only a single performance measure and fail to take account of how learning affects other outcome variables such as quality or the speed of introduction of new products. Second, they focus on only one determining variable – namely, cumulative production volume (for which time is frequently a proxy). But learning by doing, though powerful, is not the only source of learning. The mere passage of time may yield growing familiarity and expertise via the repetition of tasks and routines. But there are more intentional, active and systematic sources of learning.

As Garvin (1993) shows, one improvement, while still retaining time as the determining variable, is the so-called "half-life" curve, pioneered by the semiconductor manufacturer, Analog Devices. It is a more versatile measure in the sense that it expresses learning in terms of how long it takes to achieve a 50% improvement in a particular performance objective. The latter could be something like defect rates, on-time delivery, time to market, etc., and is plotted on the vertical axis on a log-scale; time in weeks or months is on the x-axis. So steeper slopes (positive or negative, depending on the performance variable) represent faster learning.

Two other approaches are, we believe, useful practical guides to the assessment of an organization's learning potential and performance. The first is derived from the highly successful U.K. *Investors in People* program and is, in effect, a simple but highly effective checklist. It links fundamental management processes − business planning, communications, performance reviews, human resource management practices, and systems for development of skills and competencies − to a set of indicators or criteria to help managers assess whether they have the policies, procedures, practices, systems and resources to support those basic management functions. Managers simply scan the indicators column to determine "yes," they do have this support in place; "no," they do not; or, perhaps, "it's in the works," or "we have something but we need to do better."

A simple variant of this approach is set out in Table 2.

Table 2: A framework for assessment of organizational learning potential

Building Blocks of OL	Question	Rating (1-10)	Best Practices	Gap Between Company's Current Practice and Best Practice
Collective Vision	To what extent does our company have the right culture to reach its goal?			
Core Competencies	To what extent does our company have the required knowledge, skills, and abilities?			
Motivation	To what extent does our company have the appropriate measures, rewards, and incentives?			
Organizational Structure	To what extent does our company have the right organizational structure, communications systems, and policies?			
Innovativeness	To what extent does our company have the ability to improve work processes, to change, and to learn?			
Leadership	To what extent does our company have the leadership to achieve goals?			

Once again the self-assessment of the organization's learning potential takes the form of responses to critical questions in each of a number of key components of organizational learning potential. The metrics here are interesting and two fold. First, managers rate the company on a scale of 1 to 10 as to the extent to which the company meets each criterion for learning.

Next, after identifying the best practice under each of the criteria, managers must judge the magnitude of the gap between the company's existing practice and the state-of-the-art.

4. INTELLECTUAL CAPITAL

It is by now well known that hidden or intangible assets and intellectual capital (IC) in particular are widely regarded as a powerful source of competitive advantage. Hidden or not, the market clearly values such assets. Tobin's q, the ratio of a company's market value to its replacement cost of capital, is typically higher for high-tech, high-knowledge companies and is said to be double-digit for Microsoft. It is instructive, in fact, to compare the giant of the industrial era, General Motors, with the software titan, Microsoft. The former's traditional assets had a market value in March 1997 of $49 billion. Microsoft, with few "hard" assets, had a market value of $119 billion. Small wonder, then, that firms, managers, and individual workers are beginning to make systematic efforts to identify, acquire, develop and manage IC. In this section, we attempt to set out some of the main conceptual aspects of IC and then address some questions of application and measurement.

Well within living memory, beginning students of economics learned that capital was an important factor of production and source of economic growth. It was usually regarded as physical (equipment and machinery, for example) or financial (stocks, bonds and money in the bank). More recent and more sophisticated definitions would include human and intellectual capital, and technological, social and organizational capital. Intellectual capital could, in turn, be broken down into technical knowledge and skills; management skills; vision; experience, know-how, knack, creativity and flair; and personal and psychological attributes including personality, ambition, energy, entrepreneurialism, etc.

Progressive companies have been paying increasing attention to intellectual assets since the beginning of the 1990s when the giant financial services group Skandia appointed Leif Edvinsson to the post of Director, Intellectual Capital. Since then, job titles such as chief knowledge officer (CKO) have begun to appear quite frequently, yet a survey by the American Society for Training and Development (ASTD) in 1996 shows that almost half the respondents had first heard about IC only within the last year. Most

(80%), however, viewed it as "important today and in the future." Despite this, the ASTD, in a joint investigation with the Conference Board, concluded that most corporate initiatives to manage intellectual capital are rather limited in scope. Few firms have an overall strategy for managing and leveraging IC, and very little progress has been made in the area of measurement.

One of the first obstacles is clearly a conceptual one. For present purposes, we use two main approaches to definition which, together, provide an adequate understanding of the concept. The first is shared by many of the influential writers in the IC field, including Edvinsson and Malone (1997) and Thomas Stewart (1997a) as well as the ASTD and Canada's Hubert St. Onge (1996a,b) (who pioneered the development of IC concepts when he was at the Canadian Imperial Bank of Commerce (CIBC)). Basically, this definition breaks IC down into three principal components:

- *Human capital* is the company's competencies, skills, tacit and explicit knowledge, vision, capacity to innovate, etc.
- *Structural capital* consists of information systems, policies, procedures to support knowledge development and application for optimum business performance.
- *Relational (or customer) capital* refers to the extent and quality of the firm's relationships with its clientele, including customer satisfaction, loyalty and the durability of the relationships.

Following Brooking (1996), intellectual capital may be somewhat more comprehensively viewed as the sum of four sets of assets (Figure 2).

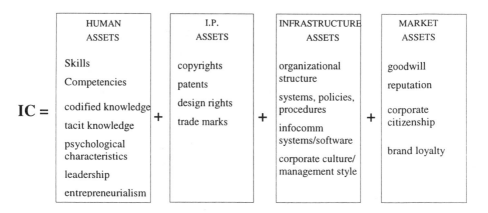

Figure 2: Intellectual capital

First, *human assets*, as in all definitions, include collective expertise, individual skills, entrepreneurial and managerial competencies, plus personal attributes such as leadership, determination, independence, helpfulness, extroversion or introversion, etc. Next, *intellectual property assets* would include copyrights, patents, licences, design rights and "trade secrets." Third, *infrastructure assets* include information and communication systems and software, organizational design, policies, practices and routines, and corporate philosophy and management style. Finally, *market assets* include goodwill, corporate image, reputation, brand loyalty and customer relations and satisfaction.

The infrastructure assets constitute the organizing framework within which human assets are developed and deployed; they constitute the policies towards, and the processes for obtaining and developing, market assets and intellectual property assets, respectively.

Following Bontis (1996), intellectual capital assets may be thought of as stocks at a point in time, whereas the dynamic processes of organizational learning may be thought of as the flows that augment those stocks. In practice, then, organizations that systematically commit to actively encourage learning can be said to be enhancing their stocks of knowledge or intellectual capital. Such efforts are many and varied. Much rarer, however, are efforts to *measure* intellectual capital. This is undoubtedly because of the formidable difficulties such measurement presents. Indeed, there is considerable debate as to whether intellectual capital can – or even should – be measured. *Forbes* magazine devoted some fifty pages of its April 7, 1997 issue to a series of articles containing strongly different points of view.

4.1   Measuring IC

The numerous attempts to grapple with the measurement of IC have spawned a burgeoning literature. A useful and very recent review is Lynn (1998). Here, we choose to concentrate on two particular approaches that are notable for their ingenuity, practicality and influence.

A comprehensive set of over one hundred measures of financial performance and structural, relational and human capital is set out in Edvinsson and Malone's (1997) popular book. Perhaps even more influential has been Norton and Kaplan's (1997) concept of the "balanced scorecard." Their fundamental point of departure is the contention that the financial bottom line is merely the dollar reflection of a range of performance factors.

The balanced scorecard therefore involves setting goals and critical indicators in four major areas:

- *Customer perspective*: time, quality, price, service, customer partnerships.
- *Internal business perspective:* identify core competencies and critical technologies and assess their suitability to achieve goals for cycle time, quality, productivity, cost, etc.
- *Innovation and learning perspective:* rates of improvement (how quickly you reach goals for reduction of cycle time, defect rates, etc.); percent sales from new products.
- *Financial perspective*: is improved operating performance (getting the long-term fundamentals right) paying off in terms of the financial bottom line?

One particularly innovative approach to measurement has been developed by Annie Brooking (1996). Her company, The Technology Broker, specializes *inter alia* in intellectual capital audits which involve an interesting and ingenious approach to metrics. The procedure is basically as follows. First, the company is asked to articulate a *goal*, such as "improve market share by X percent in Y months." The audit procedure then identifies the assets (market assets, intellectual property assets, infrastructure assets, and human-centred assets, as in Figure 2, above) required to achieve the goal and identifies their relative strengths and weaknesses. What Brooking calls the *"dream ticket"* is the optimal set of assets to achieve the goal. The audit per se is the activity of gathering information on the firm's actual relative strengths or weaknesses in the areas identified on the dream ticket. Various methods are used to elicit information, depending on the asset under consideration. To measure brand recognition, for example, a survey might be used. Or, if the value of a certain kind of infrastructure was to be determined, then "fit-for-purpose" evaluation might be invoked.

The next step is to assign an *index*, or ranking, to each of the assets. If the asset is strong enough to match the dream ticket it is accorded a value of 5; if the match is very weak, the score is 1. Finally, the scores are displayed on a *target* as in Figure 3 where the quadrants represent the four kinds of IC assets and the bullet holes represent scores for individual assets. Where an asset matches the requirement of the dream ticket, it scores a "bull's eye."

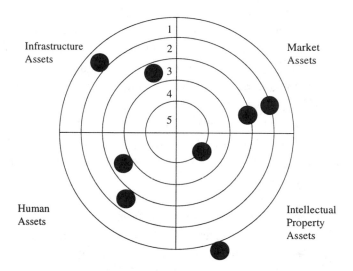

Figure 3: The target

In sum, the target provides a snapshot of the organization's strengths and weaknesses and a basis for assessing whether the situation is expected to improve or deteriorate.

5.   EMPIRICAL EVIDENCE

There is by now a large literature on OL/LO and certainly a burgeoning one on IC, as the recent spate of popular books such as Brooking (1996), Edvinsson and Malone (1997) and Stewart (1997a) attests. A large part of this literature is prescriptive: what do firms have to do to become learning organizations, and how do they "harness the power" of intellectual capital, for example. Much of the empirical work that informs such normative work is based on case studies, and interested readers can find hundreds of informative examples in the pages of such journals as the *Harvard Business Review*, the *Sloan Management Review* and the *California Management Review, inter alia*, as well as in business magazines such as *Forbes* and *Fortune*. In addition, organizations such as the Conference Board (see, e.g., Conference Board, 1997) and the American Society for Training and Development (see, e.g., Bassi, 1997) provide useful treatments based on case studies, surveys, etc.

In Canada, the Ontario Premier's Council (1995), with the support of the Canadian Institute of Chartered Accountants, has attempted to highlight examples of initiatives in the OL/LO and IC fields. A useful overview of IC, containing some real-life illustrations, is provided by the Society of Management Accountants of Canada in a recent study (CMA, 1998). Most of the empirical studies, however, are descriptive and predominantly qualitative in the nature of their analysis. Here we choose to highlight three studies that are somewhat more analytical and more quantitative in nature: one from the U.S., one comparing the U.S. and Canada, and one examining public- and private-sector firms in Canada.

The first of these, by Bassi and Van Buren (1998), reports on an analysis of survey results from 500 U.S. firms. The focus was on intellectual capital investments (firms' investments in education and training), complementary work practices and compensation policies, and subjective measures of organizational performance. For a subset of 40 publicly traded companies, data were also obtained on other corporate financial investments (physical capital and R&D) and objective measures of corporate performance such as net sales per employee, gross profit per employee, and market-to-book value.

The training investment measures included training as a percentage of payroll and training expenditure per employee in 1996, the percent changes in these figures from the previous year, and the *type* of training (technical skills or other). Factor analysis of the complementary workplace practices identified four clusters: high-performance work practices (including employee involvement in decision-making, employee access to corporate information, and self-directed work teams); innovative compensation practices (including profit- or gain-sharing, ESOPS, team-based and incentive pay); innovative training practices such as train-the-trainer programs; and competency practices such as skill certification.

In the first stage of their analysis, the authors found a significant and positive relationship between the two subjective measures of organizational performance ("better than, worse than, or same as 1995" and "better, worse or same as other organizations in the same kind of work") and firms' use of innovative training practices, high-performance work practices and innovative compensation plans. The training measures were positively correlated with 1996 performance compared to other firms, but not with the change in performance since 1995. Rather (and as one might expect) the *change* in performance is correlated with the *change* in the percentage of employees receiving training.

The second stage looked at the intellectual capital investment variables and the objective measures of financial performance for the rather limited sample of publicly traded firms. Not surprisingly, few significant correlations emerged. What is interesting, however, is that both training as a percentage of payroll and training expenditure per employee were significantly, positively correlated with 1996 market-to-book value. It seems surprising that the training variables are statistically significant when others (including the various high-performance work practices) that have been found significant by other researchers do not prove to be significantly correlated with financial outcomes.

The final stage was to run an ordinary least squares regression between market-to-book value (a classic measure of IC) and training expenditures as a percentage of payroll, with a dummy to control for the high-tech industry, which has notoriously high market-to-book values. Both right-hand-side variables are significantly related to the dependent variable in 1996 and 1997.

The authors caution that the work is tentative and preliminary but it points suggestively to important links between investments in intellectual capital and measures of firm performance, and specifically between such investments and a classic measure of intellectual capital – namely, Tobin's q.

A comparative study of the management of intangible assets in U.S. and Canadian firms is Stivers et al. (1996). Based on a mail questionnaire to Chairmen of the Board, CEOs, and Chief Financial Officers in 124 Canadian and 89 U.S. firms, the study has four main parts. In the first, participants were asked to express, on a 5-point scale (1= strongly disagree, 5 = strongly agree), their reactions to a set of statements about how their companies manage knowledge. These included: knowledge is our company's most critical resource; intellectual capital is an integral focus of our performance measurement system; intangible resources are more important than tangible resources for gaining competitive advantage; and others of a similar ilk. The relatively high values of the mean scores for both countries attest to the importance placed on human and intellectual assets. Although the scores were higher for the U.S. for all statements except one, there were only two (out of nine) cases of statistically significant difference. In a subsequent paper, Covin and Stivers (1998) augmented the list of knowledge-management practices (relabelled "knowledge-focus scale items") with a set of innovation-focus scale items. The latter included: our performance measurement system is designed to foster innovation; assistance in developing new ideas is widely available in our company; adequate resources are devoted to innovation in our company; and, there is adequate time to pursue new ideas. Scores on the two scales were used to partition firms into high-, medium- and low-knowledge and innovation categories.

Some of the results of this exercise are rather interesting. First, 45% of the U.S. firms, but only 23% of Canadian ones, were in the high-knowledge and innovation category. The authors suggest this may derive from differences in industry composition between the two countries' samples. The vast majority of the U.S. firms were in manufacturing while the majority of the Canadian firms were in services. So the result might be interpreted to reflect the fact that there is more focus on knowledge and innovation in manufacturing than in service firms.

Second, in both the U.S. and Canada, the high-knowledge, high-innovation firms were characterized by a greater technology focus, more organic (less rigidly hierarchical) organization structures, and greater concern about the future importance of intellectual property; they also placed more importance on employee-involvement-related nonfinancial performance measures.

Third, high-focus firms tended to be larger in terms of assets and numbers of employees. However, surprisingly, this study showed no consistent relationship between a focus on knowledge and innovation and financial measures of performance such as sales and net income.

In fact, for the Canadian sample these measures were highest for low-focus firms.

In the next stage of the analysis, respondents were asked to indicate on a 10-point Likert scale the level of contribution to overall business success in 1990-2000 of 17 intangible resources. Companies in both countries attached the highest importance to company and product reputation and employee know-how. For the year 2000, employee know-how, information systems and corporate culture are regarded as critical by firms in both countries. The major finding is that respondents expect *all* the intangible assets listed to become significantly more important by the year 2000.

The final section of the analysis examined critical areas of employee know-how and asked respondents to rank their importance in 1990 and the year 2000. In both countries, human resource management and management information systems become relatively more important in the year 2000. The last empirical study we examine (Richards and Goh, 1995) addresses the issue of organizational learning. It is interesting in that it is an employee-based survey that poses 21 questions clustered into five dimensions or scales: clarity of mission and purpose; leadership and facilitation; experimentation and rewards; knowledge transfer; and team and group problem-solving. The questions were posed to employees in each of five organizations. Organization 1 (ORG 1) was a federal government department of about 300 people engaged in research. ORGs 2 and 3 were Special Operating Agencies (SOAs) of about 200 people each. SOAs operate on a cost-recovery basis and enjoy some freedom from the rules that typically constrain government departments. At the time of the survey, ORG 3 had been in existence four years and ORG 2, one. ORGs 4 and 5 were private sector telecom firms, the former large and the latter with a particular emphasis on R&D.

The authors expected ORG 1 to score lowest because of the relative rigidity of the federal public sector. (Knowledge transfer is a case in point: often, the bureaucracy sets up rules about who may communicate with whom, and senior managers have "gatekeepers" to insulate them from inferiors; so information is often diluted, confused or lost.) ORG 2 was expected to score a little higher than ORG 1 because of its SOA status, while ORG 3 should have been higher than ORG 2 because it had more SOA experience and because the nature of its work is conducive to OL. It was expected that ORGs 4 and 5 would score highest since they are both highly competitive, knowledge-intensive private-sector companies. However, ORG 4 had been formed through a merger and was in the process of reassessing its mission, strategy, etc.

Generally the predictions were upheld by the results, with one major exception: ORG 2 actually scored lower than ORG 1. Despite its SOA status, the authors suggest that, having been in existence only a year, it was still addressing a number of leadership and design issues. The authors conclude that the research-based organizations scored best, especially in the teamwork and experimentation dimensions, and that this bears out the contention that an organization's task has an impact on how well it learns.

One further interesting dimension of this study is that scales for employee satisfaction and for formalization (rigid rules and procedures) were also included. As might be expected intuitively, the results show empirically that employee satisfaction increases with OLS (organizational learning survey) score, while the relationship between formalization and OLS score is negative. Overall, the OLS appears to afford a useful way for an organization to systematically assess its OL potential, compare itself with others, and track developments over time. An important extension, in the authors' view, would be to examine whether, and to what extent, superior OL potential translates into superior organizational performance.

6.   THE CASE STUDIES

The basic purpose was to identify some Canadian companies with exemplary practices. (A minor – non-academic! – motive was to celebrate some Canadian successes.) But, more generally, the purpose was to examine some companies that appeared to have made efforts to espouse the principle of OL and to husband their IC assets. It was clear, given the scope of the project, that it would not be possible (at this stage, at least) to undertake the kind of in-depth and comprehensive analysis that would yield definitive and generalizable results. However, it was felt that from an extensive literature review it would be possible to frame a useful "template" – an organizing framework for analysis of some cases. From these cases, it was felt, we might be able to identify and highlight certain strategies, practices, policies, and procedures that echo the exemplary concepts that we encountered in the literature. We might, in short, be able to distil a few lessons, a few generalizations, that constitute the ingredients of success.

Our sample, therefore, would not gladden the hearts of statisticians. In Canada today the companies that are making the most overt move to explicitly acknowledge the importance of IC are in banking and insurance. We looked at four of these. "High-tech" companies, of course, are regarded as the epitome of knowledge-intensity, and we examined four of them: two huge MNEs in the ITC field and two small, R&D-intensive companies in the field of software development and application. A recently privatized Crown Corporation afforded an opportunity to examine how an organization is adapting to the learning requirements of a new market environment. And a management consulting group specializing in corporate head-hunting is a firm whose stock in trade is, literally, intellectual capital. The eleventh and final case is an example of the way in which a time-honoured profession that – technically – has existed for millennia has taken on the tools of the KBE. More detailed descriptions of the individual cases may be obtained in the form of a background paper by the authors. What follows is our general model of OL/LO and IC, a very brief description of the instrument used for the case studies, an analysis of the cases, and our results and concluding comments.

The general framework of analysis is derived from the literature review underlying sections 3 and 4. As depicted in Figure 4 it sets out some common elements of organizational learning that come into play at the various levels of learning within the organization. This flow process of learning develops the firm's stocks of intellectual capital assets. Success then depends on managing and leveraging the knowledge embedded in these assets to enhance corporate performance.

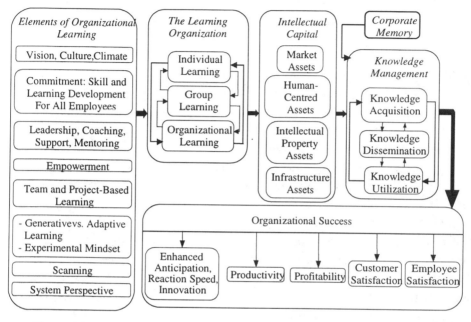

*Figure 4:*A general framework for analyzing the elements of a learning organization and intellectual capital

This framework provided the foundation for designing the questionnaire used to structure the interviews for the case studies. In addition to the usual "tombstone data," the organizations were asked about mission and overall business strategy. Two sections contained questions dealing with the firm's technological and organizational innovations. The major part of the questionnaire (12 of the 33 questions) was devoted to OL/LO. It enquired about the motives for adopting OL and the policies, practices, systems and facilities used to implement and develop it. Organizations were then asked to assess the impact of OL on a variety of performance indicators. Further questions related to the organizations' identification and measurement of IC and finally to the extent to which they participate in partnerships, consortia, etc., for joint learning and knowledge acquisition.

At the outset, although we had not framed precise research hypotheses, we expected to find evidence of some of the salient features in the OL/LO and

IC literature – namely, the importance of vision, leadership and commitment to learning; the need for technological and organizational ("structural") capital; the role of customer and quality orientation as a driver of OL; and a wide variety of practices, policies and approaches. We also expected to learn that such strategies pay off in terms of performance. And while we anticipated that many firms and individuals would agree on the importance of IC, we expected that few would be measuring it. Finally, it was expected that industry and firm size might be determinants of commitment, and/or the particular form of approach to OL/LO and IC. What did we find?

In fact, we found evidence, in varying degrees, of practically all of the features in our general model and in our set of expectations. In this necessarily brief section, we present synthetic examples in a number of such areas. Detailed case descriptions are contained in a background paper by the authors. One case description exemplifying many of the features of the model is contained in Appendix A.

Vision, commitment and leadership were important in all the cases we studied. Some examples include CIBC's explicit strategy to enhance its organizational capital to learn better and faster than competitors; Matthew Barrett's vision of a Learning Institute for the Bank of Montreal or Hubert Saint-Onge's (1997) vision of the power and importance of IC; the championship role of leaders in small high-tech companies such as Kyberpass in Ottawa, and Perigon Solutions Inc. in Calgary; and the mentoring ("critic-and-consultant") role of the principal at Barry Padolsky Architect Ltd.

Next, empowerment and teamwork often seemed to go hand in hand. The former may take the form of employee access to corporate information as well as participation in decision-making. But in several cases it takes a special form that is a distinctive feature of OL. An essential feature of CIBC's competency model approach is the concept of a "culture of personal responsibility." That is, the firm provides the commitment and the resources for the individuals to assess their needs and take charge of their skills and knowledge acquisition. This contrasts with "passive training," which reflects a culture of dependency and paternalism (Kiernan, 1996). Hubert Saint-Onge at the Mutual Group in Kitchener-Waterloo told us: "We don't talk about 'training.' We provide the opportunities for individuals to pursue their own learning goals." Similarly, Xerox Canada's *management competency framework* stresses the idea of shared responsibility: the company and its managers provide the opportunity and the resources and it is then the individual's responsibility to pursue her own learning agenda. Teams – cross-functional and cross-organizational – were also important at Xerox but appeared to be a central feature of the small firms we examined. Ron George at Perigon Solutions Inc. favours high-performance work teams composed of individuals with differing skill sets but in which everyone has responsibility for all aspects of the project. In this way, he contends, they maximize learning, ensure complete sharing of all information, and spread risk.

Technology played an important role in all cases, particularly in providing data banks and information and communication systems. Three cases were of special interest. One is the Royal Bank's "virtual academy" which permits employees, right at their own terminals, to climb the steps and enter the portals of an academy where (having been counselled by a manager) they "sign up" for their required courses. Another is the sophisticated Inter-vu video-conferencing system that gives head-hunting firm Caldwell Partners International Inc. face-to-face meetings with clients and/or candidates, and their on-line database of over 80,000 Canadian managers and hundreds of Canadian and foreign companies. A third is the systematic way in which Kyberpass employees use the Internet to exchange information with other experts and glean new knowledge from myriad sources around the world: the Internet is, in this case, the principal learning tool. One rather unexpected finding about technology, particularly in the smaller firms, was that, in addition to being a necessary condition for learning, it was also a motivator. "Techies," to put it crudely, are turned on by fast, powerful and sophisticated equipment and software.

A system perspective – a holistic view that encompasses all the various facets, processes and activities of an organization and the way they interlink – is crucial if the synergies of OL are to be reaped. All successful LOs have this. One special and specific example of this is at the Mutual Group in the form of "putting yourself in the other guy's shoes." The sales, technical and administrative staff change roles so that individuals in each group may understand the needs and challenges of the other major corporate functions and, through feedback, enhance the effectiveness of all.

Generative or (double loop, as opposed to adaptive or single loop) learning is familiar to a number of cases in our sample. The process of privatization at Canada Post, for example, called for a fundamental rethinking of corporate beliefs and strategies, and a thoroughgoing review of the learning implications, in order to address the exigencies of a new market reality. Then there is Xerox Corporation, once poised on the brink of bankruptcy and then hauled back to solvency by commitment to a TQM paradigm that contained a number of crucial LO principles. That radical realignment has provided the foundation for Xerox Canada's enviable reputation as a learning organization today. As described in Appendix A, Barry Padolsky challenges his architects to "be creative; throw away the rules" – a classic example of Argyris' double loop learning.

On the question of models and metrics, it is clear that companies are influenced by the management thinking of the day. CIBC and the Mutual Group owe much to the pioneering efforts of the Skandia Group, for example, as well as to Saint-Onge's personal *imprimatur*. As to metrics, Saint-Onge has been working on a model incorporating human, structural and relational capital assets and the flows among them, with a view to simulating and operationalizing it for practical use. Meanwhile, the Bank of Montreal is exploring the possible application of the balanced scoreboard, and CIBC has developed a number of IC indicators including (in the context of relational or customer capital) speed to market with new products and services, resolution of customer complaints, and customer retention rates.

Next, partnerships. Many, if not all, the cases we examined had some kind of external relation for knowledge creation and transfer. Newbridge, for example, is a leading player in the Ottawa-Carleton Learning Foundation, a consortium which includes many high-tech firms and local universities, colleges and schools. Canada Post has an advisory board involving representatives of the university and research communities and systematically draws on the teaching and research resources of institutions in various parts of the country.

As expected, we found a wide variety of approaches, philosophies, policies, etc. One example that struck us was the difference between the bricks-and-mortar learning institute of the Bank of Montreal, and Royal Bank's virtual academy. The former is a state-of-the-art multimedia, residential facility in Scarborough, Ontario, where the basic idea is to get people (from across the country) away from their desks and into a milieu that encourages reflection, interaction, imagination, creativity and exchange. At the Royal, by contrast, the approach is to afford individuals the opportunity to create their own learning agenda and follow it on their own volition right in the workplace.

As also expected, we found much enthusiasm about the concept of IC, but, with the few exceptions mentioned above, little evidence of success, or even systematic attempts, in identifying and measuring it. As for the size variable, we observe that the small firms in our sample exemplified many of the OL/LO attributes described in earlier sections and, in fact, we highlight one of those small firms in Appendix A.

7.   POLICY IMPLICATIONS

Why should governments be involved in the diffusion of high-performance management practices such as organizational learning and the management and development of IC? The simple answer is that the empirical evidence points to two conclusions. First, innovative HR management strategies appear to pay off in terms of crucial economic goals. Second, there are reasons to believe that firms are not adopting these strategies as rapidly, as extensively, and as comprehensively as efficiency considerations would warrant.

The more theoretical case for involvement is well known and need be restated only very briefly. First, there is the question of externalities. The new learning strategies under consideration obviously require substantial investment in people. So there may be legitimate concerns about investors' ability to capture sufficient benefits if the workforce is highly mobile. The second consideration is imperfect information. It is notoriously difficult for firms (particularly small firms) to assess the costs and (especially) the benefits of these strategies. This fact is mirrored in the paucity of information on performance outcomes. A third rationale for a government role is that there is a "public good" element to investment in such strategies that is analogous to the case of R&D and diffusion of "hard" technologies. To the extent that firms investing in these approaches compete more effectively there is a collective benefit in the form of wealth creation and jobs.

So what might governments – preferably in partnership with the private sector – usefully do? The following are some areas in which initiatives might be undertaken.

*   *Strategic Information*
    Collecting and distributing print and electronic documents responding "just in time" to the needs of the workplace parties; utilizing state-of-the-art information technologies and databases to remain abreast of local, provincial, national and international developments.
*   *Orientation and Diagnostic Advice*

Identifying needs, developing action plans, linking employers, workers, and unions to credible change leaders.

- *Brokerage and Referral*
  Once needs and opportunities are identified, guiding people and organizations to existing service providers such as supportive government programs, private sector consultants, and financial support sources.

- *Consultant Inventory*
  Maintaining an inventory of experienced, credible facilitators, and outlining the guidelines under which consultants operate in an organization.

- *Research/Evaluation*
  Undertaking or supporting publication of research on critical success factors, reasons for failure, benchmark data, case studies, support for leading-edge research.

- *Conferencing/Learning*
  Arranging opportunities for joint learning through regional and sectoral symposia. Working with educators to influence curricula, engaging Deans of Business and Engineering Schools, Industrial Relations Institutes, etc.

- *Site Visits and Study Missions*
  Arranging visits to innovating organizations and joint missions to innovating jurisdictions. Connecting "Best Practice" organizations.

- *Awards Program*
  Running an awards program for identification of leading individuals and organizations; arranging financial incentives to award winners to disseminate their experience.

With specific reference to the item above entitled "research/evaluation," a major conclusion of the paper is that there is a dearth of empirical work in this area in Canada. There are few case studies of OL/LO and IC, and even fewer surveys. Research is needed to find out where such management strategies and practices are being deployed, how, to what extent, and with what results. Numerous related surveys – on training (see, e.g., Betcherman et al., 1998), on the relationship between HR development and innovation (see, e.g., Baldwin and Johnson, 1995), and on the high-performance workplace (see, e.g., Newton, 1998) – provide pieces of the puzzle, as do several brief and scattered case descriptions. The work of Stivers et al.

(1996), Richards and Goh (1995) and various papers by Nick Bontis (see, e.g., Bontis, 1996) are a useful start in this country. And the work of Bassi and Van Buren (1998) in the U.S. seems to point in the right direction. But here is a field crying out for a focused, large-scale, comprehensive project, possibly combining a survey and case studies and (preferably) longitudinal and international comparative dimensions, as well as design features that facilitate firms' self-diagnosis and benchmarking against competitors.

APPENDIX A: BARRY PADOLSKY ARCHITECT LTD.

This small (seven persons), specialized architectural firm in Ottawa illustrates many of the characteristics and applications of the concepts of organizational learning and intellectual capital development described above. Quite simply, but most importantly, the very nature of this kind of work is fundamentally intellectual. It requires high levels of technical skill, but also vision and creativity. And all of these attributes must be continuously enriched in order for the firm to survive and prosper.

A number of facets of the firm's operations illustrate its knowledge-based, continuous-learning character. First (and, of course, this is by no means unique) it relies on advanced CAD technology and the continuous learning that experimentation with such systems and their applications requires. In this case, however, there is an interesting twist to the story. Sensing the growing importance of technological sophistication, the firm's principal deliberately sought out and acquired a special set of intellectual assets in the form of a graduate architect whose skills were less traditional and more computer-based. This in itself, created an opportunity for team learning as the acquisition of technological competence by the incumbent staff was facilitated by the new employee. The latter, in turn, benefited from the broader experience of new colleagues.

A second example illustrates what the literature variously refers to as "interactive learning" and "learning from clients." Such interaction is the lifeblood of architectural research and development. Take the case of the firm's commission to design a new hospital extension to accommodate Alzheimer's patients. Clearly, this involves an intensive and lengthy iterative process with the clients to articulate performance standards for the facility: eating arrangements, sanitation, and the spatial and psychological features of the environment. (The latter includes "meaningful wandering paths" for the patients – secure and comfortable but with therapeutic themes and events along the way – that clearly call for creativity and ingenuity.) Based on the principle of "design economics," Padolsky and his team would then offer several design options for criticism and feedback. Before submitting a redesign the team would typically undertake additional research, such as, in this case, drawing on the expertise and experience of the Australian ADARDS (Alzheimer's Disease and Related Disorders) model in Hobart,

Tasmania. The iterative process ultimately approaches a mutually acceptable consensus that reflects a rich learning process and new knowledge.

The term R&D typically conjures up images of white-coated boffins tending test tubes and retorts. But R&D, albeit of a different kind, is essential to this architectural firm, too. Some years ago the firm was called in to address problems stemming from subsidence at Ottawa's historic Victoria Memorial Museum building, a massive stone castle-like structure with turrets and crenellations. In analyzing the problem and recommending the methods and materials for repair, the team seized the opportunity to develop a comprehensive system for evaluating and monitoring the building by establishing the coordinates of the entire building, entering them on a CAD system, and establishing a management information system for maintenance and costing. This Global Positioning System is, in effect, a knowledge baseline for management in future generations.

Another example of the firm's R&D also illustrates its unique leveraging of specialized or "niche knowledge" relating to the restoration of heritage properties – "reinstating features that were long lost," in Mr. Padolsky's words. Ever on the lookout for abandoned items of historical significance that could be brought back to practical or ornamental significance in a contemporary setting, Padolsky came across a copper weather vane in the form of a flying Mercury. Custom-crafted by American sculptor W.H. Muller for Sun Life in Ottawa in 1898, the Mercury went into the custody of the Ottawa Historical Society when the building it adorned was demolished in 1949. The rescued vane now stands atop a domed clock tower, one of the new features the firm incorporated into the renovation of a vacant 65-year-old department store now known as Mercury Court.

For several other characteristics of learning organizations, the firm is also an exemplar. Take teams and mentorship. The firm encourages a team approach that combines complementary skill sets and gives everyone a taste of the various aspects of project management. Cross-functionality extends outside the firm, too: many projects call for partnerships with external experts, such as structural engineers, for example. Padolsky's mentoring role vis-à-vis such teams is interesting: "set up the team, agree on the broad parameters, and let them be creative."

His encouragement to "throw away the rules" is entirely congruent with Argyris' key concept of *double loop learning*. He avers that, in this context, he sees himself as a kind of critic and consultant.

Learning, in any firm of this kind, must be continuous. In addition to the means described above, this firm, like most, encourages staff to keep up with and surpass the skill sets of other organizations through self-learning, and participation in trade and professional organizations. In addition, there are two forms of learning that are specific to the architectural profession. The first is the institution of internship, in which new graduates are required to proceed through a systematic, monitored, and documented process of practical skill acquisition and expertise. This, in itself, is a contributing element to the climate and culture of innovation and learning that are the hallmark of the architectural firm. The other is interesting and perhaps less well known. Architecture, like medicine and law, is potentially subject to liability suits. Naturally, it is in the interest of insurance companies to minimize the frequency and incidence of claims, and therefore the maintenance and development of expertise is a major priority. Accordingly, the insurance companies strike a deal: follow a prescribed program of training to keep up and enrich your skills, and we will give you a break on the premiums.

Finally, a useful practice in this firm is the *post-mortem*. What did we learn from this project? What worked, what didn't, and what can we do about it? This is in keeping with what Garvin (1993) has dubbed the "Santayana review," after the famous American philosopher who asserted that those who do not learn from history are condemned to repeat it. It is through retrospective evaluation that organizational memory is developed.

All in all, this case clearly illustrates many of the features of the knowledge-intensive firms set out in the earlier sections of this paper. It is in many ways a classic small-firm exemplar that emphasizes a synergistic, multiskilling team approach in which "everyone learns a bit of everything," and in which leadership is crucial in defining the learning culture of the organization.

NOTES

[1] These include occupations in natural sciences, mathematics, and engineering; education; managers and administrators; social sciences; law; medicine and health; and writing.

REFERENCES

Argyris, C., "Double Loop Learning in Organizations." *Harvard Business Review*, September – October, 1977.

Baldwin, J. and J. Johnson, *Human Capital Development and Innovation*. Ottawa: Statistics Canada Research Paper No. 74, March, 1995.

Bassi, L., *Harnessing the Power of Intellectual Capital*. Alexandria, VA: ASTD, 1997.

Bassi, L. and M. Van Buren, "Investments in Intellectual Capital: Creating Methods." Paper presented at the World Congress on Management of Intellectual Capital, 1998.

Betcherman, G., K. McMullen and K. Davidman, *Training for the New Economy*. Ottawa: Canadian Policy Research Networks, 1998.

Bontis, N., "Intellectual Capital: An Exploratory Study That Develops Measures and Models." Paper presented at the 17th McMaster Business Conference, 1996.

Brooking, A., *Intellectual Capital: Core Asset for the Third Millennium Enterprise*. London: International Thomson Business Press, 1996.

CMA, *The Management of Intellectual Capital: The Issues and the Practice*. Hamilton, ON: Society of Management Accountants of Canada, 1998.

Conference Board "Leveraging Intellectual Capital." *HR Executive Review*, 5(3), 1997.

Covin, T.J. and B.P. Stivers, Knowledge and Innovation Focussed Business Practices: Profiting Canadian and U.S. Firms.Paper at McMaster University Business Conference, 1998.

Edvinsson, L. and M.S. Malone, *Intellectual Capital: Realizing Your Company's True Value by Finding Its Hidden Brainpower*. New York: Harper Business, 1997.

Forbes Magazine, Special Section: "Measurement", April 17, 1997, 35-82.

Garvin, D.A., "Building a Learning Organization." *Harvard Business Review*, July-August, 1993, 78-91.

Gera, S. and P. Massé, "Employment Performance in the Knowledge-based Economy." Industry Canada Working Paper No. 14, 1996.

Gera, S., G. Wulong and Z. Lin, *Technology and the Demand for Skills: An Industry-Level Analysis*. Ottawa: Industry Canada, 1998.

Huber, G., "Organizational Learning: The Contributing Processes and the Literatures." *Organization Science*, 2, 1991, 88-115.

Kiernan, M.J., *The Eleven Commandment of 21ʰ Century Management.* New Jersey: Prentice Hall, 1996.

Leckie, N., Can Skill Requirements Trends in Canada, 1971-1991. Mimeo; Canadian Tolia Research Networks, 1996.

Lee, F. and H. Has "A Quantitative Assessment of High Knowledge Industries Versus Low Knowledge Industries" in P. Howitt (ed.) *The Implications of Knowledge-Based Growth for Microeconomic Policies*. Calgary: University of Calgary Press, 1996

Levitt, B., and J.G. March, "Organizational Learning.", *Annual Review of Sociology*, 4(2), 1988, 319-340.

Lundvall, B.-A. and B. Johnson, "The Learning Economy." Paper presented at the EAEPE Conference on Structural Change and the Regulation of Economic Systems, Paris, 1992.

Lynn, B.E. "Perform once Evaluation in the New Economy", *International Journal of Technology Management*, 16, 1997.

Marquardt, M.J. and A. Raynolds, *The Global Learning Organization*. BuvrRidge: Irwin, 1994.

Nevis, E. C., A. J. diBella and J. M. Gould, "Understanding Organizations as Learning Systems." *Sloan Management Review*, 36(2), 1995, 73-85.

Newton, K., *The Human Factor in Firms' Performance: Management Strategies, Productivity and Competitiveness*. Ottawa: Industry Canada Occasional Paper No. 15, 1996.

Newton, K., "The High Performance Workplace: HR-Based Management Innovations in Canada." *International Journal of Technology Management*, 1998.

Nonaka, I., "The Knowledge – Creating Company" *Harvard Business Review*, November-December, 1991.

OECD, *Technology Productivity and Job Creation*. Paris: OECD, 1996.

Ontario's Premier's Council *Performance Measures in the New Economy*, 1995.

Richards, G. and S. C. Goh, "Implementing Organizational Learning: Toward a Systematic Approach." *Optimum*, autumn, 1995, 26(2), 25-31.

Saint-Onge, H., "Tacit Knowledge: The Key to Strategic Alignment of Intellectual Capital," *Strategy and Leadership,* March-April, 1996a, 24(2), 10-14.

Saint-Onge, H., "The Learning Organization at CIBC...A Framework for Application." Paper presented at the 17th Annual National Business Conference, McMaster University, 1996b.

Senge, P., *The Fifth Discipline: The Art and Practice of the Learning Organization.* New York: Doubleday, 1990.
Shrivastava, P.A., Strategic Decision – Thanking Process: The Influence of Organizational Learning and Experience. University of Pittsburgh, Ph.D. dissovation, 1981.

Soete, L., "Some Thoughts on the Economics of Knowledge." Paper prepared for the Advisory Committee on Science and Technology, Industry Canada, Ottawa, 1997.

Stewart, T.A, *Intellectual Capital: The New Wealth of Organizations.* New York: Doubleday, 1997a.

Stivers, B. et al., *The Management of Intangible Assets: A Study of US and Canadian Firms.* Prepared for Canadian Institute of Chartered Accountants, 1996.

Swieringa, J. and A. Wierdsma, *Becoming a Learning Organization: Beyond the Learning Curve.* Reading, MA: Addison-Wesley, 1992.

Swieringa, J. and A. Wierdsma, *Becoming a Learning Organization.* Wokingham: Addison-Westey, 1992.

Tsang, E.W.K. (1997) "Organizational Learning and the Learning Organization", *Human Relations*, 50(1), 1997.

Wolff, N.E. and W.J. Baundt "Sources of Post-War Eventh of Information Activity in the U.S. in the Information Economy: the Implications of unbalanced Granth", lars Osberg, E.N. Woff and W.J. Baumol (eds.), (IRPP), 1989.

5. U.S. MANUFACTURING: TECHNOLOGY AND PUBLIC POLICY IN THE "KNOWLEDGE AGE"[1]

John E. Ettlie
Rochester Institute of Technology

1. INTRODUCTION

The U.S. economy generally, and manufacturing in particular, are nearing the end of a decade of nearly unprecedented growth and high performance. Manufacturing productivity grew by a rate of 4.4% in 1996[2] and 1998 industrial output is expected to be about 3% above 1997 levels.[3] Durable goods manufacturing, in particular, has been very strong, with increased output of 9.5% in 1997[4]. The stock market is up 150% in the last four years.[5]

Unemployment levels are low[6] and, since productivity is up, the hourly cost of U.S. production workers is still relatively low when compared to the major developed regions of the world. In the U.S., the 1996 hourly cost of a production worker was $17.70, up 3% from the previous year. In Europe, the 1996 cost per hour for a production worker was $22.37 but this was only 1.2% higher than in 1995. In Japan, hourly production worker rates fell by 12.4% from 1995 to $20.84 in 1996. If one uses the measure of cost per unit of output as the comparison base, the U.S. was enjoying a 5%-10% labour advantage over Japan (using an exchange rate of 130 yen to the dollar) and a 25% labour advantage over Europe.

What accounts for this continuing vitality in the economic statistics for the U.S.? One possible explanation of this high performance is the strategic drive for increased effectiveness and efficiency with new products, new production technology and improved methods in U.S. industry. Further, U.S. technology policy may also be instrumental in this success. We explore these hypotheses below. First, we analyze the data on the relationship between investment in R&D and performance of the largest companies in the U.S. (section 2). Then we confront the investments in manufacturing technologies, equipment and information systems (sections 3 and 4) and public policy question directly (section 5).

2. TECHNOLOGY AND ECONOMIC PERFORMANCE

Does technology have a positive impact on company performance, as so many have argued? We explored this question by compiling data from public sources on R&D investment and financial performance as proxies for new technology utilization and economic success. In these Fortune 1000 companies, 1997 sales growth and earnings growth were significantly correlated, r = .191 (p < .01, n = 780)[7]. R&D has traditionally had a greater direct impact on market growth than financial indicators[8] and the results are true to this precedent. R&D intensity (R&D as a percentage of sales) is the only statistically significant predictor of sales growth for the complete data cases in the Fortune 1000, beta = .10 (p = .02, n = 558)[9]. That is, only R&D intensity, not sales per employee (productivity), not the number of employees (size), and not return on equity (ROE), can account for a significant (albeit small) variance in percentage of sales growth in the largest U.S. companies.[10]

It seems clear from these results that technology matters. But how does technology matter? New technology changes the knowledge base of organizations by enhancing the product or service capacity of units, and underwrites the processing capability of operations. About 60% of new products introduced in the U.S. are successful, once commercialized. The majority of R&D dollars are in fact currently allocated for the development of new products or new services, but this varies greatly by industrial sector.[11] As a consequence, processing technology, including information technology systems, is usually purchased rather than developed. There is an effort to tailor these information systems to support new product development and standardized operations like purchasing in successful companies.[12] However, the reengineering of business processes has proven to be a risky business, with failure rates running as high as 70%. So even though $250 billion is spent on new computer systems every year in the U.S., appropriation of the benefits of these investments remains elusive. Therefore, we concentrate here on investments in new plant, equipment and information systems, in particular manufacturing technology (section 3).

3. MANUFACTURING TECHNOLOGY

New processing technologies do not implement themselves. New systems are usually purchased outside and their development is episodic, especially for major modernizations or new product and service launches. Therefore, appropriation or capture of benefits from these investments is problematic, primarily because the technology is theoretically available to anyone who can pay for it, including competitors.[13] The extant literature on appropriation of manufacturing technology rents suggests two important conclusions:

- *Successful modernization hinges on the specific mosaic of technologies adopted; and*
- *Performance of manufacturing technology depends on which (if any) organizational innovations are adopted in conjunction with deployment.*

These two generalizations are quite far-reaching and complex, so they are taken up separately below. To the extent that the resources of a firm determine how outcomes will be pursued, the role of government becomes more important.[14]

3.1 The Adoption of Manufacturing Technologies

During the last decade, the relative absence of rigorous applied research on the adoption of manufacturing technology has been replaced by a number of important contributions in both the academic and applied press. Much of this literature has been reviewed elsewhere, so we focus here on just a few of the most relevant studies germane to the central questions of this inquiry. For the time being, we will set aside the limitations of this work, and return to future research needs as an ancillary issue later.

Perhaps the most comprehensive data available on investment in manufacturing technology, primarily in the durable goods and assembled products industries, was collected in two panels by the U.S. Department of Commerce (DOC) in 1988 and 1993. Fortunately, comparative data were also collected in Canada at approximately the same time (1989). These data have been analyzed by several research teams, but we focus on just a few here for brevity. Efforts to duplicate this effort in Europe are also relevant but, again, will be only mentioned in passing so that the focus of this report can be maintained.

Seventeen specific manufacturing technologies used in durable goods manufacturing (SIC 34-38) were included in the DOC survey. These data have subsequently been augmented with statistics from the Census of Manufacturing and data from other sources in order to develop a comprehensive picture of technology impact for 7,000 plants.[15]   Earlier results from nearly identical data showed that the more technologies plants adopted ("technology intensity"), the higher the rates of employment growth and the lower the closure rates, controlling for other explanatory factors. Plants adopting six or more of these 17 possible choices, such as numerically controlled machine tools (NC), were found to pay premiums of 16% for production workers and 8% for non-production workers. As much as 60% of the variance in wage premium paid by large plants can be explained by adoption of these manufacturing technologies. Between 1988 and 1993, increases in computer-aided design and local area networks were most prominent. Labour productivity, generally, is significantly enhanced by adoption of these technologies, which is typical of the patterns established in earlier generations of research on this subject.

Analysis of the comparable Canadian data (1989) has yielded similar results, with the added finding that manufacturing technology adoption is coincident with R&D spending by larger plants, and with variance across industries. Adoption of inspection and programmable control technology appears to promote growth faster than other technologies, but it is not clear whether controlling for other factors would sustain this result. Most important, there is an indication in the Canadian data that the mosaic of technologies adopted does matter, and not just the number of technologies purchased. A comparable result for information technology has also emerged in one applied study introduced later (adoption of EDI or electronic data interchange).

There is considerable variance in the adoption mix of technologies in these data. In the U.S., the most frequently used technologies, adopted stand-alone or in combinations, are computer-aided design (CAD) and numerical control (NC), even though this pattern is found in only 2%-4% of the cases. About 18% of these plants adopt unique combinations of technologies, e.g., common to only one or two plants, and adoption patterns generally do not follow industry groups.

The highest rate of job growth is associated with adoption of 11 of the 17 technologies studied in the U.S.   In particular, local area network technologies, either combined with computer-aided design or used exclusively for the factory, were associated with a 25% faster employment growth rate than in plants that did not adopt any of the surveyed technologies from 1982-1987. CAD and NC were associated with a 15% higher job growth rate during the same period. Programmable logic (PLCs) and NC yielded a 10% higher employment growth rate. On the other hand, CAD and digital representation of CAD for procurement experienced a 20% slower job growth rate but very fast productivity growth.

Productivity levels were 50% higher (than nonadopters) among companies that used the following technologies: CAD, CAD output for procurement, local area networks, intercompany networks, PLCs, and shop floor control computers. Earnings for production workers versus non-production workers are more directly associated with adoption of these technologies. For example, production worker employment growth was 35% higher in plants that adopted local area networks and shop floor control. But in 60%-80% of the technology categories, there were higher earnings levels for both job categories.

Two general conclusions can be drawn from these results in addition to the primary finding that the pattern of adoption determines performance, rather than simply the number of technologies used. First, outcomes vary depending on which technologies are adopted and the type of performance measured. This was called the organizational effectiveness "paradox" in earlier research.[16] Secondly, it is the combination of stand-alone technology like CAD and integrating technologies like local area networks that has the greatest impact on performance, regardless of outcome measure. Linking fabrication with assembly in successful plants suggests that functional coordination is essential to appropriation of adopted technology benefits. It is this integrating aspect of manufacturing technology that is taken up in the next section.

To summarize, the literature and empirical findings on manufacturing technology adoption indicate the following:

- Technology matters generally – R&D investments are significantly associated with sales growth which, in turn, is significantly correlated with earnings growth in the Fortune 1000 firms.
- The mosaic of manufacturing technologies matters – not just the extent or number of technologies adopted (e.g., local area networks adopted with or without CAD account for 25% faster employment growth in adopters versus non-adopters).

3.2 Appropriation of Manufacturing Technology Rents

William F. Ogburn originally proposed a theory of "cultural lag" in society: that technological and technical advances always precede the adaptations needed to adjust to them or use them effectively without harm.[17] This idea was applied to organizations by William M. Evan as the organizational lag hypothesis[18], which was expanded to two alternative models tested by F. Damanpour and W. Evan.[19] The two alternative models of organizational lag allow for either technical system impact on the social system or mutual impacts. Administrative innovations were defined as those that affect the organization's social system.

The authors studied 85 public libraries, 40 technical innovations and 27 administrative innovations and found the following:

1. Libraries adopt technical innovations (e.g., automated acquisition control systems) faster than administrative innovations;
2. Administrative and technical innovations have a higher correlation in high-performance organizations;
3. The organizational lag in adoption of administrative innovations after technical innovations are in place is negatively related to performance; and
4. Adoption of administrative innovations tends to trigger the adoption of technical innovations more readily than the reverse.

These results are in clear agreement and are extended by applied research findings in manufacturing reported indepth elsewhere : the more radical the technology departure for the project, the more radical the organizational innovations required for success. The adoption of certain types of administrative or organizational innovations, coincident with new manufacturing process technologies, enhances loose coupling and integration in organizations. In particular, the integrating mechanisms of both the vertical hierarchy (general management linked with middle management linked with the rank and file), and internal disciplines and functions (R&D, engineering, design, and manufacturing), as well as context (i.e., suppliers and customers), significantly promote successful modernization of facilities. Performance outcomes were measured across a wide spectrum: e.g., greater throughput, better utilization and cycle times, higher quality and greater flexibility.

What is challenging about these results is that there is both theory and evidence to suggest that organizational cultures that can be leveraged for higher performance are *valuable* (enhance capabilities and learning), *rare*, and *difficult to imitate*.[20] There is even historical evidence on the diffusion of organizational forms, practices and structures. For example, in states in which civil service was not mandated during an initial period (1885-1904), larger cities with more immigrants, and more white-versus blue-collar workers were more likely to adopt reform.[21] But these institutional reforms, which had a built-in standard of conformity, might be quite far removed from the organizational or administrative innovations needed to change the culture of a company to capture value from a new technological innovation.

E. Reza studied the adoption of 29 resource recovery systems (RRSs, e.g., mass burn systems with heat recovery) implemented by local community governments (city, township or regional board) in the U.S. in the early 1980s. The sample covered Akron, two sites in Chicago, Duluth, Milwaukee, Nashville, Tacoma, and Wilmington, DL.[22] A summary of Reza's results follows.

1. Larger cities are more likely to have more knowledge about resource recovery systems (RRSs) and the alternative technologies to achieve recovery goals.
2. The participation of non-elected internal actors (e.g., civil servants with a longer-range view) at the early stages of the innovation process had a positive impact on the ultimate reliability, financial viability and overall success of the RRS project (using expert panels of engineers to judge each case).
3. At the design stage of the project, the participation of external actors (e.g., private firms, federal government) promoted ultimate success.
4. Overall reliability of the RRS system is enhanced by greater local government control of the project during the development stage and by adopting relatively simple and unsophisticated technologies.

These results in the public sector are consistent with both the anecdotal, case and survey results in the private sector: through benchmarking and other means, representatives of organizations are able to find inspiration both inside and outside their own context for change. This is not to say that technological change comes easily, nor to imply that every organization finds a way to meet the most challenging goals of global standards. Organizational innovations and changes that do not fall nicely in either category are also instrumental in significant performance enhancement.[23] Duplication of a successful culture seems quite unlikely, and for most, undesirable, since circumstances vary. However, learning does take place and technology can be transferred from one locale to another – even if it is essentially "reinvented" at the new site.[24]

An illustration from the manufacturing sector of this phenomenon of "rare" breakthrough technology appears in Box 1 below. This is the story of Shamrock Fastener Technologies. Discontinuous technology changes more than just one company, it can change a whole industry. There are many other case histories like this, with relatively little fanfare, showing how U.S. manufacturing has reinvented itself, one company at a time.[25]

Box 1: Shamrock's "Learning Factory"

Why would anyone want to invest in a high technology plant for a commodity business? Ask Paul Morath, President of Shamrock Fastener Technologies, and he will tell you. First the results, in case you were skeptical about the answer: 1 ppm. That is, and let me repeat, one-part-per-million quality failure levels – or virtually zero defects in supplied bolts and fasteners to the auto industry. Toyota's best supplier is currently operating at 23 ppm. But can you make money doing this when you have to supply billions of fasteners a year?

On March 17, 1995, Shamrock opened its new $12-million plant in Sterling Heights, Michigan, jointly developed with Ring Screw Works and several suppliers. This effort included National Machinery, which installed its first FX 64XL former, the first machine in its Formax line for fastener manufacturing at Shamrock's "Learning" factory they call a "research and production facility." Can-Eng also developed a new roller hearth mesh belt hardening furnace for the new plant to reduce damage to bolts during processing. It was quite a St. Patrick's day.

The goal was simple, according to Morath: "We want to see why fasteners fail and why they work. Let's see why cylinder bolts used in aluminum blocks tend to bend in heat treating. Let's be able to reliably predict the results." Morath is often quoted as saying that this is literally the "nuts and bolts of the automobile industry," and he has made good on his promise to share what he has learned. He has opened his doors to everyone who is interested. The pay-off is that Shamrock now has to turn down business from its biggest boosters, Ford, GM and Chrysler. However, Shamrock will supply the new Chrysler V-8 engine plant on Mack Avenue in Detroit, also rumored to be the "best in class." Birds of a feather.

Who visits the new plant? Dozens of Japanese and German firms come, but you can count on one hand the number of North American firms that have visited. More Koreans have seen the plant than Americans.

But why high technology in this business? Paul Morath says he always had a dream to build the perfect plant and when National Machinery came to him and said the only way they could survive their foreign competition was to "leap-frog" the industry with a new, computer-controlled technology with a trial customer (beta site), he said yes. "Why shouldn't the North American auto producers have the best suppliers in the world? Why should equipment industries have to move off-shore to survive or perish in the process? That was the stake in the ground with the Shamrock flag on it and the Big Three rallied around this plant."

What's next? Morath says: "We are out of capacity."

Note: Sources for this case are multiple and include personal communication with Paul Morath, President, Shamrock Fastener Technologies, April 1998.

4. THE KNOWLEDGE REVOLUTION

U.S. companies spend about $250 billion annually on computer technology, yet one survey found that 42% of corporate information technology projects are terminated before completion. In order to put this statistic in perspective, over a dozen studies have reported the same failure rate, about 40%, for new products after they have been introduced. Yet, the quest for better performance using computer technology continues. In the auto industry alone, it is estimated that use of electronic data interchange[26] between suppliers and original equipment companies could save $1.1 billion or about $71 per car according to a U.S. Department of Commerce Study released in April 1998 (U.S. DOC, 1998). Many of these massive investments in computer technology coincide with business process reengineering[27] but these projects fail to meet their objectives in 50% to 70% of the cases documented. It appears that the more radical the process change being attempted, the higher the failure rate.[28]

One of the primary vehicles used to guide investments in new computer systems is enterprise integration, often called enterprise resource planning (ERP). Organizations attempt to standardize their information systems in the modern world of distributed processing, among other reasons, in order to avoid the high cost of hardware-software system maintenance. For example, Owens-Corning, which is in the process of installing a SAP, Inc. enterprise-wide information system, expects to avoid an annual expense of $35 million in information system maintenance with this new technology (White, Clark and Ascarelli, 1997). Owens-Corning started by redefining its markets to be global and broader than just insulation in an attempt to increase the proportion of materials it supplied in a typical building like a home. The company reengineered the finance process first and then went on to reengineer other business processes, replacing all but a few legacy systems that were inherited through recent acquisitions (see Box 2 below).

In this paper, it is argued that the challenge of enterprise integration, which is the driving force behind so much of the investment in computer systems today, is yet another example of what economists call the "appropriation" of benefits problem. That is, since the bulk of enterprise technology systems, like other process technology, is now supplied, rather than developed internally, organizations tend to invest R&D in new products and services, not new process technology. The technology behind the new conversion processes, which are outsourced, is, therefore, theoretically available to all organizations – including competitors. Further, because of the popularity of these new hardware-software systems, all customers are now competing for the scarce resource of supplier attention, since there are only a handful of companies that can provide this technology.

Consulting companies do take up some of the shortfall by providing the temporary labour and advice needed to plan and implement these systems. However, consultants learn from their hosts and sell their accumulated knowledge to the next client, further eroding the innovator's proposed advantage. Therefore, the appropriation or capture of benefits from innovating in this way becomes an even more difficult challenge than value capture from proprietary product or service technology. Anecdotal reports indicate considerable variance in success with enterprise integration programs (White et al., 1997), so this appears to be a fertile context in which to investigate the research question. The one report that did make an attempt to document reported differences in information technology investments found that EDI (electronic data interchange) was where payoffs occurred, similar to integrating technologies in manufacturing.[29] How do we account for the differences in outcomes of adoption of new process technology, e.g., enterprise integration computer systems? This challenge is summarized in Box 2 below.

Box 2: The Enterprise Resource Planning (ERP) Challenge

> The late Professor Carl Sagan, planetary scientist at Cornell University, used to be famous for saying "...billions and billions and billions...of stars." Now I will say it too, in a slightly different way: *billions and billions of dollars*. That is how much is going to be spent every year in the foreseeable future on ERP (Enterprise Resource Planning) systems, often just called enterprise integration systems. Now the bad news. My best estimate is that about 25% of that money will be wasted because of a lack of understanding of how to manage major change in a company.
>
> Hastened by the need to fix the "Year 2000 Bug," which typically causes information systems to recognize dates for 2000, usually entered "00", as 1900, companies have found that most of their current information resources are badly out of date and incompatible.
>
> Most big companies have upgraded, or are in the process of revamping, their information systems. General Motors Corporation, for example, wants SAP, the German software supplier of ERP systems, to establish an office just to support their needs. Suffice it say that GM and many, many other large and small companies have had a checkered history in installing new technologies during the last decade. Dell Computer cancelled its software contract in January 1997 after spending $150 million, up from the originally estimated $115 million. Dell finally determined the system it was installing couldn't handle the sales volume it was anticipating. Furthermore, the more companies that adopt SAP systems, as opposed to BAAN or some other supplier, the scarcer SAP resources become.
>
> So a lot can be learned from the companies undergoing major upheaval and installing ERP systems and those managers who are willing to talk about it. Mike Radcliff, Vice President and Chief Information Officer of Owens-Corning, is one of these people.
>
> Radcliff has been featured in many of the national business publications like *Fortune* and the *Wall Street Journal* and we were quite fortunate to have him in class recently to talk about the Owens-Corning experience with ERP installation. Based on the experience at Owens-Corning, my estimate of 25% wasted effort in installing these new systems is not far off. In fact, others have reported similar experiences. Just as they approach the final selection decision on which hardware and software systems to buy, they run out of money.

Box 2 (continued): The Enterprise Resource Planning (ERP) Challenge

The consultants, or "rent-a-bodies" as Radcliff refers to them, are just part of the unanticipated expense. They can help you get down the learning curve fast, but most companies very soon know just as much as consultants about how to change their culture. At Owens-Corning (OC), they originally budgeted 7% for training. In reality, training cost about 13% - so they were off by half. Further, since OC was in the process of growing through acquisitions at the time it launched its SAP installation, adding 17 new businesses before it was through, they went off their two year installation timetable almost immediately. Now they estimate that it will take twice that long to do it right.

Key learnings from OC? There are many. The most fundamental decision you have to make is **not whether** to reengineer, **but which** business processes to reengineer and in what order. In the OC case, it was finance first. Get finance on board, and the rest, which will have a common accounting system, will come along. Filling customer orders was next, and so on.

You are betting a lot to save a lot. OC had estimated that it was spending $30-$35 million a year maintaining antiquated information systems. Now they estimate at OC that they will save $50 million a year.

OC started by redefining its markets. Growth at home was difficult because of its dominant position in the U.S. Further, OC went to delivery of building systems, going from an average $1,000 per house in 1992 to $6,000 per house today. It took many acquisitions to do that, plus "reinventing" the supply chain to implement this new strategy, but the company has doubled in size as a result.

After OC redefined its market, it realized that its current information systems would not even come close to being able to implement this new strategy. Further, management realized that a "technology band-aid" would not solve the problem. So they decided on a total enterprise integration solution to their problem, throwing out nearly 200 legacy systems and commonizing the entire corporation for the first time in its history.

The key to success - you've heard this before - was organizational culture change. OC's version of culture change focused on very specific business outcomes, like order fill rates of 99%, determined by benchmarking best practices to target action. Each member of the staff had training to get a "operator's licence" to use the new systems. Those that couldn't or wouldn't get this "licence" could no longer continue in their jobs, and as many as 20% of OC employees were affected in this way. This is major organizational change, not "nibbling at the margins."

Note: Sources include the following as well as personal communications with Mike Radcliff, Owens-Corning: White, Clark and Ascarelli, (1997); Stewart, (1997); Romei, (1996).

4.1 E-Commerce

No technology symbolizes our age like the Internet. The infobahn. Cyberspace. The resulting impact on business is known as electronic "e" commerce, for short. This radical shift in our way of working and playing is essentially caused by the convergence of two technologies: ***computers and telecommunications***. Akin to any other discontinuous historical example that merged more than one existing technology, like the creation of the factory system in England in the 1700s around technology for spinning and weaving cotton, our century's version of the Industrial Revolution is at hand.

The number of Americans using the Internet was approximately 5 million in 1993 and this had grown to about 62 million in 1997. In July 1993, there were approximately 1.8 million Internet hosts and in 1997 this had grown to over 19.5 million. According to one estimate, Internet traffic doubles every 100 days in the U.S.[30]

I can remember the day in late August 1984 when I first walked into my office at the Industrial Technology Institute on North Campus at the University of Michigan, in Ann Arbor. It is hard to believe that was 14 years ago. I sat down at my computer screen, where 132 e-mail messages had accumulated before I had even logged onto the ITI computer network for the first time. It was a rude awakening to the Internet and the Unix-based system – my peers had made fun of it. Although most of those messages on that very first day were from colleagues and co-workers, some were from far away. It all seemed so exotic, even if some of the messages were on the lines of "the refrigerator is going to be cleaned out Friday afternoon." Today, 134 countries have access to e-mail and the Internet, and many of us take it for granted. When our local area network goes down, work grinds to a near immediate standstill. We are utterly dependent upon it.

What is this signature technology of our age?[31] The Internet is essentially a communication and transaction tool. Before the Internet, communication was analogue – like a telephone: it was done through pictures and sound. The Internet is digital – it links the computer with telecommunications technology. A CD (compact disc) converts an analogue signal (like sound) into a long string of numbers (digital) to recreate an analogue sound. These numbers are encoded on a CD so they can be "read" with light from a laser and no physical contact is needed to replay the CD – it does not wear out from use (although some of my CDs have been abused).

Computer networks are essentially combinations of hardware and software systems – computers programmed with software languages connected to transmission lines by modems (which is stands for modulation and demodulation). If two computers are connected by a wire, one needs a device to send (modulate) and receive (demodulate) messages. Actually, two sets of wires are dedicated, one for each purpose. The wires could be telephone lines, and in that case, the modem has the additional capability of being able to dial up another computer assigned a telephone number. Any kind of digital data can be sent, including a voice transmission.

So, naturally, telephone companies are a little nervous about the Internet. Character codes use standards, like the Morse Code. One standard that is popular is the American Standard Code for Information Interchange (ASCII) – which determines a bit sequence for each letter in English as well as other symbols used in communication like punctuation, digits, upper-and lower-case letters, etc. One of the improvements of digital over analogue communication is that early research worked on detecting errors in analogue encoding, transmission and decoding, and added parity bits to strings to check for errors.

Local area networks (LANs) were first in the development of the Internet, appearing in the late 1960s as computer systems began to decentralize away from exclusive dependence upon mainframes. The first stage of this technology was the connecting of a circuit board in one computer by a cable to a circuit board in another computer. Then came three computers and finally a LAN, networking many computers together. This last stage requires that computers have network interface hardware, so now we have three elements in the system – circuit boards, cable and connections to the LAN. Xerox's version of this LAN was called *Ethernet*, which became a leading technology of the day.

All this would have led rather quickly to the Internet had it not been for one little detail. Not all LANs were alike. So unless two organizations had the same LAN system, they could not network computers across town – or across the room, for that matter. I know some manufacturing plants like that. Research on wide area networks (WANs) designed specifically to span large geographic areas emerged about the same time as LANs. WANs do more than just link two computers, they also used a dedicated computer to organize a set of transmissions at each site into a coordinated system, while keeping each individual computer separate and independent. At the time, just a few WAN projects were under way, while there were many LANs proliferating; every computer company had its own, for starters. It seemed hopeless that any type of standard would be adopted, let alone optimized.

Along came Uncle Sam. During this same period (late 1960s), the military became interested in using network communication, and projects began to be funded through ARPA, the Advanced Research Projects Agency (later called DARPA, the D was added for Defense). By the end of the 1970s, several wide area networks were operating, including ARPANET, and others using satellites and radio transmission. Further work resulted in an integrated "internetwork", was shortened to "Internet", which linked WANs and LANs for the military. The prototype was capitalized: Internet. There were two key innovations that made this all happen. The first was the Internet Protocol (IP) software for basic communication and Transmission Control Protocol (TPC) software. The two were usually combined with the other systems needed and called the TCP/IP Internet Protocol, and this was adopted by the military in 1982.

From 1986 to 1996, the Internet went from a few thousand networked computers, primarily at universities, to nearly 10 million linked computers. This was the result of parallel development at Bell Labs and the University of California at Berkeley, merging the work on two network research projects. The National Science Foundation took this signal to adopt the goal of linking all scientists and engineers to promote U.S. competitiveness. The NSFNET was a project of IBM, MCI and the University of Michigan's MERIT organization, which linked the university units at the time, and became operational in 1988.

By 1991, the Internet was growing too fast for NSFNET capacity, and the federal government could no longer afford to pay for the service, so a nonprofit company called Advanced Networks and Services (ANS) was formed out of the original three organizations (IBM, MCI, and MERIT). In 1992, ANSNET was running at 30 times the capacity of its predecessor. By 1995, MCI Corporation had a new, high-speed network, *vBNS*, and the Internet had been privatized.

There is, of course, much, much more to the story. There is the technology of routing messages, addresses for computers, the HTML (Hypertext Markup Language) used for web pages, and, naturally, the competition between network suppliers. Or is it competition? Consider the antitrust case pending against Microsoft at the time of writing.

Here, space only permits a simple illustration: UPS and Federal Express track all orders digitally, and the U.S. Postal Service is experimenting with e-mail services. All this happened in the short span of 30 years – one generation.

4.2 Public Policy and E-Commerce

U.S. government oversight of the modern Internet has a created a cottage industry in Washington. Three primary concerns have emerged for lawmakers.[32] First, U.S. governors have moved aggressively to tax Internet commerce, and a bill has already been passed in the House to stop this movement. Second, parents are concerned about pedophiles stalking children on the net, and the House has passed legislation to help prosecutors track these offenders. Third, Hollywood and publishers are concerned about how to protect movies, software and copyrights, which is under study. Encryption of data is also under discussion as part of a larger privacy issue. Gambling and junk e-mail are also problematic. Overseas competitive issues, like

IBM's use of "e-business," will also likely continue to crop up as issues needing resolution by governments.[33]

Academicians have subsumed the Internet, along with other computer technology issues, under the general rubric of knowledge and knowledge management.[34] After Peter Drucker said that knowledge had become *the* major economic resource (after land, labour and capital), it was OK to study it as a legitimate subject. Forget the history of academic thought that has studied and classified knowledge for centuries, and more recently for decades, and that knowledge has been the subject of dozens of applied academic fields including R&D management, management information systems, cognition, computer science, and many others.

One recent survey of 431 U.S. and European organizations found that actually changing behaviour in the face of Internet expansion and cultural barriers to knowledge transfer were most important (as opposed to general management and lack of strategy, which were secondary).[35] Another study done in the U.K. found that it is the complementarity of assets - knowledge and functional assets - that better accounts for new product development performance.[36] It is clear that information technologies are the key to supporting this knowledge revolution, but without strategies and understanding of technology management, no technology can be leveraged economically.[37]

E-commerce is the ultimate outcome of technology management for the Internet. More than half of all the computers in the United States are linked to LANs, and each month 2,000 businesses join the Internet and the 20,000 companies already there, doing business in cyberspace. Nearly everyone has heard or read the story of Amazon.com, which is a virtual bookstore and one of the fastest growing companies in the history of business. Perhaps the most important development in e-commerce to date is the AT&T-TCI merger, which links telephones to cable and enables "digital convergence" on the most massive scale yet imagined in cyberspace.[38] The *Telecommunications Act* of 1996 eliminated nearly every barrier between communication markets, and now that the Internet has become, prima facie, the platform for all digital transmission, there are almost no limits to what could be accomplished by such an integrated company. It is the first U.S. nationwide communications firm to emerge since AT&T was broken up into its constituent companies.[39]

5. PUBLIC POLICY AND SCARCITY OF TECHNICAL RESOURCES

Two unstoppable trends in the business environment of today are alliances and globalism. One of the consequences of the convergence of the total quality movement and the natural environment is the diffusion of ISO 14000 standards, which also comes into play when technology decisions are made, as we will see below.[40] Alliances and public policy are addressed first, focusing on technology issues.

5.1 CRADAs

The Low Emission Paint Consortium (LEPC) to be discussed later was formed, in part, under the 1984 *National Cooperative Research & Development Act* (NCRA), which permits (but does not exempt antitrust action concerning) precompetitive technical collaboration in the United States. Thousands of CRADAs (Cooperative Research & Development Agreements) have been formed since this act was passed, between companies, government laboratories and universities. Do they work? The answer is yes and no - that is, the empirical evidence and theoretical models show mixed results and are subject to interpretation.[41]

Olk and Xin compared collaboration in the U.S. to four other countries (France, Germany, the U.K. and Japan) and say that the "U.S. has been only marginally successful in mimicking the foreign organizational arrangement."[42] Bozeman and Pandey (1994) compared just the U.S. and Japan and focused primarily on government laboratories' collaboration with industry. Although the mission and motives of these laboratories in both countries are similar, there are also differences including the fact that U.S. labs have twice as many cooperative agreements as the Japanese. Further, U.S. labs with agreements have more patents and rate their technology transfer efforts as more effective.[43] When Bozeman and Choi (1991) compared 134 government labs to 139 university labs in the U.S., they found that cooperative R&D, as measured by number of interlaboratory agreements, is not a strong predictor of technology transfer to either firms or government.[44] See what I mean by "mixed" results?

One economic model comparing cost and value of R&D investments by firms before and after the 1984 NCRA predicts that appropriability can be increased by both diversification and cooperation among firms but the cooperative R&D will sacrifice the competition that is present with diversification alone. Diversification in the absence of the NCRA may have been more socially desirable and the effect of the law could be to decrease investment, moving firms away from the social optimum.[45]

Olk and Young (1997) studied 184 CRADA memberships in the U.S. and found that continuing membership was a function of how much discretion an organization had over resources used in the collaboration - making the party less dependent upon the relationship. Rather, transaction cost theory was found to be a significant predictor of continuity of the consortium. Poor performance increased the likelihood members would leave and good performance was associated with staying. Further, membership conditions did influence continuity, but only a few select conditions applied. Having "fewer alternatives to the consortium increased the likelihood of leaving rather than decreasing it," (p. 866) which led the authors to conclude that "a joint venture represents a different kind of alternative than contracting or internal research" (p. 866). Network ties and involvement based on knowledge-related issues were good predictors of continuity. Learning had a negative relationship. Involved members will continue to stay in a consortium that is performing poorly, consistent with the idea of "technical side-bets." Knowledge-related involvement was important when performance was poor, while ties were credited with more importance when performance was good (which is inconsistent with transaction cost theory, where ties represent hostage arrangements).[46]

While these results may seem contradictory prima facie, Van de Ven, Angle and Poole (1989) found similar patterns in intensive case studies of the innovation process over time on such innovations as cochlear implants to defeat hearing impairment. That is, researchers typically do not drop a line of inquiry in the face of failure, and persist well beyond what outside observers would consider to be logical and prudent.[47] In particular, there are many instances in the innovation process at the bench level for individuals where "little rational learning appeared to occur," (p. 204) and further, "superstitious learning occurs when the subjective experience of learning is compelling but the connections between actions and outcomes are loose" (p. 204). That is, evaluations can be formulated as to whether outcomes are positive or negative and companies act accordingly in funding or not funding continued action. But this occurs whether learning is rational or superstitious. In good times, only "exceptionally inappropriate courses of action will lead to judgments of innovation failure," while in bad times, no course of action will lead to "outcomes judged to be successful" (p. 205). It is not surprising that the misspecification of causality in the innovation process is common, given the uncertainty of the endeavour. And, this, in part, explains the story imparted earlier by the senior R&D manager at

Canon, who said that bench researchers and project engineers are judged more for their persistence on a project than for the "objective" technical merits of progress.

This insight into the relationship between learning models and the way the innovation process unfolds in many settings accounts for the counter intuitive notion that makes management in these uncertain settings favour the so-called "consistency" or "congruence" idea of goals and policies. Resource controllers and research managers often diverge in their thinking. Quinn and Cameron reinforce this notion generally when they suggest that it is incorrect to over-emphasize one set of organizational effectiveness criteria as opposed to another and advocate balance or capacity to respond to multiple effectiveness criteria.[48]

It should also be remembered that departure and continuity are not the same as success and failure. For example, the discontinuance of a joint venture is a frequent occurrence, where one party purchases the interests of one or more of the others, but the "entity" continues in an alternative form and has a successful life. AT&T has had a policy in the past of eventually ending all joint ventures in this way.

Consistent with the anecdotal evidence in the Low Emissions Paint Consortium (LEPC), members in the Olk-Young sample may be considering the future benefits of collaboration somewhat independently of current returns. In the LEPC, a widely promulgated contention by the members and USCAR was that this initial consortium was going to serve as a "model" for future collaboration among the Big Three auto producers. True, a dozen more consortia have been added under USCAR, but there is no systematic evidence that these subsequent collaborations are using this "model." In fact, there is at least an anecdote that suggests that learning within the USCAR consortia actually makes it easier to form consortia outside of this model, to work with non-competitors on new technology projects. This calls into question the single explanation of "consortia as precursors to more embedded relationships," (p. 873), advanced in the literature and cited by Olk and Young (1997). There are also other models for major technological change enhancement and the natural environment.[49] The LEPC is summarized next.

5.2 LEPC

An example of collaborative R&D in manufacturing is the Low Emissions Paint Consortium (LEPC) in the U.S. automobile industry.[50] This consortium was developed using the enabling legislation of the 1984 NCRA in order to help Ford, GM and Chrysler comply with increasingly stringent air quality standards and EPA regulation.

In 1985, surface coatings and coating operations accounted for 27% of all industrial emissions of volatile organic compounds (VOCs). When exposed to sunlight, these VOCs contribute to the formation of lower atmosphere (tropospheric) ozone. Amendments to the *Clean Air Act* passed in 1990 were designed to significantly reduce VOC emissions of both stationary (point) and mobile (e.g., transportation) sources. Methods for abatement were suggested in the legislation, and the 1991 annual EPA survey of VOC emissions indicated that 1.86 million metric tons of VOCs were emitted by industrial surface coating operations - a 15% reduction from 1986 when 2.2 million metric tons were emitted. Other sources of VOC emissions increased by 5% during that same period. The U.S. position in the world trade in paints remained strong even though only a few European countries regulated VOCs and no regulations existed in Japan. The EPA was encouraged by these results and appeared to be determined to push even harder with VOC regulation.

Approximately 90% of all pollution resulting from automobile manufacturing occurs during final assembly, and 90% of these waste streams result from painting and coating processes. The majority of paint facilities in North America at the time (circa 1991) involved a four-step process of 1) wash (phosphate) and ELPO (an electro-deposition dip process for rust-proofing), 2) primer application, 3) base (colour) coat application, and 4) clear or finish coat application.

The key to understanding the persistence of this consortium is embedded in the case itself: "The pre-consortium committee had tentatively agreed on one important principle: if the Big Three did not stick together, the supplier community could not be persuaded to invest in the development costs needed to implement the pilot production facility. The supply community would ultimately benefit, but the pay-off had to be large enough to "make a leap 10 times greater than anything we have done before in paint, as Ernie McLaughlin, the Chrysler representative said" (Ettlie, 1995, p. 4).

From more or less the beginning of the collaboration between Ford, GM and Chrysler, it was assumed that some government funding would be available for the powder coating project. Proposals were submitted to NIST (National Institute of Science and Technology, U.S. Department of Commerce), which failed to be funded, and then EPA, and copied to the DoD and DoE. The Environmental Technology Initiative (ETI) proposal at EPA was outstanding until December 1994, when it became obvious, after several feedback deadlines were passed by the EPA, that Congress was not going to fund the ETI. Many members of the consortium were against EPA funding, thinking it would harm the effort in the long run anyway, because of the past adversarial relationship between the auto industry and the EPA. A funding crisis was precipitated by these events and all the options for resolving it were difficult to implement.

Crucial learnings in the case appear to boil down to two issues:

- Is it necessary for competitors to stick together in order to achieve full participation in R&D collaboration among suppliers?
- Are environmental issues truly non-competitive and exempt from the normal concerns about "spillovers" and "appropriation" of the benefits of investments in new technology?

A pre-production R&D facility was eventually located at the Ford Wixom Assembly plant in Michigan, and that is why it was selected for the collaborative R&D example. The case is both leading-edge practice and accessible. In spite of the fact that this collaboration is touted as a model of cooperation among competitors under the umbrella of the USCAR organization, the final results of this experiment may not be known until the 12-year contractual period has expired. Clear coat paint is being applied to cars in the pilot facility (as early as 1996), but the goal of elimination of all VOCs from the painting process is still far off. Experiment design continues to seek an optimal proven process. The partners continue to ask: who will be the first to commercialize the process? Further, is the exclusion of the other world players in the auto industry (i.e., the Japanese and Europeans) a critical issue in the persistence of this R&D consortium?

The largest collaborative R&D organization doing cross-industry consortia in the U.S. is the National Center for Manufacturing Sciences (NCMS) located in Ann Arbor, Michigan, with an office in Washington, D.C. Begun in 1987, NCMS has grown to be supported by over 220 dues-paying members. This unique case of R&D collaboration is taken up next.

5.3 NCMS

The NCMS is a not-for-profit industrial consortium of U.S., Canadian and Mexican corporations. With over 200 members, NCMS accumulated R&D revenues from 1987 to 1996 of over $400 million, of which 94% went to manufacturing projects. In 1996, the NCMS R&D program totaled $64 million, and the organization managed $285 million spread among 100 DoD (Department of Defense) projects. It has been estimated that, for every dollar spent on NCMS research, $5 has been returned to participating companies.[51]

The management structure of NCMS clusters activities in strategic interest groups (SIGs), and attempts to improve on this structure have been futile – member firms appear to thrive on this organizational mechanism.

However much the structure appears to resemble the original configuration of the hierarchy when NCMS was established, it should not be confused with the way NCMS actually operates. As originally conceived, NCMS was "industry-driven" and it continues to operate in that mode. But a strong membership and weak corporate organization, or essentially a decentralized form of governance, has gradually evolved into a strong central direction from members' representatives who have migrated to NCMS's central office. Corporate initiation of projects and coordination of efforts is, then, essential to any success that this large consortium organization achieves – even though most of the budget is allocated to member locations.

NCMS has enjoyed considerable success since it was launched as a multiple-consortia "neutral turf" facilitator of joint R&D. One indicator of this long-term success of the organization is the decreasing dependence on federal funding over time. Another rather significant development, given the very conservative intellectual property restrictions NCMS operated under, is the inclusion of first Canadian, and now Mexican, companies as members. NCMS was originally founded as a "U.S. only" consortium, much like USCAR, which hosts the LEPC.

Although NCMS represents just one example of a successful R&D consortium in the United States that has enjoyed a reasonably steady evolution with appropriate government seed funding, there are others that could also be discussed, like SEMATECH. Rather than review all these consortia, it might instead be more instructive to make just a few observations.

1. NCMS is really a "neutral turf" setting that takes a leadership role in allocating public and private funds for leverage in knowledge creation.
2. Successful structures and policies for managing this consortium have evolved slowly over time, and would not have developed without consistent and persistent government support
3. All consortia like NCMS seem to independently report a four-or five-to-one benefit return, which suggests a considerable positive effect, albeit "pooled" for this type of R&D collaboration.

5.4 Government Procurement of New Technology

The U.S. government acquires considerable technology through various sources, and outside of military procurement, the history has been checkered. The FAA and U.S. Postal Service are recent examples.[52]

The FAA is currently involved in an air traffic control technology "mess." A $500 million budget to upgrade air traffic control is now at least tripled, it is estimated, to actually make even the incremental changes needed for safety and avoidance of costly airplane delays. This is not a model of how to modernize and encourage technology.

The situation at the Post Office is not much better and even more controversial, given the anti-competitive issues raised by investments there. New legislative proposals to segment postal services into competitive and non-competitive services accompany these continuing investments in new technology, which are projected to be $3.6 billion through 2001. There is discussion about segmenting postal service into regulated, overnight first-class delivery and deregulated package delivery, following examples in Europe.

6. SUMMARY AND RECOMMENDATIONS

A number of broad generalizations can be made about the literature and new empirical findings introduced in this chapter on knowledge management and manufacturing in the United States today.

1. Investment in technology has an economic pay-off. It seems clear that the government's role in fostering infrastructure for science and engineering has been a persistent force in knowledge creation which, obviously, has had both a direct and an indirect impact on these economic benefits. Funding of basic research and universities, which industry will not likely back, especially when standards and the common good are apparently at stake, has worked in the United States. It is unlikely that there would be an Internet, at least in the form we have today, if the U.S. DOD and NSF had not funded work in that area.

2. R&D consortia, in part enabled by the 1984 NCRA, appear to have enough of a track record to conclude that they do add significant value and knowledge creation. The "pooled" estimate of this leveraged effect is about 4- or 5-to-1.

3. In manufacturing, the way in which resources are allocated makes a big difference, regardless of funding source. The mosaic of technology investments in manufacturing, not just the magnitude of investment, explains the considerable variance in performance outcomes of manufacturing firms. Both in manufacturing and enterprise integration, coordinating technologies like EDI have shown the way. Further, the administrative and organizational changes attendant on technology investments in manufacturing can make the difference between success and failure of these investments. The government has only a small and indirect impact on this effect.

4. Government does procure technology and can make a substantial difference in the direction of technology development, as a result. Examples cited in this report include the FAA and the U.S. Postal Service. These "experiments" in technology acquisition have had very mixed results, and policy-making in this area should be approached with great caution.

5. In the area of the natural environment, which was discussed under investments in pollution abatement and prevention in this report, the U.S. government has a better record than in procurement and service provision. Both at the coordination of local initiatives and with state and local government and in the encouragement of consortia in the auto industry, there has been a positive impact.

6. With respect to e-commerce, the U.S. government has continued to foster free and open development without the burden of local taxes and intervention but, at the same time, the government has moved to protect children and inventive rights. Private-sector forecasts of the impact of Internet developments are nearly devoid of substance.

NOTES

[1] © John E. Ettlie, 1998, all rights reserved, not to be reproduced by any means, mechanical or electronic. The project was supported in part by CIRANO, Montreal, Canada. The research assistants on this study were Mr. Glenn Gibson and Ms. Kelly Rinehardt. Comments on this work by my fellow CIRANO panel members are gratefully acknowledged. The opinions in this paper are those of the author and do not necessarily reflect the official position of the funding agency.

[2] See *National Productivity Review* (1998).

[3] See *Graphic Arts Monthly* (1998).

[4] See Raddock ((February 1998).

[5] See Farrel and Foust (1998).

[6] Unemployment among married men fell in June 1998 to 2.2% of the total civilian work force, from 2.4% in May, based on data from the U.S. Department of Labor and joblessness among married women rose to 2.9% from 2.8% during the same period (*Wall Street Journal*, 1998).

[7] According to the statistical analyses carried out by the author.

[8] See, for example, Ettlie, (1998).

[9] See note 7.

[10] Although the correlation matrix is not given with these regression results, the coefficient for R&D and sales per employee was $r = -.03$, n.s. (not significant), and for R&D with ROE, and number of employees, $r = .01$, n.s., and $r = .02$, n.s., respectively. In other words, no significant interaction effects were detected.

[11] Wolfe (1994) reports that about 43% of R&D spending is for new products – but service R&D is also increasing, which suggests that this new product activity requires some "fixing" in the field.

[12] See Ettlie (1997).

[13] See, for example, Echevarria (1997, p. 35), who reports that "only 25% of the Fortune 500 were able to obtain significantly increased profitability."

[14] It is important to control for industry effects in these generalizations: experience varies widely by economic sector, see Lau (1997).

[15] Much of this section is based on Beede and Young (1998).

[16] See Quinn and Cameron (1983).

[17] See Ogburn (1922).

[18] See Evan (1966).

[19] See Damanpour and Evan (1984).

[20] See Barney (1986).

[21] See Scott (1995).

[22] See Reza (1993).

[23] See Burman, Gershwin and Suyematsu (1998).

[24] There are also many sources available to get started on benchmarking: Wheatley and New (1997), Taninecz (1997); and *Business America* (1997).

[25] So as not to present the misleading picture that all this progress came about easily, it may be worth stopping for a moment and pondering the performance comparisons in the U.S. domestic auto industry that precipitated, in part, the UAW strike in Flint, Michigan, against General Motors Corporation. Ford requires 34.7 hours to produce a vehicle, Chrysler, 45.5 hours and GM, 46.5 hours. Ford makes an average of $1,520 per vehicle, Chrysler, $1,336 per vehicle and GM, $825 per vehicle. See Haglund (1998). There is also evidence that the "lean production model" of manufacturing success my be difficult to generalize outside the auto industry or even outside the specific context of firms in the industry): (Lowe, Delbridge and Oliver, 1997).

[26] "In the 1970's and 1980's, businesses extended their computing power beyond the company's walls sending and receiving purchase orders, invoices, and shipping notifications electronically via EDI (Electronic Data Interchange). EDI is a standard for compiling and transmitting information between computers, often over private communications networks called value added networks (VANs)." U.S. Department of Commerce, (1998, p. 12).

[27] "Throughout our discussion, the terms Business Process Redesign and Business Process Reengineering (BPR) are used interchangeably referring to *the critical analysis and radical redesign of existing business process to achieve breakthrough improvements in performance measures*," Teng, Grover, Fielder (1994, p. 12).

[28] Numerous examples of low-tech change efforts are documented in the change literature too. In the auto industry, a recent case is Rae (1998). The Jeep plant in Toledo, Ohio, is quite well known locally for innovative union-management labour practices and joint activities to promote productivity like ISO 9000 certification.

[29] See Deloitte & Touche, LLP (1997).

[30] See U.S. Department of Commerce (1998). However, the Internet cannot expand indefinitely - eventually, all computers will be linked and traffic will reach its physical limits.

[31] Much of this section is based upon Comer (1997).

[32] See Alvarez (1998).

[33] See Narisetti (1998).

[34] See Cole (1998).

[35] See Ruggles (1998).

[36] See Taylor and Lowe (1997).

[37] See, for example, Demarest (1997).

[38] See Hudson (1998).

[39] See Elstrom, Arnst and Crockett (1998).

[40] See, for example, *Journal of Operations Management* (1998). Also see Jaffe and Palmer (1997). The authors found little evidence that an industry's inventive output (patent applications) was related to natural environmental regulation compliance.

[41] The implied assumption here is that all collaborative activity is supported by the federal government, but that is not the case: see, for example, Grahl (1998). This centre was originally funded by the South Carolina Higher Education Commission.

[42] See Olk and Xin.

[43] See Bozeman and Pandey (1994).

[44] See Bozeman and Choi (1991).

[45] See Scott (1988).

[46] See Olk and Young (1997).

[47] See Van de Ven, Angle and Poole (1989).

[48] See Quinn and Cameron (1983).

[49] See Ferguson (1998). It is also clear that technology licensed from one firm to another can be a significant alternative way to impact firm performance. See Leaversuch (1998).

[50] See Ettlie (1995).

[51] The rate of return on other consortia involving federal laboratories and universities is also about 4-to-1. See, for example, Brown (1997). In 1996, the proposed federal budget for all R&D was $7.3 billion, or about 40% of all U.S. R&D, estimated to be about $18.25 billion. Hanson (1995) and Bozeman, Papadakis and Coker (1995), however, find little job creation as part of these programs.

[52] The FAA case is covered in Cole (1998). Literature on the technology investments at the Post Office include: Bot, Ivo, Girardin and Neumann (1997), Anthes (1997), Andelman (1998), Rosen (1998), Minahan (1998) and Duffy (1996).

REFERENCES

Alvarez, L., "Internet is New Pet Issue in Congress." *New York Times*, June 28, 1998, 14.

Andelman, D.A., "Pushing the Envelope." *Management Review*, 86 (6), 1998, 33-35.

Anthes, G.H., "Postal Service Technology Budget Misdelivers." *Computerworld*, 31(23), 1997, 33.

Barney, J., "Organizational Culture: Can It Be a Source of Sustained Competitive Advantage?" *Academy of Management Review,* 11 (3), 1986, 656-665.

Beede, D.N. and K.H. Young, "Patterns of Advanced Technology Adoption and Manufacturing Performance." *Business Economics*, 33 (2), 1998, 43-48.

Bot, B., J.H. Ivo, P.A. Girardin and C.S. Neumann, "Is There a Future for the Postman?" *McKinsey Quarterly*, 4, 1997, 92-105.

Bozeman, B. and M. Choi, "Technology Transfer from U.S. Government and University R&D Laboratories." *Technovation*, 11(4), 1991, 231-245.

Bozeman, B. and S. Pandey, "Cooperative R&D in Government Laboratories: Comparing the US and Japan." *Technovation*, 14 (3), 1994, 145-149.

Bozeman, B., M. Papadakis and K. Coker, "Industry Perspectives on Commercial Interactions with Federal Laboratories." Report to the National Science Foundation, Contract No. 9220125, January 1995.

Brown, M. A., "Performance Metrics for a Technology Commercialization Program." *International Journal of Technology Management*, 13 (3), 1997, 229-243.

Burman, M., S. Gershwin and C. Suyematsu, "Hewlett-Packard Uses Operations Research to Improve the Design of a Printer Production Line." *Interfaces*, 28 (1), 1998, 24-36.

Business America, "Four U.S. Companies Are Named Winners of the 1997 Malcolm Baldrige National Quality Award.", November 1997, 33-34.

CIO, "Neither Rain, Nor Sleet, Nor Shrinking Bandwidth." May 15, 1996, 22.

Cole, J., "Near Miss: How Major Overhaul of Air-Traffic Control Lost Its Momentum." *Wall Street Journal*, March 2, 1998, A1, A10.

Cole, R.E., "Knowledge and the Firm." Special Issue of *California Management Review*, 40 (3), 1998.

Comer, D. E., *The Internet Book*. Upper Saddle River, NJ: Prentice-Hall, Inc., 1997.

Damanpour, F. and W. Evan, "Organizational Innovation and Performance: The Problem of Organizational Lag." *Administrative Science Quarterly*, 29, 1984, 382-409.

Deloitte & Touche, LLP, "Leading Trends in Information Services." Ninth Annual Survey of North American Chief Information Officers, Deloitte & Touche Consulting Group, 1997.

Demarest, M.,"Understanding Knowledge Management." *Long Range Planning,* 30(3), 1997, 374-384.

Duffy, T., "Signed, Sealed and Delivered." *Communication Week*, No. 604, April 3, 1996, 43.

Echevarria, D., "Capital Investment and Profitability of Fortune 500 Industrials: 1971-1990." *Studies in Economics and Finance,* 18(1), 1997, 3-35.

Elstrom, P., C. Arnst and R. Crockett, "At Last, Telecom-Unbound." *Business Week,* July 6, 1998, 24-27.

Ettlie, J.E., "Low Emissions Paint Consortium." University of Michigan Business School, 1995.

Ettlie, J.E., "R&D and Global Manufacturing Performance." *Management Science,* 44 (1), 1998, 1-11.

Evan, W. M., "Organizational Lag." *Human Organization,* 25, 1966, 51-53.

Farrel, C. and D. Foust, "Are You Listening, Mr. Greenspan?" *Business Week*, July 13, 1998, 120-121.

Ferguson, K., "Weyerhaeuser Modernizes Flint River with Continuous Digester Overhaul." *Pulp & Paper,* 72 (6), 1998, 43-47.

Graphic Arts Monthly, "Manufacturing Boom to Continue in 1998." 70 (3), 1998, 16.

Haglund, R., "Study: GM Struggles to Compete." *Ann Arbor News,* July 16, 1998, D7.

Hanson, D., "Study Confirms the Importance of Federal Role in Technology Commercialization." *Chemical & Engineering News*, 73 (48), 1995, 16.

Hudson, H. E., "Global Information Infrastructure: Eliminating the Distance Barrier." *Business Economics*, 33 (2), 1998, 25-31.

Jaffe, A. and K. Palmer, "Environmental Regulation and Innovation." *Review of Economics and Statistics*, 79 (4), 1997, 610-619.

Journal of Operations Management, "An International Comparison of Environmental Management in Operations: The Impact of Manufacturing Flexibility in the U.S. and Germany." Vol. 16, 1998, 177-194.

Grahl, C., "Clemson Center Propels the Brick Industry into the 21st Century," *Ceramic Industry*, 148 (4), 1998, 109-115.

Lau, R.S.M., "Operational Characteristics of Highly Competitive Firms." *Production and Inventory Management Journal,* 38 (4), 1997, 17-21.

Leaversuch, R., "Enhanced Process Technologies Pay Off Big in Film and Molding." *Modern Plastics*, 75 (3), 1998, 38-42.

Lowe, J., R. Delbridge and N. Oliver, "High-Performance Manufacturing: Evidence from the Automotive Components Industry." *Organization Studies*, 18 (5), 1997, 783-798.

Minahan, T., "Strategy Shift Pushes More Business to Parcel Carriers." *Purchasing*, 124 (4), 1998, 87-89.

Narisetti, R., "IBM Battles Start-Up Over 'E-Business'." *Wall Street Journal*, July 2, 1998, B10.

National Productivity Review, "Data Bank." 17 (3), 1998, 91-94.

Ogburn, W. F., *Social Change*. New York: Viking, 1922.

Olk, P. and Y. Candace, "Why Members Stay or Leave an R&D Consortium: Performance and Conditions of Membership as Determinants of Continuity." *Strategic Management Journal*, 18, 1997, 855-877.

Olk, P. and K. Xin, "Changing the Policy on Government-Industry Cooperative R&D Arrangements: Lessons from the U.S. Effort.", *International Journal of Technology Management,* 13 (7,8), 710-728.

Quinn, R.E. and K.S. Cameron, "Organizational Effectiveness Life Cycles and Shifting Criteria of Effectiveness." *Management Science*, vol. 29, 1983, 33-51.

Raddock, R., "Industrial Production and Capacity Utilization: Annual Revision and 1997 Developments." *Federal Reserve Bulletin,* 84 (2), 1998, 77-91.

Rae, A., "Jeep Plant Goes Modern." *Manufacturing Engineering*, 120 (6), 1998, 74-78.

Reza, E.M., "Actors and Roles in Organizational Innovating Processes: Issues for the Recovery of Valuable Resources from Trash.", Unpublished Ph.D. dissertation, University of Michigan, Department of Psychology, 1993.

Romei, L. K., "New Technology Strengthens New Commitment." *Managing Office Technology*, 41(7), 1996, 18-20.

Rosen, S., "More than Postage Stamps Sends Messages at the Postal Service." *Communication World*, 15 (5), 1998, 43.

Ruggles, R., "The State of the Nation: Knowledge Management in Practice." *California Management Review*, 40 (3), 1998, 80-89.

Scott, J.T., "Diversification versus Co-operation in R&D Investment." *Managerial & Decision Economics,* 9 (3), 1988, 173-186.

Scott, W.R., *Institutions and Organizations*. Thousand Oaks, CA: Sage, 1995.

Stewart, T. A., "Owens Corning: Back from the Dead." *Fortune*, reprint, 1997.

Taninecz, G., "World-Class Manufacturers." *Industry Week*, 246 (22), 1997, 44-47.

Taylor, P. and J. Lowe, "Are Functional Assets or Knowledge Assets the Basis of New Product Development Performance?" *Technology Analysis and Strategic Management*, 9 (4), 1997, 473-488.

Teng, G., Fielder, 1994, p. 12.

U.S. Department of Commerce, *The Emerging Digital Economy*. National Technical Information Service, PB98-137029, April 1998.

Van de Ven, A., H. Harold, L. Angle and M.S. Poole, (Eds.), *Research on the Management of Innovation*. New York: Harper & Row, 1989.

Wall Street Journal, July 21, 1998, p. A1.

Wheatley, M. and C. New, "Factories to Emulate." *Management Today*, 1997, 74-75.

White, J. B., D. Clark and S. Ascarelli, "Program of Pain: This German Software is Complex, Expensive and Wildly Popular." *Wall Street Journal*, March 14, 1997, A1, A8.

6.   INDUSTRY-UNIVERSITY-GOVERNMENT RESEARCH PARTNERSHIPS FOR ECONOMIC DEVELOPMENT IN THE U.S.

Frederick Betz
University of Maryland

1.   INTRODUCTION

In a knowledge-based economy, technical progress is ultimately based upon progress in science and upon subsequent progress in technology. This linkage between science and technology has been called "scientific technology" – continuing progress in technology that directly uses progress in science. Scientific technology was the technical basis of the first industrial revolution in the eighteenth century and has continued to provide the technical basis for economic development in the world. During the twentieth century, research universities became the locus of scientific progress while industrial research was the locus of technological progress. At the same time, modern governmental R&D support became a major source of funds for scientific research and for much of the early development of scientific technology research. Thus universities, industry, and government R&D all have become important for fostering continuing progress in scientific technology for a knowledge-based economy.

Traditionally, governments have usually supported university research by providing basic research grants to individual investigators in academic disciplines. This has been an excellent mode of promoting advancement in science in the narrowly focused disciplines of science. Unfortunately, this is not an efficient way to promote advancement in technology, since all technologies draw upon more than one subdiscipline of science as knowledge bases. To efficiently promote advancement in technology from advancements in science, a systems approach to research is needed that ensures coordinated research on all the science knowledge bases needed for advancing basic technology.

This systems' mode of research support for directly advancing technology requires multiple-investigator, interdisciplinary, industry/university research cooperation. An interdisciplinary research team is necessary to advance technology because all technologies draw upon more than one science base. Industry and university research cooperation is necessary because industry has the expertise to know where technology needs improvement, while universities have the science focus and graduate students to carry out innovative research.

From a government science and technology (S&T) policy perspective, government support of basic research in both modes is important because (1) the disciplinary single-investigator mode develops communities of deep scientific experts, while (2) the interdisciplinary industry/university centre mode constructs multidisciplinary research teams for the interdisciplinary focus on future industrial technological opportunities.

Promoting strategic research partnerships between university, industry, and government is now an important S&T strategy for maintaining a nation's technological competitiveness. However, this strategy is not easy, due to the different institutional missions, interests, and time-frames of the differing sectors. For science to contribute to technological innovation, important factors are proper focus, scope, completeness, and timing of research. These are influenced by both the contexts and the methodologies of research. Under context, there is a need to organize a bridging form between the sources of science and the implementors of technology – university and industry. Under methodology, there is a need to adjust the approaches of science with the approaches of technological innovation through next-generation technology strategies. We will review the (1) organizational, (2) methodological, and (3) technology-transfer issues in strategic research partnerships.

2. ILLUSTRATION – THE UNITED STATES NATIONAL SCIENCE FOUNDATION CENTERS PROGRAMS

But let us first provide an illustration of these issues. Because of these different challenges facing the advancement of science versus the advancement of technology, a research agency of the United States government, the National Science Foundation (NSF), developed programs specifically focused upon building strategic research partnerships for both science and technology. Two of these, the Industry/University Cooperative Research Centers (IUCRC) Program and the Engineering Research Centers (ERC) Program, started over a hundred cooperative centres at over a hundred U.S. Universities. From these and other programs, lessons have been learned about how to encourage productive industry/university/government research partnerships for science and technology (see, for example, NSF, 1990). The major conclusions from this experience were:

(1) that it is possible for government to facilitate the building of strategic research partnerships between industry and university, and

(2) such partnerships are effective both in advancing science and technology together and in providing appropriate competitive knowledge bases for advancing a knowledge-based economy.

The NSF Engineering Research Centers are organized as strategic research partnerships between university researchers and industrial researchers and they are partially funded by the NSF as five-year grants (for a possible total period of 11 years). Site-visit peer reviews are held on an annual basis, with renewal decisions in years three and five of the Center's grant. Reviewers are outside academics and industrial researchers within the multidisciplinary areas of the Center. Criteria for review are substantial progress in the Center's research, education, and industrial collaboration programs. Table 1 lists the Engineering Research Centers that have been supported by this program since 1985. One notes that many modern technologies for a knowledge-based economy have been included in this program.

Table 1: National Science Foundation Engineering Research Centers

Bioengineering
Bioprocess Engineering, MIT, 1985
Emerging Cardiovascular Technology, Duke University, 1987
Biofilm Engineering, Montana State University, 1990
Neuromophic Systems, California Institute of Technology, 1995
Bioengineered Materials, University of Washington, 1996
Engineering of Living Tissue, Georgia Tech and Emory University, 1998
Marine Bioproducts, University of Hawaii and University of California, Berkeley, 1998
Computer Integrated Surgical Systems, Johns Hopkins and MIT, 1998

Product Design
Systems Control, University of Maryland, 1985
Advanced Combustion, BYU and University of Utah, 1986
Engineering Design, Carnegie Mellon University, 1986
Advanced Technology for Large Structural Systems, Lehigh University, 1986
Computational Field Simulation, Mississippi State University, 1990
Advanced Engineering of Fibres and Films, Clemson University and MIT, 1998

Manufacturing and Production
Intelligent Manufacturing Systems, Purdue University, 1985
Net Shape Manufacturing, Ohio State University, 1986
Interfacial Engineering, University of Minnesota, 1988
Advanced Electronic Materials Processing, North Carolina State University, 1988
Offshore Technology, Texas A&M and University of Texas, Austin, 1988
Particle Science and Technology, University of Florida, 1994
Environmentally Benign Semiconductor Manufacturing, University of Arizona, Stanford and MIT, 1996
Reconfigurable Machining Systems, University of Michigan,1996
Competitive Product Development, MIT, 1996

Information Technology Systems
Telecommunications, Columbia University, 1985
Compound Semiconductor Microelectronics, University of Illinois, 1986
Optoelectronic Computing Systems, University of Colorado, Boulder and Colorado State, Fort Collins, 1987
Data Storage Systems, Carnegie Mellon University, 1990
Low Cost Electronic Packaging, Georgia Tech, 1995
Integrated Media Systems, University of Southern California, 1996
Power Electronic Systems, VPI, Wisconsin, RPI, NC A&T, and University Puerto Rico, 1998

An example of one of the NSF Engineering Research Centers was the Data Storage Systems Center (DSSC) at Carnegie Mellon University (CMU). It arose to continue progress in an area important to both computer science and computer technology – data storage. In 1957, IBM innovated the first magnetic disk drive; and until the 1980s, most of the research in magnetic and optical recording technologies was performed in industry in a proprietary mode. Later research (and the competitive position in magnetic recording) began to change when new firms were formed by former IBM employees and Japanese companies began developing competing products. University-based research in the United States even then was still limited (with, for example, some work in magnetic recording at the University of Minnesota). However, in 1978, Mark Kryder left IBM to join CMU and began research on magnetic bubble memories, magnetic and magneto-optic recording (Kryder, 1997). In 1982, Kryder organized a research workshop with university faculty and industrial researchers in the field. From the workshop came a fundamental research agenda of issues, and Kryder then began an industry/university research centre at CMU to focus science and engineering research on disk storage technology, based upon industrial funding and participation. In May 1983, the centre started as the Magnetics Technology Center (MTC), with $750,000 in financial support by IBM and 3M Corporation. From 1983 to 1989, MTC's budget grew to $5 million in support from industrial firms and government mission-oriented agencies.

However, the industrial and mission-oriented support emphasized primarily shorter-term research issues and incremental technology progress. In 1990, Kryder and his faculty colleagues proposed for and won an Engineering Research Center award from NSF to add a longer-term research focus to their centre. The centre's name was changed from MTC to DSSC to emphasize the new balance between short-term and long-term research (continuous and discontinuous technological progress). To accomplish this balance, DSSC formulated a new research strategy based on next-generation technology (NGT) visions. The long-term research was planned as a sequence of goals for discontinuous technical progress over a ten-year period.

In 1990, the Center's first NGT goal for a next-generation technology of the storage disk was to achieve a storage density of 4 Gbit/sq in magnetic disk recording and 7 Gbit/sq in magnetic-optic recording by 1995. Later in 1992, the Center revised its first-generation NGT goal to add a demonstration of blue wavelength laser magneto-optic recording (with a carrier-to-noise ratio of 50 db) and added a second-generation NGT goal of 10 Gbit/sq by 1998. Thus, the NGT goals of the Center are periodically revised as progress in the technology system is achieved.

Industry has provided continuing support for the Center and organized its support in an industrial research consortium, the National Storage Industry Consortium (NSIC). Since then, the Center has played the role of a shared central research laboratory both for industry and for university education of graduate students. Along the way toward the NGT research goals, over 196 specific technology transfers to the industrial sponsors of the Center have occurred (and even some new companies have been started). In education, over 120 students have received advanced degrees from the Center since 1990 (including 58 PhDs and 62 master's degrees). Most of these graduates work in industry, implementing technological innovation guided by the NGT visions. This illustration shows the need for new science and technology in the data storage industry in the 1980s.

2.1   Organization

We now review some lessons learned about the effective organization of strategic research partnerships that are university-based. The example showed how the U.S. hard-disk industry was able to deliberately use university scientific capability for its science and advanced technology needs.

Centres, such as the NSF Engineering Research Centres, are useful for connecting the different cultures of technological progress and scientific progress. The culture of fundamental science has a long-term, generic perspective on what is important. The culture of technology fosters a shorter-term view of knowledge, focused on solving a particular technical problem in the near future. Scientists are motivated by achievement of scientific fame, which also translates into career opportunities for scientific employment. In contrast, technologists and engineers are motivated by the satisfaction of solving a technical problem, and rewarded by commercial employment and/or entrepreneurial financial success. The two cultures of scientists and technologists/engineers form two research communities with different cultures, values, and reward systems.

Industry has adopted and evolved the culture of technology because it directly uses technology, but industry has never wholly adopted and evolved the culture of science because it only indirectly uses science. Industry uses technology directly. Industry needs new science when technological progress in an existing technology cannot be made without a deeper understanding of the science underlying the technology, or when new basic technologies need to be created from new science.

In contrast, universities have adopted and evolved the culture of science because they directly use science in education. But universities have only partially adopted and evolved the culture of technology (and then only in professional schools of engineering and of medicine but not in schools of arts and science). For this reason, a bridging organization, an industry/university research centre, has been found useful to promote active research partnerships between industrial firms and universities.

Industrial researchers are very sophisticated about current technology and, in particular, about its problems and where the roadblocks to technical progress lie. However, because of the applied and developmental demands on industrial research, they have limited time and resources to explore ways to leap over current technical limitations. On the other hand, academic researchers have the time, resources and students to explore fundamentally new approaches and alternatives that might leapfrog current technologies.

An industry/university centre for cooperative research bridges these two cultures, creating a balance between:
- technologically pulled research and scientifically pushed research,
- short-term and long-term research foci,
- proprietary and non-proprietary research information,
- science-depth education and professionally skilled education.

In a knowledge-based economy, industry must look to the university for science – yet universities traditionally have not advanced science in forms or times *directly* usable by industry. Also, because of their narrow emphasis on disciplinary specialization, the university disciplinary departmental structures have not been very effective in training scientists and engineers directly for industrial development. While disciplinary depth is important in training scientists and engineers for industry, it is not sufficient. Industry needs its scientists and engineers also to have a breadth of skills and knowledge, in order to participate in cross-disciplinary and cross-functional teams focused on technological innovation and product realization (for example, see Rosenberg and Nelson, 1994).

Responding to such needs through government-sponsored research programs necessitates a change in the traditional practices of how government sponsors research. Earlier government programs either (1) performed internal research for government missions or (2) supported research in university and/or industry. Internal research in government laboratories has rarely succeeded in directly stimulating technological innovation because of significant innovation barriers related to focus, cost, market, legal status, etc. Also, government laboratories lack an educational mission and do not train the next generations of scientists and engineers needed by industry, so much technology may not get transferred. (It is the next generation of scientists and engineers, trained in the new science and technology bases that provides the means for industry to implement major new technological innovations.) Government programs that do provide external research support to universities and industries need to foster strategic partnerships between universities and industry to effectively stimulate technological innovation. These are the issues inherent in industry and university cooperation and, properly handled in a centre, they can create a situation of creative tension:

- linking technology and science in real-time progress,
- linking the missions of science and education with the mission of industrial competitiveness.

2.1.1   Organization – University And Industry Requirements For Industry/University Centres

There is a set of requirements that have been learned concerning what a university must do to establish and operate a successful industry/university centre in a strategic research partnership; they include the following issues:

(1) The university needs to provide contiguous space for the centre and arrange for its instrumentation needs to be at the cutting edge of science and engineering.

(2) The university needs to have recruitment, tenure and promotional policies that reward and properly balance faculty contributions both to scientific achievement and to engineering progress.

(3) The centre needs to be multidisciplinary and complementary to the departmental educational structure of the university.

(4) The centre must be large enough to perform a critical mass of research useful to industry.

(5) The centre needs to actively coordinate the educational requirements of programs and students with the research requirements of industry.

(6) The centre needs to formulate research projects that result in open publication in the literature.

(7) The centre needs to inform faculty and students how to cooperate with industry while still fulfilling the principle missions of the university in education and research.

(8)   The centre needs to work with large firms as well as small firms, with the large firms providing the principal industrial support.

(9)   The centre needs to be capable of strategic research planning for targeted basic research on a technological system.

(10) The centre needs to be capable of performing scientific and engineering research at the systems level of a technology.

(11) The centre needs to provide a dual-structure organization unit which can perform both scientific research and early technology development for industry.

Conversely, there is also a set of requirements industry must meet.

(1)   A diversified firm must have a corporate research lab as well as divisional labs, and the corporate research lab must be tightly linked with the divisional labs.

(2)   The company should work with multidisciplinary strategically focused university research centres.

(3)   Such centres should link with both the corporate research lab and the divisional labs of a company.

(4)   Company personnel should participate in both the governance and the research of the university centre.

(5)   The corporate research lab and divisional labs should be performing joint applied and development projects parallel to the research projects of the university centre.

(6)   The firm should join with several other firms and with government in financially supporting the university centre.

(7)   The firm should participate in and support several university centres sufficient to provide it with a long-term competitive edge in all its strategic technologies.

2.2   Methodology

We next turn to lessons learned concerning effective research methodologies employed in strategic research partnership centres. The use of cooperative research centres to provide scientific advances for industrial technology advancement also needs to take into account the methodology of research.   It is important that the system approach to science-based technology research focus on the methodology of "next-generation-technology systems."   This kind of technology advance, "next-generation-technology," is one of the different steps on the scale of technological innovation.

We should recall that technological innovation varies along the scale of radical, incremental, or next-generation technology. Radical innovation establishes a new functionality (e.g., steam engine or steam boat); whereas incremental innovation improves an existing technology system's performance, features, safety, quality or cost (e.g., governor on a steam engine). A next-generation-technology (NGT) innovation is a major change that dramatically improves performance, features, safety, quality or cost and opens up new applications (e.g., substitution of jet propulsion for propellers on airplanes). An incremental technological innovation is called "continuity of technological progress," while radical and next-generation-technological innovations are called "discontinuities of technological progress."

Research for technology progress cannot be planned until *after* a basic technological invention occurs. Only incremental and NGT research can be forecast and planned. Research for incremental innovations does not necessarily require new science, but research for NGT innovation *always requires some new science*. For a research strategy focused on NGT, the three partners, university, industry and government, are needed. Research planning for NGT innovation provides an effective methodology for strategic research partnerships between university, industry, and government.

Planning for NGT innovation provides an effective means for formulating strategic research partnerships between industry and university as they together plan "targeted" basic research. Targeted basic research in science can be *focused* by the technological needs of industry, aiming to overcome the technical barriers in an existing technology. The *scope* of the research must be appropriate to advance technology by determining how deeply or broadly phenomena in science need to be studied and manipulated. Since all technologies are systems, research must be *complete* in covering the aspects of the technology system that allow advances in performance of the whole system. Also, since technological innovation provides a competitive advantage to industry only during "windows" of commercial opportunity, the proper *timing* of the research is important to industry. In contrast, for academic and government science, these criteria (focus, scope, completeness and timing of research) are less critical than they are for industry.

Thus, the problem of technology transfer in strategic research partnerships between university and industry begins with ensuring that the focus, scope, completeness and timing of the proposed research will facilitate eventual technology transfer.

2.2.1 Methodology – Focusing Science for Technology

Science can be focused upon the physical or logical phenomena underlying technologies, i.e., "targeted basic research" may be scientific research focused upon the physical or logical phenomena underlying a technology system. In this way, university science can be planned for industrial needs through NGT-focused research upon:
 (1) generic technology systems and subsystems for product systems,
 (2) generic technology systems and subsystems for production systems,
 (3) physical phenomena underlying the technology systems and subsystems for product systems and for production systems.
In any of these technology systems, science can be focused upon improving the system through understanding the physical phenomena underlying technologies and inventing technical improvements in any aspect of the system:
 (1) improved system boundary,
 (2) improved components,
 (3) improved connections,
 (4) improved materials,
 (5) improved power and energy,
 (6) improved system control.
NGT-focused research strategically bridges the shorter-term technology focus of industry with the longer-term science focus of university and the generic technology focus of government. Together, industry, university and government researchers can see how to effectively bound a technological system in order to envision a next-generation technology.

The boundary of a next-generation-technology vision is an important judgment, combining:
 (1) judgments upon possible technical progress and research directions which together might produce a major advance, and
 (2) judgments over the domain of industrial organization in which such an advance might produce a significant competitive advantage.
For planning targeted basic research for a next-generation technology, strategic procedures should be implemented in an industry/university centre which can:
 (1) *Characterize the present technology as a system:*
    (a) Identify technical bottlenecks in the current system,
    (b) Describe the functionality, performance and features that are

very desirable but cannot be obtained in the current generation of technology,

(c)   Imagine how current applications could be better accomplished with the new technology and new applications that might be possible but which cannot be accomplished with the current technology.

(2)   *Explore the scientific basis of a next-generation technology system*:

(a)   Imagine if and how new research instrumentation, instrumental techniques, algorithmic techniques, or theoretical modeling could be focused upon the bottlenecks,

(b)   Imagine how to improve the understanding and manipulation of the phenomena causing bottlenecks or to develop alternative phenomena to substitute new technical manipulations at the bottlenecks.

Because an NGT vision requires both understanding of current technology and imagination of new research approaches, the strengths of the different partners, industry, university and government, can be effectively focused on new science for new technology. NGT research requires not only dramatic improvement in performance of a technology but also new science to achieve that dramatic improvement.

2.2.2   Methodology – Scoping Science for Technology

The scope of the research efforts to explore the vision of an NGT requires identification of the multidisciplinary engineering and science areas that need to be included in the cooperative centre. This provides the basis for the organization of the centre.

For example, a biotechnology process cooperative research centre at Massachusetts Institute of Technology includes the disciplines of molecular biology, chemistry, and chemical engineering in its research areas. As another example, a biofilm cooperative research centre at Montana State University includes biology, chemical engineering, civil engineering, and mathematics in its organization.

All technology systems used by industry today depend on knowledge bases in several science and engineering disciplines. Therefore, a distinctive characteristic of a cooperative research centre is its multidisciplinary character, wherein the disciplines relevant to the scope of the NGT integrate through interdisciplinary research efforts. Thus, technology transfer begins by planning not only the focus of the research effort as an NGT but also the scope of the multidisciplinary efforts and the interdisciplinary integration needed for an NGT.

2.2.3   Methodology – Completing Science for Technology

Since all technologies are systems, the research effort for an NGT requires that it be completed as a system, in order to demonstrate its technical potential and limitations to industry.

For example, the NSF cooperative research centres have chosen to do this by constructing a research testbed for a prototype of the NGT.   It is a research testbed because it integrates the research projects toward demonstrating the NGT concept; and it is begun early in the research of the cooperative centre (even while the research to be integrated is yet incomplete).   Thus, as both a demonstration testbed and a vehicle for integrating research, the NGT research testbed can show the potentials of the research and the shortcomings of present research as a means complete the NGT.   Finally, when the testbed is well enough along, industry can provide empirical applications to determine how much performance the NGT prototype can attain.

2.2.4   Methodology – Timing Science for Technology

Since the competitive benefits of technological innovation occur only within a "window" of commercial opportunity, a business must be concerned about when a technical goal can be achieved.   The timing of a centres research and the timing of its demonstration in an NGT prototype testbed are extremely important for technology transfer.   The principal benefit of research by universities and government for an industry is to lower the technical risks in the new technologies in which the industry might invest. The sooner technical   risk is lowered, the sooner industry may begin the development process and the more rapidly competitive benefits will accrue to industry.

For example, Ralph Gomory and Roland Schmidt emphasized that there are two innovation processes: a linear and a circular process (Gomory and Schmidt, 1988). The linear process connects science to the marketplace and is effective for radical innovation.   The circular process lies within the product development cycles of companies and is effective for incremental innovation. The two processes can be coupled for next-generation-technology research (Betz, 1993). Figure 1 sketches the processes, linear and circular, and their integration in next-generation-technology innovation.

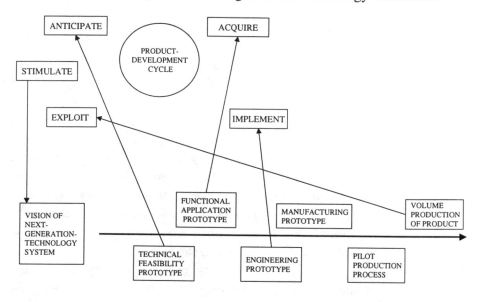

Figure 1: Integration of cyclic innovation with linear innovation in a next-generation-technology product.

For NGT innovation, the cyclic innovation process can stimulate the need for new technology by fostering the *vision of a next-generation technology*, within the linear innovation process. The *technical feasibility prototype* in the linear innovation process provides the grounds for anticipation of new technology in the cyclic innovation process. The *functional prototype* in the linear innovation process provides the information for acquiring new technology in the cyclic innovation process. The implementation phase in the cyclic innovation process designs the *engineering prototype* in the linear innovation process (which, with concurrent engineering practice, also fosters the manufacturing prototypes and pilot production). *Volume production* in the linear innovation process of the next-generation product provides the opportunity for exploitation of the new technology in the cyclic innovation process.

By establishing "technical feasibility," the linear innovation process can generate *anticipation* in the cyclic innovation process of a possible new generation of a technology. The step of "functional prototyping" in the linear innovation process establishes the *timing* for introduction of a next generation of a technology to be acquired by the product development cycle. The engineering prototype of a new-generation-technology product next allows the product development cycle of a strategic business unit to *implement* the new technology.

When one produces and markets the new product, the design, the manufacture, the timing of the introduction, the pricing of the new product and establishing distribution are all critical events. The more radical the innovation in the next-generation technology of the new products, the more likely a correction to these events will be necessary. Accordingly, the accumulating market experience with the new product will likely require industry to have a fast recycle capability though the product development cycle. The greater the technology discontinuity in a next-generation technology, the greater the necessity for a redesign of a new product.

2.3   Technology Transfer

Given effective organization and a methodology for jointly advancing science and technology in strategic research partnerships, there remains the important issue of transferring the new technology into industrial and commercial innovation. Several requirements have been learned concerning how industry can effectively transfer NGT developed in industry/university centres:

(1) Corporate research should strategically plan next-generation technology, and this is best done through participation in an industry/university cooperative research centre.

(2) The firm should be hiring university graduates from the university centre to effectively implement technology transfer.

(3) Corporate research should plan NGT products jointly with product development groups in the business divisions.

(4) Marketing experiments should be set up and conducted jointly with corporate research and business divisions, with trial products using ideas tested in the consortium's experimental prototype testbeds.

(5) The CEO team should encourage long-term financial planning focused upon NGT.

(6) Personnel planning and development are required to transition knowledge bases and skill mixes for NGT.

2.3.1 Technology Transfer – Graduate Education for a Knowledge-Based Economy

Technology transfer occurs both by the movement of information and the movement of people. A most important output of university-based strategic research partnerships is the university graduates. Thus, it is also important to emphasize that education, as well as research, is a central feature in strategic university/industry partnerships. In a knowledge-based economy, graduate education should prepare students to be employed in industry as well as academia. Graduate education in the context of industry/university strategic research partnerships provides an excellent means for this dual preparation.

Studies on technology transfer have demonstrated that technology is more effectively transferred through people than through communications. The reason for this is that basic research provides the ideas and understanding for technological development, but not the practices for embedding technology useful products, production, or services. There must be further ideas for how to use science in technological applications that can best be created and developed on the job. Thus, one of the major benefits industry receives from industry/university centres is access to students to hire who have been trained at the cutting edge of next-generation technology. The coupling of university graduate education with strategic research partnerships for NGT provides training at the forefront of future technology for a knowledge-based economy.

This is particularly important for master's-level education in engineering, since this level of engineer is the usual designer of new products, processes, and services in industry. Thus, basing a NGT research centre for industry on a university campus for both PhD and master's education is a good strategy because it facilitates graduate training on a next-generation-technology vision.

3. CONCLUSION

Strategic research partnerships between university, industrial and governmental sectors provide an important basis for Science and Technology policies aimed at improving and maintaining national competitiveness for knowledge-based economies. The parallel advancement of science and technology requires effective organization, methodology, and technology transfer. Continuing and increasing cooperation between the government, industry and university sectors is playing a central role in advancing knowledge in modern knowledge-based economies.

REFERENCES

Betz, F., *Strategic Technology Management.* New York: McGraw-Hill, 1993.

Gomory, R. E. and R. W. Schmitt, "Science and Product." *Science*, 240, 1988,1131-1204.

Kryder, M., *ERC in Data Storage Systems: Seventh Year Annual Report.* Pittsburgh, PA: Carnegie Mellon University, 1997.

National Science Foundation, *Highlights of Engineering Research Centers Technology Transfer.* Washington, DC: Directorate for Engineering, 1990.

Rosenberg, N. and R. R. Nelson, "American Universities and Technical Advance in Industry." *Research Policy*, 23, 1994, 323-348.

7. A FIRM-BASED APPROACH TO INDUSTRY CLASSIFICATION: IDENTIFYING THE KNOWLEDGE-BASED ECONOMY

John R. Baldwin
Statistics Canada

Guy Gellatly
Statistics Canada

Acknowledgements: We would like to thank Ted Wannell of the Analytical Studies Branch at Statistics Canada for his helpful comments. We also wish to acknowledge the programming assistance that we received from Daniel Stripinis and Bob Gibson during the preparation of this paper.

The ideas in this paper are those of the authors and do not necessarily reflect the opinions of Statistics Canada.

1.   INTRODUCTION

In recent years, economists have expressed considerable interest in the growth of new technology-based firms (NTBFs). Often at the forefront of product development and advanced technology use, these firms are seen to be critical to an economy's transition to knowledge-based production. Two factors, however, have created a tendency to regard the evolution of NTBFs as highly industry-specific. The first is the high visibility of new rapidly growing sectors (e.g., biotechnology, information technology). The second is the emergence of taxonomies – such as that used by the Organization for Economic Cooperation and Development (OECD, 1997) – that score industries as being either high- or low-tech.[1] Is it true that NTBFs are largely sector-specific, as existing classifications would suggest, or, alternatively, are these firms found in many industries? This issue has important implications for public policy. If the former is true, sector-specific policies to encourage the growth of NTBFs are appropriate; if the latter is the case, such policies may be misplaced.

It is the purpose of the present paper to ask four questions. First, how adequate are existing classification schemes that are used to argue that the new knowledge economy is highly concentrated in some sectors? Second, can a new set of indices be devised that are more appropriate for industry classification? Third, if so, what do these new measures reveal about the identification of high-tech industries and the location of high-tech firms? Finally, what do these indices tell us about the usefulness of classification schemes that produce a unique industry ranking?

This paper examines these issues, making use of a new data set to investigate how industries differ in the extent to which they contain advanced firms and the extent to which alternative concepts of technological prowess yield different industry rankings. In doing so, the paper develops a multidimensional framework for industry classification based on the advanced competencies of new small firms. We argue that this framework represents an advance over previous efforts, while recognizing that any single ranking derived from this multidimensional index cannot provide the definitive basis for classification.

The paper is organized as follows. Section 2 examines a series of measures that are commonly used to classify industries as more or less technologically advanced or as being high- or low-knowledge. Three standard measures of technological prowess – R&D intensity, innovation, and technology usage – are investigated in detail. We argue that each of these measures, when applied alone, is subject to a series of shortcomings that limit the utility of its corresponding taxonomy, both in general and when applied to subsets of the business population such as NTBFs.

Section 3 examines the firm-level characteristics that form the basis for our competency-based framework. Based on survey data, the innovation, technology, and human capital characteristics of new small firms are investigated in detail, as is their incidence within the entrant population.

Section 4 develops an alternative classification scheme using a competency-based framework for new small firms. This method draws on a firm's innovation, human capital, and technology characteristics to produce a multidimensional measure of its technological prowess. In developing this measure, we create three separate indices, each centred on a strategic dimension of firm behaviour. These are then combined to form an overall index that captures the advanced competencies of new firms in a parsimonious fashion. Two issues are then examined. First, we investigate differences in industry rankings based on the innovation, technology, and human capital indices, respectively. Second, we use these measures to investigate the concentration of high-tech firms in both high- and low-tech industries.

Section 5 compares our overall survey-based index to existing classification schemes – such as the high-tech/low-tech taxonomy used by the OECD – that are derived from aggregate industry characteristics. We find that these aggregate indices produce different high-tech groupings than our index based on the advanced competencies of new firms.

Section 6 investigates the limitations of a single-index approach to classification. Since the summarization inherent in any index may be too parsimonious, we ask whether the firm-based competency approach should be used to yield a unique ranking to identify high- and low-tech industries, or whether it should be used to generate a set of rankings. We conclude that there are several different dimensions to technological prowess, and that the use of a single index would obscure some of these. Moreover, there are many combinations of advanced competencies and almost every industry could be classified as a high-tech leader based on at least one of these combinations.

We conclude in Section 7 by exploring the relevance of our findings for policies designed to encourage the growth of NTBFs. In our view, policy prescriptions that presume that NTBFs are confined to particular sectors may, in fact, be misplaced.

2.   EXISTING CLASSIFICATION SCHEMES OF HIGH-TECH OR KNOWLEDGE-BASED INDUSTRIES

The use of nomenclature such as "knowledge economy" or "high-tech sector" or "innovation economy" is not generally accompanied by precise definitions of the phenomenon in question. Failure to specify how the high-knowledge sector is defined leaves discussions about its location empty and vapid. However, specifying which sectors are high- or low-knowledge is a difficult proposition since the very concept of knowledge is hard to define and even more difficult to measure. This is because a knowledge-based industry has a wide range of characteristics. To some researchers, it means an innovative sector where new products and processes are being produced. To others, it means the use of advanced technologies that either have a high degree of complexity or incorporate advanced scientific and engineering techniques, such as biotechnology. To others still, it means the embodiment of high levels of human skills in the production process.

Most attempts to systematically define high-tech sectors have focused on broad aggregate characteristics when classifying individual industries. In our view, this approach has several deficiencies. First, many of the concepts used for classification are narrow or incomplete. The OECD's high-tech classification scheme (1997) provides one of the most visible examples of this. Second, existing classification schemes treat industries as homogeneous, that is, all firms within an industry are regarded as the same. In reality, however, an industry is made up of many different types of firms, some of which are more advanced than others. It follows that some firms in low-tech industries may have higher technological skills than an average firm in a high-tech industry. Classification schemes that label an entire industry as low-tech may thus unfairly suggest that there are few advanced firms within these industries. Moreover, these classification schemes may be inappropriate for particular firm subpopulations, for example, NTBFs. As these firms are often smaller than established incumbents, classification based on an average industry variable, whose value is generally determined by the larger firms in the industry, will misrepresent the influence of NTBFs if their characteristics differ systematically from those of larger firms. This is a serious deficiency given the relative importance of NTBFs.

An additional difficulty with the high-tech or knowledge-based taxonomies that have come into use is that their narrow focus may incorrectly classify sectors. An R&D-based classification may not correspond to a more comprehensive definition that considers both inputs to, and outputs from, the innovation process. Similarly, such a scheme may have little to do with the extent to which the workforce of an industry is highly skilled. Finally, it may not be closely related to the extent to which sectors develop or make use of advanced technologies.

There are several concepts of technological prowess currently used for the purposes of industry classification. Prominent examples include R&D, innovation, and the use of advanced technology. Each of these will be discussed in turn.

2.1   Intensity of R&D as Technological Prowess

The high-tech classification scheme used by the OECD is based primarily on the R&D intensity of an industry.[2] Using R&D-to-sales ratios, the OECD divides certain industries into high-, medium-, and low-tech for several studies. This approach suffers from a number of deficiencies.

First, it is not a direct measure of at least one aspect of an industry's technological prowess. Technology involves the use of advanced processes; those not directly stemming from R&D expenditures are ignored in this classification scheme. Nor does the OECD classification scheme capture the skill levels of the workforce that are essential to growth in new firms (Baldwin, forthcoming).

Second, it measures inputs to the innovation process and not the innovations themselves. In fact, it focuses on a single input while neglecting others. Studies of innovation systems have emphasized the importance of inputs other than traditional forms of R&D (see Mowery and Rosenberg, 1989; Baldwin and Da Pont, 1996).

Third, the official statistics on R&D miss some important activity.[3] Kleinknecht, Poot and Reijnen (1991) argue that informal or discontinuous R&D is an important input into the innovation process and that it is generally omitted in the R&D data that are used by the OECD. This has particular importance for countries whose industrial structure consists of smaller firms, since these firms tend to perform more informal R&D. Baldwin (1997) confirms that in Canada small firms are more likely to conduct R&D on a discontinuous basis.

Fourth, R&D is more likely to be associated with product innovations than process innovations (Baldwin, Hanel and Sabourin, forthcoming). More importantly, small firms are more likely to use production and engineering facilities than R&D departments. This means that a simple R&D-based index will understate the relative importance of industries where process innovation is more important and where small firms account for a larger percentage of employment.

Finally, the OECD classification scheme focuses exclusively on the manufacturing sector and ignores the services sector. This bias in favour of the goods sector leaves a void in our understanding of the knowledge economy since the manufacturing sector accounts for less than 20% of employment in Canada. Innovations in services have an important effect on social welfare. Services sectors such as transportation, communications, utilities, retailing, and computing services have all been introducing innovations that not only directly affect consumers but also feed into the productivity of goods industries. What is more, new small firms are more prevalent in services than in the manufacturing sector. A study of NTBFs is therefore incomplete without consideration being given to the services sector.

2.2   Innovation as Technological Prowess

To overcome the possible distortion occasioned by an emphasis on R&D inputs alone, the technological prowess of a firm could be defined as its ability to innovate. If we are ultimately interested in the extent to which new products and processes are introduced, then it is more sensible to focus on the outputs of the innovation process rather than on inputs like R&D.[4] While seemingly uncontroversial, translating this principle into practice is difficult, as we shall see. This means that indices based on a single measure of innovative output should be treated with caution.

The innovative capabilities of a firm can be measured in several ways. Robson, Townsend and Pavitt (1988), for example, used a database of major innovations produced by a panel of "experts" to classify industries by their tendency to innovate. The industry rankings produced by this classification are quite similar to those produced by Scherer's (1982) data on U.S. patents.

In contrast, a second expert database has been constructed by The Futures Group for the Small Business Administration (Acs and Audretsch, 1990) using information from technology, engineering, and trade journals in manufacturing industries. When innovations are assigned to their industry of origin, the relative importance of certain sectors differs from that suggested by the Robson classification.

The reason for these differences is that deciding on whether a new product is an innovation involves considerable subjectivity, even when assembled by panels of experts. One bias is readily acknowledged: lists of innovations that are drawn from trade publications will be dominated by product innovations and will underrepresent process innovations (Kleinknecht, Reijnen and Smits, 1993). An equally important problem stems from the fact that new products involve a continuum of novelty and deciding on the cutoff point that should be used to define an innovation is problematic.

In place of using expert panels or trade publications, firm-based surveys have also been employed to investigate interindustry differences in innovation tendencies. Examples of these surveys are to be found in those being undertaken by the European community (the Community Innovation Surveys – CIS). These rely on a firm to identify its status as an innovator as well as the type of innovation that it is introducing. While advantageous in terms of coverage, such surveys may lead to imprecise definitions of what constitutes an innovative industry; for example, few of these surveys investigate whether the firm considers the innovation to be "major or marginal" in nature. Secondly, as with innovation lists, bias presents a problem. Survey respondents may be more willing to identify product innovations than process innovations, even though the cumulative effects of the latter may prove equally significant. As a consequence, the data that they yield will be skewed towards product innovations and will incorrectly attribute innovativeness to industries that have relatively more product than process innovations.[5]

2.3 Technology Use as Technological Prowess

As attractive as innovation is as a measure of technological prowess, it does not directly capture the extent to which an industry's production processes incorporate advanced technologies. Innovation classifications may readily miss the extent to which firms are incorporating the latest machinery and equipment into their plants since the purchase of such equipment is often not considered to involve the creation of an innovation. Nevertheless, being able to incorporate advanced equipment into the production process is a mark of a firm's technological prowess.

Several surveys have been conducted in Canada, Australia, and the United States to estimate the intensity of use of equipment or processes that are associated with advanced technologies.[6] These are technologies such as computer-aided design and engineering, flexible manufacturing cells, computer numerically controlled machines, materials-working lasers, robots, automated inspection equipment, local area networks, programmable controllers, computer-integrated manufacturing systems and artificial-intelligence systems. While the intensity of use of these advanced technologies can be employed to classify industries into high- and low-tech groups, it should be stressed that no list of technologies should be viewed as exhaustive. Some advanced technologies from this list are more relevant to certain industries than to others. The latter group of industries will thus rank lower for this reason, as opposed to any underlying technological backwardness, since they may use advanced technologies but these technologies may not be covered by the commonly used list. This simply emphasizes the caution that should be used in employing any of these measures in isolation, whether it be an R&D, an innovation, or a technology index.

3. A COMPETENCY-BASED APPROACH

3.1 Measurement of Industry Competencies

As the previous discussion has recounted, technological prowess has different meanings to those who have attempted to develop classification schemes that can be used to study differences across sectors and industries. Therefore, taxonomies that are aimed at classifying industries by a measure of advanced technological prowess have alternative standards from which they can choose. The taxonomy may focus on innovative output. Alternatively, it may concentrate on some aspect of the production process – whether firms perform research and development, whether their production processes and equipment are advanced technologically. In addition, a taxonomy could focus on whether firms employ workers with higher skill levels. Skilled labour has been recognized as being critical for the implementation of new technology (Bartel and Lichtenberg, 1987). Others have noted the impact of new technologies on wage differentials that relate to skills in the U.S. (Bound and Johnson, 1992; Berman, Bound and Griliches, 1994; Doms, Dunne and Troske, 1997). Baldwin, Gray, and Johnson (1997) and Baldwin and Rafiquzzaman (forthcoming) show that there is a strong connection between the use of advanced technologies and plant wage rates in Canada. These studies suggest that consideration also be given to the presence of skilled labour when defining those industries that have the most technological prowess.

Previous attempts at classification have had several deficiencies. First, they have tended to adopt a partial approach. In doing so, they have presumed that there is a single taxonomy that adequately summarizes the characteristics that define technological prowess. Yet it is clear that there is more than one characteristic that defines a new high-technology firm. By examining the extent to which several advanced competencies exist in new firms, progress can be made in formalizing what has been until now a somewhat amorphous exercise.

We now turn to develop a classification scheme based on several advanced competencies that are recognized as being critical to the success of NTBFs.

3.2 Data and Definitions: The Survey of Operating and Financing Practices

For this exercise, we make use of firm-level data taken from Statistics Canada's 1996 *Survey of Operating and Financing Practices*, which focuses specifically on new smaller firms in both goods and services industries. The inclusion of new firms in both the goods and services sectors overcomes the traditional manufacturing industry bias that has been associated with studies of NTBFs. The richness of the survey database allows both output- and input-based measures of the innovation, technological, and skill-based competencies of smaller firms to be developed, which are then used to characterize industries by an average measure of advanced competencies.

The survey focused on new entrants that emerged from childhood and survived to their early teen years, 11 to 14. In light of the high death rate of new firms, these are the more successful entrants. The frame consisted of all entrants to the commercial sector (both goods and services) in the period 1983-1986 that survived to 1993. The sample included 3,991 firms; the response rate to the survey was 80%.

In order to develop our taxonomy, we make use of numerous questions that capture concepts related to technological prowess. These include the innovation capabilities of firms, their human-resource competencies, their technological capacities, and their competitive strategies.

Two types of questions are used to provide information on the competencies of entrants. First, we use questions that characterize an entrant as following certain strategies – as producing a product innovation, as having formal training programs, or the percentage of investment devoted to R&D or to training. These take on 0-1 values or are expressed as percentages. Second, we use questions about an entrant's emphasis on factors, such as R&D capabilities or training activities, that contributed to the ongoing success of the firm. These questions were scored on a five-point Likert scale of 1 (low importance) to 5 (high importance) and are used to gauge an entrant's competencies. In what follows, entrants are deemed to possess a particular competency or to be stressing a particular strategy if they score either 4 or 5 on the five-point Likert scale.

3.3   Innovation Competencies

As was previously described, innovation is not easily pigeonholed in one compartment. Some innovations involve new products; others involve new processes. Innovations will differ in terms of their novelty. In order to measure the diversity of innovative activity taking place, the stress that new small firms place on innovation is measured with 10 different variables. Each captures a different, though related, concept of innovation.

The first set uses a question that asked whether an entrant had introduced an innovation and investigated the type of innovation. An innovation was defined as the introduction of a new or improved product or process; aesthetic changes that did not affect the technical construction or performance of the product were not included in the definition of an innovation. These innovations were, in turn, characterized as being either entirely new products, modifications of existing products, entirely new processes, or modifications of existing processes. Finally, entrants indicated whether these innovations were protected with intellectual property rights. Combinations of these measures are then used to define whether the entrants were introducing innovations of varying degrees of novelty and importance. These variables are:

- INGEN – whether an entrant reports any innovation.
- INIMP1 – whether an entrant reports an innovation and it is protected by an intellectual property right such as a patent, or the firm reports that a strategy of protecting its innovations with intellectual property is important or very important (a score of 4 or 5).
- INIMP2 – whether an entrant reports an innovation that is either a completely new product or a completely new process.
- INPROD – whether an entrant is a product innovator.
- INPROC – whether an entrant is a process innovator.
- INCOMP – whether an entrant is both a product and a process innovator.
  We also include variables related to innovation inputs. These are:
- INRD – whether an entrant scores 4 or 5 on the importance given to R&D capabilities.
- INIMP – whether an entrant's percentage of investment devoted to R&D is above the median of all entrants that report positive levels of R&D expenditure.

Finally, we include two additional measures that capture a broader concept of innovation. These are:

- INFREQ – whether an entrant scores 4 or 5 on the extent to which it frequently introduces new/improved products.

- INTRAD – whether an entrant scores at least 18 out of a possible 20 points on the importance attributed to quality, customer service, flexibility in responding to customer needs and customization.

3.4 Technological Competencies

The second advanced competency focuses specifically on whether technological capabilities – the application of advanced technologies as opposed to general prowess – in an entrant are important. As was the case for innovation, technological competency has more than one dimension and, as a consequence, is measured here in several different ways. Technological innovation involves a different though related dimension of innovation – the extent to which an entrant focuses on advanced technology. These variables are meant to capture the wide variety of changes that occur in the production process that would not necessarily be captured by a simple question that asked whether process innovation is occurring. The variables used here are:

- INTECH1 – whether an entrant scores 4 or 5 on the importance attached to developing new and refining existing technology.
- INTECH2 – whether an entrant scores 4 or 5 on the importance attached to purchasing technology from other firms.
- TEDEV – whether an entrant both develops/refines new technology and purchases it.
- TECOMP – whether an entrant scores 4 or 5 on the importance given to using computer-controlled processes in production.
- TEINFO – whether an entrant scores 4 or 5 on using information technology for management purposes.
- TEINP – whether an entrant's percentage of investment devoted to technology acquisition is above the median of all entrants that report positive levels of investment devoted to technology acquisition.

Finally, we use a more inclusive technology variable to capture an aspect of production technology commonly emphasized by firms. That is,

- PROD1 – whether an entrant scores 4 or 5 on improving efficiency of input use in the production process and on reducing production times.

3.5 Human Capital Development

The final set of competencies considered here are worker skills. Entrants incorporate these skills either by focusing their human-resource strategies on hiring skilled workers or by developing these skills themselves through training programs. In both cases, a firm's innovation competencies are facilitated by the amount of human capital that it possesses. Baldwin and Johnson (1996) report that a human-capital strategy is pursued more intensely by innovators in both the goods and the services sectors. In the goods sector, an emphasis on training is often combined with an emphasis on R&D or the development of new machinery and equipment. In the services sector, the innovation strategy often *is* the human-resource strategy. Baldwin, Gray, and Johnson (1997) establish the close connection between the adoption of advanced manufacturing technologies and a firm's emphasis on training.

The emphasis on human capital is measured here by the value that an entrant attaches to recruiting skilled labour, by the emphasis it gives to training, and finally by the extent to which it implements a formal training program and invests in training. The variables are:

- LABSKL – whether an entrant scores 4 or 5 on the importance given to recruiting skilled employees.
- LABSCOR – whether an entrant scores 4 or 5 on the importance attached to training.
- LABFOR – whether an entrant conducts formal training.
- LABTRAIN – whether an entrant's share of investment devoted to training is positive.
- LABINT – whether the percentage of investment that is devoted to training is above the median for all entrants that have positive levels of investment in training.

3.6   Incidence of Innovation, Technological Competencies, and Focus on Skills in the Entrant Population

Most entrants are innovative in one or other of the ways outlined above, but the percentage of the population of entrants that are innovative differs considerably depending upon which of the summary measures is used. This is illustrated in Figure 1.

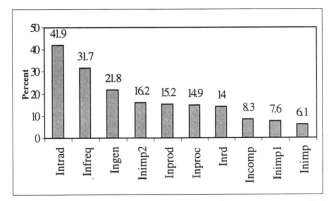

Figure 1: Incidence of innovation measures within entrant population

Many firms are experimenting with the type of innovation that requires bundling a service or quality with a good. About 42% of the population place a heavy emphasis on varying quality to provide a unique product to the consumer (INTRAD). Somewhat fewer are introducing new products. Some 32% place more than average importance on frequently introducing new products (INFREQ). When "new" is interpreted to mean an "innovation," fewer firms fall into this category. Some 22% have introduced an innovation over the 1992-1994 period (INGEN). Some 14% of entrants emphasized an R&D strategy (INRD) but some 29% either report an innovation or that they place above-average importance on R&D – about the same percentage that emphasize the frequent introduction of new products.

When the constraint of genuine novelty is imposed on the innovation, the percentage declines by amounts that vary depending on the definition of novelty. Only 16% introduced what they consider to be an entirely new product or process (INIMP2). Some 8% introduced an innovation that was protected by formal intellectual property rights (INIMP1). Despite these differences, it should be noted that the vast majority of entrants are innovative by one or other of these standards: roughly 70% of all firms fall into one of the categories defined here. Innovation is an activity that is widely pursued.

The various measures of the firm's technological capabilities indicate a diversity of technological competencies. These are examined in Figure 2.

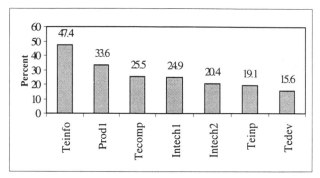

Figure 2: Incidence of technology measures within entrant population

In accord with the finding of Baldwin and Sabourin (1995) that communications technologies have been expanding fastest, the largest group of firms (47%) emphasize the importance of computer-based information technologies (TEINFO). The next largest percentage of entrants (34%) focus on methods to reduce the cost of inputs and to reduce production times (PROD1). Roughly 25% place heavy emphasis on developing new technologies (INTECH1) or use computer-controlled processes in production (TECOMP). There are about 20% who stress the purchase of new technologies (INTECH2). Finally, 16% of firms both develop new technologies and purchase new technologies from others (TEDEV). Once again, a clear majority of entrants are engaged in some form of technovation; here too, approximately 70% fall into at least one of the technovation categories.

There is also a large percentage of firms who stress the importance of worker skills and training. This is examined in Figure 3.

Roughly 56% indicate that training is important (LABSCOR) and devote considerable importance to recruiting skilled labour (LABSKL). About the same percentage perform formal training to upgrade their employees' skills. Some 52% have implemented a formal training program (LABFOR). Even if we judge whether firms are performing substantial activity in this area – on the basis of whether they report that they devote part of their investment to training (LABTRAIN) – 31% of new firms are still seen to be serious participants in upgrading human capital. Thus, a large percentage of entrants are part of the knowledge economy in the sense that they place a high value on human capital.

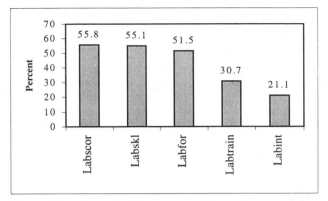

Figure 3: Incidence of skill measures within entrant population

These data show that a substantial proportion of new entrants consider themselves to be innovative or technologically advanced or to depend on skilled workers. When we consider the characteristics jointly, the percentage of entrants that fall into at least one category increases. For example, 22% of new firms report an innovation, 14% place a very high importance on R&D, and 29% report at least one of these two characteristics. Similarly, 25% of entrants report that they develop new or refine existing technology, while 20% bring in outside technology; but some 30% perform at least one of these two. Some 47% of entrants use information technology in management and 26% use computers for process control; however, 53% of entrants exhibit at least one of these characteristics. When we expand our definitions of innovation to encompass a characteristic from more than just the innovative group, the percentage of entrants that can be said to be innovative is quite large. Some 39% report an innovation, or perform R&D, or emphasize either the development or purchase of technology. Some 65% report one of the above competencies, or emphasize computer-controlled processes, or stress the use of information technologies.

4.   AN INDUSTRY TAXONOMY

The previous section examined the incidence of advanced innovation, technology, and skill-based competencies within the entrant population. These data, in turn, can also be used to classify industries on the basis of their technological prowess. With this in mind, the current section has several objectives. We first use the above data to derive competency-based indices for each dimension of technological prowess under study – one each for innovation, technology use, and human capital, respectively. These indices are then combined in order to construct our multidimensional measure of advanced competency. We then use these indices to explore differences in the identification of high-tech and low-tech industries. In doing so, we ask whether the innovation, technology, and human skill indices provide the same information – that is, do they rank industries identically? Our goal is to ascertain whether there is one simple classification that more or less captures the various aspects of technological prowess that many observers have associated with the new knowledge economy. Finally, we use each of these indices to investigate the incidence of high-tech firms in high-tech and low-tech industries.

4.1   Devising Firm-Based Indices

In order to examine how industries differ across the dimensions that our survey measures, the respondents' scores on each of the above characteristics were averaged for a set of 48 industries in order to produce three indices – one for innovation (INAV), one for skill-based competencies (LABAV), and one for technology (TEAV). The industries used for this analysis consist of combinations of standard three-digit classifications. The combinations chosen depend, in the first instance, on the availability of sufficient observations on respondents to yield meaningful estimates for the industry. Second, where possible, an industry segment was split into those industries where R&D is important and those where it is not.[7] A more extensive discussion can be found in Baldwin and Gellatly (1998).

The innovation index produces a score for each industry based on the responses of all firms within the industry. This score was calculated by taking the average of select core innovation variables (INGEN, INPROC, INPROD, INIMP1, INIMP2), variables that capture the importance of R&D (INRD, INIMP), as well as the percentage of firms introducing new products (INFREQ).[8]

The technology index was constructed in a similar fashion. Industry scores were calculated based on an average of the various technological competencies. The index included the core technology variables (INTECH1, INTECH2, TEDEV, TECOMP, TEINFO, TEINP) as well as the more inclusive measure (PROD1).

Finally, we devised a skill-related index based on our five measures of human capital development (LABSKL, LABSCOR, LABFOR, LABTRAIN, LABINT).

We found that each of the three indices – innovation (INAV), technology (TEAV), and skill (LABAV) – ranks industries more or less continuously from those with the lowest to those with the highest scores. Moreover, the three measures capture similar though not identical dimensions of advanced competencies. Table 1 reports the correlation coefficients for the various indices. The correlation between the industry scores on the innovation index and the skills index is .55, while it is .62 between the innovation and technology index for all industries. The correlation between skills and innovation is about the same in both the goods and services sectors, but the relationship between technology and innovation and between technology and skills is higher in the goods sector than in the services sector.

Table 1: Correlation of competency-based indices

	INNOVATION			SKILLS		
	Goods	Services	All	Goods	Services	All
SKILLS	.58	.60	.55			
TECHNOLOGY	.76	.47	.62	.66	.46	.57

4.2   Industry Differences Using the Competency Approach

In order to further assess the relation between indices and ultimately to compare the ranking given by our competency-based index to rankings produced by other indices, we created an overall index by averaging the individual innovation, skills, and technology indices. To investigate the extent to which the innovation, technology and skills indices yield comparable rankings, we ranked all industries by the overall index and plotted each of the individual components. This is done for goods industries in Figure 4 and for service industries in Figure 5. By construction, the index measures the percentage of firms that are advanced in an industry, where innovation, technology, and skill development are considered.

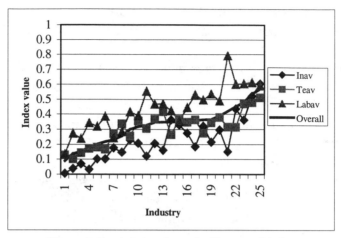

Figure 4: Goods industries ranked by overall index

For the goods sector, the skill and innovation indices (LABAV and INAV) track the overall index, at least in the sense that dividing the sample at the median on the basis of the overall index would also divide the sample into industries that generally have the highest and lowest values for the innovation and skills indices.[9] This does not occur for the technology index (TEAV). In the goods sector, there are a number of industries that are in the bottom half of the distribution when classified by the overall index, but that possess values for the technology index that are at least as high as many in the top half. This suggests that the technology index has several dimensions that are different from the innovation and human capital variables. New firms may consider themselves among the most technologically advanced without reporting that they are among the most innovative or that they place the heaviest emphasis on skilled workers. This highlights the need to utilize more than one dimension to measure the advanced competencies of industries.

In the services sector, the technology index (TEAV) tracks the overall index quite well, but the innovation index (INAV) does less well. Here, there are a number of industries that are classified in the top half of the distribution on the basis of the overall index, whose innovation value is not greatly different than for industries in the bottom half. There is also considerably more variability in the skills index (LABAV) in the services sector than in the goods sector.

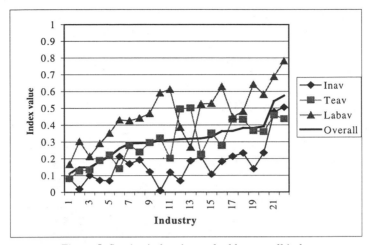

Figure 5: Service industries ranked by overall index

The differences in relationships between the goods and services sectors suggest that classification of industries into high- and low-tech using one dimension is more problematic in the latter than in the former.

4.3 The Location of High-Tech Firms

While taxonomies are often utilized for the purpose of classifying industries as high- as opposed to low-tech, low-tech industries should not be considered to be devoid of technically advanced firms, nor, for that matter, should high-tech sectors be viewed as consisting entirely of high-tech firms. To demonstrate this, we separated both the goods and services industries into high- and low-tech sectors based on each of our indices outlined in Sections 4.1 and 4.2. In the case of the innovation index, industries with scores above the median were classified as high-tech, whereas those with scores below the median were deemed low-tech. In this context, then, the high-tech sector represents those industries with a greater proportion of innovative firms, and the low-tech sector those industries with relatively fewer innovative firms. When the technology index is used, the high-tech sector represents those industries with a greater emphasis on advanced technology use, as measured by the proportion of firms that use these technologies, whereas the low-tech sector represents those industries with less emphasis on advanced technology use. In a similar vein, when the division of industries into high- and low-tech sectors is based on the skills index, the former comprises industries in which firms place a greater emphasis on human capital development, and the latter those industries where this emphasis is less pronounced. This separates industries into high-knowledge and low-knowledge sectors, respectively. Finally, the division of industries into high- and low-tech sectors based on the overall index separates industries in which firms place a relatively greater emphasis on all dimensions of technological prowess – innovation, advanced technology use, and human capital development – from those where this emphasis is less pronounced. Table 2 reports, for each of the above distinctions, the average score for the index value – the percentage of firms within the sector that excel in the competency being measured.

Table 2. Average index values for firms in high- and low-tech sectors (%)

	Innovation Index	Technology Index	Skill-Based Index	Overall Index
High-tech (goods)	31	39	56	41
Low-tech (goods)	9	21	32	23
High-tech (services)	25	39	58	40
Low-tech (services)	7	18	32	23

Herein, examples are illustrative. For service industries classified in the low-tech sector using the technology index, the average score is 18%. For the high-tech sector, the index value stands at 39%. That is, the low-tech services sector contains about half as many firms (18%) that excel in technological competencies as the high-tech services sector (39%). We find a comparable relation in terms of goods industries, with low- and high-tech scores of 21% and 39%, respectively. When the skills-based index is used, the percentage of high-knowledge firms in low-tech industries is more than half those in high-tech industries (i.e., 32% and 56% for goods, 32% and 58% for services, respectively). By contrast, when the innovation index is used, there are relatively fewer high-innovation firms in low-tech industries for both the goods and services sectors. In summary, industries that might be classified as low-tech on the basis of these indices are not devoid of firms with advanced competencies. Nor do industries that might be classified as high-tech comprise exclusively firms that exhibit these competencies. When the three indices are averaged to create an overall index, industries that are ranked in the low-tech sector contain at least half as many high-tech firms as industries that are ranked in the high-tech sector.

5.   A COMPARISON OF FIRM-BASED AND OTHER INDUSTRY-BASED CLASSIFICATION SCHEMES

In this section, we compare the rankings produced by the competency-based indices to several alternatives based on aggregate industry statistics. We generate the first alternative ourselves from aggregate characteristics designed to capture the "knowledge" components of industries. In the case of the goods sector, several variables were used to classify industries. First, the percentage of sales devoted to R&D was used to replicate the emphasis on R&D found in the OECD high-tech classification system. Second, the percentage of firms using advanced technologies was used to capture the technological bent of the industry. Third, we used a measure of an industry's tendency to be innovative as given by the Robson classification system. Fourth, we included the industry's average wage rate to capture its knowledge base. Fifth, we included the value of the industry's multifactor productivity measure since it captures the extent to which knowledge that is not embedded in labour or capital is important for productivity growth.

These variables were then combined into an index using principal components analysis. We then used the value of the first principal component to divide the industries into two groups. The top half were defined as being high-knowledge, the bottom half were deemed to be low-knowledge.

A similar procedure was employed for services industries, except here there are fewer meaningful variables that can be generated at the industry level. The variables used included GDP per hour worked, the proportion of workers with post-secondary education, and the average wage rate. Once again, the value of the first principal component was used to divide the industries into high- and low-knowledge groups.

This high/low-knowledge classification was then compared to our overall competency-based classification. To do so, the aggregate knowledge-based index was used to divide the universe of three-digit industries at the median. This classification was then applied to our sample giving us a number, n_1, of high-tech industries, and n_2, low-tech industries. We then chose the same number of high-tech industries and low-tech industries using our overall competency-based index to rank our sample from top to bottom. In both cases, a binary variable was created that assigned a value of 0 to a high-tech industry and a value of 1 to a low-tech industry.

We first compared the two classification schemes by correlating the 0/1 binary variable for each classification. Correlations between the two classification schemes are reported in Table 3. For goods and services industries combined, the correlation was only .07. The aggregate industry-based index has a higher correlation with the goods sector (.24) than with the services sector (-.08). Indeed the latter is negatively correlated with the entrant-based competency index. We also examined whether this pattern differed across the subcomponents of the overall index – the innovation, skill, technology indices – to see if any of these components might be more closely related to the aggregate knowledge-based index. None are. In conclusion, the aggregate knowledge-based index is not closely related to new-firm competencies in the areas of innovation, knowledge, or technology.

Table 3: Correlation between indices

	Aggregate Index
Survey Index	.07
Goods	.24
Services	-.08

In addition to correlation analysis, we compared the two classifications by asking how many industries are classified identically under the two schemes. For the goods sector, only 52% of industries are correctly classified. For the services sector, only 48% are correctly classified. Finally, we performed a chi-square test and concluded that the two classification schemes are independent of one another.

The above comparisons rely on an index of firm-based characteristics that is the simple sum of the innovation, knowledge, and technology subcomponents, a procedure that weights all variables equally. We also performed a principal components analysis on our competency variables to create a second entrant-based overall index, using the first principal component. When we compared the high/low-tech categorization of industries using this component to the aggregate knowledge-based categorization, the correlation was found to be no better than those reported above. Thus, the use of the key component derived from our firm-based measures does not change our conclusion that a rich and varied set of small-firm characteristics – as revealed by the firms themselves – shows a different pattern of industry rankings than those based on aggregate industry characteristics.

To further investigate the adequacy of aggregate indices, we compared the results using our firm-based index to the results derived from using an aggregate measure developed by Lee and Has (1996) that divides industries into "high-knowledge" and "low-knowledge" groups on the basis of three R&D measures – the R&D-to-sales ratios, the proportion of R&D personnel to total employment, and the proportion of professional R&D personnel to total employment – and three measures of human capital – the ratio of workers with post-secondary education to total employment, the ratio of knowledge workers[10] to total employment, and the ratio of the number of employed scientists and engineers[11] to total employment. Industries were then assigned to a high-knowledge category if they fell in the top third on the basis of two of the R&D indices *and* two of the human-capital indices.

In order to compare our firm-based classification scheme to the Lee and Has measure, we assigned each of our industries to one of three categories – high, medium, and low. To do so, we used the Lee and Has taxonomy to classify the industries included in our analysis. This yielded x high-tech, y medium-tech and z low-tech industries. We then ranked our sample by our index and chose the first x as high-tech, the second y as medium-tech and the remaining z as low-tech. Industries were assigned a value of 1, 2, or 3, depending on the category they fell in. The correlation between the two classifications was only .38. The correlation is .46 for goods industries but only .18 for services industries. Once again, it is apparent that the firm-based classification yields a different view of how to divide industries into those that are more and less advanced.

We then asked how our competency-based index compares to the OECD index for manufacturing industries. To facilitate this comparison, we ranked manufacturing industries based on the ratio of R&D to production (OECD, 1997) and divided them at the median into the highest and lowest groups. The correlation between our high/low breakdown and the high/low breakdown derived from OECD R&D ratios is only .57. Once more, it is apparent that the firm-based classification scheme yields a different high/low dichotomy.

These differences suggest that there are a number of industries where small-firm profiles differ quite substantially from large-firm profiles. These differences are particularly acute in the services sector. If we are going to search for new, small, high-tech firms, we had best not focus our search solely on small firms in what are commonly perceived to be high-tech industries.

6.   INNOVATION, SKILL INTENSITY, TECHNO-VATION: DO THEY HAVE SEPARATE DIMENSIONS?

In Section 5, we demonstrated that a multidimensional index based on the innovation, technology use, and labour skill characteristics of new small firms yields a different set of high-tech industries than those based on aggregate industry measures. Given that, in our view, the former is superior on conceptual grounds, is it reasonable to infer that the rankings based on this multidimensional index constitute the definitive basis for classification? At first blush, one may suspect that this is indeed the case; other schemes – like the one advocated by the OECD – implicitly consider there to be only one ranking scheme that is important. What follows, however, suggests that reliance on any single ranking may be ill-advised.

This section explores, in greater depth, the dimensionality of advanced competencies, and asks whether various combinations of advanced competencies will identify the same industries as high-tech leaders. In Section 4, we demonstrated that the various dimensions of advanced competencies – innovation, technology, and labour skill – do not necessarily yield identical industry rankings. Industries that fare well in one dimension (e.g., innovation) need not fare well in other dimensions (e.g., technology use). The various measures of innovation, labour skill, and technology were related, but imperfectly so. In this section, we explore the dimensionality of these differences, using principal components analysis. We include in the analysis the innovation, technology, and skill-based variables defined previously, as well as three new variables that capture the degree of innovation occurring in the industry. These are:

- OBSPROD – the degree to which products become obsolete in an entrant's industry.
- OBSPROC – the degree to which processes become obsolete in an entrant's industry.
- RTL – whether a firm reports investment spending on research and development, technology acquisition, and training.

The first two variables are derived from a question that asked firms to score, on a scale of 1 to 5, the extent to which the forces that create obsolescence were important in their industry. For this paper, we classify a firm as finding these obsolescence conditions to be important if it scores a 4 or 5 on the question. The third variable is included to capture the extent to which a firm emphasizes all three of the dimensions – research and development, technology and human resources – that are used here to capture the advanced competencies of firms.

Principal components analysis will be used to summarize the extent to which the competencies that we have measured are different from one another – or the extent to which we can discover the number of independent dimensions that they measure. After the components are calculated, an industry score is obtained by averaging the principal component scores of all firms in an industry.

Principal components analysis[12] on the innovation, technological competency, and skill measures produces eight important principal components.[13] The first (used previously in Section 5) accounts for 26% of the total variation in the sample, the second accounts for about 10%, and the eight together account for 75% of the variance. The eigenvectors are presented in Table 4. The components are described in Table 5.

Table 4: Eigenvectors from the principal components analysis

	PC1	PC2	PC3	PC4	PC5	PC6	PC7	PC8
INGEN	0.24	0.36	0.21	0.06	0.22	-0.12	-0.04	0.05
INIMP1	0.12	0.15	0.04	0.09	0.02	-0.05	-0.06	0.04
INIMP2	0.19	0.28	0.17	0.04	0.20	-0.02	-0.01	0.09
INTRAD	0.20	-0.07	-0.12	-0.00	-0.09	0.65	-0.24	0.32
INFREQ	0.17	-0.02	-0.07	0.21	0.21	0.52	-0.05	0.09
INIMP	0.04	0.05	0.01	0.00	0.08	0.05	0.06	0.08
INTECH1	0.27	0.07	-0.04	0.02	-0.40	-0.14	-0.09	0.07
INTECH2	0.22	0.09	-0.06	0.03	-0.43	-0.11	0.07	0.23
INRD	0.16	0.03	0.02	0.21	-0.08	0.06	-0.02	-0.02
OBSPROD	0.22	-0.43	0.52	-0.03	0.06	-0.08	-0.05	0.05
INPROD	0.20	0.27	0.11	0.13	0.19	-0.00	-0.06	0.09
INPROC	0.19	0.29	0.15	0.00	0.09	-0.13	-0.05	-0.03
INCOMP	0.14	0.19	0.05	0.06	0.07	-0.02	-0.06	0.01
TEINP	0.07	-0.01	0.01	-0.16	-0.15	0.03	0.35	0.29
TEDEV	0.21	0.09	-0.03	0.02	-0.42	-0.10	-0.03	0.18
TECOMP	0.19	-0.06	-0.07	0.25	-0.15	0.11	0.08	-0.36
OBSPROC	0.22	-0.47	0.43	-0.02	0.03	-0.07	-0.08	0.10
TEINFO	0.19	-0.09	0.01	0.38	0.02	0.09	0.75	-0.18
PROD1	0.22	-0.11	-0.13	0.23	-0.12	-0.06	-0.41	-0.54
LABTRAIN	0.27	0.08	0.01	-0.49	-0.03	0.11	0.08	-0.26
LABINT	0.17	0.03	-0.03	-0.46	-0.09	0.13	0.09	-0.22
LABSKL	0.23	-0.21	-0.43	0.04	0.28	-0.25	-0.08	0.22
LABFOR	0.29	0.03	-0.16	-0.34	0.25	0.06	0.11	-0.14
LABSCOR	0.25	-0.23	-0.42	0.01	0.21	-0.28	0.04	0.16
RTL	0.07	0.07	0.02	-0.02	0.03	0.03	0.04	-0.04

Table 5: A description of the principal components

Component	Positive Weights	Negative Weights
PC1	Weights on all of Innovation, Technology and Labour	
PC2	Innovation	Obsolescence, Emphasis on Recruiting and Training
PC3	Innovation and Obsolescence	Emphasis on Recruiting and Training
PC4	Introduces New Products, R&D, Computer Processes and Information Technologies	Training Activities
PC5	Innovation, Introduces New Products, Emphasizes Recruiting Skilled Labour and Performs Training	Both New Technology and Adaption of Technology, Technology Expenditures and Computer Processes
PC6	Traditional Innovation, and Frequent Introduction of New Products	Emphasizes Recruiting and Training Skilled Labour
PC7	High Technology Expenditures and Emphasizes Information Technology in Management	Focuses on Efficiency of Input Use and Traditional Innovation Mode
PC8	Traditional Innovation, Adopts Technology, and Recruits Skilled Labour	Focuses on Efficiency of Input Use, Use of Computer Processes and Trains Employees

The first component describes the general innovator – weighting as it does innovation (INGEN), important innovations (INIMP2), the two technology variables (INTECH1, INTECH2), and several training variables (LABFOR, LABSCOR, LABSKL). Other variables like research and development (INRD), computer technology (TECOMP), and uncertain industry conditions (OBSPROD, OBSPROC) also have relatively high positive weights.

The interpretation of the first principal component is relatively straightforward. Firms with a high score in this dimension will generally be doing more than one of these activities intensively. Since each of the original variables is a binary variable scaled from 0 to 1, a firm must be generally be engaged in the activities that receive the highest weights for it to receive a high score here.

The interpretation of the other components is less straightforward because each of the components has some variables with positive and others with negative weights. For example, the second component has relatively large positive weights on INGEN, INIMP2, INPROD, INPROC, and INCOMP. It has relatively large negative weights on OBSPROD, OBSPROC, LABSKL, and LABSCOR. Thus, this component captures firms that are innovators but that do not face much obsolescence and do not value recruiting skilled labour or training, or the reverse. It should be noted that a firm can receive a high absolute score on this component score either by emphasizing innovation and not training, or by emphasizing training and not innovation.

The third component positively weights innovation (INGEN) that is novel (INIMP2) and has a great deal of product and process obsolescence (OBSPROD, OBSPROC), but negatively weights recruiting and training (LABSKL, LABSCOR). This component then inversely weights important innovation and human resource strategies.

The fourth component has positive weights on frequently introducing new products (INFREQ), emphasizing R&D (INRD), computer-process technology (TECOMP), computers in management (TEINFO), and improving efficiency (PROD1). Negative weights are given to training activity variables (LABTRAIN, LABINT, LABFOR). This component inversely weights an emphasis on new products that is based on R&D expenditures and specific uses of computer technologies on the one hand and training activities on the other.

The fifth component positively weights innovation (INGEN), labour skills (LABSKL, LABSCOR), and training (LABFOR), but gives negative weights to technology variables involving the adoption of new technologies (INTECH1, INTECH2) and the use of computer processes (TECOMP). This component then is the innovator that emphasizes human capital but does not focus on technology.

The sixth component gives positive weights to traditional forms of innovation (INTRAD) and the frequent introduction of new products (INFREQ), but negative weights to recruiting (LABSKL) and training (LABSCOR). This represents the traditional innovator that does not emphasize human capital.

The seventh component gives a positive weight to high technology expenditures (TEINP) and the use of information technologies (TEINFO), but negative weights to traditional innovation (INTRAD) and production efficiencies (PROD1). This represents a technology firm that does not concern itself with the more traditional emphases that are found in small firms.

The eighth component positively weights traditional innovation (INTRAD), a high expenditure on technology acquisition (TEINP) and recruiting skilled labour (LABSKL), but negatively weights an emphasis on efficiency (PROD1), computer processes (TECOMP) and training (LABTRAIN, LABINT). This represents the more traditional innovator that also emphasizes technology, but does not worry so much about traditional efficiency considerations in the production process.

These components provide a rich and varied picture of the innovation archetypes that can be found in the population. Three of these components are characterized by an emphasis on the narrow definition of innovation. The first component involves a comprehensive approach combining innovations, new technologies, and training. Firms in components two and five also stress innovation. In two instances, there is an emphasis on labour training skills in conjunction with innovation (components one and five). In one instance, there is an emphasis on R&D spending and the introduction of frequent product changes (component four).

Two components (six and eight) both emphasize the traditional forms of quality and service competition. The latter combines this with a positive emphasis on training; the former with a negative emphasis.

It should also be noted that there is an inverse emphasis in a number of cases with the stress given to either innovation or human resources (components two, three, and six). In these cases firms are either heavily emphasizing human resources but not focusing on innovation, or doing the reverse.

Three important observations emerge from this.

First, the emphasis on innovation is quite diverse – ranging from the momentous to the more incremental. Some entrants report that they are introducing product and process innovations. Others do not innovate in the narrow momentous sense, but they do emphasize the fact that they continuously introduce new products and that they perform R&D. Still others focus on the traditional forms of competition that involve innovating with respect to quality, flexibility, and customization and also stress R&D or a skilled labour force.

Second, R&D is not restricted just to those reporting momentous innovations; it can also be found in those archetypes that emphasize a broader concept of innovation.

Third, an accent on labour skills is widespread. Four of the archetypes place a heavy emphasis on labour skills, some with an emphasis on frequently introducing new products, some with an emphasis on more momentous innovation.

Up to this point, we have discussed how the dimensions revealed by the principal components differ. Each dimension has been examined separately, because they are constructed to be independent of one another. It is natural, however, to ask whether the separate dimensions, when considered as a whole, reveal which industries are more advanced. This is difficult to answer. By construction, the dimensions that are defined by each principal component are orthogonal to one another. Thus, the scores that are assigned to each industry by the principal components are not related to one another for the entire industry set. This means that any attempt to sum the scores across the components to produce an overall ranking is inherently superfluous. It provides little overall additional information. For example, the ranking obtained using the first principal component is identical to the ranking obtained using the sum of the first component and the other components.[14]

This independence necessarily exists only for the entire set of observations. It is still possible that the top industries are the same for each of the archetypes. To investigate this matter, the industries were ranked by each of the components. Each component was used to choose the top six goods industries and the top six services industries. Choosing the top six in the first component is straightforward because all weights are positive. They are simply the industries with the six highest scores. However, for the other components, the pattern that is identified by the component is simply the inverse weighting of separate factors, which can occur with one receiving a large positive emphasis and the other no emphasis or the reverse. An industry can receive a large positive score on a particular component if its firms stress those strategies that have a positive weight in the component and they do not stress those with a negative weight, or it can receive a large negative score if its firms do not stress those with a positive weight and do stress those with a large negative weight. In each case, the industry fits the dimensions of the component since its stress on those variables that are positively and negatively weighted is negatively correlated. Because of this, we chose the industries with the three highest positive scores and the three largest negative scores for each component. Table 6 lists the goods industries that fall in the top six using each component; a "+" indicates that the industry is one of the top three with positive scores, a "–" indicates that it is in the top 3 with regard to negative scores. Table 7 does the same for the top six services industries. In each table, the right-most column contains the sum of the number of times an industry falls into the topmost category.

Almost every industry falls into the topmost group using one of the principal components considered here. Twenty-three of the 25 goods industries are classified in the top six by one of the dimensions and are represented in Table 6; 19 of the 23 services industries are in Table 7. This is indicative of the universality of at least one dimension of advanced competencies. Not only are there differences in the types of competencies that are used at the industry level, but at least one aspect of these competencies is found in almost every industry.

It is also true that some industries appear more frequently in the topmost group. The most advanced industries have some overlap in their membership across the archetypes represented by each component. In the goods sector, the science-based electrical industry occurs in the top group three times. Printing and publishing, primary metal, and refined petroleum and chemical products occur even more times, respectively. Similarly, in the services sector, several industries are repeatedly found to be at the top of the list. These include computer business services, farm services, recreation services, personal services and other services.

While a small number of industries are found at the top using several different dimensions, this should not be interpreted to mean that there is a common ranking across all industries produced by the different components. There is not a large amount of overlap in the industries chosen by the various components. Advanced competencies are combined in different ways and almost every industry is found to stress at least one of the combinations. Moreover, different combinations of advanced competencies will yield different sets of high-tech leaders.

Table 6: Ranking for goods industries using principal components

Industry	PC1	PC2	PC3	PC4	PC5	PC6	PC7	PC8	Sum
Science-Based Electrical	+	+		+					3
Electrical - Product Differentiated	+					+		+	3
Printing and Publishing	+	-	+		-		+	+	6
Food and Beverages				+					1
Plastic	+						-		2
Rubber							+		1
Refined Petroleum and Chemical Products	+		+		+		-		4
Crude Petroleum and Natural Gas			-			-	+		3
Farm Operations			+	+					2
Machinery					+	-		+	3
Clothing					+				1
Primary Metal	+		-	-		+		-	5
Primary Logging and Mining						-			1
Miscellaneous Non-Scientific						+			1
Fabricated Metal – Miscellaneous		+							1
Fabricated Metal - Product Difference		-			-				2
Furniture			-	-				-	3
Non-Metallic		+							1
Wood - Miscellaneous		-							1
Construction Developers							-		1
Scale-Based Wood			-						1
Motor Vehicles and Transportation					-				1
Construction - Heavy								-	1

Table 7: Ranking for services industries using principal components analysis

Industry	PC1	PC2	PC3	PC4	PC5	PC6	PC7	PC8	Sum
Business Services - Personnel Agencies and Advertising Agencies	+					+			2
Business Services - Architects, Engineers and Other Technical Services	+								1
Business Services - Computers and Related Services	+		+		+				3
Business Services - Other			+	-					2
Business Services - Accounting, Lawyers, and Management Consultants				-	-				2
Real Estate Agents		-					+		2
Farm Services			+	-	-		+	+	5
Services for Forestry, Petroleum, and Natural Gas			+					-	2
Services - Food and Beverages					+	+			2
Services - Accommodation		-	-						2
Services - Other		-					+	+	3
Services - Personal		+		+	-	-	-	-	6
Services - Amusement and Recreation	+	+	-					-	4
Retail - Food						-			1
Retail - Motor Vehicles	+	-							2
Retail - Other			+		+			+	3
Transportation and Storage							-		1
Wholesale - Electric, Machinery, Metal and Motor Vehicles				-			-		2
Construction Services		+						-	2

7. CONCLUSIONS

In this paper, we advanced a series of arguments, supported by statistical analysis, that question the extent to which current approaches to measuring the knowledge economy actually yield useful metrics for studying new technology-based firms. Our motivation for doing so is twofold: first, the debate surrounding the knowledge economy is, in its use of conceptual and operational measures, too often simplistic, and, in its use of descriptive terminology, too obviously emotive. Second, if seen as a basis for interventionist practices, the taxonomies that are often used to support this debate may lead policy-makers to direct resources inappropriately. In making these claims, our discussion has touched on several, often related, themes. For the benefit of readers, we summarize our major points below, placing particular emphasis on their relevance to policy issues.

7.1 What Does the Label "High-Tech" Actually Mean?

A new technology-based firm does not possess a single, uniform set of characteristics. A high-tech firm may focus on developing innovations, for example, by rapidly bringing new or improved products to market. Alternatively, a high-tech firm may stress the development of new technologies, or the integration of existing technologies into current production routines. Lastly, a high-tech firm may be one that invests heavily in improving worker skills. In certain cases, these three areas – innovation, technology use, and human-capital development – are highly complementary (as is often tacitly assumed); in other cases, however, innovation, technology use, and human-capital development represent disparate activities, undertaken in support of different objectives, and emphasized to varying degrees.

Our evidence supports this latter view. Many new technology-based firms in the goods sector see themselves as technologically advanced without necessarily reporting that they are highly innovative, or that they invest heavily in human capital. In the services sector, new technology-based firms that stress innovation are not necessarily those that emphasize the development of advanced technologies.

In our view, policies designed to encourage the growth of new technology-based firms should be mindful of these distinctions. Incentives to encourage more innovation, for example, should recognize that there may be concomitant gains supporting other areas related to technology use or labour skills. Prudent policy should be directed at all three objectives.

7.2 How Straightforward is the Identification of High-Tech Sectors?

Even if clear distinctions between objectives are made, policies to encourage the growth of the knowledge economy may be of little value if they target firms incorrectly. In our view, the danger of misclassification, based on current approaches, is substantial. There are two reasons for this.

First, many of the existing approaches to classification focus on conceptual and operational measures that are narrow and incomplete. An index based solely on R&D-intensity is one such example. R&D is an important input in the innovation process, but it is not the sole input. Even if such a measure is highly correlated with innovation – and is thus able to distinguish more from less innovative sectors – it may not succeed in separating industries into those that are more or less technologically advanced, or those that place more or less emphasis on human capital. Accordingly, then, policy objectives designed to encourage a certain characteristic (such as technology adoption) must be based on methodologies that allow for sensible distinctions between industries in accordance with this characteristic (i.e., that allow for the identification of more or less technologically intensive sectors).

In practice, the fact that classification often relies on industry aggregates complicates this process. Rankings based on industry aggregates (again, R&D-intensity is a useful example) are often driven by the characteristics of large firms, and may be misleading if large firm profiles differ systematically from those of smaller firms. And yet, it is small firms that are often more relevant to discussions of the knowledge economy. Following our earlier example, while an R&D-based index may identify one sector as more "innovative" than another, this may simply be due to the fact that large firms in the former invest more heavily in R&D. Small firms in the first industry may be no more innovative than in the second.

7.3   Are There Really High-Tech Sectors to Identify, or Only High-Tech Firms?

The above arguments assume that "sectors" constitute the appropriate unit of analysis, and hence, the appropriate unit for policy intervention. Sectors are, after all, simply collections of firms with similar product or process characteristics. However, firms classified to broad sectors are heterogeneous. The firms that comprise any sector often exhibit vastly different commitments to, and competencies in, key strategic areas – e.g., innovation, technology use, human resources, financing, management, marketing, and growth. Our research shows that, when viewed from a strategic or performance-orientated perspective, as opposed to one that emphasizes product or production characteristics, an industry is a collection of heterogeneous units, not homogeneous ones.

Is this relevant to the debate over new technology-based firms?   Yes, because policies that treat all firms within certain sectors as the same will miss large numbers of advanced firms in what are deemed to be "low-tech" sectors. This paper has argued that simply citing certain industries as being more advanced is acceptable neither on a priori nor on empirical grounds. Focusing only on "high-tech" sectors will miss those "high-tech" firms in the so-called "low-tech" sectors. Moreover, it will reward "low-tech" firms in "high-tech" sectors.

A substantial percentage of entrants (ranging from 65%-70%) demonstrate some commitment to at least one facet of technological prowess, either in terms of innovation, technology use, or human capital development. This suggests that the size of the knowledge economy is larger than conventional views, many of which focus disproportionately on certain highly visible sectors, would suggest. Accordingly, it is not surprising that so-called "low-tech" sectors contain substantial numbers of advanced firms (depending on one's metric for defining advanced). In a related vein, it is misleading to view high-tech industries as comprising exclusively advanced firms. Advanced firms in a "low-tech" sector are often more sophisticated, in one or more dimensions, than "average firms" in a "high-tech" sector. Policies that do not acknowledge these distinctions risk penalizing advanced firms in certain sectors, and rewarding average firms in others, simply on the basis of their industry of origin.

7.4   Is There a Case for Policy?

The evolution of new technologies has led to attempts to measure the extent to which different sectors are benefiting from the application of these technologies. Some of this interest stems from a simple wish to understand how technology diffuses across sectors, or to understand how the spread of new technology affects a country's comparative advantage and trading patterns.

Measuring the knowledge economy, however, is far from a trivial task. Much of the present analysis has drawn attention to what we regard as deficiencies in the debate over new technology-based firms – deficiencies that often arise out of inappropriate, or inadequate, measurement.

Our intent in making these claims is not to suggest that the case for supporting the development of advanced capabilities is a futile one. Rather, our intent is simply to draw attention to those facets of the debate over new technology-based firms that, in our view, too often go unnoticed or unstated.

We do not raise these issues in order to trumpet ours as the definitive approach to classification, or to argue that the taxonomies developed herein should be adopted for policy purposes. Prior to making such claims, we would want to subject our competency approach to other data sources, that is, to the discipline that comes from replication.

That said, we feel that our competency approach has two major advantages over previous efforts. First, it focuses squarely on the correct population – new, small firms, the very firms that are spearheading the new technological revolution in many industries. The firms that we identify as advanced in this study have one or more of the characteristics associated with new technology-based firms. They are innovative; they introduce new products and processes; they place great emphasis on technology; they invest in their workers. The second advantage of our competency approach rests with its recognition of this multidimensionality – by developing indicators of technological prowess that span a range of activities pertaining to innovation, the use of advanced technologies, and investments in human capital.

These advanced competencies are "combined" by firms in a large number of legitimate ways – indeed, as we argue in Section 6, while certain industries repeatedly score well based on different combinations of advanced competencies, almost all industries can be viewed as high-tech based on one or another of these legitimate combinations. There is more than one dimension to advanced knowledge. Product and process innovation tends to be done by different firms. An emphasis on advanced technology is pursued by a different group than that which focuses on R&D and product innovation. Some firms combine an emphasis on labour skills with R&D spending, others with technology. While prudent policy may choose to favour certain facets of technological prowess over others, it should not view the high- and low-tech distinctions between firms or industries as trivial or simplistic.

NOTES

[1] See OECD (1994, 1997).

[2] See OECD (1997, pp. 69 and 109).

[3] Schmookler (1959) raised this issue in a debate over whether, on the basis of official R&D statistics, it was correct to conclude that small firms were less innovative than large firms. He argued that informal R&D was more prevalent in small firms and that its incidence was not highly correlated with formal measures of R&D.

[4] Unless, of course, the two are so closely linked that one is a perfect proxy for the other.

[5] As pointed out in Section 2.1, this bias also arises from the use of the OECD-type R&D index.

[6] See Australian Bureau of Statistics (1989), Baldwin and Sabourin (1995), and U.S. Bureau of the Census (1989).

[7] See Baldwin and Rafiquzzaman (1994) for a discussion of this classification.

[8] In constructing the index, we tested the sensitivity of our industry rankings to the inclusion or exclusion of variables that capture broader concepts of innovation (INFREQ and INTRAD). As we found little difference between the various combinations, we arbitrarily chose to include INFREQ in the innovation index. For a more detailed discussion of the innovation and other indices, see Baldwin and Gellatly (1998).

[9] We focus on this criterion since a similar dichotomous division is used when others divide their sample into high-tech and low-tech sectors.

[10] Occupations in the natural sciences, engineering and mathematics, education, managers and administrators, social sciences, law and jurisprudence, medicine and health, and writing.

[11] Occupations in the natural sciences, engineering and mathematics.

[12] Because each of the variables has the same scaling, and for ease of interpretation, we have not standardized the variables when calculating the principal components.

[13] These components have eigenvalues that are greater than one.

[14] It would also be the same if you compared the ranking of the second and the second plus all others. Of course, the ranking of the first and second are different.

REFERENCES

Acs, Z.S. and D.B. Audretsch, *Innovation and Small Firms*. Cambridge, MA: MIT Press, 1990.

Australian Bureau of Statistics, *Manufacturing Technology Statistics*. Cat. No. 81230. Canberra, 1989.

Baldwin, J.R., *The Importance of Research and Development for Innovation in Small and Large Canadian Manufacturing Firms*. Research Paper No. 107. Analytical Studies Branch. Ottawa: Statistics Canada, 1997.

Baldwin, J.R., *A Portrait of Entry and Exit*. Research Paper No. 121. Analytical Studies Branch. Ottawa: Statistics Canada, forthcoming.

Baldwin, J.R. and M. Da Pont, *Innovation in Canadian Manufacturing Enterprises*. Catalogue No. 88-513. Ottawa: Statistics Canada, 1996.

Baldwin, J.R. and G. Gellatly, *Are There High-Tech Industries or Only High-Tech Firms? Evidence From New Technology-Based Firms*. Research Paper No. 120. Analytical Studies Branch. Ottawa: Statistics Canada, 1998.

Baldwin, J.R., T. Gray, and J. Johnson. "Advanced Technology Use and Training in Canadian Manufacturing." *Canadian Business Economics,* 4, 1997, 51-70.

Baldwin, J.R., P. Hanel and D. Sabourin. *The Determinants of Innovation in Canadian Manufacturing Industries*. Research Paper No. 122. Analytical Studies Branch. Ottawa: Statistics Canada, forthcoming.

Baldwin, J.R. and J. Johnson, "Human Capital Development and Innovation: A Sectoral Analysis," in P. Howitt (ed.) *The Implications of Knowledge-Based Growth for Micro-Economic Policies*. Calgary: University of Calgary Press, 1996.

Baldwin, J.R. and M. Rafiquzzaman, *Structural Change in the Canadian Manufacturing Sector (1970-90)*. Research Paper No. 61. Analytical Studies Branch. Ottawa: Statistics Canada, 1994.

Baldwin, J.R. and M. Rafiquzzaman, "The Effect of Technology and Trade on Wage Differentials Between Non-Production and Production Workers in Canadian Manufacturing," in D.B. Audretsch and R. Thurik (eds.) *Innovation, Industry Evolution and Employment*. Cambridge: Cambridge University Press, forthcoming.

Baldwin, J.R. and D. Sabourin, *Technology Adoption in Canadian Manufacturing Enterprises*. Catalogue No. 88-512. Ottawa: Statistics Canada, 1995.

Bartel, A.P. and F.R. Lichtenberg. "The Comparative Advantage of Educated Workers in Implementing New Technology." *Review of Economics and Statistics,* 69, 1987, 1-11.

Berman, E., J. Bound and Z. Griliches, "Changes in the Demand for Skilled Labour Within U.S. Manufacturing Industries." *Quarterly Journal of Economics,* 109, 1994, 367-398.

Bound, J. and G. Johnson, "Changes in the Structure of Wages in the 1980s: An Evaluation of Alternative Explanations." *American Economic Review,* 82, 1992, 371-392.

Doms, M., T. Dunne and K. Troske. "Workers, Wages and Technology." *Quarterly Journal of Economics,* 112, 1997, 253-290.

Kleinknecht, A., P.T. Poot and J.O.N. Reijnen. "Formal and Informal R&D and Firm Size: Survey Results from the Netherlands," in Z.J. Acs and D.B. Audretsch (eds.) *Innovation and Technological Change.* New York: Harvester/Wheatsheaf, 1991.

Kleinknecht, A.H., J.O.N. Reijnen and W. Smits, "Collecting Literature-Based Innovation Output Indicators. The Experience in the Netherlands," in A.H Kleinknecht and H.D. Bain (eds.) *New Concepts in Innovation Output Measurement.* London: Macmillan, 1993.

Lee, F.C. and H. Has, "A Quantitative Assessment of High-Knowledge Industries Versus Low-Knowledge Industries," in P. Howitt (ed.) *The Implications of Knowledge-Based Growth for Micro-Economic Policies.* Calgary: University of Calgary Press, 1996.

Mowery, D.C. and N. Rosenberg, *Technology and the Pursuit of Economic Growth.* Cambridge: Cambridge University Press, 1989.

Organization for Economic Cooperation and Development, *Science and Technology Policy. Review and Outlook.* Paris, 1994.

Organization for Economic Cooperation and Development, *Science, Technology and Industry. Scoreboard of Indicators.* Paris, 1997.

Robson, M., J. Townsend and K. Pavitt, "Sectoral Patterns of Production and Use of Innovations in the UK: 1945-83." *Research Policy,* 7(1), 1988, 1-14.

Scherer, F.M., "Interindustry Technology Flows in the United States." *Research Policy,* 11, 1982, 227-246.

Schmookler, J. "Bigness, Fewness and Research." *Journal of Political Economy,* 67, 1959, 628-632.

U.S. Bureau of the Census. *Manufacturing Technology: 1988.* SMT(88)-1. Washington, DC, 1989.

8. THE COST OF CAPITAL FOR KNOWLEDGE-BASED ENTERPRISES IN CANADA

Cécile Carpentier
Université Laval

Jean-François L'Her
École des Hautes Études Commerciales and CIRANO

Jean-Marc Suret
Université Laval and CIRANO

1. INTRODUCTION

Financing of knowledge-based enterprises (KBEs) most commonly involves equity financing. The concept of capital cost is thus a key factor in the financing of KBEs. Capital cost, which is also the rate of return required by investors to commit funds to a project, directly influences the value placed on shares, and consequently the extent of control that the promoter must surrender. It is also clear that capital is a vital resource for technology firms. High financing costs will lessen the competitiveness of these firms and their ability to undertake new projects (Pecaut, 1993). Further, in the context of economic policy, the notion of capital cost[1] is vital because of its link to business competitiveness (Baldwin, 1986). In a 1992 report, the Canada Consulting Group (CCG) argues that the cost of capital in Canada is abnormally high, and concludes, "We have a high cost of capital . . . many of our companies can no longer carry that burden because it does not allow them to grow, diversify and invest to stay competitive. The only option for these firms, should they continue to bear this yoke of high capital cost, is to shrink, limit their product and market development, and disinvest. This problem experienced at the individual company level translates into disaster for the economy as a whole" (p. I-3). According to CCG, the problem is far more serious among knowledge-based firms, which require major research and development (R&D) investments, and hence more capital. However, calculation of the cost of capital must take into account various tax provisions, notably depreciation and R&D credits. The CCG report shows that the cost of capital remains higher for knowledge-based enterprises in Canada than for their competitors in other countries, even when we take into account relatively favourable R&D tax provisions in Canada.

It is therefore essential to measure correctly the cost of capital for knowledge-based firms, but this task proves difficult. Even for traditional firms listed on the stock exchange, assessing capital cost remains problematic and fraught with error. The situation of knowledge-based firms is even more difficult to analyze, and it becomes extremely difficult to assess the capital cost of privately held firms, to which the usual methods based on the study of market data cannot be applied. There are few recent studies on the cost of capital for Canadian firms and, to our knowledge, none focusing on KBEs. Accordingly, the aim of this study is to measure the cost of capital for such firms in Canada, using the latest estimating methods. The study contains three sections: the first presents the different methods of estimating capital cost; the second examines the cost of capital for Canadian knowledge-based enterprises; finally, the third draws conclusions and notes future directions for research in this field.

2.   ESTIMATING THE COST OF CAPITAL

2.1   Methods

The cost of capital – a major consideration in investment decisions – is a key factor determining the level of economic activity and competitiveness of a firm. It has been widely argued in the United States that Japan's economic performance is partly due to lower capital costs, giving that country's firms a significant (and unfair) competitive advantage. For example, Regan (1990) suggests that "With the Japanese prime rate at half the level of the U.S. rate, and with stock price/earnings ratios at five times the level of ours, the Japanese cost of capital is the lowest in the world." The advantage thereby conferred on Japan is related to the country's strong exporting capacity (Poterba, 1991). This argument has provided the basis for many studies (Frankel, 1991; McCauley and Zimmer, 1989; Ando and Auerbach, 1988, 1990), which generally conclude that Japanese firms have a real advantage in this respect. The same argument has been used in Canada, which is considered to be at a disadvantage compared with other industrialized countries (Canada Consulting Group, 1992; Pecaut, 1993), although a Finance Canada report (1991) and a study by Ando, Handock and Sawchuk (1997) qualify these assertions to a considerable extent. According to Caldwell, Sawchuk and Wilson (1994), capital costs are significantly higher for small than for big firms in Canada, with the difference amounting to 400 basis points for the cost of equity capital. These studies measure the average weighted cost of various sources of financing and then estimate three main variables: the cost of debt, the cost of equity capital and the debt/service ratio. The calculations are performed at the aggregate level, making it possible to estimate the average national cost of capital, something that raises major methodological problems. In particular, the differences noted may have as much to do with the industrial structure as with a country effect; in addition, one of the main components of capital cost, the cost of equity capital, cannot be precisely determined at the national level and is still harder to compare from country to country.

Studies of capital cost differ primarily in their methods of estimating the cost of equity capital. These methods fall into three categories, each with significant deficiencies. The methods all derive from the same principle: equity financing is basically internal rather than external. To a very large extent, firms use self-financing and only rarely resort to issuing shares. Equity financing covers neither the costs of issuing shares nor taxes, with the result that a firm's equity capital cost equals the rate of return set by the market for investing in its shares. As there are generally several investments with comparable risk levels, the cost of equity capital is also the yield of stock A that must be forgone to invest in stock B, involving the same risk.[2] In the first category are methods that seek to measure total before-tax stock yields over a holding period long enough that the rate of return achieved is close to that required. Using that method, Ando and Auerbach (1988) estimate the rate of return at 12.3% in the United States, compared with 6.5% in Japan, for the period 1967–1983. Errunza and Miller (1998) use this method to highlight the effect of a liberalization of emerging markets on the capital cost of firms. This category also includes methods that seek to evaluate the risk premium, that is, the historical gap between the rate of return on stocks and on Treasury bills. Some authors, notably Caldwell et al. (1994), measure the accounting rate of return on equity capital (the return on equity, or ROE). These *ex post* methods capture the entire return achieved by shareholders but produce estimates that are skewed in the short term (McCauley and Zimmer, 1989).[3] Estimates obtained by these methods are highly sensitive to the period chosen and to the firm's financing structure, especially when accounting rates of return are used. Finally, these tools are of limited use when the evaluation period is relatively short.

The sensitivity of *ex post* measurements to the chosen period explains why most studies use estimation methods of the second category, based on inverse price/earnings ratios (PER) or on dividend ratios plus the expected growth rate. The ratios are aggregated for each country, after correcting earnings to account for differences in accounting methods and changes in certain macro-economic variables. Price/earnings ratios are directly dependent on the underlying accounting principles, on macro-economic conditions and on the interaction of these conditions with accounting practices. For example, the impact of inflation on earnings varies depending on the methods of depreciation or inventory recording.[4] These methods are also difficult to defend in the case of technology firms, many of which do not pay dividends or even make a profit. Using such methods makes it necessary to estimate the future rate of growth of earnings or dividends. At the aggregate level, researchers use economic growth forecasts while company studies make use of forecasts of earnings growth (Harris and Marston, 1992).

In the third category are methods used infrequently in international comparisons. These tools derive from the capital asset pricing model (CAPM) or variants of it that add to systematic risk other risk factors, such as size or financial distress. Most works on finance seek to estimate firms' equity capital using the *beta* coefficient, a measure of the systematic risk of a security compared with the overall market. The cost of equity capital is thus assessed using the CAPM.[5] However, while this method has the advantage of simplicity and a rigorous conceptual basis, its value is severely questioned because the model itself is subject to criticism, and also because applying the

CAPM to small firms and technology firms is difficult and risky. A CAPM-based model that draws from empirical observations rather than a theoretical construction seems to be gradually emerging as an alternative tool for calculating the cost of equity capital. It is the three-factor pricing model (TFPM) proposed by Fama and French (1997). The expected rate of return of a stock would depend on the sensitivity of the stock's yield to three factors: market yield; a size premium; and a premium linked to the ratio of book-to-market value of equity (BE/ME) of shares, associated by several authors with the risk of financial distress (Fama and French 1992). This model emerges from many empirical studies that have highlighted the (abnormally) higher rate of return of small firms and of firms with a high BE/ME ratio (Fama and French, 1992). The present study is based mainly on methods falling in the third category, but we also show historical rates of return.

2.2   Estimating the Cost of Equity Capital: CAPM and TFPM

2.2.1   Cost of Equity Capital: CAPM and TFPM

In the CAPM equation, the cost of equity capital for security i equals the sum of the risk-free rate and a market premium adjusted by the *beta* coefficient, which measures the systematic risk of a security (in other words, the risk that cannot be eliminated by diversification):

$$E(R_i) = R_f + \beta_i[E(R_m) - R_f] \tag{1}$$

where,

R_f = the expected rate of return of risk-free assets (Treasury bills);

β_i = the *beta* coefficient or systematic risk of company i;

$E(R_m)-R_f$ = the market premium or the difference between the expected market yield and that of the risk-free assets. It represents the extra return required by investors for investing in shares rather than in risk-free securities.

The CAPM model has been called into question in many empirical studies (Fama and French, 1992, 1993) showing that certain features of firms, notably size and the BE/ME stock ratio, systematically influence yields. The controversy over the validity of the CAPM has not ended, but the TFPM is becoming the preferred tool for measuring the cost of a firm's equity capital (Fama and French, 1993, 1995; Annin, 1997).

In the TFPM, the return on a security is determined by its sensitivity to three factors: market yield, size and the ratio of book equity to market equity. The hoped-for excess yield of firm i is thus expressed by the following equation:

$$E(R_i) - R_f = b_i[E(R_m) - R_f] + s_i E(SMB) + h_i E(HML) \qquad (2)$$

where,

$E(R_m)–R_f$ = market premium

SMB = small minus big (variable relative to ME size) or size premium;

HML   = high minus low (variable relative to BE/ME ratio) or premium for financial distress;

b_i, s_i and h_i = level of risk associated, respectively, with the market premium, the size premium and the premium for financial distress.

The average difference between the market rate of return measured by the TSE 300 and the rate of return of risk-free securities represents the price of risk. Similarly, *SMB* and *HML* represent the gain or the price of risk (small minus big) represents the difference in yield between a portfolio of firms with low capitalization (*S*, for small) and a portfolio of firms with high market capitalization (*B*, for big). The TFPM predicts a positive difference, or yield premium, for firms with low capitalization. The variable *HML* (high minus low) corresponds to the difference in yield between a portfolio of firms with a high BE/ME ratio and a portfolio of firms with a low BE/ME ratio. The TFPM predicts a positive difference, or yield premium, for firms with high BE/ME ratios. Chan and Chen (1991) associate the BE/ME ratio with an indicator of financial distress. Lakonishok, Shleifer and Vishny (1994) and Fama and French (1995) show that firms with a high BE/ME ratio (i.e., a high book value relative to the market value) generally have low earnings (financial distress), but offer above-market average future yields; these are value stocks. In contrast, a low BE/ME ratio (high market value compared with book value) is typical of firms with high earnings but lower future yields (growth or glamour stocks).

Coefficients b_i, s_i and h_i represent, respectively, the amount of risk associated with the risk factors related to market, firm size and the BE/ME ratio. The interpretation of the b_i coefficient is identical to that of the systematic risk in the CAPM model; it is the elasticity coefficient of a security's yield compared with the market yield. The s_i and h_i coefficients have virtually the same interpretation except that they are standardized not to 1 but to 0. The level of risk associated with risk factors pertaining to firm size and the BE/ME ratio equals 0 in the case of firms whose capitalization is equal to the average market size and to the average BE/ME ratio. It is negative (positive) if the firm has a market capitalization higher (lower) than the average market size and the average market BE/ME ratio. Lakonishok et al. (1994) and Haugen (1995) maintain that the average yield premium relative to value stocks can be explained by the fact that the market undervalues the securities of firms in financial difficulty. In contrast, the markets overvalue firms with a good track record, i.e., glamour stocks. Once estimation errors are corrected, value stocks yield higher average returns.

2.2.2   Estimating the Cost of Equity Capital by CAPM and TFPM

CAPM

To measure the cost of equity capital, it is thus necessary to estimate the systematic risk of the shares (b_i), and the market premium ($(E(R_m)–R_f)$). To do so, we regress the excess yield of stock i ($R_i–R_f$) on the excess market yield ($R_m–R_f$) and we estimate the systematic risk by the slope of the regression, or the sensitivity of stock yields to market yields.[6] The regression may be undertaken for a shorter or longer period (Fama and French, 1997), but 60 months is customary. Risk-free assets' yields are determined by measuring yields on Treasury bills, while market yields are determined by measuring yields of the market portfolio, in this case the TSE 300. The model used is expressed as follows:

$$R_{it} - R_{ft} = a_i + b_i (R_{mt} - R_{ft}) + e_{it} \quad t = -60\, to -1 \tag{3}$$

Once coefficient $\hat{b}_i$ is estimated for an earlier period [–60, –1], the cost of equity capital for stock i at time 0 is assessed as follows:

$$E(R_{i0}) = R_{f0} + \hat{b}_i \overline{(R_m - R_f)} \tag{4}$$

where the market premium is assessed on the basis of the historical difference in yield between the TSE 300 and the risk-free assets.

TFPM

In the case of the three-factor model, the methodology is more or less the same. One first measures the amount of risk (b_i, s_i and h_i) associated with the three factors, and then multiplies them by the corresponding risk premiums, or the yield differences (1) between the market yield and the yield on risk-free assets, (2) between securities with low and high market capitalization, and (3) between securities with high and low BE/ME ratios. The last two premiums are more complex to estimate and, in the following paragraphs, we attempt to clarify the procedure.

A firm's size (measured by its market capitalization) and the BE/ME ratio are considered to be CAPM abnormalities, for the following reason: if portfolios are built on the basis of these variables, the future yields of the portfolios differ, even if we take into account their systematic risk. However, accounting data are not available immediately at the end of the fiscal year. It is often necessary to wait several months before the information is published. The calculations given here take this time lag into account: the yield calculation for a given year starts only four months after the end of the preceding fiscal year. On that date and for each fiscal year,[7] stocks traded on the Toronto Stock Exchange are classified according to their market capitalization and divided into two groups, separated by the median value; in this way, a distinction is made between small firms (S) and big firms (B). The sample is sorted a second time according to the BE/ME ratio, independently of the first sorting by size. Three groups are thereby formed using the proportions of 30%, 40% and 30%, respectively for low (L), medium (M) and high (H) ratio groups. The BE/ME ratio is obtained from the database, and corresponds to the fiscal year-end. Firms with negative shareholders' equity are removed from the sample. After sorting, the 12 monthly yields are calculated for each of six stock portfolios (SL, SM, SH, BL, BM and BH). For the fiscal year ending in December of year t, yields are calculated from May of the year $t+1$ to April of the year $t+2$. Portfolio yields are equi-weighted. The value SMB is calculated by finding the difference between the average yield of the three portfolios made up of small firms (SL, SM and SH) and the average yield of the three portfolios made up of big firms (BL, BM and BH). The value of the HML premium equals the difference between the average yield of the two portfolios made up of firms with high BE/ME ratios (SH and BH) and the average yield of the two portfolios made up of firms with low BE/ME ratios (SL and BL).

Once these series ((R_m–R_f), SMB and HML) of monthly yields have been calculated, it is possible, as with the CAPM, to estimate the amount of risk associated with these premiums. To do so, the same method is used as for CAPM, regressing excess yields of stock i (R_i–R_f) on excess market yields

(R_m–R_f), as well as *SMB* premium (size effect) and *HML* premium (effect of the BE/ME ratio). The following regression equation is used:

$$R_{it} - R_{ft} = a_i + b_i(R_{mt} - R_{ft}) + s_i SMB_t + h_i HML_t + e_{it} ; t = -60 \ to -1$$

(5)

Once the three coefficients $\hat{b}_i$, $\hat{s}_i$ *and* $\hat{h}_i$ have been estimated, the cost of equity capital is assessed by multiplying the coefficients by the yearly historical risk premiums of the three factors:

$$E(R_{i0}) = R_{f0} + \hat{b}_i(\overline{R_m - R_f}) + \hat{s}_i \overline{SMB} + \hat{h}_i \overline{HML}$$

(6)

While this method eliminates several abnormalities observed when the CAPM is used, the cost of capital calculated remains an approximation: the different parameters involved are subject to estimation errors and, overall, Fama and French (1997) consider that this error for the industry cost of capital is on the order of 5%. Nevertheless, this is the most refined of all methods that have been proposed.

2.2.3   Estimating R_m–R_f, *SMB* and *HML* Risk Premiums

The data used to calculate the R_m–R_f, *SMB* and *HML* premiums cover the period 1966 to 1996. The stock yields and market equity (ME) of Canadian firms come from the Ruban Laval database (for the period 1966–1984, 1992 version) and the TSE Western database (for the period 1984–1996). The book equity (BE) figures come from the *Financial Post* database (for the period 1966–1992, 1994 version) and from Compustat (for the period 1992–1996, 1997 version).[8]

Over the entire period, the monthly market premium is 0.601% with a standard deviation of 4.75% (Table 1). This premium is significantly different from 0 ($t = 2.45$) and it is higher than that estimated for the United States by Fama and French (1997),[9] but it is very close to historical values reported for the United States by Kaplan and Ruback (1995), who assess the premium at 7.68% annually.

Over the same 30-year period, the average monthly yield linked to size of Canadian firms (*SMB*) is 0.676%, or 8.11% annually. The premium is of the same order of magnitude as the market premium, but the standard deviation (2.46%) is almost one-half that of the market premium. Thus, we must reject the hypothesis that the premium is of null value ($t = 5.32$).

The *HML* premium is substantially similar in size to the two previous premiums, with a monthly yield of 0.616% and an annual yield of 7.39%. This annual premium is 60 basis points lower than the size premium, but we must still reject the null hypothesis ($t = 4.00$), even though the standard deviation is higher than that for *SMB* (2.97% compared with 2.46%). Table 1 lists these findings and offers a comparison of these premiums with those obtained by Fama and French for the United States for a slightly shorter period with the same method. In general, premiums are seen to be higher in Canada than in the United States.

The findings in this first part of the study are significant for estimating the cost of capital of KBEs. They suggest that in Canada, size and *HML* premiums (which must be taken into account in estimating the cost of capital) are still higher than in the United States. It is thus impossible to calculate and compare KBEs' cost of capital without taking into consideration their size and BE/ME ratio.

Table 1: Estimation of premiums influencing the cost of capital in Canada and comparison with comparable U.S. data on the basis of average monthly yields, standard deviations and mean tests for the three factors R_m-R_f, *SMB* and *HML*, over the period 1966–1996

Results from Canadian data, 1966-1996

1966–1996	Market premium (R_m-R_f)	Size premium (*SMB*)	Premium associated with book-to-market ratio (*HML*)
Monthly average	0.601%	0.676%	0.616%
Standard deviation	4.75%	2.46%	2.97%
t value	2.45	5.32	4.00
Average annual premium	7.21%	8.11%	7.39%

Results from U.S. data obtained by Fama and French (1997), 1966-1993

	Market premium (R_m-R_f)	Size premium (*SMB*)	Premium associated with book-to-market ratio (*HML*)
Average	0.43%	0.27%	0.45%
Standard deviation	4.39%	2.86%	2.56%
t value	1.87	1.80	3.46
Average annual premium	5.16%	3.34%	5.40%

3.   THE COST OF CAPITAL OF KNOWLEDGE-BASED ENTERPRISES

Section 1 shows how equity capital is calculated for Canadian firms using the latest models, but without taking into consideration intensity of research and development efforts. In the second part of the study, we seek to answer the following question: do publicly listed Canadian KBEs face higher capital costs than traditional firms?

3.1   Cost of Equity Capital for Knowledge-Based Firms

Calculating the cost of equity capital for knowledge-based enterprises (KBEs) raises a double problem which can be resolved only by using an appropriate model. First, KBEs are, on average, smaller in size than firms in the traditional economy. Any comparison between the two groups must therefore take into account the size effect: unless provision is made for this effect, it could be wrongly concluded that R&D influences yields where in fact only the size effect is involved. Second, R&D expenditures can simultaneously influence the book value and the market value of stocks, the BE/ME ratio, which seems to be significantly linked to yields and thus to the cost of capital. The book value of stocks is lower when a firm invests in R&D instead of making traditional investments, since only development expenditures can, in certain circumstances, be capitalized.[10] Further, R&D expenditures are likely to create future growth opportunities that should stimulate share prices (Coleman, 1997a, b). It may also be that the effect of the BE/ME ratio on yields, which has not been explained in a convincing manner, is linked to this double impact of R&D activities.

To determine the extent to which Canadian technology firms do or do not face abnormally high capital costs, the following steps are thus required: (1) calculation of premiums under the three-factor model, which provides a formula for calculating the cost of capital for all firms (this was performed in the first part of this study); (2) breakdown of Canadian firms in terms of intensity of R&D effort, which will be used as an indicator of the level of knowledge; and finally (3) calculation of the rate of return required on equity capital (adjusted for the three factors of the TFPM) for each group of firms. In addition, we shall undertake two types of calculations corresponding to the two categories of methods for estimating the cost of capital: comparison of the historical rates of return of technology firms and traditional firms, and analysis of the cost-benefit (C/B) ratio for the group of technology firms in the start-up stage.

3.2 Measuring R&D Intensity

Measurement of R&D intensity is based on an in-depth analysis of the Evert specialized business data[11] as well as accounting databases,[12] particularly the Stock Guide.[13]

First, from Evert we obtained information on 179 firms listed from 1990 to 1997. The information was then systematically compared and rounded out using the Stock Guide database, by applying the following rules:

Data for the years 1990 and 1991 were omitted because of the high proportion of missing data.

A systematic search was undertaken for firms likely to have R&D activities, first by using the sectoral classification proposed by Lee and Has (1996), and then by keyword search of the on-line descriptions of corporate activities. Firms for which R&D data appeared in the Stock Guide database, but not in Evert, were added to the sample. When the databases showed differing R&D information for a particular company, priority was given to Evert data since Evert undertakes adjustments and checks data on R&D expenditures.

Firms for which information on R&D expenditures was not available for at least two of the seven years were eliminated. Some firms found in the Evert database did not have R&D expenditures within the period of study; they too were eliminated.

Firms in the Stock Guide database for which R&D information was given, but which were not covered by Evert, were added except in the following sectors:[14] gold and precious minerals; integrated mines; integrated oils; mining; mining exploration; oil and gas producers; and oil, mining, gas and forest.

Sales data were added from the Compustat database. The ratio of R&D expenditures to sales was calculated, and all instances of significant variation were examined. In several cases, the variations resulted from transfers or acquisitions of firms or divisions, substantially changing sales. Extreme data were also analyzed: some ratios exceeded 100% (in the case of firms at the R&D stage that as yet were generating no or very low sales).

The analysis of the data allowed us to identify a group of 187 firms reporting R&D activities. Next, we added to the data the returns in the TSE

Western database, which covers 647 firms actively doing business between 1975 and 1997; some 20 observations were thus lost because of a discrepancy in the time of update of the two databases. The G1 group of firms engaged in R&D for which market yields are available thus comprises 167 firms. They are divided into three sub-groups, based on the intensity of their R&D activities, by means of two criteria: the average ratio of R&D to sales[15] and the average annual amount of R&D.[16] The classification is thus the result of a cluster analysis, with a close examination of extreme data:

Group G11 consists of firms at the R&D stage (reporting virtually no sales and with revenues coming mainly from R&D credits) or at the take-off stage, for which the ratio of R&D to sales was decreasing very rapidly; an example is Cangene Corp., whose ratio went from over 100% to nearly 29% within a few years. Firms in this group spent over 25% of their total revenues for the period on R&D or still showed an R&D ratio exceeding 50% in one year. The 28 firms in this group are the subject of a more in-depth analysis in Section 2.5.

Group G12 includes moderately R&D-intensive firms, that is, firms that had moved beyond the stage of start-up or take-off, spending under $5 million per year on R&D or (if they exceeded this amount) having a ratio of R&D to sales lower than 0.005%. There are 85 firms in this group.

Group G13 includes R&D-intensive firms that spent over $5 million per year on R&D, and that had an R&D-to-sales ratio exceeding 0.005%. There are 55 firms in this group.

To complement the sample, we also identified a control sample, Group G2, which included 244 firms for which it can reasonably be said that they did not conduct R&D activities. These firms did not present R&D data in their financial statements, did not mention such activities in the detailed description of their operations (Stock Guide corporate profile), and were not listed by Evert as conducting such activities. Table 2 shows the annual breakdown of the number of firms in each group.

Table 2: Number of yearly observations in the sample of firms engaged in R&D and in the control sample

Year	Firms engaged in R&D				Firms not engaged in R&D
	G11 Firms taking off	G12 Moderately R&D-intensive	G13 Heavily R&D-intensive	G1 Total	G2 Control sample
1992	14	53	42	109	199
1993	21	66	46	133	226
1994	25	78	52	155	240
1995	26	81	54	161	242
1996	28	85	54	167	243
1997	28	85	53	166	244

Among the firms listed in the various databases, 234 were excluded because of their particular features or because it was impossible to reliably determine how they should be classified.[17] Note that firms were classified on the basis of recent data, while the analysis of yields covers a longer period. The study is thus based on the hypothesis that the relative position of firms on the scale of R&D intensity is fairly stable. An examination of yields over shorter periods does not, however, change the conclusions of the study, and findings by sub-period have not been reported.

3.3   Analysis of Historical Yields

Calculating the historical yield of firms or portfolios is the simplest way to assess their cost of capital, on the hypothesis that the expected rate of return is, on average, equal to the rate of return achieved. For each of the groups considered, yields were calculated for the period January 1975 to July 1997.[18] Table 3 shows the rate of return of various equi-weighted portfolios formed on the basis of intensity of R&D activity. The average yield of firms used in this study (including the excluded firms making up Groups 3 and 4[19]) was 16.99% per year, which is higher than the yield of the TSE 300 Index for the same period (13.46%).[20] The two groups studied, G1 (firms with high R&D levels) and G2 (firms not engaging in R&D), had yields higher than the overall yield of all the firms studied. R&D firms had an average monthly yield of 1.45%, while firms not engaging in R&D had an average monthly yield of 1.58%, with lower volatility. Annualized yields were 17.42% for the R&D group and 18.98% for the non-R&D group. From the viewpoint of investors, such a finding indicates that during this period it was preferable to invest in firms not engaging in R&D activities. From the viewpoint of firms, the finding shows that financing via share capital is less costly for a knowledge-based firm than for a traditional firm. This finding may seem counter-intuitive. Some authors explain it by the fact that investors attach great, not entirely logical, value to R&D activity and to technology firms, and are ready to pay high prices to own shares of technology firms. The result of this fad is a relatively lower financing cost for KBEs. However, KBEs vary greatly, as shown in Table 3.

Table 3: Main distribution characteristics of historical (equi-weighted) rates of return of portfolios based on the intensity of R&D activity in Canada, 1975–1997

	Overall observations	Groups formed based on the relative intensity of R&D activity				
		G1	G2	G11	G12	G13
Monthly yields						
Average	1.42%	1.45%	1.58%	−0.20%	1.46%	1.51%
Standard deviation	5.03%	4.79%	4.50%	9.58%	5.25%	4.72%
t value	4.62	4.98	5.77	−0.35	4.58	5.27
Annualized yields						
Annual average	16.99%	17.42%	18.98%	−2.43%	17.55%	18.16%
Minimum	−26%	−25%	−23%	−29%	−27%	−24%
Maximum	16%	15%	25%	33%	17%	14%

G1: Firms reporting R&D expenditures
G2: Firms reporting no R&D expenditures
G11: Technology firms in start-up phase, for which R&D credits represented a significant proportion of revenues
G12: Firms with low R&D intensity, on the basis of two criteria: total amount of R&D, and relative amount of R&D (R&D-to-sales ratio)
G13: R&D-intensive firms.

Firms classified as being in the "start-up phase" (G11) were listed on the stock exchange but their activities did not yet generate significant sales during most of the period studied. Their stock yield was negative (−2.43% per year), "actually, statistically not different from zero," whereas the sample as a whole had a yield of close to 17%. The existence of this group raises important financing questions: investors seem to be ready to pay high prices for shares of technology firms that have recently entered the market, even though the prospects of earning a profit are relatively low and longer-term. A more in-depth analysis of firms making up this sub-sample was therefore performed and is presented in Section 3.5.

The intensity of R&D efforts, as we measure it, did not seem to significantly influence the yield (and hence the cost of capital) of firms in the sample. Firms with high R&D intensity had an annualize yield of 18.16%, compared with 17.55% for firms with low R&D intensity. On the basis of monthly yields and their dispersion, we cannot conclude that there is a significant difference between the two groups of firms.

But there are various shortcomings in the analysis of historical yields to estimate the cost of capital. In particular, we did not take into account firm characteristics other than R&D intensity, which may be done using the three-factor pricing model.

3.4   Analysis of the Cost of Capital Using the Three-Factor Pricing Model

The cost of equity capital (k_E) was estimated using the CAPM and the TFPM, for each of the groups formed on the basis of R&D intensity. In each case, we have also presented various performance measures to assess whether a portfolio's yield can or cannot be described as abnormally high or low.[21] These findings are given in Table 4.

CAPM
In the CAPM, only one risk factor is taken into account: the market. The systematic (*beta*) risks of groups G1 and G2 are practically the same: 0.86 for G1 and 0.80 for G2. With an average annual risk-free rate of 9.37% and a market premium of 7.28% during the entire period studied, the estimated cost of equity capital is on the order of 15% to 16% for the two groups. The systematic risk is thus practically insensitive to the intensity of R&D activity. It is, however, noteworthy that while the cost of equity capital is approximately the same, the abnormal yield measure, i.e., Jensen's *alpha* coefficient or intercept, is significant only for Group G2 (*alpha* = 0.26% and t (*alpha*) = 2.15). As a result, the group of firms not engaging in R&D activities seems to have had an abnormal positive yield given the systematic risk. This is not observed in the case of Group G1, for which the estimated abnormal yield is 0.12% and the corresponding t statistic is 0.91%. However, neither of the other two performance measures generally used (the Sharpe

and Treynor indexes) supports the conclusion that the performances of the two portfolios differ significantly in one or the other group.

Table 4: Abnormal performance and cost of equity capital for portfolios of Canadian firms based on the intensity of R&D activity, 1975–1997 (t-statistics are in parenthesis)

	Groups based on relative intensity of R&D activity				
	G1	G2	G11	G12	G13
Calculation of cost of equity capital with the CAPM					
k_E (CAPM)	15.62%	15.17%	14.43%	15.19%	16.06%
Jensen's *alpha*	0.12	0.26	−0.01	0.20	0.08
	(0.91)	(2.15)	(−1.54)	(1.36)	(0.54)
Beta (CAPM)	0.86	0.80	0.69	0.80	0.92
Sigma	4.79%	4.50%	9.58%	5.25%	4.72%
Sharpe's index*	0.77%	0.99%	−1.43%	0.84%	0.79%
Treynor's index**	13.83%	17.60%	−10.35%	12.84%	15.36%
Calculation of the cost of equity capital with the TFPM					
k_E (TFPM)	14.03%	15.23%	17.11%	15.20%	12.23%
TFPM *alpha*	0.25	0.26	−1.47	0.15	0.45
	(1.90)	(2.09)	(−1.94)	(0.99)	(3.03)
Beta (TFPM)	0.89	0.85	0.56	0.97	0.85
s (TFPM)	−0.20	−0.12	0.46	−0.18	−0.34
	(−4.12)	(−2.53)	(1.81)	(−3.12)	(−6.08)
h (TFPM)	0.04	0.16	−0.18	0.11	0.02
	(0.98)	(4.62)	(−0.91)	(2.61)	(0.47)

* Sharpe's performance index = $(R_i-R_f)/sigma$
** Treynor's performance index = $(R_i-R_f)/beta$
R_i represents the portfolio yield; these two indicators give an estimate of the portfolio's excess yield per unit of risk. They differ in the risk measure used.
Values in parentheses are Student's *t* values.

G1: Firms reporting R&D expenditures
G2: Firms reporting no R&D expenditures
G11: Technology firms in start-up phase, for which R&D credits represented a significant proportion of revenues
G12: Firms with low R&D intensity, on the basis of the two criteria of total amount of R&D, and relative amount of R&D (R&D-to-sales ratio)
G13: R&D-intensive firms.

TFPM

For each group, we estimated the cost of equity capital according to the TFPM, that is, taking into account the three risk factors. We also assessed the intercept to examine whether the yields of some of the portfolios could be described as abnormal. The systematic (*beta*) risks of groups G1 and G2 are slightly higher than those estimated with the CAPM: 0.89 for Group G1 and 0.85 for Group G2. The coefficients s_i, relative to the size premium, are both negative (–0.20 and –0.12) and very significant. On average, we can therefore say that the firms making up the portfolios studied are of a larger size than the average firm in the market index used. These two coefficients, although slightly negative, will help reduce the estimated cost of equity capital. The coefficients h_i, relative to the premium for the BE/ME stock ratio, are both positive, the first being 0.04 and the second 0.16. Only the second, that of Group G2, is significant (*t* test = 4.62). This could have been expected since the portfolio is composed of firms said to be high-value, i.e., firms with a higher BE/ME ratio. The effect is to increase the cost of equity capital for firms in this group. With an average annual risk-free rate of 9.37%, a market premium of 7.28%, a size premium of 10.14% and a BE/ME share premium of 5.48% over the entire period studied, the estimated cost of equity capital is in the range of 14% to 15% for the two groups. When the three risk factors are taken into account, there is no significant difference in the financing costs of firms that could be linked to the intensity of their R&D activity. Accordingly, it cannot be argued that the cost of share capital for Canadian technology firms is abnormally high, if we associate this characteristic with the relative importance of R&D expenditures.

The cost of equity capital is approximately the same in the two groups. However, the intercept of the three-factor model measuring abnormal yield is of the same order in both groups. It is statistically significant for Group G2, with a *t* value of 2.09. Thus, over the period of analysis, firms reporting no R&D expenditures achieved an abnormally high yield given their systematic risk, their size and their BE/ME ratio. The abnormal yield of Group G1 is not significant at the 5% threshold but is significant at the 10% threshold. The yields of the two sub-groups are thus high, and a study of firms excluded from the sample because of uncertainty about the real level of their R&D activity shows that abnormally low yields were found in this part of the original sample.

The estimated cost of capital for the Group 1 subset of firms is of the same order when the three-factor model is used (G11, 17.11%; G12, 15.20%; G13,

12.23%). The highest cost of capital is found for young firms that have not yet completed the R&D phase and do not generate sales. Firms with moderate R&D intensity have an equity capital cost of 15.20%, while the most R&D-intensive firms have a lower cost of capital. This finding may seem counter-intuitive. It results from the fact that firms with high R&D intensity are also bigger in size, as indicated by the significant negative size premium. These firms also have a systematic risk lower than that of firms with moderate R&D intensity.

Whether one uses historical yields, a CAPM-based estimate of the cost of equity capital or a more complex three-factor model, it is impossible to reject the null hypothesis that firms with high R&D intensity benefit from the same cost of capital as firms not engaging in R&D. In Canada, technology firms thus seem to finance themselves with equity capital at a cost equal to or lower than that faced by firms in traditional sectors. These findings have at least two implications that are examined in greater depth and discussed in the last part of our study. However, before proceeding to that stage of the study, we should analyze in more detail the group of firms in the start-up phase, whose weak performance and low systematic risk level influence all of Group 1.

3.5   Detailed Analysis of the Group of Firms at the Take-Off Stage (Group G11)

Firms in this group were not start-ups in the agreed-upon sense of the term, which is generally reserved for the very first stages of forming and launching a firm; instead, the securities studied were listed on the stock exchange. They were issued by firms that had undertaken an initial public offering, something that in principle requires them to have been in existence for several years. However, the 28 firms in this group (Table 5) were in a "take-off" situation since a considerable portion of their reported revenues in all likelihood came from R&D tax credits. In this group were firms that, for at least one year, had reported revenues less than double their R&D expenditures. On average, these expenditures amounted to more than 25% of sales during the five to six years studied; for example, at Imutec Pharma Inc. the average R&D-to-sales ratio was 2,300%. This situation, however, was temporary since over the entire period (1991–1997) the ratio exceeded 50% only for three years, although the company did not achieve a net profit. Accordingly, this is a take-off situation: the company was approaching (or launching) its commercialization phase but had not yet reached that point and (except in three cases) reported no profit for at least two consecutive years. Some firms maintained a ratio of R&D to sales higher than 50% over more than half the period. This was the case for nine firms in the group, which (with the exception of Aeterna Laboratories Inc.) did not achieve sustainable profits.

Nevertheless, against all expectations, these firms succeeded in maintaining high share prices. Between 1991 and 1997, four of them increased their stock price significantly: from $2.65 to $3.85 in the case of Hyal Pharmaceutical Corporation, and from $6.63 to $10.00 in the case of Allelix Biopharmaceuticals Inc. The five others saw their share prices fall and then stabilize: for example, Biomira's share price went from $7.75 to $6.05 between 1991 and 1997, during which time the company did not report a profit in two successive years and R&D expenditures equalled over 50% of revenues in each of these six years. Some firms experienced a sharp rise in stock price without having achieved sustainable profits; for example, QLT Phototherapeutics Inc. saw its share price rise from $8.38 to $28.30 between 1991 and 1997, while the share price of MDSI Mobile Data Solutions Inc. rose from $1.30 to $37.00 between 1992 and 1997. Neither of these two firms reported profits in two consecutive years during the period studied.

We arrive at the following conclusions: first, firms with very distant prospects of becoming profitable were able to issue shares at high prices, compared with the discounted value of the cash flow available to shareholders. The value of shares at the beginning of the period and the discounted value of the cash flow to be paid to shareholders eventually can be reconciled only if the discount rate is very low. This rate represents the cost of share capital financing. Second, the stock market does not seem to severely penalize firms that, while undertaking major R&D expenditures, have no sustainable profits. This confirms the findings of earlier works (Swanson, 1998), which indicate that investors seem to regard amounts invested in research as an investment and not as an expenditure (despite what accounting principles say). On this basis, it would seem that listed knowledge-based firms had no problems with their cost of capital: KBEs maintained or increased their share prices even without sustainable profits. Contrary to the assertion of the 1992 Canada Consulting Group report, it would seem that Canadian firms engaging in R&D activities are not at a disadvantage and are indeed favoured by investors for doing so.

Table 5: Characteristics of Group 1-2 Firms : Start ups

GVKEY	Name of firm	Year of entry*	Number of years in period	Profit > 0 throughout the period ?**	Nbr of years in period where R-D/sales > 0.5	Av ratio of R-D/ sales	Init. price	Clos. price	Date of initial & closing prices
810062	HYAL PHARMACEUTICAL CORPORATION	1991	6	no	6	11.3351	2.66	3.85	July 91 & 97
815467	QSOUND LABS, INC	1991	6	no	2	0.4434	10.75	2.90	Mar. 91 & 97
815803	QLT PHOTOTHERAPEUTICS INC	1991	6	no	3	3.7012	8.38	28.30	July 91 & 97
820245	BIOMIRA INC	1991	6	no	6	1.9337	7.75	6.05	July 91 & 97
820800	TELEPANEL SYSTEMS INC	1991	6	no	1	0.2094	0.90	3.60	July 91 & 97
821959	MDSI MOBILE DATA SOLUTIONS INC	1992	5	no	1	0.1117	1.30	37.00	July 92 & 97
824726	CANGENE CORPORATION	1991	6	yes, 1995	2	0.4726	4.65	2.00	July 92 & 97
824854	ALLELIX BIOPHARMACEUTICALS INC	1991	6	no	6	1.3817	6.63	10.00	July 92 & 97
825578	SPECTRAL DIAGNOSTICS INC	1991	6	no	4	10.2660	20.63	7.15	July 94 & 97
825750	IMUTEC PHARMA INC.	1991	6	no	3	23.3236	2.16	0.98	July 93 & 97
825841	XILLIX TECHNOLOGIES CORP	1991	6	no	6	1.2971	2.34	2.65	July 93 & 97
825920	PROMIS SYSTEMS CORPORATION LTD	1991	6	yes, 1996	0	0.3607	6.00	4.75	July 93 & 97
826821	SOFTQUAD INTERNATIONAL INC	1992	5	no	1	0.2148	5.00	1.40	July 93 & 97
827332	INFOCORP COMPUTER SOLUTIONS	1993	4	no	1	0.2280	0.34	0.95	July 93 & 97
827522	ID BIOMEDICAL CORPORATION	1991	6	no	3	3.7738	0.87	4.00	July 92 & 97
827889	BATTERY TECHNOLOGIES INC	1991	6	no	1	0.1567	2.95	0.41	July 95 & 97
828150	HEMOSOL INC	1991	6	no	6	4.7498	7.13	2.20	July 93 & 97
828355	PLAINTREE SYSTEMS INC	1991	6	no	1	0.2646	7.00	4.45	July 93 & 97
828724	BALLARD POWER SYSTEMS INC	1991	6	no	5	0.9200	6.75	44.25***	July 93 & 97
829324	ALPHANET TELECOM INC	1991	6	no	1	0.1346	12.00	10.90	July 94 & 97
829407	MOSAID TECHNOLOGIES INCORPORATED	1991	6	yes, 1992	1	0.2736	8.00	17.00	July 94 & 97
829477	ABL CANADA INC	1991	6	no	1	0.3609	3.25	1.25	July 94 & 97
829759	BIONICHE INC	1991	6	no	3	0.5825	3.60	1.10	July 94 & 97
829879	METROWERKS INC.	1993	4	no	1	0.3434	1.40	9.00	July 94 & 97
829955	BIOVAIL CORPORATION INTERNATIONAL	1991	6	yes, 1993	1	0.1913	8.751	36.05	July 94 & 97
831616	SYSTEMS XCELLENCE INC	1991	5	no	1	0.1753	1.95	1.51	July 96 & 97
862475	INEX PHARMACEUTICALS CORP.	1993	4	no	4	2.8997	10.55	7.10	July 96 & 97
863562	AETERNA LABORATORIES INC	1994	3	yes, 1994	2	0.8721	21	8.60	July 96 & 97

* The year of entry is the year during which the firm first appeared in the Evert database.

** Profits are durably positive if they are so in at least two consecutive years without becoming negative subsequently. The year indicated is that in which the profit period started.

*** After reaching $130 in March 1998, the stock price had declined to $27 by year-end.

4.   IMPLICATIONS AND AVENUES FOR RESEARCH

4.1   Discussion of Findings

The main conclusion of this study is that Canadian knowledge-based firms with shares listed on a stock exchange do not face abnormally high capital costs that could place them at a disadvantage compared with other firms. This holds true even when the firms are still at the stage at which the ratio of R&D expenditures to sales is very high (25% or more).

Historically, the rate of return on a portfolio made up of firms classified as being in the KBE sector is 17.42%, while it is 18.98% for firms in the control sample. This measure of capital cost is, however, incomplete since it does not take into account other factors known to influence the cost of equity capital. When these factors are integrated, we find that the required rate of return for KBEs can be estimated at 14.03%, as compared with 15.23% for other sectors. Firms with high R&D intensity at the take-off stage seem to be particularly highly valued by the market; they sustain relatively high prices over long periods even when reporting no profits. Once again, the implicit cost of capital is very low.

These findings accord with those of many studies that, without directly measuring R&D intensity, have examined differences in yield between growth stocks (which may be associated with the most technologically advanced sectors) and value stocks (generally associated with less R&D-intensive sectors). Fama and French (1998) present findings from a study of 13 developed markets and 16 emerging markets. From 1975 to 1995, the average annual premium of value stocks over growth stocks in developed markets was 7.60%, and value stocks outclassed growth stocks in 12 of the 13 markets studied. In the 16 emerging markets examined for the period 1987 to 1995, the average annual premium was 16.91% for weighted portfolios, or 14.13% for equi-weighted portfolios. Again, value stocks outclassed growth stocks in 12 of the 16 markets. However, additional studies would be needed to evaluate the extent to which these findings hold true when stocks are classified not by their BE/ME ratio but according to their R&D intensity; this would be a major undertaking given that in most countries firms do not divulge this type of information. The findings obtained here are consistent with those reported by Coleman (1997a, b), who shows that the R&D yield premium is generally negative when there is no clear relation between these expenditures (ratio to sales) and yield, whether adjusted or not for different factors.

The findings reported for Canada in our study are also entirely consistent with those reported in a later study undertaken in the United States by Chan, Lakonishok and Sougiannis (1999). The authors use measures of intensity of R&D expenditure similar to those used in the present study. Their conclusions are as follows: "The evidence does not indicate that firms engaged in R&D experience superior stock price performance, compared to firms with no R&D. Rather, the average return on the two sets of stocks is comparable" (p. 4). In the case of small firms, however, R&D intensity seems to be associated with a higher yield, but the difference is only 1.8% per year. The authors also show that shares of R&D-intensive firms are more volatile and that, when they choose such stocks, investors must accept greater volatility for a similar yield. For the authors, these findings indicate that market investors correctly integrate the future net value of R&D benefits. Investors seem clearly more sensitive to R&D efforts that result in patents, whose rate of citation seems positively related to share value. Hall, Jaffe and Trajtenberg (1999) show that stocks of firms holding frequently cited patents (more than 20 times) outperform shares of comparable firms without patent citations by 50% to 60%. This result is comparable to those reported by Deng, Lev and Narin (1999), who associate high stock yields with widely used patents rather than with intensity of R&D effort.

The results obtained in the case of firms at the take-off stage which have recently been listed on the stock exchange are also consistent with those of studies of the movement of newly issued shares. They show that prices are knowingly falsified by brokers (Krigman, Shaw and Womack, 1999) and that the medium-term performance of these initial issues is generally disappointing, especially in the case of smaller firms that are not supported by venture capital investors (Brav and Gompers, 1997).

An explanation of this phenomenon is far beyond the scope of the present study. There are few plausible explanations if we suppose that markets are efficient and investors rational. The only way to find a possible explanation is to go beyond this frame of reference and acknowledge that market investors have long attributed to R&D expenditures a value they do not have.[22] Shares of very R&D-intensive firms would thus seem to have been overvalued for many years, without providing yields that would justify the investors' optimism. It may also be that firms, attracted by the generous R&D tax credits, allocate too much money to these activities, particularly since R&D yields seem to be falling (Swanson, 1998). Recent OECD studies show that, in most countries, the investment category most highly valued is investment in R&D yielding short-term profits (Gordon and Tchilinguirian, 1998); this is particularly true in Canada, which (after Australia and Spain) offers the most advantageous tax treatment for short-term R&D projects of any OECD country (Gordon and Tchilinguirian, 1998, Table 4, p. 19). The situation is almost identical for long-term projects. It may thus be that R&D tax treatment has a link with the phenomena observed here. Before considering the implications of these observations for economic policy, it is worth broadening the area of study to address the more complex problem of the cost of financing for privately held firms.

4.2   The Cost of Capital for Privately Held Firms

In the case of privately held technology firms, estimation problems are still greater for the following reasons: (1) Determining the *beta* coefficient is impossible without market data and it remains very difficult when shares are traded in low volumes. Among small firms, instances of financial distress are relatively frequent and have a strong influence on measures of systematic risk (Chan and Chen, 1991). Finally, according to Ibbotson, Kaplan and Peterson (1997), the *beta* coefficients of small firms are systematically undervalued. (2) It may be considered that the portfolios of managers of these firms cannot be totally diversified, because outside investors generally require that managers hold a relatively large proportion of the shares. Damodaran (1997, Ch. 30) also seeks to measure the cost of equity capital for privately held firms by taking into account total risk, not only systematic risk. Finally, knowledge-based firms are subject to specific risk factors that may be difficult to diversify: this is true, for example, of the risk represented by a refusal on the part of the Food and Drug Administration (FDA) to authorize the introduction of a new pharmaceutical product on the market.

Based on values commonly used and current rates,[23] the CAPM indicates a 14% to 16% cost of equity capital for a firm with a systematic risk of *beta* = 2 (a plausible value for a very volatile technology firm). However, it is common to see the venture capital industry use rates higher than 45% for start-up firms. The rate varies from 30% to 45% for firms at the intermediate financing stage (Wright and Robbie, 1996). The addition of a size premium and a value (BE/ME) premium does not enable us to reconcile the rates predicted by the models and those prevailing in the market. Thus, direct observations and the practices of venture capital firms seem hard to reconcile with theoretical concepts, but some partial explanations may be adduced for this situation.

The discrepancy between the cost of capital calculated according to the CAPM and that commonly used in start-up situations comes from the existence of a liquidity premium. The premium is commensurate with the ability to get a stock exchange listing, rules concerning the resale of shares before a public offering (right of exit), etc. Estimates of these premiums vary but are often in the area of 40% (Pratt, Reilly and Schweihs, 1995). However, there is a lack of Canadian data on this subject and these premiums alone cannot account for the discrepancies observed.

Control premiums (that is, discounts for minority holdings) could also partly explain the high costs of financing via share capital for start-up technology firms. Once again, estimates of these premiums vary but are often in the area of 35% (Pratt, Reilly and Schweihs, 1995).

However, it is noteworthy that control and liquidity premiums seem to explain only in part the very large differences noted between rates of return predicted by the models and those used in practice.

Among the possible explanations is the following: the rate used by investors in such situations takes into account the probability of a total failure of the start-up firm (60% to 90%, depending on the sector). Thus, a biotechnology firm with a capital cost of 15% (taking into account only systematic risk) will face a doubling of this rate if investors consider that there is an approximately 50% probability that the FDA will not approve the firm's product (causing the company to close or significantly delaying its commercialization phase). The additional risk is not incorporated into the systematic risk since it is difficult to diversify.

Accordingly, further studies are needed on the issue of the cost of capital for privately held KBEs. Studies should first focus on measuring the cost of capital, using other methods than those applied here, given the lack of market data. They should also examine factors that might explain and justify a very high cost of capital while publicly traded KBEs benefit from a very advantageous cost of financing through share capital. Finally, it seems important to develop more accurate methods of determining rates that shareholders may require, since these rates are at the centre of negotiations on the financing and development of privately held firms, notably by venture capital lenders.

4.3   Economic Policy Implications

The first economic policy implication is thus clear: the cost of capital for KBEs must not attract government intervention once KBEs are listed on a stock exchange. They benefit from an entirely normal cost of capital given their risk level. Two points follow from this first observation.

First, insofar as the cost of capital is normal and R&D expenditures are profitable, is the generous assistance offered by governments for R&D in the form of tax expenditures indispensable for firms whose shares are listed on an exchange? We have highlighted the fact that firm yield seems lower when R&D intensity is higher. That being the case, one may wonder whether the low after-tax net cost of R&D expenditures does not encourage firms to invest beyond the desirable optimum and undertake unprofitable projects. The lack of a positive relation between R&D intensity and the rate of return on stocks is a disquieting finding in an economy that is heavily influenced by the notion that R&D is beneficial and desirable. Have we not gone too far in giving Canadian R&D privileges seemingly without parallel except in a very few countries?

Second, if listing on a stock exchange greatly facilitates the financing of knowledge-based firms, public policies must be aimed at helping firms that have not yet reached this stage of development. As well, a study should be conducted on how listing can be facilitated.[24] Several policies that were expected to resolve these problems have not yet achieved the desired results.

Start-up KBEs seem to face some scarcity of funds and a high cost of capital. This situation has long been noted and has given rise to large-scale government actions that have sought to increase the supply of venture capital, especially by means of tax expenditures granted to labour funds. As Riding (1998) comments, it is far from certain that these initiatives have achieved the intended objective. Despite a real excess in the supply of so-called venture capital, KBEs in the start-up phase still face serious financing difficulties, and the cost of capital required by institutions heavily subsidized directly or indirectly by governments still stands at around 70% for an initial round of financing.

Difficulties have also been encountered in trying to encourage firms to list their shares on a public exchange by means of tax expenditures (stock savings plans), especially in the case of smaller firms. Smaller firms are encouraged to be listed by relaxing prospectus-filing requirements and by measures that could reduce the very high costs involved in listing. To a large degree these costs are not proportional to the size of the public offering and are therefore a major obstacle for small public offerings. The findings of this study thus give greater weight to the observations and recommendations of various groups that have examined the process of listing shares on a stock exchange (Riding, 1998).

5.   CONCLUSION

The objective of this study was to measure the cost of share capital for knowledge-based enterprises in Canada, and to evaluate the relevant public policy implications. The study focuses mainly on firms listed on a stock exchange, and the conclusions cannot be generalized to other firms, especially privately held small firms. Estimates of the cost of share capital have been performed for various groups of firms, classified according to the relative importance of their R&D activities. Whatever method is used to estimate this cost, we cannot conclude that firms with high R&D levels face higher capital costs than firms reporting no such activities. On average, the yield of the former is also lower than that of the latter, a fact that raises serious questions about the profitability of R&D activities. One possible explanation is that firms spend more than the optimum amount on R&D, because of the very advantageous tax treatment applying to this type of expenditure.

The cost of capital for stock-exchange-listed KBEs cannot be regarded as an obstacle to their development. The same is not true for privately held firms, which seem to face very high financing costs despite massive intervention by governments to increase the supply of available venture capital. Other avenues for reducing the cost of share capital for privately held technology firms should therefore be explored, and strategies seeking to facilitate stock market listings should also be envisaged for these firms.

Few studies have examined the cost of capital of knowledge-based enterprises, although financing is vital to their development. Accordingly, further research efforts should be undertaken. These could seek to expand the focus of the present study. Because of the considerable difficulties encountered in trying to find data on R&D expenditures, firms were classified using relatively recent data while yields were studied over a 20-year period. Further, no attempt was made to formulate estimates for privately held firms.

NOTES

[1] The cost of capital is a weighted average of the costs of various sources of financing. Given the relative importance of the cost of equity capital in the financing of knowledge-based enterprises, we focus on this component; the study deals mainly with the cost of share capital.

[2] The concept of capital cost is discussed in basic finance textbooks, such as Damodaran (1997). The various methods of estimating this cost are examined by Patterson (1995) and Ehrhardt (1994), while Ibbotson and Associates (1997) offer cost estimating services for U.S. firms. For Canada, Ando et al. (1997) and Jog (1997) present more detailed analyses of the methods based on accounting data and on the capital asset pricing model (CAPM).

[3] For example, if long-term interest rates fall, a corresponding drop in the cost of equity capital is expected (by simple arbitrage between financial stocks). In the short term, however, a share price increase entails a rise in the realized return.

[4] Adjustments have been studied, particularly in the case of Japan, where price/earnings ratios have historically been higher than in the United States. Ando and Auerbach (1988) adjust this ratio in relation to inflation and its effect on depreciation, inventory and interest payments. These adjustments increase the earnings of Japanese companies and therefore lower their price/earnings ratio; but for U.S. firms they do not change price/earnings ratios significantly. See also Frankel (1991) and Aron (1987).

[5] See Damodaran (1997, Ch. 6) for descriptions of this calculation method, which is most commonly adjusted to take into consideration variations in debt level.

[6] Inasmuch as excess yields are used, the constant a_i should have a zero value. If it is found not to have a zero value, this indicates abnormal yields.

[7] Fama and French do not make the same distinction by final month of fiscal year, and more conservatively consider that all business information is available by June (plus six months). For fiscal years ending between July and November of year t, they calculate yields starting from January of the year $t+1$. For fiscal years ending between January and June of year $t+1$, they calculate yields starting from July of the year $t+2$.

[8] As no recent data cover a long enough estimation period, we have had to juxtapose several databases.

[9] The premium is much lower if we measure the market yield by the rate of return of the TSE 300 Index (monthly average of 0.237% and standard deviation of 4.57%, for a yearly average of 2.84%) rather than by the equi-weighted yield of stocks making up the sample.

[10] Canadian accounting principles specify that research expenditures must be charged against output for the fiscal year in which they are undertaken. Development expenditures may be capitalized if, and only if, the following five conditions are met: (1) the product or process in question is well defined and the expenses involved are identifiable; (2) from the technical angle, the feasibility of the product or process has been demonstrated; (3) the management of the firm has indicated its intention to produce and commercialize or use the product/process; (4) the potential market for the product/process is clearly defined or, if the firm itself intends to make use of it, the product/process is shown to be useful to the firm; and (5) the firm already has or can obtain the resources needed to complete the project (*CICA Manual*, Chs. 3450.16, 3450.21). For an analysis of the effect of R&D expenditure accounting methods on book values, see Swanson (1998) and Healy, Myers and Howe (1999).

[11] The Evert Canadian corporate R&D database reports amounts invested in R&D before allocation of tax credits and other government subsidies. The database is described at the following address: http://www.evert.com. The R&D data used in this study are for all companies covered in the Evert database and listed on the Toronto Stock Exchange.

[12] We first used the classification of Lee and Has (1996) who, on the basis of Statistics Canada data for the period 1984–1988, propose a breakdown of 52 Canadian industrial sectors into three groups: high knowledge, medium knowledge and low knowledge. This classification does not allow for firm-by-firm analysis and places companies with very different R&D efforts in the same category; it was therefore abandoned.

[13] The Stock Guide database presents the financial statement and a descriptive notice of the activities of each company listed on the Toronto Stock Exchange. Two complementary data sources have been used here since it is difficult to obtain reliable R&D data on Canadian companies, which are not required to divulge that information.

[14] Some companies in this sector, tracked by Evert, separated exploration expenditures from R&D activities. These observations have accordingly been kept.

[15] The ratio is obtained by dividing total R&D expenditures by total spot sales during the period.

[16] Amount of annual R&D = total R&D expenditures divided by the number of years in the period under study.

[17] These include 172 firms tracked by Evert for which we do not have sufficient data (less than two years of R&D), plus firms in resource sectors whose R&D expenditures could not be separated from exploration costs (gold and precious minerals; integrated mines; integrated oils; mining; mining exploration; oil and gas producers; and oil, mining, gas and forest). These firms make up Group 3. Also included in the group are firms mentioning R&D activities in their corporate profile but not divulging any amount. Added to these observations are 64 companies for which we lack sufficient information to determine whether or not they engaged in R&D; they make up Group 4.

[18] For Group G11, yields could be calculated only from January 1984.

[19] See note 17.

[20] The firms studied here are not those that make up the Index; they are generally smaller in size. Further, the yields are equi-weighted while Index yields are calculated taking into account market capitalization. These two factors explain the differences observed.

[21] The abnormal performance indexes used in this section are described in all basic textbooks on portfolio management. See, for example, Reilly and Norton (1999, p. 778 ff).

[22] In particular, investors seem partly to value R&D expenditures as if they represented acquired assets with a long-term value. See Swanson (1998) for a review of the relevant studies.

[23] The risk-free rate is around 6% and estimates of the risk premium are generally from 4% to 6%.

[24] See Riding (1998) for a review of initiatives in this field and for a summary of the report of the McCallum Task Force.

REFERENCES

Ando, A. and A.J. Auerbach, "The Cost of Capital in the United States and Japan: A Comparison," *Journal of Japanese and International Economics*, 2, 1988, 134-158.

Ando, A. and A.J. Auerbach, "The Cost of Capital in Japan: Recent Evidence and Further Results", *Journal of Japanese and International Economics*, 4, 1990, 323-350.

Ando, A., J. Handock and G. Sawchuk, "Cost of Capital for the United States, Japan and Canada: An Attempt at Measurement Based on Individual Company Records and Aggregate National Accounts Data," in P. Halpern (ed.), *Financing Growth in Canada*. Calgary: University of Calgary Press, 1997.

Annin, M., *Fama-French and Small Company Cost of Equity Calculations*, Working paper, Ibbotson & Ass., http://www.ibbotson.com/Research/Fama/page0000.asp, 1997.

Aron, P., *Japanese Price Earnings Multiples*, Daiwa Securities America, 1987.

Baldwin, C.Y., "The Capital Factor: Competing for Capital in a Global Environment," in M. Porter (ed.), *Competing in Global Industries*. Boston: Harvard University Press, 1986.

Brav, A. and P. Gompers, "Myth or Reality? The Long-Run Underperformance of Initial Public Offerings: Evidence from Venture and Nonventure Capital-backed Companies," *The Journal of Finance*, 52 (5), 1997, 1791-1821.

Caldwell, D., G. Sawchuk and J. Wilson, *Do Small Firms Face Higher Financing Costs?* Special Study, Statistics Canada, Cat No. 61-008, 1994.

Canada Consulting Group, *Under-Funding the Future: Canada's Cost of Capital Problem* Ottawa, 1992.

Chan, L.K.C., J. Lakonishok and T. Sougiannis, *The Stock Market Valuation of Research and Development Expenditures*. NBER Working Paper 7223, http://www.nber.org/paper/w7223, 1999.

Chan, K.C. et N. Chen, Structural and Return Characteristics of Small and Large Firms, *Journal of Finance* 46, 1991, 1467-1484.

Coleman, R.D., *The R&D Effect with Static Stock Pricing*. Working Paper, http://www.cyberramp.net/~investor/download/rdstext.pdf, 1997 a.

Coleman, R.D., *The R&D Effect with Dynamic Stock Pricing*. Working Paper, http://www.cyberramp.net/~investor/download/abstract.pdf, 1997 b.

Damodaran, A., *Corporate Finance: Theory and Practice*. Toronto: Wiley, 1997.

Deng, Z., B. Lev and F. Narin, "Science and Technology as Predictors of Stock Performance." *Financial Analysts Journal*, vol. 55 (3) 1999, 20-32.

Ehrhardt, M.C. *The Search for Value, Measuring the Company's Cost of Capital.* Cambridge, MA: Harvard Business School Press, 1994.

Errunza, V.R. and D.P. Miller, *Market Segmentation and the Cost of Capital in International Equity Markets.* SSRN Working Paper, http://papers.ssrn.com/paper.taf?abstract_id=99833, 1998.

Fama, E.F. and K.R. French. "The Cross-Section of Expected Stock Returns." *The Journal of Finance*, vol. 1992, 427-466.

Fama, E.F. and K.R. French, "Common Risk Factors in the Returns on Stocks and Bonds." *The Journal of Financial Economics*, vol. 1993, 3-56.

Fama, E.F. and K.R. French, "Size and Book-to-Market Factors in Earnings and Returns." *The Journal of Finance,* 50, 1995, 131-155.

Fama, E.F. and K.R. French, "Industry Cost of Equity," *The Journal of Financial Economics*, 43 (2), 1997, 153-193.

Fama, E.F. and K.R. French, *Value Versus Growth: The International Evidence.* SSRN Working Paper, 1998.

Finance Canada. "The Real Cost of Funds for Business Investment." *Quarterly Economic Review,* Special Report, 1991, 55-67.

Frankel, J.A., "The Japanese Cost of Finance: A Survey," *Financial Management*, Spring, 1991, 95-127.

Gordon, K. and H. Tchilinguirian, *Marginal Effective Tax Rates on Physical, Human and R&D Capital.* Economic Department Working Paper No. 199, OECD, Paris, 1998.

Hall, B.H., A. Jaffe and M. Trajtenberg, *Market Value and Patent Citation: A First Look.* NBER Working Paper, 1999.

Harris, R.S. and F.C. Martson, "Estimating Shareholder Risk Premia Using Analysts' Growth Forecasts." *Financial Management*, Summer, 1992, 63-70.

Haugen, R., *The new finance the case against efficient market*, prentice-Hall, 1995.

Healy, P.M., S.C. Myers and C.D. Howe, *R&D Accounting and the Tradeoff Between Relevance and Objectivity.* SSRN Working Paper, 1999.

Ibbotson, R.G., P.D. Kaplan and J.D. Peterson, *Estimates of Small Stock Betas Are Much Too Low.* Working Paper, Ibbotson Ass. and *The Journal of Portfolio Management*, http://www.ibbotson.com/Research/Small_Stock_Betas/, 1997.

Jog, V.M., "Investing in Canada: Estimation of the Sectoral Cost of Capital and Case Studies for International Comparisons," in P. Halpern (ed.), *Financing Growth in Canada.* Calgary: University of Calgary Press, 1997.

Kaplan, P.D. and J.D. Peterson, *Full-information Industry Betas.* Working Paper, Ibbotson & Ass.,http://www.ibbotson.com/Research/Industry_Betas/Full_Information_Industry_Betas.pdf, 1997.

Kaplan, S.N. and R.S. Ruback, "The Valuation of Cash Flow Forecasts: An Empirical Analysis." *The Journal of Finance,* 50 (4), 1995, 1059-1093.

Krigman, L., W.H. Shaw and K.L. Womack, "The Persistence of IPO Mispricing and the Predictive Power of Flipping." *The Journal of Finance,* 54 (3), 1999, 1015-1044.

Lakonishok, J., A. Shleifer and R.W. Vishny, "Contrarian Investment, Extrapolation and Risk." *Journal of Finance,* 49 (5), 1994, 1541-1578.

Lee, F.C. and H. Has, "A Quantitative Assessment of High-Knowledge Industries Versus Low-Knowledge Industries," Iowit Peter (ed.), *The Implication of Knowledge-Based Growth for Micro-Economic Policies.* Calgary: University of Calgary Press, 1996.

Lippens, R.E., "The Cost of Capital: A Summary of Results for the U.S. and Japan in the 1980s." *Business Economics,* 26 (2), 1991, 19-24.

McCauley, R.N. and S.A. Zimmer, "Explaining International Differences in the Cost of Capital." *Federal Reserve Bank of New York Quarterly Review,* 14 (2), 1989, 7-28.

Mohnen, P. and J. Mairesse, *R-D et productivité: Survol de la littérature.* CNRS Working Paper No. 99019, Collection Les cahiers de l'innovation, 1999.

Patterson, C.S., *The Cost of Capital Theory and Estimation,* Quorum Books, Westport, Conn. 1995, 344 p.

Pecaut, D., "Canada's High Cost of Capital: A Barrier to Investing for the Future." *Canadian Investment Review,* Summer, 1993, 9-16.

Poterba, J.M., "Comparing the Cost of Capital in the United States and Japan: A Survey of Methods." *Federal Reserve Bank of New York Quarterly Review,* Winter, 1991, 20-32.

Pratt, S., R.F. Reilly and R. Schweihs, *Valuing a Business: The Analysis and Appraisal of Closely Held Companies,* 3rd ed., Homewood, Illinois: Irwin, 1995.

Regan, P. J., *"Japan Bashing and the cost of capital",* Financial Analyst Journal January-February 1990, 10-11.

Reilly, F.K. and E.A. Norton, *Investment,* 5th ed. Forthworth, Texas: The Dryden Press, 1999.

Riding, A.L., *Financement des entreprises de pointe: Enjeux d'ordre juridique et réglementaire.* Research Paper prepared for the Task Force on the Future of the Canadian Financial Services Sector, Ottawa, 1998.

Swanson, Z.L., *R&D, Firms' Fundamentals, and Diminishing Returns for the Stock Market.* SSRN Working Paper, 1998.

Wright, M. and K. Robbie, "Venture Capitalists, Unquoted Equity Investment Appraisal and the Role of Accounting Information." *Accounting and Business Research,* 26 (2), 1996, 153-168.

9. INNOVATION, M&AS AND INTER-NATIONAL COMPETITION WITH AN APPLICATION TO PHARMACEUTICALS AND BIOTECHNOLOGY

Maria-Angels Oliva
MIT Sloan School of Management

Luis A. Rivera-Batiz
McGill University, Universitat Pompeu Fabra
And Inter-American Development Bank

1.   INTRODUCTION

Multinational corporations carry out a substantial and increasing share of business research and development (R&D). For instance, the amount of R&D conducted by the top 20 multinationals is greater than the combined R&D spending of France and Great Britain. As a result, multinationals have become increasingly important as innovators. During the eighties, multinationals accounted for 75% of all patents granted in the United States. Foreign companies comprised 50% of the total.

Multinationals' activities create a global innovation network that operates through multiple channels. First, the results of multinationals' R&D flow within enterprises that operate plants around the globe and have a strong outward orientation. Foreign sales account for about half of the top 100 multinationals' sales (United Nations, 1997). Second, a substantial share of R&D is actually conducted abroad, that is, outside the multinationals' home countries (Florida, 1995). Third, foreign investment flows constitute a major channel for both the diffusion of innovation abroad and the appropriation of innovation generated abroad. These channels have contributed to globalizing innovation and R&D. However, the supply side of new global knowledge is still highly concentrated. Income on account of royalties and fees is concentrated among a small number of developed economies, particularly the U.S., France, Germany, Japan, the Netherlands, and the U.K.

This paper examines the role of foreign investment through mergers and acquisitions (M&As) in international technological competition in research-oriented industries, particularly in the pharmaceutical and biotechnology industries. With this subject in mind, we propose a knowledge-based approach to multinationals and their foreign investment activities. These activities generate knowledge that reduces firms' marginal costs, increases product quality and leads to the creation of new products. In contrast with traditional foreign investment literature, which stresses capital investment and plant openings, the knowledge-based approach points toward the productive role of knowledge and technology. In contrast to the usual portfolio diversification approach, the knowledge-based approach focuses on risk diversification across R&D projects.

Many models of the international diffusion of innovation focus exclusively on technology spillovers that do not require any interaction between firms. If it is true that foreign investment serves as a channel for appropriating spillovers, technological benefits must often be gained through organizational strategies directed at exploiting firms' interactions. Two of them are strategic alliances and M&As. Most business literature still stresses the former, even if M&A trends parallel those of interfirm technology agreements and M&As have become gigantic in recent years (United Nations, 1998, p. 24).

A large number of recent M&As have taken place in high-tech and medium-tech industries driven by intense technological competition based on product, quality and process innovation. These M&As represent strategic investments taking place to create competitive advantages by appropriating spillovers and exploiting potential technology synergies. The term synergy refers to the gains generated by various firms working together as opposed to the spillovers generated by individual firms working in isolation. M&As can generate many different types of synergies, serving as a means for capturing distribution channels, obtaining administrative and production cost savings, and reaping research and know-how benefits. The subsequent discussion of the case of pharmaceuticals and biotechnology concentrates on the benefits from shared know-how, pooled research skills that are used to generate product innovation, and product marketing.

The appropriation of spillovers and the exploitation of synergies through M&As are key elements of firms' strategies because they generate marginal cost reductions, contribute to better tailor products to consumers' needs, and can increase market share and confer greater monopoly power. A delicate policy dilemma arises because technology benefits may come together with a potentially harmful increase of industrial concentration.

The paper is organized as follows. Sections 2 and 3 describe international patterns of business R&D, examine the technology role of multinationals and foreign investment, and document the dominant role of M&As in foreign investment. Section 4 sketches a model of strategic multinationalization and research spending. Sections 5 to 7 examine the pharmaceutical M&A wave of the 1990s, the creation of competitive advantages between pharmaceuticals and biotech firms, and the internationalization of the biotech industry. Sections 8 and 9 examine policies toward innovation and M&As, and Section 10 concludes.

2.   BUSINESS RESEARCH IN INTERNATIONAL COMPETITION

In most industrial countries, business R&D is concentrated in manufacturing industries. There is an increasing amount of R&D in the service sector, but reliable and comparable international data sets covering this type of R&D are not available. In the U.S., R&D in service and other non-manufacturing industries represents a quarter of total corporate R&D expenditures.

When we restrict ourselves to the manufacturing sector, a key stylized fact emerges. Around 90% of all business R&D spending in the major industrial economies (France, Germany, Japan, the U.S. and the U.K.) is concentrated in medium- and high-tech industries.[1] With the exception of Germany, where R&D is evenly divided between medium- and high-tech sectors, most R&D spending is directed toward high-tech industries.

2.1   R&D Specialization Patterns

Technology-intensive industries account for a substantial portion of industrial countries' international trade. In Canada, about 25% of total exports can be attributed to high-technology sectors. A main element of high-tech competition is R&D spending directed to reduce costs (i.e., process innovation) or to produce new goods and increase their quality (i.e., product innovation).

Table 1 shows the distribution of business R&D for several technology-intensive industries. The principles of international specialization are clearly at work at industry-level R&D spending. R&D activities are heavily concentrated in a few high-tech and medium-tech industries. For instance, the aerospace and chemical industries spend 40% of U.S. business R&D. These industries, plus instruments, electronic equipment, and motor vehicles, make up 80% of U.S. business R&D spending.

Table 1: Cross-country sectorial distribution of business R&D (1993 data, as a percentage)

	U.S.	U.K.	France	Germany	Japan
Aerospace	18	12	17	8	1
Instruments	12	1	1	2	4
Industrial Chemicals and Drugs	22	35	19	20	18
Office Machinery and Computers	6	6	4	3	9
Electrical Machinery	1	8	4	9	11
Electronic Equipment and Components	13	13	23	19	16
Motor Vehicles	13	9	13	20	12
All Sectors /Total R&D	85	84	81	81	71

Source: OECD, 1996.

Innovation is oriented toward different industries and types of technologies in different countries. The distribution of R&D spending across countries mirrors the arenas of high-tech international competition, reflecting the role of knowledge and information in high-tech industries. The massive aerospace research spending of the U.S., France and the U.K. reflects the keen competition between Boeing and Airbus as well as the significant role of British industry in supplying world markets. In contrast, Japan spends 1% of its R&D in aerospace. Electrical machinery accounts for a mere 1% of U.S. R&D, while it amounts to 11% in the case of Japan. In the U.K., R&D is heavily concentrated in chemicals, which account for 35% of total R&D. In fact, pharmaceuticals alone account for 23% of total R&D. Sixty percent of France's R&D is invested in aerospace, chemicals, and electronic equipment and components. Clear patterns of R&D specialization are also observed in Germany and Japan.

3. FOREIGN DIRECT INVESTMENT AND M&AS

A key feature of business research is that its funding is largely a private matter. Between 70% and 98% of the major industrial countries' business R&D is privately funded. The fact that business R&D is largely privately funded calls our attention to the role of firms, particularly multinationals, in financing and designing strategies for national competitiveness. The importance of multinationals' international activities has changed dramatically in the last two decades. Table 2 shows that the stock of world foreign investment increased from $479 million in 1980 to $3,455 million in 1997. Foreign investment is dominated by industrial countries, which account for about 68% of the stock of world direct foreign investment.

Table 2: Foreign direct investment inward stock (in US$ millions)

	1980	1985	1990	1995	1996	1997
World	479	745	1726	2732	3065	3455
Industrial Countries	373	538	1371	1929	2123	2349
Industrial Countries/World (%)	78	72	79	71	69	68

Source: United Nations, 1998.

3.1 M&As' Dominance of Medium- and High-Tech Foreign Investment

It is not always recognized that foreign investment among industrial countries consists largely of mergers and acquisitions (M&As). Tables 3 and 4 show data on selected U.S. industries. M&As overwhelm establishments in the high-technology sector as well as in food, a major manufacturing industry. The dominance of M&As is not a phenomenon of the 1990s. Table 4 shows the dominance of M&As in chemicals, as well as in the pharmaceutical subsector of the chemical industry, since 1980.

Why are M&As such an important element of foreign investment in research-based industries? To see why, recall that technology management motivates high-tech firms to invest in innovative countries. Foreign investment is often undertaken to exploit technological advantages, generate new research and knowledge synergies, and appropriate foreign technologies. Synergistic and knowledge-based foreign investment encourages M&As rather than new plant openings. The latter represent expansions or reallocations of production that become attractive when market penetration, low-cost outsourcing, and tariff jumping motives are present.

Table 3: Acquisitions versus establishments in the U.S. (in percentage)

Industry	1992		1993		1996	
	M&A	Est.*	M&A	Est.*	M&A	Est.*
Food and Kindred Products	65.6	34.4	99.5	0.5	90.0	10.0
Chemicals and Allied Products	90.9	9.1	100.0	0.0	96.7	3.3
Machinery (except Electrical)	61.5	38.6	99.2	0.7	75.4	4.6
Electric and Electronic Equipment	95.5	4.5	99.8	0.2	48.2	51.8

* Establishments
Source: U.S. Department of Commerce, 1997 (Table 4-5, p. 20).

Table 4: Mergers and acquisitions in chemicals

	1980	1989	1993
Chemicals			
Acquisitions	96%	93%	100%
Establishments	4%	7%	0%
Drugs			
Acquisitions	90%	93%	100%
Establishments	10%	7%	0%

Source: U.S. Department of Commerce, 1991 and U.S. Department of Commerce, 1995.

3.2   M&A Waves

Mergers and acquisitions have experienced recurrent boom episodes over the last hundred years. In the U.S., these waves go back to the trust-related activity of the end of the nineteenth century, the combination mergers of the 1960s and the 1980s' explosion of hostile takeovers and very large acquisitions with frequent payments in cash. In the 1990s, M&A dealings proliferated, including multiple megadeals in technology-intensive industries. The opening of new markets, shifting technologies, and the rising number of strategic alliances and M&A deals have led to an ongoing restructuring process in technology-intensive industries.

The 1990s wave is the largest ever in nominal terms. It overwhelms the wave of the 1980s both in real terms and relative to the size of the U.S. economy (i.e., measured in terms of U.S. GDP). The 1990s wave had a global character. Similar patterns are indeed noticeable in the U.S., the European Union and Canada. These features suggest that there are common shocks behind the waves and raise the possibility of contagion effects.

Why did M&A activity increase in the late 1980s and the 1990s? Globalization, deregulation, European integration, and other developments had significant implications for strategic management, industrial productivity, R&D activities, and the innovation process. Restructuring through M&As, such as the pharmaceuticals M&A wave examined in detail below, represented a response to a changed market environment.

3.3   R&D Orientation and Technological Outsourcing

What is the evidence concerning the role of R&D and technological outsourcing in international acquisitions? Relevant evidence is still scarce. Harris and Ravenscraft (1991) analyze the performance of 1,273 U.S. firms acquired by foreign firms during 1970-1987. The authors find that international acquisitions mostly occur in research-intensive industries, and that 75% of cross-border transactions involve firms with closely-related product lines. This result is interpreted as evidence of the important role of R&D in foreign investment. Moreover, cross-border acquisitions tend to result in higher profits for U.S. targets than is the case for targets in domestic U.S. acquisitions.

Neven and Siotis (1996) examine whether firms invest abroad to appropriate technology developed abroad. The authors use data from 1984 to 1989, disaggregated at the sectorial level. Research spending abroad is a significant explanatory variable accounting for U.S. and Japanese foreign direct investment outflows to the U.K, France, Germany, and Italy (i.e., the largest countries in the European Union), but not when referring to intra-European foreign direct investment flows. They conclude that U.S. and Japanese investments might be driven by a technology-sourcing motivation.

4.   MODELLING M&AS IN RESEARCH-BASED INDUSTRIES

International acquisitions (or mergers) involving multinationals arise naturally as a channel for technology appropriation and exploitation. How do firms realize technology synergies and what is the role of M&As in international competition? We sketch a theoretical model of M&As that are knowledge-based. M&As have also been analyzed as a mechanism to change the management of badly managed firms, increase market concentration, realize diversification, and exploit firms' synergies. The synergy approach presented here offers a complementary view to the approach to takeovers as a market for managers acting under imperfect information (Jensen and Ruback, 1983; Jensen, 1988).

4.1   Modelling International Takeovers and Technology Networks

The synergy-spillover perspective stresses that M&As serve to create competitive advantages through process or product innovation. Oliva and Rivera-Batiz (1999) develop a model in which post-takeover profitability depends on the extent of the M&A cost-reduction effect. Consider a two-country duopoly partial equilibrium model of two related goods. In a pre-stage, two firms labelled "1" and "2" compete in the domestic market, and two foreign firms labelled "1*" and "2*" compete in the foreign market. The multinationalization game solved has three stages. At stage 1, firms choose whether or not to multinationalize and negotiate the M&A takeover fee. At stage 2, firms choose the level of R&D, and at the last stage they determine the volume of production.

The price paid in the M&A transaction depends on post-merger profits, firms' opportunity costs, and parties' bargaining power. The post-merger operating profit functions of cross-product groups formed by firms 1 and 1* and firms 2 and 2* are given by adding up their demands and operating cost functions. The feature that justifies a takeover or merger is the search for variable cost reduction. Cost-reducing M&As are modelled by introducing a cost function embodying technology transfers among the firms forming a conglomerate and technology spillovers.

The variable cost reductions generated by process innovation can be decomposed into:

(1) the direct cost-reduction effect of a firm's own research investment,

(2) the cost-reduction gain due to the R&D activities of the other group members (i.e., the intrafirm technology transfer or synergy effect),

(3) the spillover gains reaped from domestic competitors (i.e., the Silicon Valley effect).

R&D synergies between firms belonging to the same combination imply that the group obtains production cost-reduction benefits. However, synergies are not cost-free. In order to benefit from the technology developed within the group, member firms must afford some adaptation costs.

Takeovers that look advantageous from the viewpoint of acquiring firms might not be beneficial from the viewpoint of overall industry profitability. If one acquisition is matched by another acquisition involving rival firms, the new groups will not be able to obtain a net competitive advantage relative to each other. Furthermore, high enough cross-plant cost reductions can work against takeover profitability if they lead to high output, lower prices and reduced oligopolistic profits. In this case, the common suggestion that low profitability from M&As means that there is a reduction in the productivity of the acquiring and acquired companies is unwarranted.

Multinationalization arises in equilibrium when intrafirm synergies are strong enough. Strong synergies can be interpreted as meaning that multinationals' technologies are easily transferable within the group. Notice that stronger local interfirm spillovers might or might not encourage foreign investment. On one hand, stronger local spillovers benefit foreign investors operating in the region (i.e., Silicon Valley externality effects). On the other hand, stronger local spillovers increase the price of acquiring a local firm (i.e., the Silicon Valley acquisition price effect). The net effect of local spillovers on foreign investment depends on the relative importance of the local externality and acquisition price effects.

5. THE 1992-1994 PHARMACEUTICAL CRISIS AND THE STRATEGIC RESPONSE

In the late 1980s and 1990s, the pharmaceutical and biotechnology industries faced major restructuring processes involving mergers and acquisitions (between pharmaceuticals, and between pharmaceuticals and biotechnology firms), the formation of numerous strategic alliances, and the organization of research cooperation ventures. These developments highlight trends that apply to other industries as well, but there are features that are specific to the pharmaceutical industry.

Since the 1970s, pharmaceuticals have gone through twin waves. The first one took place in the late 1980s and the second during 1993-1995. The wave of M&As in the pharmaceutical industry in the 1990s differed from the aggregate U.S. and worldwide wave. The pharmaceutical wave began earlier and had slowed down by 1995 while the worldwide wave built up steam in the late 1990s. Also, the pharmaceutical M&A waves did not evolve in a random walk fashion but rather like two outbursts that died out as activity returned to normal levels. This idiosyncratic outburst pattern suggests the presence of industry-specific factors explaining the timing of the waves.

We focus here on the 1993-1995 wave in the U.S., and how M&As became an important element of the strategic response to specific structural and economic developments. A number of factors motivating pharmaceutical M&As are industry-specific. Restructuring activity was due to competitiveness factors, cost-reducing pressures, and regulatory changes faced by pharmaceutical firms. A redirection toward new technologies, and away from the traditional reliance on chemicals, increased pressures for cost reductions and the development of new pharmaceutical products.

The U.S. pharmaceuticals M&A wave of the 1990s took place in a period in which the industry's financial performance sharply deteriorated. During 1992-1994, price-earnings ratios collapsed, and the future of the industry became uncertain. The critical conditions prevailing at the time were the result of the combination of various contributing factors. These include the rise of competitive factors such as the generic drugs, delays in regulatory agency product approvals, bunched patent expirations, and the anticipated adverse effects of the Clinton administration's Health Reform. These events encouraged restructuring, domestic and international M&As, and a closer relation between pharmaceutical and biotech firms.

5.1   The Rise of Generics

In the U.S., the rise of generics after the enactment of the *Drug Price*

Competition and Patent Term Restoration Act (DPC-PTRA) of 1984 was a major factor putting competitive pressures on brand-name pharmaceutical products. This Act made generic drug testing requirements less stringent, facilitating the copying of prescription drugs with expired patents by generic drug companies. The Act reduced development time by only requiring a manufacturer to realize bioavailability or bioequivalence testing. This testing is designed to prove that a generic version produces the same level of the drug in the body as the brand-name drug, and thus in principle the same biological effects as the brand-name drug. Prior to 1984, a manufacturer of generics was subject to the same requirements as brand-name manufacturers. In particular, it was subject to expensive clinical trials to show the generic drug's safety and effectiveness.

The rise of generic drugs posed a serious threat to brand-name manufacturers. By the mid-1990s, generics held a 40% share of all U.S. prescriptions. A similar increase in market share took place in the U.K., but generics did not have a similar market impact in Spain and other countries. Typically, the expiration of a patent leads to the production of generic drug substitutes that significantly reduce the brand-name market share. Brand-name manufacturers have responded by producing generics and increasing advertising to keep brand-name prices up. The ultimate response to generics, though, is to bring in new patented products.

Generics also had a negative impact on international brand-name sales. Many Latin American and other countries that do not enforce international patent protection became producers of generic drugs.

5.2 Cost Containment and the Clinton Health Plan

U.S. policy initiatives related to the health plan advanced by the Clinton administration hit pharmaceuticals hard in 1992-1993. A component of the Clinton Health Plan, widely discussed in 1993, involved imposing price controls on pharmaceuticals. This initiative would have reversed the traditional policy of free determination of drug prices. Price controls were considered in order to reduce the high U.S. prices to levels closer to those in Europe and Canada. The plan was defeated in 1994, putting an end to the threat of price controls.

5.3   Patent Applications, Approval Delays, and Patent Expirations

The regulatory environment surrounding patents played a key role in leading to restructuring and new strategies in the U.S. pharmaceutical industry, the world's largest pharmaceutical market. M&As were encouraged by the stagnant number of drugs approved by the Food and Drug Administration (FDA), substantial approval delays, and patent expirations.

The total number of drugs approved by the FDA declined during the critical 1992-1994 period. Approvals went down from 26 in 1992, to 25 in 1993, and 22 in 1994. The decline in drug approvals in 1992-1994 coincided with the peak of the pharmaceutical companies M&A wave in the U.S. Because the stagnation in drug approvals limited the supply of new drugs by pharmaceutical companies, it played a role in encouraging M&As. Approvals sharply increased after 1994. There were 28 in 1995, 53 in 1996, 39 in 1997, and 30 new drugs (and 9 biologics) in 1998.

Mean approval times for pharmaceutical products declined from 34.1 months in 1986 to 29.9 and 26.5 in 1992 and 1993, respectively, but these approval times were still considered excessively long by industry sources. Subsequently, mean approval times declined substantially to 17.8 months in 1996. The *FDA Modernization Act*, approved in 1998, allowed further reductions in drug approval times. It took 11.7 months, on average, for the FDA to review the 30 drugs approved in 1998. The 9 biologics approved during 1998 were reviewed by the FDA in 13.5 months on average. The reviewing process benefited from user fees paid by pharmaceuticals to enable the FDA to hire additional personnel to review new drug applications.

The difficulties arising from the stagnant number of drug approvals and relatively long FDA delays in the early 1990s were compounded by the bunch expiration of patents on major products during 1993-1995 (see Table 5).

The associated reduction in revenues, jointly with the fact that most of the big pharmaceuticals depend on a few blockbusters, led the pharmaceuticals to search for new research areas to replace their product lines with new inventions. M&As can provide new products that satisfy market needs and sustain the acquirer's market-share position.

Table 5: Blockbuster patent expirations between 1993-1995 (US$ million)

Company	Product	Total Sales per Product in 1992
Glaxo	Zantac	$3,198
Bristol-Myers Squibb	Capoten	$1,652
Ciba-Geigy	Voltaren	$1,164
	Lopressor	$350
SmithKline Beecham	Tagamet	$1,075
Marion Merrel Dow	Seldane	$878
Sandoz	Sandimmune	$859
Syntex	Naprosyn	$785
Upjohn	Xanax	$650
Warner Lambert	Lopid	$552

Source: Ernst & Young. *Biotechnology Industry Annual Report*, 1994.

6. THE CREATION OF COMPETITIVE ADVANTAGES BY PHARMACEUTICAL AND BIOTECH FIRMS

The revenues of pharmaceutical firms depend on a few high-sales products developed through risky R&D spending. Patents held, patent expirations and government drug approvals play a key role in the incentives for innovation in the pharmaceutical industry (Boston Consulting Group, 1996). A key response to competitive pressures and regulatory barriers entails the search for new products. These factors have motivated increasingly close interactions with an allied industry: the biotechnology sector.

Biotechnology refers to any process based on manipulating DNA, the genetic blueprint of living organisms. Most biotech firms are devoted to the development of diagnostic and therapeutic products, particularly pharmaceuticals. In the 1990s, developments such as gene therapy were revealed to be promising areas for the development of new products.

Biotechnology research is a strategic asset for pharmaceuticals. Biotech research is complementary to pharmaceutical research and can serve as a platform to quickly expand the pipeline of pharmaceutical products. This factor explains why pharmaceuticals actively took over biotechnology firms in the 1990s and engaged in numerous strategic alliances, cooperative research ventures, agreements to market biotech-based drugs, and other forms of cooperation.

6.1   The Growth of the Biotechnology Industry

The biotechnology industry is a relatively young industry (close to 40% of U.S. biotech firms were founded after 1986) that currently comprises about 1,300 firms in the U.S. Biotechnology is not a large-firm industry. In 1997, approximately one-third of U.S. companies had fewer than 50 employees and more than two-thirds had fewer than 135 employees. Only about 10% of the companies employed more than 300 people.

The biotech industry has grown rapidly in the past decade. The value of product sales from biotechnology products increased from $1 billion in 1986 to $8 billion in 1985, $11 billion in 1996 and $13 billion in 1997. Industry sales are dominated by a small number of companies. In 1997, the three top-selling biotech drugs (Procrit, Epogen and Neupogen) were developed by Amgen (U.S.) and together sold over $3,200 million. Biotech drugs correspond to about 5% of drug sales worldwide.

After almost a decade of slow growth of value, Biotech stocks became hot during 1998-1999. The Amex Biotech Index of 15 stocks of major biotechs increased about 90% from August 1998 to August 1999, finally matching the previous record level of the index in 1992. However, the behavior of the 15-stock index hides large differences in the stock market performance of individual companies.

The biotechnology industry has traditionally been centred in the U.S., but it gradually extended worldwide in the 1990s. The Canadian biotech industry currently comprises about 50 firms. While increasingly globalized, biotechnology is not as globalized as the pharmaceutical industry. The U.S. Bureau of the Census reported that U.S biotechnology exports amounted to $1.0 billion in 1994, while imports were $0.1 billion.

6.2   Pharmaceutical and Biotech Research and Innovation

Research intensity is usually measured by the ratio of research spending to total sales. According to this index, pharmaceuticals and biotechnology firms are among the most research-intensive of all industries.

During 1973-1993, the median R&D intensity in all industries was 11% for U.S. firms, 7.3% for U.K. firms, 7.4% for French firms, 6.1% percent for German firms, and 4.3% for Japanese firms (OECD, 1995). The pharmaceutical industry has become more and more research-intensive over time (see Cockburn and Henderson, 1994, Henderson and Cockburn, 1996). Research intensity has increased from 3.7% in 1951 to 7% in the late 1950s, 8%-9% in the 1960s and 1970s, and 20% in 1997. According to Pharma, the U.S. pharmaceutical industry spent over $19 billion and $24 billion in R&D in 1996 and 1998, respectively.

The R&D intensities of pharmaceuticals are overwhelmed by the biotech industry. In 1997, R&D spending in the biotechnology industry amounted to $9.9 million. This amount corresponded to 74% of the $13.4 billion total industry sales (Ernst & Young, 1998). This is the highest research intensity level of any industry.

Table 6 reports the percentage of sales that top biotechnology and pharmaceutical firms devoted to research expenditures in 1993-1994. The magnitude of biotech research is high even when compared with current pharmaceuticals' R&D, and has increased phenomenally by any reasonable standard.

Table 6: R&D intensity of pharmaceutical and biotechnology firms

	Total Sales ($ million)		R&D ($ million)		R&D/Sales (%)	
	1993	1994	1993	1994	1993	1994
PHARMACEUTICAL INDUSTRY						
Johnson & Johnson	14,138	15,734	1,182	1,278	8.4	8.1
Merck	10,498	14,970	1,173	1,231	11.2	8.2
Bristol-Myers Squibb	11,413	11,984	1,128	1,108	9.9	9.2
Pfizer	7,478	8,281	974	1,139	13.0	13.8
Eli Lilly	6,452	5,712	955	839	14.8	14.7
Rhône-Poulenc Rorer	4,019	4,175	561	600	14.0	14.4
Hoechst	6,899	7,794	258	313	3.7	4.0
BIOTECH INDUSTRY						
Amgen	1,306	1,550	255	324	19.6	17.3
Genentech	457	601	299	314	65.4	52.2
Chiron	148	276	140	166	94.6	60.1
Biogen	136	140	79	91	58.1	65.0
Genzyme	234	290	97	67	41.5	23.1
Immunex	119	136	72	78	60.5	57.4

Source: Firms' Annual Reports, 1994-1995.

6.3   Biotech Patents and Approval Delays

Facing expiration of numerous patents as well as delayed and uncertain approval of new drugs, the pharmaceuticals looked for sources of new drug products. The biotechnology industry turned out to be the right alternative. After many years during which the biotech industry was more a promise than a source of new products, the prospects changed in the 1990s.

During the critical years 1992-1994, the number of patent applications presented by biotechnology firms to the U.S. Patent and Trademark Office augmented about 20%. However, the average pendency time for a biotech patent approval increased from 20.8 months in 1994 to 27.1 months in 1997 (according to the Biotechnology Industry Organization 1998 report). Still, the number of biotechnology drugs approved by the FDA increased steadily from 1994 on, reaching a record of 20 in 1998.

6.4   Restructuring and Competition

The relationship between pharmaceuticals and biotechnology strengthened in the mid-1990s as a consequence of competitive pressures. Pharmaceuticals' managers looked for new products and global efficiency achievements by combining biotech and pharmaceutical firms with complementary product lines and research. On one side, M&As and strategic alliances gave financial stability to biotech firms, allowed them to overcome marketing difficulties, and launched product internationalization. On the other side, pharmaceuticals found new research pipelines, technological synergies from biotechnology research groups, and access to new products.

Due to the nature of the industry, M&As involving biotech firms either exploit the marketing-production advantages of pharmaceuticals or are based on knowledge complementarities. The complementarity between pharmaceuticals' and biotech firms' capabilities, and the pursuance of similar goals, explain the M&A wave involving U.S. biotechnology companies and large European and U.S. pharmaceuticals. The exploitation of synergies between similar technologies has contributed to promote pharmaceutical-biotechnology linkages. The type of high-cost research projects that many biotechnology companies are developing could not be implemented without the support of pharmaceuticals.

7. INTERNATIONALIZATION AND CLUSTERING OF THE BIOTECH INDUSTRY

The internationalization of the biotech industry is reflected in emerging biotech industries in different countries around the world, and the large number of international strategic alliances, joint ventures and M&As in recent years. Globalization has proceeded rapidly, contingent on the presence of a skilled and highly specialized labour pool. There are currently about 1,300 firms in the U.S., 500 in Europe, 100 in Israel, 50 in Canada, and many in Japan, Korea, Singapore and other countries. The developments discussed below signal greater international diffusion and keen global competition in the future.

7.1 U.S. Biotech Firms Abroad

A relatively new phenomenon is that U.S. biotech companies are investing abroad. Although biotechnology firms do not have the marketing power of the large pharmaceuticals, they often commercialize their own products abroad.

Many of the top U.S. biotechnology companies conduct their foreign operations through numerous subsidiaries abroad. For instance, Baxter

Healthcare Corp. currently operates in around 50 countries (in Western Europe, Latin America and Asia). In 1992, the foreign markets and foreign operations of Genzyme amounted to 16% of total sales. The foreign share increased to 29% in 1993, 37% in 1994, and over 46% in 1997. By 1997, Genzyme had subsidiaries installed in more than 14 countries.[2] During 1992-1994, between 11.8% and 14.3% of Centocor's revenues were obtained in Europe. In 1997, the percentage had risen to 26% of Centocor's total revenues.

7.2   Foreign Investment in the U.S. Biotech Industry

A remarkable feature of cross-border acquisitions of biotech companies is that they have been largely unidirectional. European pharmaceuticals' acquisitions of U.S. biotech firms exceed the number of deals between U.S. pharmaceuticals and European biotechnology firms. In 1998, domestic deals between U.S. firms dominated while European firms remained outside the target area of American raiders.

Foreign direct investment in U.S. biotechnology firms has been increasing in importance in the past two decades. According to the International Trade Commission, about 54 U.S. firms related to the biotech industry were acquired by foreign investors in the 1980s. The peak was reached in 1989 with the acquisition of 9 firms, among them the purchase by Bayer (Germany) of Miles Pharmaceuticals Inc., a large U.S. biotech firm located in West Haven, Connecticut.

Acquisition activities involving biotech companies and European pharmaceuticals surged in the 1990s. Table 7 shows data on national and international investments involving pharmaceuticals and biotechnology companies. In 1990, Hoffmann-La Roche (Switzerland) paid $2,110 million to acquire 60% of Genentech Inc, a large U.S. biotech company located in San Francisco. By 1995, La Roche already owned 66% of Genentech and held an option (expiring in 1999) to increase its stake to 79.9%. A further move by La Roche to open new markets was the 1997 $11,000-million purchase of German-based Corange, the parent company to the world's second-largest diagnostics firm.

Foreign investments in U.S. biotechs continued throughout the 1990s. In 1993, Rhône-Poulenc Rorer (France) paid $113 million, for Applied Immune Sciences. In 1994, Ciba-Geigy (Switzerland) paid $2.1 billion to acquire

49.9% of Chiron (U.S.). In 1995, Glaxo Wellcome (U.K.) purchased Affymax, and Sandoz (Switzerland) acquired Genetic Therapy Inc. As shown in Table 7, strategic cross-border acquisitions of U.S. biotech firms are not restricted to the major European giants.

Table 7: Selected international and national investments between pharmaceutical and biotechnology firms (in $ millions)

Pharmaceuticals	Biotechnology Firms	Amount
1990		
Roche (60%)	Genentech	$2,100
1991		
American Home Products (60%)	Genetics Institute	$666
Sandoz (60%)	SyStemix	$392
1993		
Rhône-Poulenc Rorer (60%)	Applied Immune Science	$113
1994		
Ciba-Geigy (49.9%)	Chiron	$2,100
1995		
Glaxo Wellcome	Affymax	$533
Sandoz	Genetic Therapy Inc.	$295
Eli Lilly	Sphinx Pharmaceuticals	$80
Marion Merrell Dow	Selectide	$60
1996		
American Home Products	Genetics Institute	$1,250
1997		
Millennium Pharmaceuticals	ChemGenics Pharmaceuticals	$93
Novartis	Systemic	$76
Agouron Pharmaceuticals	Alanex	$61
1998		
Arris (U.S.)	Sequana (U.S.)	$166
Pharmacopeia (U.S.)	Molecular Simulations (U.S.)	$133

Source: Ernst & Young. *Biotechnology Industry Annual Report*, 1994 and 1997.

Several factors explain the U.S. deals involving foreign firms in recent years. First, the regulatory environment is favourable compared with other countries such as Germany. Second, the important basic research efforts of universities and public organizations represent a magnet for research-oriented industries. Third, there are flexible and extensive financial facilities. Fourth, biotech product commercialization is centred in the U.S., which is the largest health-care market worldwide (about a third of all pharmaceuticals are sold in the U.S.).

7.3   Local Clustering and Knowledge Externalities

U.S. biotech clusters have been attractive for foreign companies searching for benefits from both the R&D investments of the target biotechnology firms and the externalities generated by the U.S. clusters. The deals involving foreign companies include acquisitions of biotech firms as well as multiple joint ventures and strategic alliances.

Table 8 shows the clustering of biotech firms in 1994 and 1996. The industry is concentrated in California (with clusters in Silicon Valley, San Diego and Los Angeles/Orange County), New England (i.e., the Boston area), and to a lesser extent in New Jersey and Pennsylvania. The location of the two major biotech clusters in the Bay Area and Boston can be rationalized by the abundance of specialized skilled labour and the easy access to trained researchers and R&D developed by the universities in these particular regions. Zucker, Darby, and Brewer (1996), and Audretsch and Stephan (1996, 1998), present evidence showing that the localized benefits arising from the presence of scientists and highly trained human capital affect the number of startups in biotechnology. This evidence is suggestive of the presence of knowledge externalities.

Table 8: Clustering in the U.S. biotechnology industry

	1994	1996
Area	Number of Firms	
SF Bay Area	192	204
New England	172	168
Mid-Atlantic	114	108
San Diego	102	94
New York	86	84
LA/Orange County	68	75
Texas	54	53
Seattle	52	53
New Jersey	49	62
Philadelphia	48	63
North Carolina	47	47
Wisconsin	33	37
Illinois	27	26
Ohio	26	27
Michigan	23	23
Iowa	23	24
Florida	21	19
Minnesota	21	22
Georgia	20	24
Colorado	20	22

Source: Ernst & Young. *Biotechnology Industry Annual Report*, 1994 and 1997.

7.4   Internationalized Research

A substantial proportion of pharmaceuticals' R&D has been conducted abroad in the past two decades. In 1980 and 1995, 27% and 28%, respectively, of pharmaceuticals' R&D was conducted abroad. The share of research conducted abroad declined to 22% in 1998.

Various companies are highly globalized in terms of research spending. For instance, Pfizer conducts as much research abroad as in the U.S. The 50,000-employee pharmaceutical giant has close to 5,000 employees in its research division. Half of them work in Groton, Connecticut, while the rest work in Sandwich, Britain, and Nagoya, Japan.

A key aspect of research globalization has to do with the formation of research alliances between biotech and pharmaceutical firms in different countries. For instance, in 1998 American Home Products (pharmaceuticals, U.S.) and Genset (biotech, France) signed a deal for developing vaccines based on Genset's gene research. Genset also signed a contract with Pharmacia & Upjohn (U.S.) to examine which genes respond to a medicine being developed by Pharmacia & Upjohn.

7.5   The Rise of European Biotechnology

An important element in the biotech industry's internationalization is the rise of European biotechnology. In the mid-1990s, British companies such as British Biotech, Scotia, Celltech, Chiroscience and Chemunex dominated European markets. There are now over 500 biotech companies in Europe, and European Union policies are keen on promoting industry development. Innogenetics (Belgium), Qiagen (the Netherlands, with operating headquarters and production in Germany), Genset (France), Transgene (France), NeuroSearch (Denmark), and many other continental European companies now compete with British firms as equals.

A number of factors have facilitated the development and consolidation of the European biotechnology industry. European equity markets expanded in the 1990s, opening the door for public stock offerings by biotech companies, which previously depended on private financing obtained from venture capital, institutional investors and strategic alliances.   In 1992, British Biotech listed in the London Stock Exchange (LSE) and almost 20 companies promptly followed suit upon the liberalization of the LSE towards the biotechnology industry.

The European equivalent of NASDAQ, the European Association of Securities and Dealers Automated Quotation (EASDAQ), has unified the European markets and opened financing alternatives to biotechs. Innogenetics, the Belgian therapeutics and diagnostics company, which rose from $10 to $74 a share on EASDAQ between April 1997 and April 1998, was the most-valued continental Europe bioscience company in 1998 ($1.65 billion). European biotechs can now list in local markets, EASDAQ and NASDAQ. For instance, Transgene has completed a dual listing in NASDAQ and in the Paris Bourse's Nouveau Marché, Chemunex lists on EASDAQ and on the Nouveau Marché, and Qiagen lists on NASDAQ and on Frankfurt's Neuer Markt.

The establishment in 1995 of the European Agency for the Evaluation of Medicinal Products, EMEA (the European equivalent of the FDA) established clearer and more unified rules of the game in Europe. The London-based organization makes recommendations about new drugs to the European Commission. Both EMEA and the European Commission have the stated goal of rapid drug approval and unification of the drug approval process.

8. INNOVATION POLICY AND PERFORMANCE IN PHARMACEUTICALS AND BIOTECHNOLOGY

Pharmaceutical invention and innovation can be measured along many dimensions. These include the number of patent applications, patents granted, the number of new products approved by regulatory agencies, product quality, and market price effects (the latter two are examined by Berndt, Cockburn and Griliches, 1996). We focus on the number of products approved by regulatory agencies. The number of new products most accurately measures the availability of new products arising from innovation. It also reflects the impact of regulatory actions such as approval lags and denials by regulatory agencies.

8.1 Innovative and Global Drugs

An analysis of the impact of innovative efforts should take into account the distinction between breakthrough drugs and drugs arising from minimal product differentiation. The latter are sometimes called "me too" efforts to produce varieties competing with breakthrough products.

Table 9 shows a classification of countries according to the innovative (i.e., breakthrough) and global drugs developed during 1975-1989. Global drugs are defined as those marketing in all of the G-7 countries (Canada, France, Italy, Germany, Japan, the U.K., and the U.S.). Sixty-six drugs are classified as both innovative and global. The U.S. holds the largest share in absolute terms, but the U.K. comes out as the best performer if innovation is measured relative to the domestic market size.

Table 9: Countries ranked by number of innovative and global drugs developed between 1975-1989

	Number of Innovative and Global Drugs (I&G)	Weight	Weighted # I&G
United Kingdom	11	8.69	95.65
United States	30	1.00	30.00
Germany	8	3.73	29.85
France	3	4.13	12.39
Japan	3	1.54	4.62
Canada	0	12.19	0.00

Source: Finkelstein and Bittenger, 1993 (Exhibit 2, p. 3).

The highly controlled and regulated countries in the sample were the least innovative during the period. These include Canada (price controls, compulsory licensing until 1987, and partial patent protection afterwards), France (price controls), and Japan (price controls, although prices are high relative to the rest of the world due to a protected market).

8.2 Regulation and Biotech Innovation in Canada

The Canadian government has traditionally followed a policy of maintaining low drug prices. This goal has been promoted through price controls and patent laws. The Patented Medicine Pricing Review Board (PMPRB) reviews new medicine prices by comparing them with prices in foreign countries and Canadian prices in the same therapeutic class. The Board has the power to investigate and negotiate to lower prices (on the basis that it has the remedial power to revoke the patent of any drug selling at prices deemed to be excessive).

In 1969, an amendment to the *Canadian Patent Act* introduced compulsory licensing to import chemicals to be used to manufacture medicines. The royalty rate to be received by the patent holder was set at the low level of 4% of the licensee's gross sales (the royalty rate was subsequently increased). The licensing requirement allowed generic firms to manufacture patented medicines developed by foreign firms and import generics from other countries (including countries that manufactured generics under weak patent protection laws). The weakening of patent protection was intended to lower drug prices. Bill C-22, passed in 1987, partially re-established patent protection by tying the protection to increased R&D spending in Canada. The bill granted 7 to 10 years of conditional protection from compulsory licensing (or 20 years for drugs invented in Canada) provided that the R&D-to-sales ratio in Canada increased step-wise from an average of 4.9% in 1986, to 8.0% in 1991, 9.0% in 1994 and 10% in 1996.

Weak patent protection in Canada was associated with low research intensities, low rates of innovation, and stagnant investments by multinationals. The 1989 Act reinforcing patent rights was followed by greater spending (particularly in clinical trials) by multinationals.

The Canadian biotechnology industry gained force in the 1990s. There are about 50 Canadian biotech firms, including Allelix, BioChem Pharma, Biomira, QLP PhotoTherapeutics, and MDS. In November 1995, BioChem's Pharma obtained FDA approval for Epivir (3TC), an AIDS drug that has been shown to be effective in treating AIDS when combined with AZT. BioChem's success allowed the company to raise $183 million through offerings in 1996, a very high amount by biotech standards. Epivir, marketed by Glaxo Wellcome, sold $973 million worth in 1998, becoming the fourth biotech drug in terms of worldwide sales.

Canadian success is not restricted to BioChem. In December 1995, QLP PhotoTherapeutics obtained FDA approval for Photofrin (to treat esophageal cancer). In April 1996, Biomira received approval for Truquant BR (a breast cancer diagnostic drug). In view of the increasing importance of the Canadian market, the large U.S. biotech firm Genzyme established a headquarters in Ottawa in 1996.

9.   TECHNOLOGY AND M&A POLICIES

This section focuses on innovation and technology policies. M&As have implications for a wide range of policy issues relating to subsidization of research expenditures, market concentration, and the regulation of M&As.

9.1   Business R&D Policy and Government Financing

What has been the role of the government in encouraging business R&D? When we restrict ourselves to business R&D spending, the role of the private sector is dominant. Between 70% and almost 100% (Japan) of business R&D is financed by the private sector. Even though the government plays a minor overall role in business R&D, this role can be important in particular strategic sectors. The policy problem is determining how to allocate scarce government resources across sectors.

Governments are likely to intervene in commercial research-intensive sectors, and routinely do so, because there are large externalities involved that are not completely internalized by the private sector. The idea of improving current and estimated future performance hinges on maximization of social benefits, including the externalities created. How to allocate subsidies among industries and firms is a decision entailing efficiency and strategic elements.

The exploitation of comparative advantages might serve as a criterion to specify R&D targets. In practice, the problem consists of determining the costs and potential efficiency levels of industries and firms. The economics of strategic research spending when there is incomplete information about firms' characteristics suggests the following principle: governments should spend on the most efficient firms, and support those that show the greatest and fastest learning-by-doing potential. There is a serious problem in identifying firms' cost functions and learning potential. But if funds are to be granted on the basis of efficiency criteria, estimates must be made even if they are not accurate. The government might not be able to pick winners, but it must at least try to do so, or abstain from intervention in technology sectors.

Optimal strategic intervention arguments in competing open economies, as detailed in Oliva and Rivera-Batiz (forthcoming), seem to be at odds with common notions of strategic government intervention. For instance, one would gather that well-performing sectors do not need funding compared with struggling industries. But international strategic arguments are based on social benefit maximization and global competition, not on industry need.

Unless estimated future growth in learning and externality-creating potential are high, it is difficult to articulate an international strategic argument for investing in under-performing industries. In international competition, if a country decides to subsidize under-performers, it is optimal for rival countries to subsidize over-performers and get the largest share of the world market. As a consequence, in a competitive world of rapid innovation, changing competitive advantages, and uncertain industrial policy success, traditional infant industry arguments are precarious.

9.2   Market Concentration and Synergies

M&As serve to generate technology synergies. This efficiency effect poses a policy problem because M&As can also increase industrial concentration and induce the exit of existing firms. These consequences arise in an obvious way when M&As take place within an industry, but can also take place when cross-industry M&As create competitive advantages that force independent firms to exit the markets. While it is true that the latter mechanism for inducing exit is not the standard predator behavior, it is also true that it can ultimately have the same adverse effects on competition. How to deal with the indirect industrial concentration effects of cross-product M&As is an issue that has not received adequate attention yet.

The combination of synergistic M&As and greater market concentration represents a clear dilemma between efficiency and excessive market power. Some observers have argued that rapid technological change will eliminate competitive advantages, and market power based on them. Firms are exposed to innovation by competitors that erode monopoly power. For instance, a strategy oriented toward leapfrogging by investing in the latest technologies that have not been fully developed by established firms can ultimately allow follower firms to surpass technological leaders.

When applied to M&As, there might be problems with the argument that we can safely "leave Microsoft alone" because rapid technological change will induce leapfrogging that will dilute its monopoly power. Concentration of research in large firms can represent a difficult entry barrier to smaller, isolated firms. The same type of argument applies at the country level.

Our discussion suggests some approaches to the acute technology versus industrial concentration dilemma. First, strategic arguments suggest that regulators should promote M&As that enhance industries' international competitiveness and do not reduce local competition. Second, government-financed basic research and science discoveries lead to the diffusion of new knowledge, encouraging the development of new technologies that in turn make technological leapfrogging possible and allow the creation of new companies. Third, a policy of promotion of clusters encourages diffusion of technology and the generation of externalities that can limit market concentration. Fourth, a policy of responding to M&As with further M&As (or strategic alliances) can paradoxically eliminate the negative effects of having large integrated firms competing with smaller firms that do not reap the synergies that are attached to M&As. The role of the government in this case entails encouraging, or at least not opposing, cooperative efforts that have the potential to undermine the monopoly power of market leaders.

9.3 Should M&As Be Prompted or Restricted?

Are M&As a negative activity from a social point of view? In general, the answer depends on the types of parties involved in the transaction, and the particularities of the industry (e.g., how competitive the industry is in the first place).

Two arguments are often utilized to defend measures restricting foreign direct investment through M&As. First, M&As often increase market concentration and entail predatory behavior that is harmful to consumers' interests. It is well known that this argument may or may not hold and can only be assessed strictly on a case-by-case basis. Second, M&As can result in a decline in R&D. For instance, if M&As generate large debts that must be paid after the restructuring, R&D spending could be negatively affected and there could be social losses.

The evidence on the effects of M&As on research is ambiguous except for highly research-intensive industries. In this case, mergers and acquisitions have been found not to induce a decline in research spending. In medium and low research-intensive industries, results tend to be negative, that is, M&As are found to induce a reduction in R&D. The available evidence is reviewed next.

9.4   The R&D Effects of M&As

A commonly voiced critical comment on M&As is that they result in lower levels of research. What are the effects of M&As on R&D spending? The evidence tends to show that research investment does not decline with M&As in high R&D-intensive industries. Also, there is some evidence that R&D increases when M&As involve related firms.

A 1985 survey done by the U.S. Office of the Chief Economist of the Securities and Exchange Commission (SEC) concludes that all firms participating in the survey increased their R&D in the post-merger period, with the exception of those in the steel industry. Jensen (1988) reports a positive correlation between M&As and R&D at the aggregate level for the U.S. economy. In fact, the volume of R&D increased in years of heated M&A activity, such as 1984.

Hall (1988) uses data on 2,519 U.S. manufacturing companies acquired 1976 to 1986. She finds that, when the parties involved in the M&A firm transaction are high R&D-intensive, post-merger gains increase and there is no evidence that R&D spending declines (although there is no evidence of increased R&D). A related study by Hall (1994) finds that takeovers involving the acquisition of new product lines have no significant impact on the level of R&D, but R&D declines when M&As are defensive-type restructurings (targets reacting against hostile takeovers).

An example of a negative effect of M&As on research is the 1985 M&A involving Datapoint and Polaroid Corporation, which resulted in a 50% decline in R&D spending. M&As among closely related firms did not produce evidence of an induced decline in R&D spending. On the contrary, when acquirer and target have closely related product lines, the evidence points to a constant level of R&D, or even an increase. For example, the transactions between Du Pont Chemical and Conoco in 1982, and Philip Morris and General Foods in 1985, led to increased R&D expenditures.

Miller (1990) studies 19 U.S. restructuring firms in the 1980s, finding that the restructurings entailed increased debt, and resources were shifted away from R&D activities to pay the debt. As a consequence, R&D spending declined after merging. However, he argues that the M&As did not negatively affect research spending of those R&D-intensive firms in which R&D is especially relevant.

10. CONCLUSIONS

This paper has examined international competition through technology creation and appropriation. Countries display clear R&D specialization patterns. R&D spending in particular industries varies widely across countries and mirrors the arenas of international competition. Mergers and acquisitions are viewed as a particular form of firm interaction to face international technological competition. There are two related but separate orientations of M&As: national and international. In both cases, they can constitute a strategy to gain market share directly, but also to increase market share indirectly by improving competitiveness. Competitive advantages are created by innovation arising from the exploitation of technology synergies and the appropriation of foreign research through subsidiaries abroad.

Pharmaceutical and biotech firms' sales are usually concentrated in a few star products. These products are developed through risky R&D spending that constitutes a high fixed-cost factor. Given these industry features and tough international competition, firms have followed two key strategic responses. One strategy involves globalization to increase sales and spread the cost of developing new drugs over many markets. The second strategic response is to engage in the search for new products and innovation through M&As, cooperative ventures, and strategic alliances. The rise and globalization of biotechnology in the 1990s constituted a major element of pharmaceuticals restructuring and search for new products.

In the early 1990s, the expiration of numerous patents and the associated reduction in revenues, jointly with the fact that most of the big pharmaceuticals depend on a few blockbusters, led them to look for biotech research to replace their product lines with new inventions. M&As brought new products into the pipeline, satisfied market needs, and sustained the acquirers' market-share position. M&As involving biotech firms led to a surge in the introduction of biotech products and constituted a diversified portfolio of products in the pipeline.

The analysis in this paper offers a knowledge-based view of competition in research-oriented industries. The approach relates closely to the literature on research and endogenous technological change launched by Romer (1990) and others. This literature stresses the role of aggregate externalities relating to human capital, physical capital and technology. In order to examine the role and extent of international externalities, we need models that can define and delimit the properties of externalities in the context of inter- and intrafirm interactions. International growth and trade patterns can then be analyzed in terms of models that have explicit microeconomic dimensions. Formulation of microeconomic models of this type might be a prerequisite for rigorous strategic policy discussions in a knowledge-based society.

NOTES

[1] See OECD (1996). The distinction between high- and medium-tech is not clear-cut. According to the OECD classification, high-tech includes aircraft; drugs and medicines; electrical machinery; instruments; office and computing machinery; and radio, TV and communication equipment. Medium-tech industries include chemicals (excluding drugs); nonelectrical machinery; nonferrous metals; motor vehicles; and rubber and plastic products.

[2] Denmark, England, France, Germany, Italy, Spain, Switzerland, Japan, Singapore, Argentina, Brazil, Australia, Canada and Israel.

REFERENCES

Audretsch, D. B. and P. E. Stephan, "Company-Scientist Locational Links: The Case of Biotechnology. " *American Economic Review,* 86(3), 1996, 641-652.

Audretsch, D. B. and P. E. Stephan, "How and Why Does Knowledge Spill Over? The Case of Biotechnology." Center for Economic Policy Research, Discussion Paper Series No. 1991, October 1998.

Berndt, E. R., I. Cockburn and Z. Griliches, "Pharmaceutical Innovations and Market Dynamics: Tracking Effects on Price Indexes for Anti-Depressant Drugs." *Brookings Papers on Economic Activity: Microeconomics,* 1996, 133-188.

Boston Consulting Group, *Sustaining Innovation in U.S. Pharmaceuticals. Intellectual Property Protection and the Role of Patents.* Boston: Boston Consulting Group, 1996.

Cockburn, I., and R. M. Henderson, *Racing or Spilling? The Determinants of Research Productivity in the Pharmaceutical Industry.* Washington, DC: American Enterprise Institute, 1994.

Ernst & Young, *Biotechnology Industry Annual Report.* Palo Alto, CA: Ernst and Young LLP, various issues (annual).

Ernst & Young, *New Directions' 98. The Twelfth Biotechnology Industry Annual Report.* Palo Alto, CA: Ernst and Young LLP, 1998.

Ernst & Young, *Bridging the Gap. 13th Biotechnology Industry Annual Report.* Palo Alto, CA: Ernst and Young LLP, 1998.

Finkelstein, S. N. and P.G. Bittenger, "Price Controls and the Competitiveness of Pharmaceutical Firms: A Preliminary Look at the Experience of Five Countries." Program on the Pharmaceutical Industry. MIT Sloan School of Management. Working Paper #8-93, 1993.

Florida, R., "Foreign Direct Investment and the Economy," in Cynthia A. Beltz, (ed.) *The Foreign Investment Debate. Opening Markets Abroad or Closing Markets at Home.* Washington, DC: Institute for International Economics, 1995.

Hall, B. H., "The Effect of Takeover Acquisition on Corporate Research and Development," in Alan J. Auerbach (ed.) *Corporate Takeovers.* Chicago: University of Chicago Press, 1988.

Hall, B. H. "Investment and Research and Development at the Firm Level: Does the Source of Financing Matter?" NBER Working Paper No. 4096, June 1992.

Hall, B. H., "Corporate Restructuring and Investment Horizons in the United States, 1976-1987." *Business History Review,* 68, 1994.

Hall, B. H. and J. Mairesse, "Exploring the Relationship between R&D and Productivity in French Manufacturing Firms." NBER Working Paper No. 3956, January 1992.

Harris, R. S. and D. Ravenscraft, "The Role of Acquisitions in Foreign Direct Investment: Evidence from the U.S. Stock Market." *Journal of Finance*, XLVI(3), 1991, 825-844.

Henderson, R. M. and I. Cockburn, "Scale, Scope, and Spillovers: Research Strategy and Research Productivity in the Pharmaceutical Industry." *Rand Journal of Economics,* 27(3), 1996, 32-59.

Jensen, M., "Takeovers: Their Causes and Consequences." *Journal of Economic Perspectives*, 2(1), 1988, 21-48.

Jensen, M. C. and R. S. Ruback, "The Market for Corporate Control: The Scientific Evidence." *Journal of Financial Economics*, 11(1-4), 1983, 5-50.

Mergers + Acquisitions International, New York: Investment Dealers' Digest. Bimonthly periodical.

Miller, R. R., "Do Mergers and Acquisitions Hurt R&D?" *Research-Technology Management,* 33, 1990, 11-15.

Neven, D. and G. Siotis, "Technology Sourcing and FDI in the EC: An Empirical Evaluation." *International Journal of Industrial Organization,* 14(5), 1996, 543-560.

OECD, *Industrial Policy in OECD Countries. Annual Review.* Paris: Organization for Economic Cooperation and Development, 1994.

OECD, *Scoreboard Indicators.* Paris: Organization for Economic Cooperation and Development, 1995.

OECD, *Scoreboard Indicators.* Paris: Organization for Economic Cooperation and Development, 1996.

Oliva, M-A. and L. A. Rivera-Batiz, "Multinationals, Technology Networks and International Takeovers." Mimeo, MIT Sloan School of Management and McGill University, 1999.

Oliva, M-A.. and L. A. Rivera-Batiz, *Strategic Trade Analysis: Theory, Policy and Evidence.* Oxford: Oxford University Press, forthcoming.

Pharmaceutical Manufacturers Association (PMA), *Trends in U.S. Pharmaceutical Sales and R&D, 1990-1993 Annual Survey Report.* Washington, DC: PMA, 1993.

Romer, P. M., "Endogenous Technological Change." *Journal of Political Economy*, 98, 1990, S71-S101.

United Nations, *World Investment Report.* New York and Geneva: United Nations Centre on Transnational Corporations, Annual report, various issues.

U.S. Department of Commerce, Bureau of the Census. *Census of Manufacturers.* Washington, DC: U.S. Government Printing Office, various years

U.S. Department of Commerce, *Foreign Direct Investment in the United States: Review and Analysis of Current Developments*. Washington, DC: U.S. Government Printing Office, 1991.

U.S. Department of Commerce, Economics and Statistics Administration, Office of the Chief Economist, *Foreign Direct Investment in the United States: An Update*. Washington, DC: U.S. Government Printing Office, 1995.

U.S. Department of Commerce, Bureau of Economic Analysis, *Survey of Current Business, Foreign Direct Investment in the U.S.* Washington, DC: U.S. Government Printing Office, 1997.

Zucker, L. G., M. R. Darby and M. B. Brewer, "Intellectual Human Capital and the Birth of U.S. Biotechnology Enterprises." *American Economic Review,* 86(3), 1996, 641-652.

10. ELECTRONIC COMMERCE AND THE INFORMATION HIGHWAY

Luc Soete
University of Maastricht & MERIT

1. INTRODUCTION

What probably strikes most readers of recent policy documents discussing the subject of electronic commerce and the information highway is the extent of the expectations business people and policy-makers have with respect to the expected growth impact of such new forms of electronic, interactive, digital commerce, particularly when compared to the current, limited, occurrence of the phenomenon. There is probably no area where, considering the relatively limited technological improvements still required, the gap between the current phenomenon and expected future use is as large as in the case of electronic commerce. For instance, Figure 1 illustrates the Internet growth forecast in Europe for the period 1998-2001 in terms of on-line population and Internet revenues. While the growth in penetration rate is substantial, a threefold increase over the next three years, the forecast growth in revenues is staggering: from just over $1 billion in 1998 to $64 billion in 2001. By comparison, U.S. revenues are estimated at more than $200 billion in 2001.

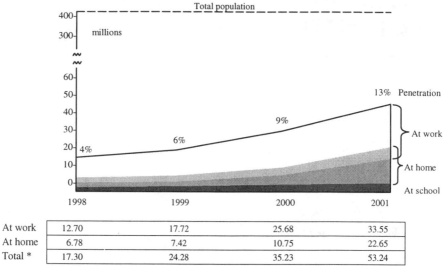

	1998	1999	2000	2001
At work	12.70	17.72	25.68	33.55
At home	6.78	7.42	10.75	22.65
Total *	17.30	24.28	35.23	53.24

* Total less than sum due to overlap. Includes School figures.

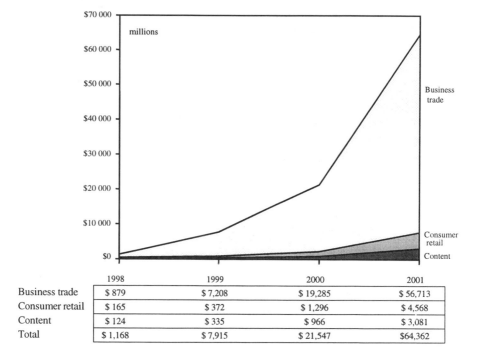

	1998	1999	2000	2001
Business trade	$ 879	$ 7,208	$ 19,285	$ 56,713
Consumer retail	$ 165	$ 372	$ 1,296	$ 4,568
Content	$ 124	$ 335	$ 966	$ 3,081
Total	$ 1,168	$ 7,915	$ 21,547	$64,362

(Source: Forrester Research, Inc.)

Figure 1: The European on-line population and growth of Europe's Internet revenues

Such dramatic forecasts lead one almost automatically to the presumption that there must be particularly strong impediments of various sorts preventing the rapid diffusion of electronic commerce so far. These barriers or impediments can be of a technical (e.g., encryption), legal (regulations), economic (costs) or simply user-friendly nature (access through PC or TV and mobile phone). The essential assumption from the policy perspective is that governments can help private industry in overcoming many of these barriers. Furthermore, overcoming those barriers is likely to involve finding international solutions, since the real growth potential of electronic commerce involves, in the first instance, "global" access by firms and individuals to suppliers of goods and services of all kinds. Hence, and not surprisingly, this has been to some extent the bread and butter of most recent policy reports on the subject, whether from national authorities (including the Canadian report "Electronic Commerce in Canada – Priorities for Action", 1997/8; the U.S. policy notes on "A Framework for Global Electronic Commerce", July 1997; the Japanese policy statement in "Towards the Age of the Digital Economy", May 1997; and the European Union's "European Initiative in Electronic Commerce", April 1997) or international organizations (see, among other things, the many contributions from the OECD in particular but also the WTO and WIPO).

In this paper, I will not discuss these relatively common policy issues. They are relatively well known by now and evolve rather quickly because of new technical solutions. There is an obvious tendency to reduce the debate to such technical issues: to finding appropriate technology-push solutions to the many security, privacy or consumer protection problems. In so doing, the basic premise is, generally speaking, that the current legal framework regulating "meatspace," as some authors are now calling real, physical commerce, can be adapted to "cyberspace." While this will certainly be the case for a number of products and consumers, whether business or individuals – a good example is given in Box 1 with respect to the licensing of downloaded music – there will also be many cases where such technical solutions will not really provide the conditions of trust and transparency typical of physical, human interactions. From this perspective, not to open the "black box" of the more human cultural and social barriers, considering, for instance, the role of shopping as a social activity, seems to ignore some of the most essential features of "commerce" activities.

Box 1: From http://www.MusicTrial.com

> The first integrated solution for licensing music in the digital age will be formally tested this autumn by U.K. music rights societies MCPS and PRS and the leading U.S.-based developer of secure on-line music delivery systems, Liquid Audio.
>
> Anyone visiting the *www.MusicTrial.com* Web site will be able to download CD-quality music for free using the Liquid Audio MusicPlayer (which can also be downloaded free from *www.LiquidAudio.com*). The music tracks available for download have been provided free of charge by PRS and MCPS members for the duration of the 90-day trial.
>
> Utilizing the Liquid Audio music distribution system, the trial partners will track music downloads and users will be given automatic copyright clearance in accordance with the licence granted to the owner of the sound recording by the copyright holder of the musical work. The prototype integrated licensing system developed by MCPS and PRS for MusicTrial.com provides a template for future audio distribution and licensing management on the Internet and represents a critical step forward for on-line music sales. MusicTrial.com demonstrates how music can be acquired and licensed for use in one simple on-line transaction.
>
> This unprecedented trial represents the first significant step towards finding a global solution for the legal trading of copyright music and sound recordings in the electronic age.
>
> More information from *acrookes@prs.co.uk*

To avoid this critique, the assumption is often made, as in Figure 1, that it is the business-to-business segment of electronic commerce that will take the lead, where such barriers are unlikely to play a significant role. For the next five years, most forecasts expect the business-to-business segment to be the driving force behind the expected rapid growth of e-commerce. This will allow for lower costs through international access to cheaper and more efficient suppliers, further opening up and enlarging market opportunities, particularly with respect to small and medium-sized firms, and through better use of available capital. In short, it will change the business fundamentals of exchange both internally and externally with suppliers and customers. From this perspective, it is likely that e-commerce represents to some extent a flood of new market opportunities. However, in making these at first sight rather reasonable assumptions, one seems to underestimate the relatively broad extent of electronic interchange that already exists between various supply chains from raw materials production down to retail sale businesses in highly developed economies such as the U.S., Canada, Japan or Europe. From this point of view, electronic commerce appears more like an evolutionary transformation, a further, undoubtedly more ubiquitous, efficiency-improving factor in a long series of improvements in logistics and wholesale and retail trade activities, from bar coding to EDI to e-commerce. As a consequence, and maybe somewhat paradoxically in terms of expectations of the huge growth and efficiency-enhancing effects of e-commerce, these improvements appear to be more of the incremental type. They will be small in sectors where large, sophisticated multinational companies already operate, as in the food or automobile sectors, in a logistically sophisticated way, but probably large in sectors with many SMEs and a more overt domestic focus.

In saying this, it will be clear that the definition of the relevant concept of e-commerce used here interacts with the information highways, i.e., the conduct of commerce activities – buying, selling and transactions of all kinds – over the new information highway, i.e., the Internet. To argue that e-commerce is not new and includes all commerce transactions involving some use of information and communication technologies, such as ordering by telephone, fax, or Minitel, or payment by credit or debit cards, would effectively mean that practically all commerce is now e-commerce. Within the European context of the existence of systems such as Minitel, such a definition does not provide sufficient insight into the new policy challenges posed by the new forms of e-commerce.[i]

In the case of business-to-consumer commerce, the long-term growth impact of e-commerce is likely to be even more significant given the greater opportunities for substitution of physical commerce for electronic commerce,[ii] the possibilities for greater market transparency allowing consumers to identify products at the lowest price, and the new opportunities for suppliers to "version" goods (Varian, 1997) more directly to consumers' needs. The balance between these consumer economic advantages versus possible social and cultural needs for shopping is likely to differ across product categories. Hence the diffusion path of such new forms of electronic commerce is likely to be very differentiated, with some goods, such as software, computer games and other content programs, CDs, and books rapidly being traded on-line on the Internet (see Table 1), while many others continue to rely on physical commerce. Although the likely growth in such electronically traded product categories may well be very high, the overall growth impact again does not really fit the overall growth expectations of electronic commerce.

Table 1: On-line purchases for various categories of goods

Category	% of users who have purchased
Software	16.0%
Books	14.0%
Computer Hardware	13.0%
Music	11.0%
Home Electronics	6.5%
Videos	5.0%
Travel Services	5.0%
Tickets for Events	4.0%
Casual Clothes	3.0%
Other Clothes	1.5%

The line taken in this paper is that the policy discussion on electronic commerce has been overly dominated, as is often the case, by the search for technological and legal solutions to cyberspace issues, assuming rather quickly that physical and electronic commerce are perfect substitutes for each other. In doing so, one is not only likely to overestimate the substitution possibilities of physical commerce and electronic commerce, one is also likely to underestimate the new growth possibilities of electronic commerce outside of traditional commerce fields. It is in this sense that the word "e-com" seems particularly badly chosen and very reminiscent of previous technological transformations such as "the wireless", which were expected merely to substitute for now old, nearly abandoned human activities. More than in these earlier, primarily technologically driven cases, the discussion of electronic commerce will have to acknowledge to a much greater extent the particular features and relative merits of physical versus electronic communication and exchange including money exchange. This discussion will also have to address the more fundamental question, as a number of economists dealing with information economics have been doing for some time now, of whether the various technological and legal attempts to create such familiar market relationships will entail the same market optimality and social welfare outcomes. We turn to this issue in the next section.

However, as we will discuss in the third section of the paper, limiting the debate on e-commerce to the distribution of goods and services would seem to miss the essence of what the information highway is all about. From this perspective, the real growth of electronic commerce does not seem to lie in the simple substitution of physical commerce and electronic commerce. Rather, it seems to reside in what we will call "e-exchange," i.e., the opportunities offered by electronic networks for new forms of exchange and communication, across businesses, between businesses and consumers, and between consumers. The main "commerce" challenge is to generate value out of such new forms of exchange. From the perspective of Europe's relative lagging position in e-commerce, two areas appear to be of special relevance: e-banking, which in the European context of Euroland might become the leading sector, establishing new conditions of security, trust, even tax compliance, and public services. In the latter case, it might be argued that, in the European context of large public sectors, e-exchange may become an enabling factor for broad public access to information highways, as discussed in section 4.

If these challenges are not addressed, the new opportunities of the information highways are likely to become part of the underground economy. They may become part of that contribution to overall well-being that economists have little grip on, since it is not measured, not paid for, and only contributes in a virtual sense to economic growth, national income, or tax revenues. We will conclude this paper by arguing that, while unfortunate, this trend may actually force economics to readdress some of the old well-being and "happiness" issues. These issues were eliminated long ago, when microeconomics turned utilitarian, but are probably of growing importance in a society in which the immaterial satisfaction of easy information and communication becomes an intrinsic part of well-being and happiness.

2. ON THE NATURE OF ELECTRONIC EXCHANGE MARKETS

There is little doubt that one of the main achievements of economics has been the pervasive illustration that prices in well-functioning markets lead both in a static and in a dynamic sense to "optimal" outcomes. In a static sense, "free-market" prices solve the distribution of scarce commodities among consumers better than any other system – anyone not willing to pay the market price will simply not be allowed to consume the commodity. In a dynamic sense, prices also signal profit opportunities to potential suppliers, and their entry and competition with the incumbent brings prices into line with production costs. Under the well-known assumptions of free, well-functioning, open markets, this market price system will create the maximum amount of social surplus. It could be argued from this perspective that the failure of the plan-based socialist system was, in the first instance, a failure to cope with these dynamic challenges. It failed to increase social surplus, at the precise moment (the 1970s and 1980s) when changes in new production methods and new product opportunities were also challenging the capitalist market system.

However, for markets to function well, three essential structural conditions need to exist: excludability, rivalry and transparency. These conditions are to some extent intrinsic to the exchange of material goods.

Thus, the exchange between seller and buyer needs to involve the exclusive exchange of ownership over the particular product. Once traded, the product is no longer the property of the seller but the exclusive property of the buyer. It is this feature which is, of course, behind the notion of economic scarcity and provides the impulse for new output activities on the part of the seller. Another feature typical of material production and open markets is the notion of rivalry. While significant economies of scale are likely to exist in the production of most material goods, the selling of a single good will still imply that the same good cannot be sold to another buyer. At the same time, while there might be significant entry barriers, the threat of new entry will imply that suppliers will not be in a position to keep prices substantially higher than costs. Rivalry is, in other words, a major and essential condition for markets to generate optimal outcomes. Finally, the exchange of material goods involves a high degree of transparency: the buyer can see, feel, test, smell, in some cases even taste the product on offer.

In the case of the exchange of a purely informational "electronic" good, it can be argued that none of these conditions hold. The owner of the digital commodity selling his product in the marketplace will have difficulty preventing buyers, or anyone else for that matter, from copying and reselling it. Excludability will typically be difficult if not impossible to achieve. Rather than a purchase and sale relationship, the exchange will look more like a gift. The creation and enforcement of excludability is thus an absolute and first condition for such markets to exist. Hence, encryption, watermarks and various other forms of tracing and monitoring property rights are a central focus of most policy documents on e-commerce. Without these rules creating excludability, no optimal level of production can be achieved and little indication can be obtained of the sort of products that are wanted by potential buyers.

Yet the creation and strengthening of such property rules has immediate implications, of course, for the openness and degree of competition in such markets. If property protection is absolute, whereas at the same time marginal production costs are minimal, possibly even nil as is typical for many digital goods, many potential users will not consume and, compared to the social optimum, too little will be produced (as in the case of the virtual monopolist). At the same time, the individual producer is now being guaranteed a fixed property income and has little to fear either from competitors and or from consumers, who can only choose to buy the particular product from him. This non-rivalry characteristic directly challenges the optimal market outcome. It raises a very large set of welfare questions characteristic of what has been called network economics and involving competition policy, regulation – for instance, price control in the case of a natural monopoly – standards and interconnectivity, etc.

Finally, despite the tremendous opening-up of trading possibilities and the increase in market transparency, the actual exchange of a digital commodity will involve, almost by definition, a high degree of information asymmetry between seller and buyer. Many of the new forms of markets emerging on the Internet are typical illustrations of such problems of information asymmetry and well known in information economics. New intermediaries emerge to assist buyers in their search; alternatively, goods may be offered for free, paid for by advertising or by subsequent upgrades; a limited preview of the good may be offered for free; etc. We will return to some of these new forms of markets and intermediaries in the following section. Yet, it is clear that the traditional physical marketplace is being replaced by a far more complex and diversified set of exchange methods in which the value of what the content seller is offering is likely to differ greatly among individual consumers – hence the crucial importance of so-called versioning (Varian, 1997) – and is distributed among many intermediaries that bring the buyer into contact with the supplier – with significant shifts in the value chain as highlighted in so-called attention or click economics.

On all three accounts, it is difficult to simply subscribe to the notion that the newly created markets will, as in the exchange of physical goods, guarantee optimality. As de Long and Froomkin (1998) put it forcefully: "What used to be second-order 'externality' corrections to the invisible hand have become first-order phenomena" in the cyberspace world. Nowhere is this more clearly illustrated than in the artificial creation of excludability. In contrast to the old notion of the invisible hand of the market, excludability is human-made. Its length, its height, its breadth, as in the case of patent protection, are likely to have major implications for market structure, competition and, more generally, welfare. Furthermore, while national rules might be enforced and hence domestic excludability could succeed in generating an optimal outcome, international differences in the protection of property rights might undermine such domestic attempts at strengthening intellectual property. In other words, the human-made rules of excludability involve, practically by definition, particular sectoral and/or national lobbies.[iii] Excludability also questions the traditional arguments about the welfare gains from trade: for example, strengthening the imposition of the international property regime worldwide might well shift the terms of trade in favour of countries specializing in digital goods and content to the disadvantage of countries that specialized more in manufactured commodities.[iv] As argued elsewhere, this might well be one of the underlying "real" factors behind the Asian crisis.

The variety of new forms of markets and exchange on the Internet also illustrates that it is very difficult to draw a distinction between electronic "commerce" and electronic exchange, whereby the former would be limited to purely commercial transactions. As different forms of information markets emerge, it will be clear that many different forms of electronic exchange will have an (in)direct impact on consumer satisfaction and costs.[v] The electronic commerce debate therefore needs to be broadened to include all forms of electronic exchange. In so doing, we would highlight the fact that the emerging information society is much broader than an electronic commerce economy and that the policy challenges are also much more pervasive. Before entering into this discussion, we shall focus on some of the more narrow "commerce" issues.

3.   FROM E-COMMERCE TO E-EXCHANGE VALUE

For the commercial exchange of goods to take place, there are a number of prerequisites well known in economic theory. Specialized infrastructures for the organization of commercial transactions are obviously needed, as they have been since the Middle Ages, such as marketplaces or trade fairs, particular trade sub-areas in towns (one may think of Shinjuku in Tokyo with respect to electronics), and more recently malls of various sorts in suburbs. As argued by Chandler and others, the organization of commerce from wholesale distribution, through various intermediaries such as representative agents and importers, down to retail shops has aimed at reducing the associated investment costs so as to better adjust to the sometimes erratic movements of final demand. Such infrastructure costs will, however, only be recuperated if commerce actually takes place. Another essential cost feature associated with commercial transactions is, of course, the information search cost preceding a possible transaction. In transaction theory, these are called the *ex ante* transaction costs.

On both accounts, information highways are likely to significantly reduce costs. The emergence of virtual malls is likely to replace the physical infrastructure; similarly, the information search costs are likely to become significantly reduced due to the ease of electronic access and the available databases on products and suppliers. Transaction costs are thus likely to fall and existing intermediary costs to decline. This argument appears to be valid for both intermediary and final demand.

Alongside these immediate short-term impacts, there are of course longer-term impacts that are more associated with new possibilities for trade and commercial exchange. Electronic exchange is likely to lead to a substantial reorganization of markets with the value chain shifting across businesses. The phenomenon of outsourcing is typical of such a reorganization. As witnessed in the rapid growth of business services, activities that are not part of the core manufacturing or service production of a firm can now be carried out more efficiently outside of the firm, by specialized companies. Similarly, with respect to final demand, goods and services can become more versioned to the particular needs of the consumer. In the extreme case, "untradable" services – "untradable" because of the physical presence of the service delivery – can now be effectively traded, dramatically raising the tradable value of such services.

Table 2 classifies these impacts for both intermediary and final demand: short-term cost impacts associated with the reduction in transaction costs and the disappearance of intermediaries (disintermediation) and long-term growth impacts associated with the reorganization of production and markets and new commercial transactions.

Table 2: Impacts for both intermediary and final demand

	Short-term	Long-term
Intermediary	Division of labour	Organization of markets
Final	Disintermediation	Reintermediation

Most of the high expected growth impact of electronic commerce is associated with this typical dual feature of technological advance: a significant cost-reduction impact, increasing efficiency and freeing up resources, and a more direct growth-enhancing impact associated with new growth opportunities.

The doubts raised with respect to the actual growth likely to occur are twofold.

First, the discussion of electronic commerce, particularly in the business-to-business segment, seems to ignore the existence of various quite common forms of electronic exchange between businesses such as electronic data interchange (EDI) or bar-coding systems. These systems, which are in operation in many sectors (the food sector being probably the most developed one), have existed for over 15 years and have to some extent formed the basis for the trend towards outsourcing. While these kinds of EDI can be viewed as early forms of electronic commerce, their widespread use across businesses leads one to question somewhat the immediate, additional growth impact of further reductions in transaction costs associated with the emergence of information highways, at least in the business-to-business segment.

Of course, in many countries EDI systems have remained limited in use to only a couple of sectors; many of the networks used have remained very costly because of their proprietary nature and their compatibility is often limited. It is most likely that the open standard, compatibility and low costs associated with information highways such as the Internet will significantly expand the possibilities for more extensive and widespread use of EDI across sectors. Particularly with respect to small and medium-sized firms and new access possibilities for international customers and suppliers, a significant new impulse can be expected. At the same time, it is important not to underestimate the widespread nature and integration of use of EDI and bar coding in many sectors. The bar-coding system, for example, has been continuously upgraded, allowing systematic integration of inventory data, payment systems, and even sales or value-added tax reporting. The security and reliability of the system is well accepted in many sectors and often contrasts sharply with the, at least perceived, insecurity of information highways and the new forms of electronic commerce. Similarly, most business transactions are already the subject of various forms of electronic final transfer. The guaranteed security and trust in such systems is likely to be an important factor in slowing down the use of other more open, Internet-based solutions.

In other words, many of the impacts described above with respect to reduction of transaction costs as a result of electronic commerce in intermediary demand have already occurred. While further growth is likely, there is a tendency to overestimate the additional growth impact.

Second, and with respect to final demand, the reduction in transaction and intermediary costs is undoubtedly also being accompanied by new information search costs. The dramatic growth in access to information has also led to information overload, to new search costs. In other words, the reduction in intermediary and transaction costs is likely to be accompanied by the emergence of new intermediaries to select relevant information. The emergence of these new intermediaries, so-called intelligent agents, while likely to solve some of the new search costs for final consumers, will also raise transaction costs. Furthermore, to the extent that such agents also take away some of the more "desirable" search activities of consumers, they are likely to be confronted with social and cultural barriers. For some products and services, commerce will remain in the first instance a social activity, where personal contact, search, and experimentation continue to be an essential feature. As the limited success of mail-order selling, at least in Europe, has illustrated, for many products the pleasure of acquiring something will remain an activity people like to be directly involved in themselves, whereby personal contact remains an essential feature. In other words, electronic commerce continues to be constrained by human beings' desire to be personally and directly involved in consumption.

Yet there is little doubt that the emergence of information highways and the Internet has led to an explosion of new activities involving the search for information: data, facts, news items in all forms, available at one's fingertips and stored in millions of books, articles, databases, libraries, websites, etc. Such new possibilities for data-mining more and more information are leading to better informed judgements not just in commercial buying and selling but in all kind of activities. Some of these are essential for one's work, others are purely of the hobby type, and still others simply contribute to one's personal general knowledge, interest in democratic control and so on. On the other hand, the emergence of information highways and the Internet has led to new opportunities for communication – not just for business or private family communication as in one-to-one "commercial" telephone conversations, but in all kinds of one-to-many communications such as virtual video conferences, debating clubs, chat rooms, and so on, identifying people elsewhere on the globe with similar work, leisure, hobby, personal and political convictions. Such forms of exchange do not appear to have any more commercial "value" than is being paid for in terms of Internet access charge and telephone costs. Nevertheless, it is obvious that such electronic communication activities represent a large part of the increased welfare associated with information highways and that they indirectly contribute to economic performance and feelings of well-being.

This explains why, in the current debate on the information society, limiting the discussion to e-commerce – the commercial exchange or the selling and buying of goods and services – appears too minimalist. It reduces the relevant growth and welfare parameters to only economically directly measurable concepts such as lower costs and larger markets.

4.   GENERATING E-EXCHANGE VALUE OUT OF PUBLIC SERVICES

There are two areas of economic activity which in essence involve only the handling of information and thus appear from the outset to be crucial "enabling" areas for the more narrowly defined e-commerce to take off: financial services and public services.

Financial services have a long history with the use of information and communication technologies. In the 1960s, they were at the forefront of a rapid process of automation, quickly becoming one of the main customers of the large mainframe computer sector. Similarly, with the advent of the minicomputer followed by the PC, the financial sector was quick to pick up these new technologies, rapidly adjusting its organizational structure to the new, more decentralized opportunities offered by the personal computer. As opposed to this more process-driven use of information and communication technologies, the advent of the ATM has allowed banks also to respond more directly to consumer needs for easier, 24-hour access to money. Under pressure from their large customers, concerned by security issues, banks have also become instrumental in the immaterial exchange of money between businesses, salary and wage payments and, increasingly, final consumer payments (PIN codes, credit cards and electronic debit cards).

With respect to electronic banking, most banks now offer home banking services to their clients, who can log in from their computer through a modem onto the bank's computer using a specific protocol. Such forms of PC banking can best be compared with EDI, in light of our discussion above. While there is a digital electronic interchange, it is a closed system. One cannot transfer savings from one bank to another bank offering better rates. Internet banking involving open access and use of the Internet is still relatively limited, with the exception probably being Finland and Sweden, and more focused on financial services of all sorts, each searching for the elusive market niche.

By itself, as Figure 2 illustrates, there is little doubt that there are substantial cost advantages to banks in shifting from physical interchange to electronic interchange. But, as Figure 2 also illustrates and in line with some of the arguments set out in the previous section with respect to the incremental nature of e-commerce as opposed to EDI and bar coding, the cost advantage of the final step from PC banking to Internet banking is relatively small. As in the case of e-commerce, the real benefit of Internet banking will, in the first instance, be linked to increased competition and consumer satisfaction. Traditionally, these features are not what existing banks are particularly interested in. Even today, Internet banking and, more generally, Internet-based financial service provision has been the domain of small players, as in Finland, or newcomers.

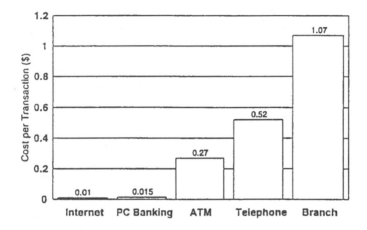

Figure 2: Internet banking is cheaper for banks (Source: Booz-Allen & Hamilton)

This is why the combination of the introduction of the Euro, with its major impact on financial restructuring and competition in the banking sector, and Internet banking looks so promising in the European context. The shift in trust, habits, and national identity which is being brought about by the replacement of a national currency with the new, unknown Euro is in many ways rather similar to the shift in trust and habits required to move to purely on-line Internet banking and other financial transactions. At the same time, the transparency brought about by prices, wages, and rates being denominated in a common currency across the 15 member states is likely to provide a major impetus to European commerce and exchange, and the Internet will probably be the tool to realize and bring about such transparency and growth. With the structural changes occurring in the banking sector, Internet banking, as an area where such on-line exchange can become complete, is likely to become the major growth area for such electronic commerce and exchange. At present, many of the existing Internet banking services are typically limited to national or domestic clients. In foreign countries, a bank will typically operate through its physical retail banking presence. The combined effect of the Euro and information highways makes such electronic pan-European services attractive to both existing and new banks, opening up their national markets and enabling clients to access their bank wherever they are in Europe.[vi]

A second area that might become a "pulling" factor for Internet uptake and e-commerce is public services.

Certainly within countries such as Canada and many EU countries, which have a large and diversified public sector, one may view public services in their broadest sense, i.e., including health, education, transport, government services, and public utilities, as the most promising area of electronic commercial and exchange value creation.

First of all, the simple fact of the matter is that public administration, whether at a national or local level, is first and foremost an information service, often involving many private and public information features. This raises not only the problems of excludability and rivalry typical of commercial markets but also important questions about privacy, access and democratic control, of direct relevance to many of the new forms of e-commerce and e-exchange.

Second, because the physical and human capital investments in such activities are often substantial, such publicly sponsored and initiated investments provide plenty of opportunities for improved connectivity, standard setting, etc. Public administration might, in many instances, take the lead, given the high risks involved in investing in new, interactive information systems, and open up new market opportunities for private partnerships in the development, execution and maintenance of new information systems.

Third, the public administration sector is probably the ideal one for internal organization experiments, bringing to the forefront the many organizational bottlenecks in public bureaucracies, and enabling diversity at the local administration level. Such experiments and pilot projects, in government's backyard so to speak, are likely to be promising in revealing more immediate solutions for and insights into some of the practical organizational and local problems associated with the introduction of information highways and electronic exchange. This can, to some extent, be viewed in parallel with the discussion in section 3: electronic exchange allows not just internal reengineering processes to take place in the public sector, but also new forms of external outsourcing and public-private partnerships. It could be argued that the effectiveness and efficiency of the public sector will become, as with infrastructural provisions, a key variable in the competitiveness of countries.

Fourth, many areas dominated by public authorities and public service providers such as education, health, culture, media, social services, immigration, police, libraries and other local services, are typically bound by the geographical limits of the country, province, region or town within which they operate and are administered.

In other words, the wide variety of public information services provides a number of opportunities for information-led growth, whereby such services might both become a cost reduction factor for business and at the same time provide some of the "killer applications" for new consumer-led growth, opening up new market opportunities for private partnerships in the development, distribution and maintenance of new information systems. At the same time, the public sector can help to guarantee reliability, trust, legal security and access and become a model of electronic service provision. The assumption that private parties and the market will by themselves take care of the many new growth opportunities induced by the information highways, is, as we have argued in section 2, seriously flawed.

5. CONCLUSIONS

The focus in most recent documents on e-commerce and the information highways has been on the challenge both for business and policy-makers to bridge the gap between the enormous growth potential offered by the Internet and the limited amount of electronic trade still taking place on the information highways. As argued in section 2 of this paper, this challenge goes far beyond some of the new technical solutions offered for encryption, watermarks, certification authorities, etc., all aimed at organizing new property rules in markets characterized by a lack of excludability. Whether one likes it or not, the development of markets in cyberspace requires a substantial amount of human intervention. To what extent such markets still correspond to the economist's ideal of social optimality must therefore be questioned.

As a result, the scope of relevant policy issues must be broadened. E-commerce will increasingly raise questions about competition policy with a tendency towards "winner takes all" features in the production of many digital, non-rivalry goods. Questions about open standards, compatibility and interconnectivity will increasingly influence existing competition rules, as will issues related to dynamic efficiency; new questions about data protection and consumer privacy will have to be addressed with the emergence of new intermediaries competing for access to customer data; attempts by firms to create artificial rivalry through, for example, continuous upgrading and versioning of goods and services will have to be closely monitored; as will many other directly policy-relevant issues going beyond traditional economic policy concerns.

A discussion of electronic commerce and electronic highways cannot be limited to just issues involving the organization of electronic commercial activities. The information highways provide a vast array of new information and communication access opportunities. The majority of those contribute only indirectly to increased efficiency in economic production and distribution, but mainly involve increased consumer satisfaction, increased well-being and freedom of communication and exchange. It is in this sense that the notion of an emerging Information Society takes on its true value. A society in which ease of communication and access to information and data are not just essential ingredients of economic activity – in the production, distribution and consumption, increasingly, of digital goods and services – but also of leisure, household and other so-called "non-work" activities, of social interaction and of democratic expression. I would argue that easy access to this variety of new "immaterial" goods and services, the largest part of which are not commercially traded, represents to some extent the new wealth of the 21st century.

Typically, these are goods and services the consumption of which does not lead to the sort of happiness paradox first identified by Tibor Scitovsky in the 1960s that is characteristic of material consumption (Scitovsky, 1976). The consumption of material goods, with its dramatic growth in product innovation and product differentiation (consumers' love of product variety), has become characteristic of the consumption societies of the 1970s and 1980s. As Frank (1997) has argued forcefully, this consumption pattern has also led to a spiral of over-consumption in which individual consumers define happiness ultimately in terms of relative consumption. Happiness is from this perspective closely linked to excludability and rivalry: possessing a more recent car than one's neighbour, wearing a more fashionable dress than one's colleague or possessing a more up-to-date computer than one's boss. By the same token, unhappiness can increase even if one's own consumption remains the same simply because of other people's consumption patterns. Consumption has, in other words, negative externalities.

By contrast, immaterial network goods and services, I would argue, are typically characterized by positive externalities. Having seen the same movie, read the same book, listened to the same band, opera, or performer – all of these create positive externalities. Consumption of such goods increases social cohesion or, to put it differently, leads to a desire to communicate, to exchange information and to share common impressions. Even if the widespread diffusion of electronic exchange and communication does not in the end create additional value in a narrow economic commercial sense, it could significantly increase well-being and happiness. From this perspective, the Information Society could well represent the trend towards a society less based on material production and consumption, thereby providing a solution to the unsustainable nature, both from an environmental and personal perspective, of material-based output and consumption growth. It is in this sense that the emerging "new economy" should be understood: new global opportunities for information-based, primarily immaterial, production and consumption, some of which might be measured and find their expression in GDP or productivity growth, but most would evaporate in cyberspace, simply increasing the opportunities for visiting, learning, interacting and exchanging ideas and views.

NOTES

---

[i] Otherwise, how can one explain the fact that security, privacy and payment issues never seemed to raise such major policy questions when Minitel was introduced in France, with its still unchallenged rapid diffusion rate?

[ii] Even though in some countries the use of mail-order and telephone or television shopping is already quite extensive.

[iii] The extension of copyrights from 50 to 70 years is a good case in point. The U.S. was instrumental in making the case for this extension, since many early Hollywood movies were in danger of falling into the public domain.

[iv] Once again, there is no superior invisible hand involved in such a shift. For many centuries, the now developed countries have freely taken ideas, technologies and knowledge from now less developed countries.

[v] A line taken, for example, by the recent OECD document on Electronic Commerce prepared for the Ottawa Conference in October 1998 (DSTI/ICCP(98) IS/PART 1-4).

[vi] See also Lavin (1998, pp. 18-20).

REFERENCES

A European Initiative in Electronic Commerce, April 15, 1997.
www.ispo.cec.be.Ecommerce/initial.html

A Framework for Global Electronic Commerce, July 1, 1997
www.iitf.nist.gov/eleccomm/ecomm.html

Bonn Ministerial Declaration, Industrial Declaration, July 8, 1997
www2.echo.lu/bonn/final.html

De Long, J. Bradford and A. M. Froomkin,"The Next Economy?" in D. Hurley, B. Kahin, and H. Varian (eds.) *Internet Publishing and Beyond: The Economics of Digital and Intellectual Property.* Cambridge, MA: MIT Press, 1997.

Electronic Commerce and the Role of the WTO
www.wto.org/wto/publicat/newpubl.htm

European Commission, "Building the European Information Society for Us All." Final report of the high-level expert group. Luxembourg: EC, 1997.

Frank, R.H., "The Frame of Reference as a Public Good." *Economic Journal,* 107, 1997, 1832-1847.

Lavin, D., "Why E-Commerce and the Euro Will Pack a Punch." *Convergence,* IV(3), 1998, 18-20.

OECD, "The Competitive Dynamics of Internet-Based Electronic Commerce." Paris: OECD, 1998.

Scitovsky, T., *The Joyless Economy.* Oxford: Oxford University Press, 1976.

Towards the Age of the Digital Economy, May 1997
www.wcoomd.org/ecjapan.html

Varian, H. R., "Versioning Information Goods." Paper prepared for *Digital Information and Intellectual Property*, Harvard University, Jan., 1997, 23-25.

11.   PUBLIC MANAGEMENT OF POSITIVE RESEARCH EXTERNALITIES

Patrick Cohendet
Université Louis-Pasteur

Dominique Foray
Université Paris-Dauphiné(France)

Dominique Guellec
OECD (France)

Jacques Mairesse
CREST & NBER

1.   INTRODUCTION

The purpose of this text is to highlight certain limitations of the traditional approach to positive research externalities, in the current context of knowledge-based economies (Section 2). We shall start by showing that the two basic assumptions equating knowledge with information and limiting agent interaction to competitive commercial exchanges are no longer valid, and that it is necessary to reformulate the theoretical framework of this approach (Section 3). Next we shall give some preliminary suggestions on how to rethink the principles and practices of public management of research externalities (Sections 4 and 5). Finally, in the conclusion, we shall stress that the importance of externalities is not the only justification for public intervention in the field of research, but that issues of intergenerational and intercommunity equity are also crucial, especially with regard to the allocation of resources to long-term scientific research.

2. THE TRADITIONAL APPROACH TO POSITIVE RESEARCH EXTERNALITIES AND ITS LIMITATIONS

The traditional literature on externalities clearly highlights the problems raised by the presence of positive externalities in the field of scientific and technological research (Bach and Lhuillery, 1999). Agents that conduct research and, more generally, innovation activities generate information and knowledge, which are disseminated and can be acquired by other agents, but without necessarily giving rise to compensation. Accordingly, if it is recognized that economic agents undertaking research and innovation activities cannot adequately appropriate their results, there will be an inadequate and inefficient allocation of resources to such activities, as well as a gap or shortfall between their "private" and "social" return on investment. More specifically, the private return (what accrues only to the innovators) will be smaller than the social return, which is appropriated partly by imitators and partly by consumers. It follows that in a decentralized economy the equilibrium level of investment in research and development (R&D) is *a priori* socially sub-optimal.

2.1   The Availability of Corrective Mechanisms

In the real world, however, the importance of these externality gaps is reduced by the presence of "natural" or spontaneous corrective mechanisms, which are often overlooked in economic theory. These stem from the very nature of knowledge and the potential for internalizing externalities within the framework of bilateral relations, or from redistribution effects. While in some cases they spare us heavy and expensive public intervention, they do not offer a complete solution or one with general application.

The first corrective mechanism has been strongly emphasized recently in the literature on the economics of innovation. It stems from the fact that knowledge does not disseminate spontaneously and is not easily acquired. Much knowledge is largely tacit in nature and takes the form of know-how. It is thus generally specific that is, inseparable from the agents who possess it and cannot be transferred without an intentional action on their part. This mechanism nevertheless has its limitations since the tacit nature of knowledge is an obstacle to its dissemination, slows the acquisition and advancement of learning, and is generally a source of inefficiency in transactions involving innovation. The tacit nature of knowledge has consequences analogous to those of secrecy, which it either allows or promotes. "Craft secrecy," for example, was the protective device used by craftsmen in medieval Europe, with major negative effects on the entry of competitors on the market. Consequently, to rely on the importance of tacit knowledge in order to reinforce private incentives for research and innovation is not desirable and cannot be regarded as a satisfactory public policy tool.

The second corrective mechanism, proposed by Coase (1960), is linked to opportunities for direct negotiation between agents, who can enter into a process of internalizing externalities in order to arrive at a mutual optimum. In the case of research, this process leads to the creation of institutional or private contractual forms of organization: an industrial or geographic association, a cooperative research and development program, or integration by merger or acquisition. These forms of organization make it possible to reduce the scale of externalities and hence the need for public intervention in order to correct market deficiencies. However, they offer only partial solutions. Internalization or integration rapidly runs up against limitations arising from internal coordination costs and information asymmetries, which make contracts imperfect, difficult to draw up and harder still to implement. (How is one to ensure that the partner or subordinate acts properly in the agreed sense?) The complexity of these effects increases as the number of agents rises. Externalities, especially those generated by general-purpose technology, by definition extend to a multitude of activities and agents. They will thus always go far beyond any set of coordinated activities, which are by nature local.

The last corrective mechanism arises from the potential redistribution effects of speculative activity linked with the commercial development of innovations. An innovator sometimes has information on future variations in the price of certain goods, and is thus able to speculate on those goods. Whoever invented the water mill, for example, was (or may have been) enabled by that very fact to buy land crossed by a river in his region before the value of that land rose (Hirschleifer, 1971). Generally, however, such a mechanism can function only on a very limited scale, particularly since very few innovations are sufficiently radical to significantly affect the pricing structure of products and resources, and hence businesses' expectations and behaviour.

2.2   Public Intervention Mechanisms and Associated Difficulties

Given the limitations inherent in the different corrective mechanisms, public intervention is justified to complement their impact and to stimulate weak private initiative. Three main forms of public intervention are considered in the traditional understanding of externalities:

- Attempting to create knowledge and invention "markets" by establishing intellectual property rights. Such property rights systems vary greatly from field to field and from country to country. Their advantages and weaknesses are discussed at length in the specialized literature. Patents, legislation on trade secrecy, trademarks and royalties offer various methods of defining and protecting "private knowledge," innovations and intellectual creations.
- Directly stimulating private research activities through various forms of assistance and incentives. These can be tax measures (tax credits on R&D expenditures), innovation premiums, financial assistance directly offered to businesses (specific grants or assistance for cooperative research), or legislative and regulatory provisions aimed at creating a favourable financial climate for the creation and development of innovative firms (venture capital, profit-sharing arrangements for research engineers).
- Substituting public production for private initiative. Governments become directly involved in the creation of knowledge, permitting its free use and applying tax revenues to finance research and innovation. This approach is central to Samuelson's analysis of effective production of public goods. The best examples are provided by the laboratories of major public research institutions and universities.

However, the different modes of public intervention face many difficulties both practical and theoretical in nature.

First, the attempt to restore market mechanisms by guaranteeing inventor appropriation (patents, legislation on trade secrets) in itself creates obstacles to the diffusion of innovations. In general, public management of research externalities cannot be viewed as simply being symmetrical to the management of negative externalities. Any measure that seeks to restrict the "absorption" activity of receivers (which is exactly symmetrical to actions seeking to limit the activity of sources of negative externalities) also has a negative impact on the social return of research. This is at the heart of the basic dilemma raised by the conflict between the need to protect inventors and the need for widespread dissemination of the new knowledge they generate: strong patents in terms of duration and, particularly, scope, and legislation strictly protecting trade secrets have the double effect of increasing incentives to private initiative and lessening the social return of innovations. This dilemma inevitably leads to second-best solutions.

Second, directly stimulating private research initiatives, through subsidies and various R&D policies, raises serious problems of "information asymmetry." Governments in general are required to behave like society's "principal." They must therefore develop monitoring mechanisms, audit procedures and other regulatory devices to ensure that the specialized tasks undertaken by various "agents" do not lead to behaviours that conflict with the principal's interests. In particular, governments have no certainty that research supported by grants would not have been undertaken otherwise (through a windfall effect or adverse selection), and it is difficult to ensure that subsidies really lead to research whose social return outweighs its private benefits. Problems of information asymmetry, identification and monitoring are especially acute in the case of tax and financial incentive policies that target a large number of firms.

Third, offsetting inadequate private initiative through publicly performed research may entail other difficulties. It is clear that government's sponsorship will raise agency problems of its own. Even if we accept that the social return is a valid objective of government intervention, does the same hold true for research institutions, laboratories and researchers themselves? A major complication arises from the fact that, with regard to the production and dissemination of scientific and technical knowledge, modern societies must turn to members of specialized communities of researchers to help them manage and control the work undertaken by those very communities. Moreover, government itself is part of a political structure where lobby groups have much weight, and it is not clear that society's interests alone always guide public decisions.

It should be noted also that the knowledge produced in a public setting, with no involvement from private firms, is not freely available to the latter. Instead, they often have to incur substantial expenditures in order to appropriate the new knowledge.

Finally, the fact that the research is undertaken by government offers no guarantee against excessive duplication of research efforts. There is a natural tendency to focus research activities on well-known areas, subjects or opportunities, leading to a collective convergence of research projects and efforts seen not only in private research undertakings. Excessive duplication could result, given that knowledge is a good "indivisible in use." There is generally no significant value added when a discovery is made for a second or third time. Only the research that first leads to a discovery receives credit for it and makes a real contribution to the social surplus.

3.   REFORMULATING THE BASIC ASSUMPTIONS OF THE TRADITIONAL APPROACH

The preceding discussion clearly shows that the traditional approach, in its basic form, does not account for the difficulties associated with policies used to manage externalities. The obvious reason is the oversimplified nature of this approach, which gives it theoretical clarity but also explains its limitations. Theoretical simplicity is achieved via two key hypotheses (H1) and (H2) about the nature of knowledge and the relationships between economic agents, which can be formulated as follows:

(H1): Knowledge is defined as "information." An analogy is made with a software program which, as soon as it is loaded on a computer, can function at full efficiency. The knowledge is coded and thus transportable from one application and user to another, without any loss or training costs. A consequence of this hypothesis is that, from a social viewpoint, it would always be beneficial to ensure the widest possible diffusion of all inventions since they could be widely used at no additional cost.

(H2): The only interactions between agents take place on competitive markets, where prices are the only information that flows and thus defines exchanges and transactions. Agents do not directly enter into specific bilateral arrangements but are controlled by prices and market conditions.

These assumptions have the advantage of allowing the construction of equilibrium models in a convenient analytical framework. For the purpose of studying public policy issues, however, they should be reformulated in a more realistic setting.

3.1   The Tacit Nature and Other Characteristics of Knowledge

The first hypothesis should be reformulated in two respects:

(H1'): First, knowledge (the circulation of which gives rise to externalities) cannot be reduced to mere information made up of codified instructions. The importance of the tacit aspect of knowledge calls into question the entire way of representing the behaviour of those who produce or receive knowledge. In many cases, knowledge cannot be separated from the medium through which it is conveyed, whether human or material. To acquire knowledge, one must make specific, costly investments. One must identify the knowledge required, locate prospective suppliers, and then grope, learn and assimilate. The cost incurred is higher the more distant the knowledge in question is from one's base of prior knowledge. The cost of even quite commonplace knowledge may be significant. In order to truly master new knowledge, it is often necessary to generate a range of complementary local knowledge. In this sense, innovation and dissemination are not totally independent functions, and policies seeking to promote them cannot be defined entirely separately (Cohen and Levinthal, 1989).

Second, for those producing it, knowledge has specific economic properties, especially that of increasing returns (or savings from experience): the more inventions or innovations one produces, the easier it becomes to produce still further inventions and innovations (Machlup, 1982). Thus, generating new knowledge increases the likelihood of developing new ideas, processes and products from new, unexpected combinations. This view is adopted by Romer (1986, 1990) in recent studies on endogenous growth, where he insists on the "non-rival" character of knowledge (i.e., its non-destruction by use) and, particularly, on the notion that knowledge stimulates knowledge and can therefore trigger "unlimited" growth in productivity and welfare. Similarly, studies by Scotchmer (1991) and David (1993) emphasize the cumulative nature of invention activity and show that the marginal returns from producing new knowledge increase rather than decrease (as traditional theory supposes).

However, this view should be put in perspective. The organization and timing of research are crucial. It is not at all certain that doubling the number of researchers working at a given time on a research project or in a research area will generate twice the number of discoveries. There are many reasons for this, particularly the fact that each field of research advances on the basis of external contributions, arising from discoveries in other fields (following a process of cross-fertilization, which is a form of externality). Obviously, these outside contributions do not double along with the specific resources allocated to a single field of research. But an increase in the resources allocated to other research areas can help overcome certain barriers, at least after some time. Of course, such a framework does not apply to all types and fields of research. Some areas of research experience rapid advances at certain times (e.g., electronics, computer technology and biotechnology today), while others make little progress. Clearly, research efforts will focus mainly on the fields advancing most quickly and will eventually generate increasing returns to scale.

Reformulating the assumption about the nature of knowledge has already significantly altered the traditional conclusions. Science and technology become imperfect public goods, the circulation of which entails training and transaction costs, and (the still costly) access to which can be partly controlled. It is no longer certain that the private return from research and innovation will indeed be lower than the social return partly because imitation can be restrained by the innovators (thereby increasing the private return) and also because it is costly to the imitators themselves (the social return is lessened). Further, in such circumstances the social return is no longer automatic but is a function of the individual and collective choices of economic agents. In particular, calculation of the social return must take into account the costs of access to and acquisition of knowledge, and the net return will differ from the gross return. These costs are partly endogenous to the economic system, as they are closely linked to the institutional structure. Controlling them and reducing them thus become potential targets of public action.

Once an overly simplistic view of science and technology is shunned, the appropriate public policy appears even less simple. Such a policy must have two objectives that may mutually conflict: to increase both the private and the social returns from research and innovation. It is no longer a matter of merely managing fixed externalities but of promoting them (from being exogenous, the externalities become endogenous).

In an essentially dynamic environment, the role that seems to have naturally fallen to government is to create the conditions for increasing returns and mutual reinforcement of innovation projects and activities by focusing on the organization of the knowledge distribution system and developing as much as possible its "distributive power." In contrast to a strictly informational representation of knowledge that conjures up a world of distrust where battle must be waged against information "leaks," the make-up of a system "rich in positive externalities" suggests a world characterized by mutual trust between agents, a considerable degree of openness and sharing of acquired knowledge, and consolidation of individual research efforts. Such a vision may seem downright utopian, especially to those familiar with the research community and its tendency toward disagreements over priorities and intellectual authorship. (One example among many is the much-publicized controversy between professors Gallo and Montagnier over the discovery of the HIV virus causing AIDS.) It is, however, relevant, or could become so, if certain institutional conditions are met. In particular, game theory defines certain conditions under which purely individualistic agents can be induced to cooperate (see below). The important point is that cooperative structures for knowledge production can be highly efficient.

3.2   Cooperation and Other Institutional Arrangements

In this regard, the second hypothesis should be reformulated as follows:

(H2'): Interactions between agents do not happen exclusively through market mechanisms. Agents interact directly with each other using contractual forms other than those resulting from pricing mechanisms. Examples of current arrangements are the guarantees offered on a product or the adoption of certified quality standards; these are important in the context of limited, asymmetrical information in the interactions between sellers and buyers.

Cooperation agreements between firms, such as are found in business networks, are institutional arrangements developed by the agents themselves, which (at least within certain limits) allow for the sharing and appropriation of externalities. They have the advantage of not requiring governments to intervene, sparing them the costs involved, especially the costs necessary to identify the agents likely to have an interest in those externalities.

In a sense, the main difficulty encountered by governments in dealing with externalities may be compared to that of somehow moving a fence whose original location is only known very approximately, while its final and perhaps "ideal" position is particularly hard to determine. Aside from the very rare cases of an externality in which there are only a few agents, all of which are identified (cases that can generally be resolved simply through direct discussion), the most common cases involve a large number of agents, of which some are identified and some are not, some are likely to be transmitters and others receivers of the externality (or both at the same time), some have the capacity to absorb new knowledge and others are entirely incapable of doing so, and so on.

If direct negotiation between agents is thus likely to enable government to avoid significant intervention costs, this approach also has its limitations since reaching agreements and contracts entails major transaction costs. For example, someone able to control access to a technology can demand compensation for granting others that access. Given the characteristics of that technology, especially more or less important differences in information and uncertainty regarding its *ex ante* and *ex post* economic value (the value of a technology is demonstrated by the market, and this process can take considerable time), contracts between agents are both complex and imperfect, and the costs involved can act as a deterrent (Guellec, 1995).

The legal and institutional context in which agents encounter each other is also a key element. While some of the corresponding costs are actually technical in nature (and thus exogenous to the economic system and not reducible by economic action), on the other hand some are economic in nature and hence endogenous. The costs may be increased or reduced by institutional arrangements put in place by government, or implemented in a decentralized manner by the agents concerned. The costs of identification (of interesting technologies and partners) for an agent are reduced by a system which induces agents to widely disclose their discoveries – such as, in principle, the patent system (if the description of the patented invention is sufficiently precise, or if it is not a ruse to put competitors on a false trail). Training costs are lower when research is undertaken jointly, at least for some of the firms involved; transaction costs are lowered by a proper system of intellectual property rights, etc. In this regard, legislation on intellectual property is very important, including the deadline for disclosing the content of a patent application (18 months after application in Europe; on issuance of the patent in the United States), plus rules on licensing agreements or the transfer of know-how. Competition policy is important as well, especially with regard to the way it treats R&D cooperation between firms.

4.   RECONSIDERING THE PRINCIPLES OF PUBLIC POLICY

To sum up, the reformulation of the basic hypothesis of the traditional approach, in its simplest form, calls for a broad re-examination of its outcomes and leads to a more comprehensive and realistic understanding. The reformulation of the first assumption suggests that the social return will not be as high as it might be if the costs of disseminating the results of research and innovation were negligible. The reformulation of the second assumption suggests that the private return will be greater than that predicted by the standard competitive equilibrium theory. In the new vision, there may seem to be a reduced need for public intervention since decentralized resource allocation is no longer at such variance with social efficiency. At the same time, however, by better identifying problems, the new vision can help define, quite precisely, the objectives and forms of public intervention.

It is thus possible to reconsider conventional policies for dealing with externalities through a modified view of the nature of goods giving rise to externalities (knowledge rather than mere information) and the nature of interactions between the agents involved (varied contractual forms, not solely competitive commercial relations). In this reconsideration, two factors should be emphasized: the need to resolve coordination problems in knowledge creation and dissemination, and the need to develop new institutional arrangements or "institutional compromises" between existing arrangements.

4.1   Solving Coordination Problems in Knowledge Creation and Dissemination

The public management of externalities raises both *ex post* and *ex ante* coordination problems:

First, once an innovation has been developed within a particular organization, how should one promote dissemination of the associated knowledge? This is an *ex post* coordination problem that requires organizing access to information and the distribution of the new knowledge. The problem is one of converting a private good into a public one, without excessively changing incentives to private enterprise in this area. The positive externalities in the use of new knowledge will be greater the higher the probability of finding *ex post* complementarities between the new and previously existing knowledge.

Second, the coordination problem can be viewed *ex ante* in the conduct of a research or innovation project. Exploitation of externalities in the creation of knowledge associated with the project is more socially profitable if the project is marked by strong uncertainties involving the need for multiple experiments in different directions, or if it requires the application of varied technologies and know-how which, by definition, cannot be mastered by a single organization.

These two coordination problems in knowledge creation and dissemination call for quite different public policies. What is needed is, on the one hand, an increase in the probability of finding dynamic complementarities between projects already completed, and on the other hand, an improvement in the division of labour in research and innovation activities now under way, especially by taking concerted actions.

4.2   Developing Institutional Compromises

Finally, the task of government is not so much to attempt to restore the conditions allowing a "knowledge market" to function properly, but instead to develop institutional compromises promoting the emergence of collective interaction dynamics that are sources of generally positive knowledge externalities.

A major difficulty stems from the coexistence of positive and negative research externalities. Negative externalities have to do with substitutability between innovations (or, more exactly, substitutability between innovative products), while positive externalities have to do with their complementarity (or, more exactly, complementarity between the elements of knowledge incorporated into these innovations). In the first case, research efforts undertaken by competing agents lead to substitutable products, such that at equilibrium the market will select only one of them. Duplication is involved, and the knowledge incorporated into the goods not selected will have no economic value. For example, when two software programs performing the same function compete, in many cases one of the two will be rejected by the market although both required high R&D investments (as happened with the OS/2 and Windows operating systems). In the second case, the innovative products do not compete on the market and the types of knowledge they incorporate are mutually reinforcing. In this case, one type of knowledge is strengthened by another without replacing it, and helps increase its social value. For example, an advance in genetics and another advance in electronics made it possible to accelerate gene-sequencing methods. A third case would be a situation in which substitutability of and goods of complementarity knowledge are simultaneously present, as in the Schumpeterian model of creative destruction (Aghion and Howitt, 1992). The new good completely displaces the old one, driving it from the market. The result is a loss in value of the knowledge incorporated into the displaced good, which is a negative externality. But the new good has benefited from knowledge incorporated into the old one, which provided it with a support base. There is thus a positive externality as well. The overall outcome (that is, the net social return, or difference between the social and private returns) is by definition uncertain: it can be positive or negative.

These considerations are particularly important in economies that are increasingly knowledge-based, especially in the light of some recent trends that may be quite worrisome. For example, companies' research programs seem to be more and more short-term in focus, and their innovating activities seem more and more aimed at product differentiation of an extremely superficial nature (Foray and Lundvall, 1997). These shifts are difficult to evaluate without proper statistics, but they can be seen in a range of anecdotes and observations (notably those concerning massive disinvestments in basic research and the closing of laboratories in well-known mega-corporations such as AT&T, IBM, General Electric, Xerox and Kodak).

The coexistence of positive and negative externalities thus cannot be ignored in public policy. If at this stage we set aside considerations having to do with the benefits of competition, it is inefficient to encourage research leading to new products that are (entirely) substitutable. The mingling of the two types of externality (and of the effects of competition) should lead governments to work toward a clear goal: continually try to develop institutional compromises that can promote the production and exploitation of positive externalities through coordination of training, while mitigating the effects of negative externalities through individual protection guarantees for agents.

An institutional compromise must therefore be designed as an arrangement permitting one to manage conflicting influences in this instance, those arising from the coexistence of positive and negative externalities. In the case of biotechnology, for example, Joly (1992) has shown that intensive knowledge exchange is compatible with strong R&D incentives, provided an institutional arrangement ensures that "free rider" behaviour is not allowed. Romer (1993) has advocated the creation of "independent industrial investment centres" to offer research assistance, especially to universities, with private funds provided by firms. And Kremer (1997) has proposed that governments purchase some of the patents of private firms to place them in the public domain, buying them at a price determined by an auction process that would better reflect their social value, which is higher than their private value. This is what the French government did in 1839, when it purchased Daguerre's patent on the invention of photography (based on the Daguerreotype process). At the time, this measure did much to promote the use and improvement of the invention, leading to its rapid success.

5.   IMPROVING PUBLIC POLICY PRACTICES

In light of these reflections on the principles of public policy, we can try to re-interpret its traditional instruments with a view to strengthening them and making them as functional as possible in real cases of externalities.

The system of property rights, and especially the patent regime, is inevitably one of the favoured instruments for correcting the lack of private incentives for investment. At the same time, the patent is a device that allows close coordination between decentralized research projects in a context of positive externalities: although the patent discloses only the codified information necessary for sufficient characterization of the innovation, it also gives a valuable indication of the potential success or real prospects of a line of research, and enables competing firms to better allocate their research resources. Strong property rights are consistent with a system dominated by distrust between agents and a low degree of openness, while weak property rights encourage the organization of a system rich in positive externalities. The desirable compromise can juggle the basic characteristics of patents by adjusting patent "duration" (the period for which protection is granted), "scope" (the range of products or processes on which the patent holder is granted sole exploitation rights) or "depth" (should it be necessary to obtain a whole series of patents to protect successive minor innovations, or should protection be reserved for major innovations?), disclosure timelines (after a set time from the date of application, or only when the patent is actually issued), conditions for licensing agreements (whether compulsory licences are to be issued on demand), etc.

Recent examples in biotechnology, among other fields (Joly, 1995), suggest that innovating firms must negotiate on two fronts: to ensure that they have property rights to protect their newly developed knowledge and to gain access rights to complementary knowledge that they need from other firms. In a knowledge-based economy, there are ongoing trade-offs between property and access rights. One of the notable reasons for the success of innovation networks is that they allow their members to easily undertake such trade-offs. The system of laws and regulations on intellectual property rights must be sufficiently flexible and adaptable to facilitate negotiations and trade-offs. It must also promote access to knowledge held by public research agencies.

Public research programs are also excellent tools for stimulating private initiative because they are likely to generate considerable externalities. From this standpoint, the way these programs are implemented is crucial, especially the selection of networks of contracting parties who will have to carry them out. In addition, the way in which calls for tenders for these programs are drafted and the means of monitoring and assessing them will affect the make-up of the networks of contracting parties and strongly influence their operational efficiency, while promoting joint training and the generation of positive externalities. According to the 1993 BETA Report on the effects of Brite-Euram contracts in the case of European research programs, for example, networks of contracting parties that mixed together industrial and university laboratories gave rise to more effective training processes than did projects drawing on "homogeneous" networks of contracting parties. The main explanation for the superiority of the former is that the university laboratories effectively ensure that the functions of codifying, formalizing and checking knowledge are properly performed within the network, and thereby greatly facilitate knowledge creation and dissemination. In networks composed solely of private partners, none of them really has the incentive or the experience to perform these tasks properly. Such findings encourage us to define less strictly the role of public research in knowledge-based economies. Not only must public research complement private research in certain fields in order to offset the weaknesses and inadequacies, but it must also provide productive collaboration opportunities for private research by exploiting its comparative advantages, and contribute to an improved division of labour in the shared production of knowledge.

Subsidies or direct individual tax incentives can be a good means of stimulating private initiative. The scope of these measures is open to debate when the beneficiaries are agents whose behaviour is not well known since the measures are vulnerable to information asymmetries (cheating, non-disclosure of real research efforts, etc.). By contrast, if the beneficiaries of individual assistance are clearly identified and monitored, and if they work in close interaction with government to consolidate a line of research (as in the case of certain Anvar-type programs), the risks are lower and there is a high probability of consolidating training activities that have positive externalities.

Incentives to direct negotiation between agents in order to internalize externalities are a traditional method of resolving negative externality problems. They can also be viewed as another means of stimulating interactive forms of training between agents that support positive externalities. Again, everything depends on the manner in which these measures are applied, especially the possibility of clearly identifying the agents. Further, the government's favourable attitude toward interfirm research cooperation can quickly come into conflict with the requirements of competition policy. Upstream cooperation can easily turn into downstream collusion, which obviously goes against the immediate interests of consumers and of firms that are not included in these agreements, and acts against the very incentives to innovate in the medium term. How to bring consistency to public policy in the two fields of cooperative research and competition is a fundamental issue that has been debated in the United States, Japan and Europe since the early 1980s. The answers must take into account current and foreseeable (or potential) market structures, and should not have a high degree of generality, notwithstanding the prevailing conditions and fields of application.

The same comments and interpretation may apply to all other public policy instruments (creation of technical infrastructures, major research facilities, or technology transfer and documentation centres, etc.). In each case, precisely defining the nature, goals and circumstances of research and assessing the potential for externalities must be central to the selection of appropriate institutional arrangements and compromises. In each case also, the design and implementation of these measures has a strong impact on the effectiveness of public policy.

6.   CONCLUSION: EQUITY CONSIDERATIONS

In conclusion, we consider it important to stress that the existence of externalities is not the sole justification for public intervention in research. In this as in other areas, equity problems, especially problems of intergenerational relations, also arise. The latter can be analyzed in terms of externalities as well as in terms of equity. There is an element of externality because future generations will greatly benefit, at no cost, from our inventions, as we benefit from those of past generations. There is an equity issue in the sense that future generations are entitled to demand from us knowledge that they can apply and develop, as we ourselves were able to do with the knowledge base we inherited from past generations. At issue here is mainly long-term and scientific research, which has a distant and uncertain time frame for completion and application. It is evident that the market is not an institution intended to resolve this issue. Agents focused on their private benefits naturally contribute to the generation of long-range externalities, but that contribution can only be a by-product. It is mainly up to the government to pursue this objective and thus ensure "intergenerational redistribution" of research resources.

Adoption of a "sustainable growth" approach, such as can be applied in the environmental field, could be useful for dealing with the resource allocation problems facing government. Such an approach can help avert the temptation of opportunism in decision-making, since past generations cannot reclaim their legacy to us and future generations cannot protest against our possible refusal to help improve their well-being. Above all, this approach can avoid excessive reliance on calculations of opportunity costs which, despite their usefulness, most often show that other types of public investment could have a greater social return (such as community, housing and education services). The principle of cost-benefit analysis is to assign present values to distant benefits. But these values are extremely dependent on the discount rate used and will always be low even with a very low rate. Some may argue, at least in theory, that anyone could manipulate this parameter in accordance with the chosen "philosophy." But when we speak of scientific research, for which the costs to be borne immediately may be considerable and the direct and indirect long-term benefits (in light of the cumulative and expansionary aspects of knowledge creation processes) may be immeasurable but of unknown probability, calculations based on variations in the discount rate no longer make much sense.

Relations between groups or communities with unequal resources and living conditions also raise serious equity problems. Although they may be cast in terms quite different from those of intergenerational relations, these problems are also a key force motivating public research policy. Without such a policy, imbalances between research seeking to satisfy attainable needs and research aimed at meeting needs unlikely to be satisfied would be sizable (even greater than they often are). Many key areas of research for poor countries (health, environment and agronomy, among others) are commonly ignored. Even today, for instance, for lack of adequate international funding, the amount spent on research to fight malaria is less than a tenth of what is spent on AIDS research, although malaria kills far more people. Even in rich countries, research on so-called "orphan" diseases (affecting only a small number of people) is neglected. In knowledge-based economies, for reasons of equity as well as economic effectiveness, the development of a strong, committed public research policy, capable of innovation in managing different means of action, will be increasingly essential.

REFERENCES

Aghion, P. and P. Howitt, "Un modèle de croissance par destruction créatrice," in D. Foray and C. Freeman (eds.), *Technologie et richesse des nations*. Paris: Economica, 1992.

Bach, L. and S. Lhuillery, "Recherche et externalités: tradition économique et renouveau," in D. Foray and J. Mairesse (eds.), *Innovations et performances: Approches interdisciplinaires*. Paris: Editions de l'EHESS, 1999.

BETA, "Les effets économiques des programmes Brite-Euram." Rapport à la Commission économique européenne, BETA. Strasbourg: Université Louis Pasteur, 1993.

Coase, R.M., "The Problem of Social Costs." *Journal of Law and Economics*, 3, 1960, 1-44.

Cohen, W.H. and D. Levinthal, "Innovation and Learning: The Two Faces of R&D." *The Economic Journal*, 99, 1989, 569-596.

David, P.A., "Knowledge, Property and the System Dynamics of Technological Change," in L. Summers and S. Shah (eds.), *Supplement to World Bank Economic Review*. Annual Bank Conference on Development Economics, Washington, DC, 1993.

Foray, D. and B.A. Lundvall, "Une introduction à l'économie fondée sur la connaissance," in B. Guilhon, P. Huard, M. Orillard and J.B. Zimmermann (eds.), Économie *de la connaissance et organisations*. Paris: L'Harmattan, 1997.

Guellec, D., "Externalités et asymétries d'information dans un modèle de croissance." *Revue Economique,* 46(3), 1995, 837-847.

Hirschleifer, J., "The Private and Social Value of Information and the Reward to Inventive Activity." *American Economic Review*, 61, 1971, 561-574.

Joly, P.B., "Le rôle des externalités dans les systèmes d'innovation." *Revue Économique,* 43(4), 1992, 785-796.

Joly, P.B., "A quoi servent les brevets en biotechnologie," in *Changement institutionnel et changement technologique*. Paris: CNRS Éditions, 1995.

Kremer, M., "Patent Buy-Outs: A Mechanism for Encouraging Innovation." National Bureau of Economic Research, Cambridge, MA, Working Paper no. 6304, 1997.

Machlup, F., *Knowledge: Its Creation, Distribution and Economic Significance – The Branches of Learning*, Vol. 2. Princeton, NJ: Princeton University Press, 1982.

Romer, P., "Increasing Returns and Long Run Growth." *Journal of Political Economy*, 94(5), 1986, 1002-1037.

Romer, P., "Endogenous Technical Change." *Journal of Political Economy*, 98(5), 1990, S7-102.

Romer, P., "Implementing a National Technology Strategy with Self-Organizing Industry Boards." *Brooking Papers in Microeconomics*, 2, 1993, 345-399.

Scotchmer, S., "Standing on the Shoulders of Giants: Cumulative Research and the Patent Laws." *Journal of Economic Perspectives*, 5(1), 1991, 29-41.

12. INTELLECTUAL PROPERTY RIGHTS AND THE TRANSITION TO THE KNOWLEDGE-BASED ECONOMY

Iain M. Cockburn
NBER and Boston University
Boston University

Paul Chwelos
University of British Columbia

1. INTRODUCTION

Intellectual property is perhaps the most important – and often the only – significant asset of knowledge-based enterprises. The legal structure of Intellectual Property Rights (IPRs) defines not just ownership of these intangible assets, but also their value, and the nature of the markets in which they can be bought and sold. The statutory framework of IPRs, associated jurisprudence, and the institutions which administer them therefore constitute a critical part of the infrastructure of the new knowledge-intensive sectors of the economy. In the transition to a knowledge-based economy, firms' strategies for creating, managing, and realizing returns from intellectual property will be a key factor in creating wealth and employment. This paper examines the extent to which new technologies and new ways of doing business present challenges for Canada's current IPR regime, and discusses possible policy responses.

As a framework for understanding these issues, we begin by reviewing global trends in international patent statistics and in intellectual property legislation. Canada's position relative to comparable nations is evaluated using some simple indicators of utilization of IPRs and resources provided to maintain the IPR system. Next, we discuss the role of IPRs in business strategy. Studies of the "old" manufacturing economy have confirmed that the strength of IPRs plays a very important role in incentives to innovate, but firms can and do use other mechanisms to appropriate returns from R&D, such as time to market, control of complementary assets, or internal policies to limit knowledge spillovers. In the new knowledge-based economy, however, it is unclear exactly how effective and important these mechanisms will be, compared to the use of IPRs, or whether new business forms and new technologies will lead firms to find new appropriability mechanisms. We note also that the framework of IPRs has broader implications for competition and business strategy. In addition to their direct role in giving firms control rights over their innovations, IPRs also play important roles in other aspects of business practice such as financing new enterprises, monitoring and motivating human capital within the firm, structuring alliances between firms, and contracting for technology transfer.

We then turn to a review of some of the challenges posed to the existing system of IPRs by the new "information-dense" technologies which support some of the most salient knowledge-intensive sectors of the economy: software, biotechnology, and electronic media "content." The debate surrounding appropriate responses to these new technologies illustrates some of the very substantial difficulties and dilemmas inherent in formulating any IPR policy. We conclude with a discussion of possible IPR policy responses to the growth of the knowledge-based economy.

2.   GLOBAL TRENDS

2.1   Patent Statistics

Formal IPRs consist of patents, copyrights, trademarks, and legal recognition of trade secrets, plus a variety of specific provisions such as protection for integrated circuit topographies. With the exception of patents, statistics on the use of these rights are difficult to obtain consistently over time and across countries. We therefore focus on patent applications as indicators of differences and changes in use of IPRs across countries, recognizing that these too are subject to serious problems of measurement and interpretation.[1]

We begin with trends over time, using data on filings at the U.S. Patent and Trademark Office. Figure 1 illustrates the remarkable and sustained growth in patent applications experienced since the early 1980s. After remaining stable at roughly 100,000 per year for much of the postwar period, total applications from both U.S. inventors and foreign-domiciled inventors have doubled since 1984. Various reasons for this have been advanced.[2] Procedural reforms in the U.S. are said to have created a "friendly court" and thus greater incentives to file for patents. The surge in patenting may also reflect fertile new technological opportunities, though the increase is too large and widespread to be attributable to particular industries such as software or biotechnology.

In our view, the likely underlying cause of this surge in patenting can be found in the combination of a number of factors. One of these is a general

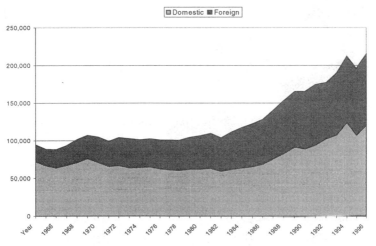

Figure 1: U.S. patent applications

increase in technological dynamism prompted by worldwide economic growth and the widespread application of "general purpose technologies," such as computing, that have opened up technological opportunities in many sectors of the economy. A second, closely related, possible cause is the increased "knowledge content" of many products, which is not confined to high-tech industries. Third, the rising trend in patent filings may reflect not only a streamlined and more patentee-friendly court system, but a substantial change in business practices and attitudes toward patents. A series of high-profile patent disputes that resulted in huge damages being awarded by the courts (or paid in out-of-court settlements) has raised the profile of IPRs, and at the same time there has been a growing understanding that IP assets can be an important source of revenue in themselves. The revelation that Texas

Instruments was making more money in some years from licensing fees realized from aggressive enforcement of patents than it was from its manufacturing operations is often cited as a "wake-up call to business."

Increased awareness of patent issues has been accompanied by much more sophisticated use of the patent system. Both inside and outside the traditional high-tech sectors, businesses have increased resources devoted to active management of intellectual property assets. While a minority of firms has always recognized the value of strategies such as "thicketing" core technologies with dozens of interrelated patents, many more firms appear to have moved to a more aggressive and proactive stance with respect to IPRs. Even if they are not actively enforcing patent rights, many firms are willing to invest significant resources in accumulating patent portfolios for defensive reasons. The simplest (and most common) means of settling legal disputes over patents is a cross-licensing arrangement, and a firm that does not have a strong IP portfolio of its own is at a serious disadvantage in such situations. Note also that there is a powerful "prisoner's dilemma" at work in industries in which one or more competitors begin to accumulate large numbers of patents. In these circumstances, strategic considerations (such as fear of legal action or of being locked out of new technological developments, or concerns that technologies practised as a trade secret may become "owned" by a competitor who files patents) create strong incentives for all firms in an industry to ramp up their patenting activity, independent of any changes in underlying technological progress.

Whatever its causes, the trend toward increased use of patents shows no signs of abating. We turn next to cross-national comparisons, and to some simple benchmarks of Canadian IPR infrastructure and activity. Data were gathered on patent filings at the Canadian Intellectual Property Office (CIPO), the European Patent Office (EPO), the German Patent Office (GPO), the Japanese Patent Office (JPO), and the U.S. Patent and Trademark Office (USPTO) for the operating year 1995-1996. Four principal findings emerge from analysis of these data.

First, Canada appears to be roughly comparable with other countries with regard to inventive activity, in terms of patent applications per dollar spent on research and development. (See Table 1.)

Table 1: Cross-country comparison of patenting and inventive activity

1996	Canada	EU	Germany	Japan	US
Domestic Applications	4,002	31,599	42,834	340,101	116,335
Applications with USPTO	4,893	29,537	11,515	39,810	116,335
USPTO Applications per Million Population	163	79	200	317	438
USPTO Applications per Million $ Domestic R&D	0.478	0.231	0.426	0.489	0.649

Notes: "EU" applications are the total from the EU-15 countries filed at EPO or USPTO. R&D expenditures are computed using 1995 OECD estimates of gross domestic expenditure on R&D converted to U.S. dollars at PPP rates.

For this comparison, we chose to use the number of U.S. patent applications filed by the country in question for the year 1996. An alternate measure of research output is the number of domestic patents filed, but this measure is hard to compare across countries because of significant differences in patent laws (particularly in those relating to the scope of individual patents) across jurisdictions. Notice, for example, the large discrepancy between the number of domestic applications filed with the JPO (340,101) versus the number of U.S. applications filed with Japan as the country of origin (39,810). While there may be some Japanese inventions for which the assignee sees no economic return in the U.S. market, this finding primarily reflects the much more narrow scope of Japanese patents. Historically, a popular rule of thumb has been that one U.S. patent covers approximately the same amount of subject matter as ten Japanese patents. Though using U.S. applications as a benchmark likely biases the numbers in favor of the U.S., the magnitude of this bias is certainly not comparable to that which would have resulted from comparing domestic application figures. Research output, measured in number of applications per million U.S. dollars spent on R&D, ranges from 0.231 for the aggregate of E the U countries to 0.649 for the U.S. Canada is the median of the five countries looked at, with a value of 0.478. Thus, we conclude that, while Canada is slightly less inventive than the U.S. on a per-dollar basis, it certainly does not lag far behind.

In terms of inventiveness per capita, however, Canada lags behind both Japan and the U.S. This result reflects the higher levels of per capita investment in R&D in these countries. Thus, while Canadians appear to be "as good as" their international counterparts in terms of the research they conduct, Canada simply does not engage in as much research per capita as do the U.S. and Japan. If the lower per capita inventive output in Canada is viewed as a problem, its cause does not lie with less innovative Canadian researchers, but with a lack of investment in research in Canada.

Second, the CIPO does not appear to be the office of first resort for Canadian inventors. As the table indicates, in any given year more patent applications are filed by Canadians with the USPTO than with the CIPO. This supports the "folklore" that the standard operating procedure for Canadian inventors is to: (i) file with the USPTO, (ii) wait for an initial determination, and (iii) file with the CIPO within the grace period if the initial determination is favourable. While data for a single year should be interpreted with caution, we believe that a detailed analysis of the international filing patterns of Canadian inventors would support this conclusion.

Third, the CIPO appears to be significantly under-funded in comparison to its international counterparts. Table 2 compares the level of funding across the five patent offices. In real terms, the CIPO budget, per application, is approximately one-fourth the USPTO budget per application. Likewise, the CIPO figure is smaller even than the GPO and JPO figures, despite their rather different patent law and administrative processes. On average, patent examiners with the CIPO are expected to deal with more than three times as many applications as their counterparts at the USPTO. Given these funding levels, it may be unrealistic to expect that CIPO examinations are as rigorous as USPTO or EPO examinations, or can be processed as quickly. This finding is at least consistent with the off-the-record contention of some practitioners that the CIPO effectively "rubber-stamps" the determinations of the USPTO. Certainly, this level of funding constrains the ability of the CIPO to make expeditious, independent patent decisions.

Table 2: Comparison of patent office activity and resources

	CIPO	EPO	GPO	JPO	USPTO
Total Applications	26,629	64,035	51,833	376,615	206,275
Patent Office Budget (US$ M)	$22.7	$567.6	$141.6	$462.0	$666.4
Budget per Application	$852.64	$8,864.68	$2,731.14	$1,226.69	$3,230.64
Patent Examiners	105	912	2,484	2,512	2,500
Applications per Examiner	254	70	21	150	83

Notes: Budget figures converted at PPP exchange rates. EPO and GPO personnel count includes management as well as examiners.

Fourth, an examination of the legal profession in Canada and in the U.S. suggests that, at least in crude terms, IP enforcement activity in the two countries is roughly comparable. Patents are only as effective as the ability of the patentee to enforce them. Consistent data on patent-related legal disputes are very difficult to find and interpret. However, the number of patent lawyers gives some sense of the scale of IPR enforcement activity. Table 3 presents the membership figures for the American and Canadian Bar Associations. For both countries, roughly 4% of bar association members were also members of the Intellectual Property Law section. However, a discussion with practitioners suggests that IP enforcement, in terms of legal actions, "goes where the money is." In most cases, this means that, given a choice, actions will be filed in the U.S. because of the history of large awards for IP infringement and the possibility of obtaining triple damages after a finding of "willful infringement." We note also that since the early 1980s the U.S. has had a dedicated legal channel for filing and litigating IP cases, the Court of Appeals of the Federal Circuit. This specialized court has removed some of the uncertainty and delay and "venue-shopping" associated with pursuing cases through the regular U.S. federal court system. IP litigation appears to be much rarer in Canada, perhaps reflecting a less litigious business community, but also the lack of such specialized legal processes. With no guarantee that cases will be heard before specialist judges, considerable uncertainty surrounds the outcomes of such cases.

Table 3: Legal resources available for enforcement of IPRs

	Canada	U.S.
Practising Lawyers (estimated)	68,433	654,000
Bar Association Members	34,822	340,000
Bar Association IP Group Members	1,277	16,000
IP Membership / Total Membership	3.7%	4.7%

Notes: Figures for the Canadian Bar Association are from personal correspondence with Lorraine Prior, Aug. 20, 1998. Figures for the American Bar Association are from personal correspondence with Michael Winkler, Aug. 19, 1998.

2.2   Legislative Reform

The past decade has been notable for a gradual, but pervasive trend toward reform and harmonization of intellectual property laws across countries. This trend has been accompanied by efforts to extend granting and enforcement of IPRs into "outlaw" jurisdictions which have historically been *de jure* or *de facto* outside the system common to OECD-type countries. The process of harmonization and extension has been pursued largely within the framework of international agreements such as the 1991 "TRIPS" Agreement on Trade-Related Aspects of Intellectual Property Rights arrived at as part of the Uruguay round of GATT negations. While most of the world's trading nations are signatories to this agreement, and are consequently obliged to put in place appropriate internal reforms, the process is far from complete. TRIPS provisions remain controversial, not only in developing nations but also in countries such as the U.S. where efforts to reform IP law have been met by vociferous internal opposition.

International differences in patent law and procedure are exceedingly complex and lie beyond the scope of this paper. It is clear, however, that variation among countries in treatment of priority, opposition procedures, duration of patents, and standards for patentability, has made obtaining and enforcing international patent rights extremely difficult and expensive. While there is as yet no such thing as a "world patent," the world's major economies have been steadily converging toward a common set of basic patent doctrines and administrative processes. This "WIPO model" for patents features a 20-year term from the date of application, a first-to-file basis for establishing priority, renewal fees, publication of patent applications after an 18-month period, and a broad notion of what constitutes patentable subject matter.

For the most part, Canada's statutory provisions for IPRs are in broad compliance with the "WIPO model," particularly in terms of administrative procedure, and where there have been important conflicts, Canada has moved relatively promptly and effectively to address them. The "devil is in the details," however, and there are a number of areas in which Canada is at variance with major trading partners. The most significant of these differences lie in the scope of patentable subject matter. In general, Canada has been much less aggressive than the U.S. in extending patent rights to cover new technologies. A conservative reading of the statutory description of patentable subject matter in the *Patent Act* by both Canadian judges and the CIPO has resulted in a number of technologies being denied patent protection in Canada. While Canada readily began awarding patents on many aspects of biotechnology, other jurisdictions such as the U.S. have gone on to extend protection beyond process technologies and modified microorganisms to higher (i.e., multicellular) life forms, which Canada has not. Other controversial areas are software inventions and methods of doing business, in which Canada has either been much slower in expanding the definition of patentable subject matter or taken a much firmer position. We return to some of these issues below.

The other main area in which Canada's framework for patents differs from competitors is in the treatment of minor inventions. Canada has no exact equivalent of the *Gebrauchsmuster* or "utility model patents" available in some (primarily European) countries, or of the design patents available in the U.S.. On the face of it, the *Industrial Design Act* offers equivalent protection to many of the inventions covered by these "petty patents," but very little research has been done on the economic aspects of these rights.

Turning to copyright law, Canada can again be said to be in general compliance with international norms and treaty obligations. There are minor differences between Canada and major trading partners relating to treatment of corporate versus individual holders of copyright, administrative procedures, and so on. The most significant differences between Canada and other countries lie in the definition of fair use, for which Canada offers somewhat more generous protection to copyright holders than does the U.S., and in the issue of "moral rights" of authors where Canada is firmly at odds with the U.S.[3] Canada is also more generous to copyright holders than the U.S. on the question of placing a levy on blank recording media. Canada has not yet followed the EU's lead on providing statutory protection for databases and other compilations of factual material.

Canada has some unfinished business in terms of conforming to international treaty obligations, and to less formal harmonization around WIPO draft treaties. The *Plant Breeders Rights Act* may not fully comply with the International Convention for the Protection of New Varieties of Plants (UPOV). Some difficult questions relating to the recognition of indigenous peoples' traditional knowledge and artistic and cultural "content" (which fall outside the "author-centric" conception of IPRs) are unresolved.

Examination and clarification of the "shrink-wrap" and "click-wrap" contracts used to assert proprietary rights over software and digital media is probably necessary. But by and large, Canada's legislative framework for IPRs conforms fairly closely to that of competitor economies.

3.   CHALLENGES OF NEW TECHNOLOGIES

Some of the most visible aspects of the transition to a knowledge-based economy are the emergence of new "information-dense" technologies such as molecular biology and software, and orders-of-magnitude changes in the cost of communicating and distributing information. These technologies are placing the traditional framework of IPRs under considerable strain. The current framework, in Canada as in other countries, is one inherited from the Age of Manufactures. Though it has proved to be surprisingly flexible and adaptable, critics claim that this framework has been stretched close to the breaking point by these new technologies. In this section, we review some of the issues and challenges presented to (i) the patent system by the cases of patenting higher organisms, gene sequences, and software, and (ii) the law of copyright by the digital media and the Internet and efforts by owners of databases to obtain proprietary rights over their creations. Difficulties have arisen in copyright because of the revolutionary change in the economics of copying and transmitting creative works brought about by digital media. For patents, new technologies have created difficulties in part because they do not fall easily into the legal definition of what can be patented, and in part because they blur a fundamental distinction in patent law between ideas and use of ideas.[4]

3.1   Patent Controversies: Biotechnology and Higher Life Forms

In 1980, a U.S. Supreme Court decision in *Diamond v. Chakrabarty*[5] opened the way to patenting life forms. By a 5-4 majority the court ruled in favour of the inventor of a genetically modified bacterium, coining the now famous phrase "Anything under the sun that is made by man is patentable." This ruling opened the gates to a flood of biotechnology and genetic engineering patents on processes for manipulating genetic material. Though the *Chakrabarty* decision raised some ethical hackles, it was relatively uncontroversial, and patent offices around the world rapidly followed suit. Many thousands of patents have now been issued worldwide on modified single-cell life forms and processes for manipulating genetic material. These patents support a very substantial investment in R&D with potentially huge payoffs for human and animal health, as well as agricultural productivity.

The logical extension of the "everything under the sun" principle by the USPTO resulted in 1988 in the highly controversial granting of the "Harvard Mouse" patent.[6] Well-founded ethical and religious objections, and widespread public concern raised by the spectre of genetic monsters, generated extensive public debate.[7] Notwithstanding these objections, the the USPTO has since issued more than 200 patents on transgenic multicellular nonhuman animals, including rats, rabbits, guinea pigs, sheep, goats, pigs and cows. The USPTO's current position is that patents will not be allowed on methods for modifying human germ cells. Ownership of human beings is, of course, unconstitutional but it is unclear exactly where the line will be drawn in terms of human-animal chimeras.

Public opposition to this extension of patentable subject matter remains intense, particularly in Europe, though lobbyists also claim widespread support in North America. In Europe, opponents of patenting life forms succeeded in blocking the issue of a significant number of patents by the EPO on the grounds that they were contrary to *ordre publique*. A lengthy and heated debate in EU member states and in the European parliament ensued, and resulted in long delays and compromises before the EU managed to gain legislative approval in 1998 for its *Directive on the Legal Protection of Biotechnological Invention*s which allows restricted patenting of higher life forms.[8] European biotechnology firms, while not entirely happy with this document, have at least had the burden of significant uncertainty lifted from them.

In Canada, the application for a patent on the Harvard Mouse has been rejected by the CIPO, and the assignee's appeal was recently denied by the Federal Court. The CIPO Commissioner's view, as upheld by the Court, was that the claimed invention falls outside the scope of patentable subject matter as laid out in the *Patent Act*. The ethical and legal bases of this decision (and continued rejection by the CIPO of patents on higher life forms) remain a source of public debate and controversy. Given the general unease about the ethical issues, a conservative reading of the *Act* may well be appropriate pending legislative review. But we note that this decision has potentially serious economic consequences for future of biotechnology investment in Canada. A recent Industry Canada Study on "Ethical Issues Associated with the Patenting of Higher Life Forms" concluded, quite reasonably, that CIPO administrative decisions as embodied in the *Manual of Patent Office Practice* are hardly an appropriate mechanism for resolving the very difficult and controversial debates surrounding this issue.

Patenting of genetic sequences raises additional problems for the patent system. There appears to be substantial and sustained public opposition to the notion that patentees can "own" genes or the entire genome of organisms. At the same time, the information-dense nature of gene sequences sits uncomfortably with a fundamental doctrine of patent law, namely that patents confer exclusive rights over the application of ideas, not ideas themselves. Faced with a "gold rush" stampede to gain proprietary rights over gene sequences with unidentified functions ("ESTs"), the USPTO and other patent offices have backed off from automatically granting patents on gene sequences whose utility has not been clearly demonstrated. However, the issue is far from settled and thousands of such patent applications are pending.[9]

3.2   Patent Controversies: Software Inventions

Computer software is a pervasive feature of modern economic life, and the software industry is a major locus of intellectual effort and wealth creation. Once thought to lie outside the realm of patentable subject matter due to their algorithmic component, software inventions were protected primarily by copyright and trade secret. However, software patents began to be issued in large numbers by the USPTO in the mid-1980s following the U.S. Supreme Court decision in *Diamond v. Diehr.*[10] The Court ruled that an otherwise patentable process is not unpatentable simply because it is executed by a computer, leading to applications for thousands of patents on computer-related inventions. Case law and patent office practice have since evolved to include "new and useful processes operated by a computer" in patentable subject matter in Canada and many other jurisdictions.

Software patents have aroused great controversy. In part, this reflects initial difficulties experienced by the USPTO (and other patent offices) in developing appropriate examination procedures. A number of high-profile cases (such as the extraordinarily broad "Compton Multimedia Patent" issued and then withdrawn by the USPTO in response to widespread protest) buttress the arguments of critics who allege that large numbers of granted software patents are invalid, or should be invalidated, since they fail to meet the standards for non-obviousness and novelty, or are inappropriately broad in scope. The Internet continues to resound with howls of derision greeting newly issued patents which appear to cover software techniques that are thought to be blindingly obvious to industry insiders, or are alleged to have been practised decades ago. The rapid pace of advance in the industry makes many of these challenges difficult to assess: given that much software is developed in secret (few software authors publish source code) or is sketchily documented, legally establishing the existence of prior art can be difficult. The assertion that "We did that at Stanford AI Lab in 1972" can be hard to back up with physical evidence. After all, who keeps backup tapes from 25 years ago, and who has appropriate hardware today to read them?

Efforts to better train examiners and to develop searchable repositories of prior art may address these difficulties to some extent. Nonetheless, many in the software industry continue to oppose software patents, arguing that they are simply inappropriate for a technology which is "grown, not made" and is essentially algorithmic. As a practical matter, software projects containing millions of lines of code accreted over many years present enormous difficulties in terms of identifying and avoiding patent infringement. The rapid pace of change in the industry relative to the speed at which patent offices can process applications presents a further serious practical difficulty: the same technique could be independently invented and applied many times, and become effectively obsolete by the time a patent is issued to one of its inventors.

It has also been argued that the rules of logic and the restrictions built into programming languages effectively constrain programmers to operate within very narrow bounds. Different programmers approaching the same problem will arrive at substantially similar solutions, even though each has created their solution independently. While some code will be superior to others in different contexts, patent protection given to one program would prevent these other solutions from being developed. Fear of infringing the broad functional protection provided by patents would, it is argued, seriously discourage creativity in writing software.

These arguments have led many observers to advocate policy changes to ensure that copyright, rather than patents, be the primary source of protection for software. Yet heated disputes have also arisen over the extent to which copyright applies to key aspects of computer programs. U.S. Courts continue to wrestle with very difficult questions surrounding the extent to which nonliteral similarities in the "structure, sequence, and operation" of programs constitute copying. The important question of whether user interfaces are copyrightable expression remains essentially unsettled even after the *Lotus v. Borland* case went to the U.S. Supreme Court.

3.3   Copyright and Digital Media

Supported by rapid technological change, the Internet is becoming faster and cheaper and ever more pervasive. Increased functionality, in concert with the rapidly growing diversity of information, products, and services available on the Internet is leading to an explosion in the number of Internet users.[11] The supply of unprecedented amounts of digital communication bandwidth and access to consumers should be very good news to copyright holders: a huge and nearly zero-cost medium of distribution holds the potential for a massive boom in the consumption of "content." However, the providers of copyrighted creative "content," be it images, music, or video, have good reason to be cautious about the Internet. For the first time, "producers" and "consumers" of content have access to the same means of production. By making the reproduction and distribution of digital material nearly instantaneous and costless, the Internet has acquired the dubious title of "one giant copying machine."

To date, the Internet appears not to account for a large proportion of total copyright infringement. Far more significant are pirate CD manufacturing plants and home duplication of music. However, new technologies, such as the MPEG Layer 3 standard (MP3), present a frightening prospect for content producers. The Motion Picture Expert Group developed the MP3 standard to compress video for high-definition TV broadcasts and digital video disks (DVDs), but MP3 has found application in the duplication and distribution of (copyrighted) digital music tracks from CDs. With a modest multimedia PC and a modem, anyone can download a song from the thousands of (illegal) sites on the Internet that make MP3 files available. The MP3 format stores songs in a highly compressed form, requiring only about 4 megabytes to store a four-minute, CD-quality song, as opposed to about 40-50 megabytes on an audio CD. Even with a 28.8-kbps modem, the song can be downloaded in about 20 minutes. Users with the next generation of faster connections (cable modems, digital subscriber lines) can download the same song in under a minute.

The rise of the Internet raises a number of interesting IP issues. First, does existing copyright legislation cover digital products on the Internet? Following the WIPO meeting in 1996, at which the WIPO Copyright Treaty was adopted by many countries, the answer is "yes." Second, are databases covered by copyright? Historically, the answer is "yes, in part." There have been calls for new *sui generis* protection of databases, and draft legislation is being considered in the U.S. and has been passed in the EU. Third, are the incidental copies that are made in distribution over the Internet considered to be an infringement of copyright? Early rulings found that incidental copies in RAM or on a browser's disk cache were not considered a "fixable medium" and hence were not an infringement; however, recent rulings have considered copies in RAM to be fixable and a violation. At the 1996 WIPO meetings, delegates declined to establish international norms on temporary copying, so the issue remains open. Fourth, does the potential for resale of digital products hold the potential to erode markets for digital content? In theory, yes, although there are business strategies that can counteract this threat. All of these issues are discussed in greater detail below.

3.3.1   Pressures for New Legislation

Industry forces, including the Creative Incentive Coalition, the Information Industry Association, and the International Intellectual Property Alliance, joined by the Hollywood studios and the American Bar Association, have been lobbying for a strengthening of domestic and international copyright legislation. The primary argument used is that, without more stringent protection of digital content, the incentives to produce quality content will be eroded by widespread piracy on the Internet. The public, in turn, will be harmed by a lack of quality products and the "Information Superhighway" will turn out to be a dead end. With the U.S. copyright industries accounting for $278 billion in value added in 1996 (3.65% of U.S. GDP), the copyright industry has become a powerful political force.[12]

Of particular concern to the compilers of on-line databases is the perceived need for *sui generis* protection of databases. U.S. copyright law has provided protection for databases provided that there was sufficient originality in the selection, organization, and arrangement of the data; however, only the original portion of the database was protected by copyright, respecting the central principle of copyright law that works with no original content are not eligible for copyright protection. Thus facts, being unoriginal, are not copyrightable. The U.S. courts have previously rejected "sweat of the brow" arguments for making collections of facts copyrightable, as in the watershed case *Feist Publications v. Rural Telephone Service.*[13] Providers of on-line databases that are large, general compilations intended to be searched by users note that their products are ineligible for copyright protection because they do not, prior to searching, display originality. Without some special form of protection, these providers argue, there are insufficient incentives to create and make available such on-line databases. The EU has adopted legislation that provides both *sui generis* protection of facts within a database, and copyright protection of any original portions of the database. Similar legislation is before the Senate in the U.S. Both the EU and the U.S. draft make it possible to extend indefinitely the period of *sui generis* protection by repeatedly engaging in "significant" revision of the database: at each revision, a new 15-year term of protection is awarded.

The validity and enforceability of so-called "shrink-wrap" or "click-wrap" licences for software is another issue that may need legislative attention. Shrink-wrap licences on software specify that, by breaking the wrapping on the box of software that you have purchased, you agree to be bound by the terms of the licence contained in the box. (Similar licences for software distributed on-line require you to click on the "okay" button prior to downloading software; such agreements are termed "click-wrap" licences.) In the past, these licences were typically regarded as invalid because the user was not deemed to have actually agreed to the terms of the contract. Court decisions typically upheld this point of view, especially where shrink-wrap licences attempted to limit rights of fair use guaranteed under copyright law. Again, recent decisions in the U.S. have created uncertainty, as the court in *Pro-CD v. Zeidenberg* ruled that Pro-CD's shrink-wrap restrictions were enforceable under state contract law. The need for clarity on the legality of shrink- and click-wrap licences and consideration of the rights of copyright holders versus consumers suggests that new, or at least carefully amended, legislation bridging copyright law and the law of contracts may be needed.

The principal challenge presented by new digital media to copyright law, is, however, that brought about by the revolutionary changes in the economics of production and distribution of "content." Copyright law has historically made both duplication and distribution of a copyrighted work an infringement. In a world in which copyright is always manifest in a physical medium, such as a book, the link between duplication and distribution was clear and sensible. If someone runs off a thousand (illegal) copies of a book, this investment in duplication is clearly part of a plan to engage in (also illegal) distribution of these copies for profit. However, in a digital world, in which copyright is "fixed" in intangible vehicles, the link between duplication and distribution becomes less clear. In the process of engaging in a legitimate sale of, say, a short story (a copyrighted work) over the Internet, the story is duplicated and delivered, with the buyer ultimately receiving a copy. In the process of delivery, however, a number of temporary copies of the story are automatically created in the servers of the seller's and buyer's Internet Service Providers (ISPs), in other network hardware between these locations, and finally in the buyer's RAM and the browser's disk cache. Unlike physical copies, however, these temporary incidental (electronic) copies embody no intent for further distribution of the copyright work. Thus, copyright law could usefully be updated to recognize the difference between "reproduction with intent to distribute" and "temporary incidental reproduction" created as a by-product of the distribution medium.

Finally, the nature of the Internet requires close international harmonization of relevant intellectual property laws. Internet transactions that span more than one country raise significant problems. In a world of copyright on content-fixed physical media, it is possible to sustain substantial differences across national IP regimes, with some countries permitting generous "fair use" while others are more restrictive, some countries respecting the moral rights of authors, and others not, and quite wide variation among countries in the duration of copyright. However, when a product copyrighted in Canada is sold from a computer in the U.S. to a customer in England, it is far from clear which country's laws should apply, and how the copyright holder might seek redress.

3.3.2   Pressures Against New Legislation

There continue to be significant and real losses due to unauthorized reproduction of intellectual property, with the software industry being one of the more visible victims. According to the Software Publishers Association: "[Of] the 574 million new business software applications installed globally during 1997, 228 million applications – or four in every ten – were pirated. Revenue losses to the worldwide software industry due to piracy were estimated at $11.4 billion."[14]   While it is generally acknowledged that industry association figures represent overestimates of the losses to piracy, by any estimate piracy is a significant economic force.

However, the fact of widespread violation of IPRs does not of itself clearly demonstrate the need for new legal mechanisms to protect intellectual property. In the case of software piracy, existing intellectual property laws *already* make such activity illegal in countries adhering to the Berne Convention for the Protection of Literary and Artistic Works and the Agreement on Trade-Related Aspects of Intellectual Property Rights (TRIPS). The prevalence of software piracy can be more convincingly used as evidence that more vigorous enforcement of *existing* laws is required, or that international adherence to these laws should be secured. On balance, the argument that new and stronger forms of IP legislation are required is far from convincing, especially in light of the technological and business strategy approaches to protecting IP surveyed below.   It is worth remembering that the software industry was born and thrived without *any* form of intellectual property protection. The application of copyright, and later patents, to software has surely had some effect on the consumers and producers of software, but it would be difficult to argue that stronger IPRs will necessarily lead to more innovation in the industry, or make it easier for small software firms to compete.

3.4   Methods for Protecting Digital Intellectual Property

Digital intellectual property, whether in the form of text, images, music, or video, is often referred to simply as "content." While the same technologies that allow content owners to create and distribute digital IP allow essentially costless duplication, a number of creative methods for protecting digital content have been developed. These methods rely on technological means of making content proprietary, or the use of particular business practices, or both.

3.4.1 Technology-Based Methods for Protecting Digital IP

In the extraordinarily dynamic competitive environment of new media and the Internet, at least four technology-based approaches to protecting content, and enabling its owners or creators to appropriate rents from its distribution can be identified: encryption, serialization, digital watermarking, and superdistribution. Digitized content, whether its underlying form is text, audio, image, video, or a computer program, can be infinitely replicated without any degradation in quality because it is stored as a series of digital bits: ones and zeros. The high quality of digitized media is both bane and blessing: bane because of the ease of illegal reproduction of content, blessing because a method of protecting any form of digital content can be applied to all forms. The methods described below can be applied to any digitized content.

Protection through encryption. Encryption scrambles the underlying content through the application of a key (or secret code). In order to decrypt the content into a usable form, the user must have an appropriate key. Private key cryptography relies on both the sender and the recipient having access to the same key; that is, prior to being able to send encrypted messages, the two parties must have exchanged the private key, presumably through a secure channel. This requirement is feasible for frequent communications between two parties, but becomes intractable when a large number of parties need to communicate in a secure manner, as is the case with digital delivery of content in electronic commerce. Fortunately, an alternative exists that does not require the sender and the recipient to share the same secret key. Public key cryptography relies on a two-key system.[15] Each user has both a public key and a private key. All users' public keys are published with a reputable third party. When Party **A** wishes to encrypt a message to send to Party **B**, **A** looks up **B**'s public key with the third party. **A** then uses that code to encrypt the message, which is then sent to **B**. **B** then uses his private key to decrypt the message. Thus, both **A** and **B** know that no one else has been able to decrypt the content.[16] However, once the purchaser has decrypted the content, it is no longer protected and can be easily replicated.

Protection through serialization. The process of assigning a serial number to a piece of intellectual property is the *de facto* standard in software distribution. In order to obtain technical support or product upgrades, the user of a software package must provide a serial number. If the publisher finds a serial number appearing more than once, it knows that either a reseller or a user has illegally reproduced the software. The ability for publishers to generate serial numbers on the fly and attach them to products is both technically feasible and low-cost. Serialization has enjoyed some success with software because there is a tangible value to being a registered user of the software, e.g., access to after-sales technical support or lower-price upgrades to future versions of the software. Serialization can be applied to other digital media, but by themselves serial numbers can be easily removed or altered. However, in combination with digital watermarks (below), serialization is not easily removed. By itself, serialization does not prevent duplication or reuse of content, but it does provide a mechanism for its detection and thus weakens incentives to copy. Recently, a standard called the Digital Object Identifier (DOI) has been promulgated by the International DOI Foundation, a non-profit organization. The DOI is intended to be the digital equivalent of an ISBN (International Standard Book Number), long used to identify books. The DOI standard will enable the identification of all digital content that has been marked with a DOI. Similarly, the recording industry has developed the International Standard Recording Code. Thus, the DOI or the ISRC are options for use in serialization.

Protection through digital watermarks. In their most common form, digital watermarks encode information in undetectable ways in content, and are thus a modern example of steganography. In an image, for example, the luminance of small groups of pixels can be altered slightly (undetectable to the human eye) in the process of inserting a watermark. Later, an image can be examined to determine whether it contains the watermark. Considerable research is under way to develop robust methods of watermarking content that are not easily altered or destroyed, either deliberately or accidentally, as through common techniques of compression. In their primary use, watermarks promise to provide a way of marking a piece of content with regard to the publisher, buyer, distributor, or all three. Again, watermarks do not prevent duplication of content, but may provide a method to prove ownership of digital content and expose violations of copyright.

Protection through superdistribution technology. "Superdistribution" describes a comprehensive approach to protecting content with four separate components: a persistent cryptographic wrapper, a trusted tool, a rights management system, and a network of fault-tolerant middleware. With superdistribution, content is encrypted and stored in a persistent cryptographic wrapper[17] that contains the business rules that govern the use of the enclosed content. These business rules determine the cost of using the content, and can be flexible, allowing for a variety of pricing schemes from pay-per-view, renting for a specific time period, ownership, and even volume discounts. Once the user agrees to the terms, payment is arranged through a "back office" system. Once payment is verified, the key to unlock the content is sent to the trusted tool (not the user), which decrypts the content and "streams" the content into memory. The rights management system ensures that the payment is appropriately allocated to the publisher of the content and value-added resellers, if any. The fault-tolerant middleware enables the user to access the content even if the user is temporarily unable to access the network that will carry out the payments.

The combination of content and its wrapper can be freely replicated and shared among users, but to gain access to the content, each user must agree to the terms and make appropriate payment. The promise of this "super" approach lies in its nearly costless method of secure distribution and its ability to administer "microtransactions" of $1 or less. Given sufficiently fast networks, almost anyone can become a publisher of digital content, and charge a fee that is close to users' marginal valuations.

While superdistribution is theoretically possible, and is being vigorously developed by a number of firms, a number of concerns about its technical and economic viability exist. The extent to which the decryption process will be transparent and painless to the end user is unknown. The difficulty of cracking the cryptographic envelope depends on the length of the key used to encrypt it, and using a longer key makes cracking the code more time-consuming. However, a longer key also increases the time (or processing power) needed to decrypt the content by legitimate means. Superdistribution requires tight coordination between a number of bodies and depends on the existence of standards to support this integration. Without the intervention of a strong standards-setting body, these mechanisms may be impossible to achieve. However, early forms of superdistribution already exist in the marketplace, for example in disposable DVDs.[18]

A concern with superdistribution is the capture of the streaming content in a form that will allow it to be reproduced. As with simple encryption, if a user is allowed to keep a decrypted copy of the content, then the content is rendered completely unprotected. Streaming technology is designed to send the content in small packages only when and for how long it is needed, as in the case of "streaming" a signal from a DVD to a TV. The streamed content is presented in a way that makes it difficult to capture and record. It is clear, however, that with sufficient effort, the streamed content can be captured. For example, reports of cracking the "Real Audio" format for streaming audio across networks have recently arisen.

The most technologically ambitious approach to protecting digital content would combine the use of superdistribution, serialization, and digital watermarking. The content is encrypted and placed in a strong cryptographic wrapper. When a user pays to access the content, the streaming content is watermarked with a serial code, such as a DOI.[19] This DOI is unique, and is recorded in a public repository, identifying the content and the details of the transaction: when it was sold, to whom, and under what terms. If a pirated version of the content appears, the watermark can be used to trace the violator.

In summary, technological methods of protecting digital content take one of two approaches: (i) scrambling the content through encryption so that only authorized users have access, or (ii) marking the content so that ownership can be established and violators of copyright identified. While the increasingly clever approaches of cryptography and superdistribution will prevent casual interception and duplication of content, mathematical relationships exist that make codes that are "impossible" to break infeasible for commercial applications, because they would simply require an inordinate amount of computing power for the user to decrypt the content. Thus, determined individuals will continue to be able to gain unauthorized access to digital content. For this reason, legal enforcement of ownership rights over intellectual property that is embodied in digital content remains crucial. Steps being taken to protect content owners' rights to use technological methods to protect copyrighted materials are to be welcomed. Technology can limit duplication, identify pirated content, and perhaps even identify the pirate. However, it is up to legal channels to prosecute these pirates and provide a deterrent to intellectual piracy.

3.4.2 Business Strategy Methods for Protecting IP

Businesses that seek to derive revenue from the creation of digital IP face two threats to their revenue stream: piracy and resale. If digital content is sold outright, under the doctrine of first sale the purchaser has the right to resell (or loan, or give away) the content after use. Because digital content does not degrade and can be transmitted very quickly, there is the potential for significant erosion of the marketplace from resale.

However, content providers have a number of strategies that mitigate the effects of resale. *Customization* of the content to the tastes of the individual buyer not only limits the "resaleability" of the content, but also increases the value of the content for the original buyer. Many providers commit to *frequent updates* of their content. If these updates are important to consumers, then old versions of the content will be less valuable and less likely to be resold. In effect, the provider is attempting to reinvent the market with each update. *Zero pricing*, in combination with advertising, is another approach to content provision. On the Web, for example, many providers give away their content to attract "eyeballs" (readers or viewers of the content). In turn, these providers sell advertising space on their websites. Since web advertising is priced by either the number of "hits" (people who see the advertisement) or the number of "click throughs" (people who click on the advertisement and go to the advertiser's website), providers seek to attract as many eyeballs as possible. Obviously, zero pricing of content completely erodes any secondary market since it is already available for free. Finally, providers may take the *multi-use* strategy, that is, striving to make their content suitable for multiple uses. Examples of multi-use digital content include software, computer games, movies, and databases, each of which can be used repeatedly by consumers, though perhaps with declining marginal utility. As long as the owner of the content values the utility from the future stream of his uses of the product more highly than the utility provided by the resale price of the content, he will continue to hold the product.

Of these four strategies, all but multi-use also serve to combat piracy by diminishing the value of pirated versions of the content. Just as tailoring a product to individuals (customization), providing the most current content (frequent updates), and giving content away (zero pricing) erode the market for resale, they also decrease the economic viability of piracy. Thus, even without any form of intellectual property protection, some types of digital content may be adequately protected by the business practices of the provider.

3.5   Dangers of New Legislation

While the emergence and popularization of digital methods of reproducing and distributing content presents new threats for content providers, the technology also provides new mechanisms, both technical and business, for protecting that content.   The need for new IP legislation, beyond clarifications and international harmonization, has not been convincingly demonstrated. Nevertheless, a number of important pieces of IP legislation have recently been proposed or passed. Some of this new legislation will significantly alter the balance of rights between producers and consumers of digital content. The consequences of these initiatives are discussed below.

3.5.1   Sui Generis Database Protection: A Dangerous Precedent?

As mentioned above, it has long been a central tenet of copyright legislation that facts, *per se*, are not copyrightable. The proposed *sui generis* legislation designed to protect proprietary rights in databases seeks to abandon that principle in order to protect the incentive to collect and compile data. Such a major change in IP philosophy should not be hurriedly enacted, especially when there is little evidence that consumers are suffering from a dearth of data due to market failure. Likewise, the proposed U.S. legislation breaks new ground in its significant curtailment of "fair use" access to the content of databases. While the legislation may lead to the creation of more databases, it is not clear to what extent these works will be available for criticism, comment, reporting, teaching, and research.

3.5.2   The Danger of Overprotection

The danger of underprotecting intellectual property is that there will be insufficient incentives for its creation.   The danger of overprotecting intellectual property is reduced efficiency resulting from a restriction on information flows and reduced ability to innovate. Intellectual property law has always sought to strike a balance between efficiency and incentives: the efficiency that comes from having information freely available versus the mechanisms required to call forth investment in the creation of new intellectual property.

Arguably, legislation providing a new form of *sui generis* protection of databases of the type proposed in recent drafts would destroy the balance between efficiency and incentives, focusing too much on producer rights and the incentives to create. Critics feel that these proposals, by curtailing fair use and removing the doctrine of first sale, are too strong in their protection of producers and too weak in their protection of consumers. There are also concerns that other forms of IP will eventually fall under the scope of the proposed database protection. These fears have some basis, since the American Bar Association, for example, favours expanding the scope of *sui generis* database protection to include "data, text, images, sounds, computer programs, computer software, databases, literary works, audiovisual works, motion pictures, mask works."[20]

One of the dangers in rushing into new legislation, particularly that which creates new statutory rights (such as *sui generis* database protection) is that it becomes difficult to subsequently justify repealing or modifying these rights. Producers can legitimately argue that they would not have engaged in the time and expense of developing the works had there not been the promise of protection of those works. As in other situations in which new forms of legal protection are introduced, a fundamental asymmetry is present in the consequences of making mistakes in formulating the law. Obviously, under-protection of IP may result in underproduction of IP to the detriment of all; however, this problem can be rectified relatively painlessly by *ex post* strengthening of IP protection. Conversely, overprotection of IP will benefit owners of IP, but at some cost to consumers, educators, researchers and the media; once recognized, however, rectifying the problem by weakening IP protection is likely to be a painful and contentious issue. Looking back at the history of IP legislation, the law has often lagged behind technological innovations. However, these lags were healthy in the sense that they allowed time for deliberation and ensured that when the law finally was enacted, it would get the balance right. Proponents of new IP legislation are asking that, unusually, IP law should lead rather than follow. Perhaps this is asking for the cart to be put before the horse.

3.5.3   Mass-Market Licensing Practices

One particularly contentious piece of draft legislation is the proposed Article 2B of the *Uniform Commercial Code*. This legislation, under development by the American Law Institute, is intended to be adopted by state legislatures. Among the contentious elements of UCC2B are (a) its explicit validation of shrink-wrap, click-wrap, and other forms of mass-market licences for software and other information products such as databases, and (b) its allowance for the inclusion of technical "self-help" capabilities in software.

The validation of mass-market licences is, in effect, a method of using contract law to circumvent federal intellectual property law. Under these licences, software, databases, or other information products are not sold, but are instead licensed. The important distinction is that, by avoiding a sale, the doctrine of first sale does not apply and the purchaser of software or a database does not have the right to resell the product. Further, these licences typically contain restrictive provisions that prohibit the purchaser from making backup copies, modifying software, or decompiling software for any purposes, despite the fact that federal copyright law guarantees the rights of consumers to all of these actions (limited to certain purposes and contexts). Further provisions of licences can invalidate perfect tender, the requirement that goods must be suitable for the purpose for which they are sold, for example by disclaiming all "implied warrants of merchantability." Even more restrictive conditions can be placed, such as those on PhoneDisc, a collection of phone numbers and addresses published by Digital Directory Assistance, the licence for which specifies that the software cannot be "used in any way or form without prior written consent of Digital Directory Assistance, Inc."[21]   Mass-market licences, if enforced, are akin to rights against the world (the domain of intellectual property law), not rights against an individual (the domain of contract law). Using contract law to circumvent IP law has been compared to eating your cake and having it too: content producers have broad, tight protection without having to clear the hurdles traditionally associated with obtaining such protection (e.g., the rigour, time, and expense of the patent process).

UCC2B could hail the transition from the sale of information to the widespread restrictive licensing of information. In the words of Pamela Samuelson, Professor of Law at UC Berkeley: "If information ever wanted to be free, it must have changed its mind because under UCC2B, information seems intent on being licensed."[22]

The provision for technical "self-help" in software is a worrisome misnomer. Far from allowing consumers to obtain help in using software, it in fact allows software publishers to include code in their products that will allow them to render the software inoperable if the consumer/licensee fails to make royalty payments. The concern with this provision is twofold. First, it will give software companies the ability to hold their customers for ransom, even in the case of a legitimate dispute as to what fees are, in fact, due. Second, software systems have become critical to the operation of many organizations to the extent that even a temporary shutdown of these systems may cause excessive harm. Allowing software vendors to hold such authority over their customers (without need for intervention of the court) again appears to swing the balance too much in favour of the producers of IP over the consumers.

These concerns about the consequences of overprotection of digital IP have led critics to envision a dismal future captured by the phrase "Digital Dark Age." Ironically, though technology for the first time enables the instant, global, and nearly costless distribution of information, new legislation may make accessing useful information more difficult or costly than ever before. Some fear stagnation in economic, educational, and inventive activity as a result of unprecedented amounts of information becoming proprietary and being licensed only under very restrictive terms. Some have envisioned a "tragedy of the anti-commons" in which creators and writers cannot easily connect because they are divided by too many gates and too many toll-keepers. These fears may overemphasize the negative aspects of new IP legislation, but they serve as a reminder of the importance of getting the balance right.

3.5.4 Status of Legislation

At the time of writing, a number of jurisdictions are considering or have implemented legislation to provide *sui generis* protection for databases. Most notably, the European Union passed a database directive in March of 1996. This legislation required member states to implement the directive by January 1, 1998, though a number of members have not yet done so (for example, France has passed the directive while the United Kingdom is considering draft legislation). Canada currently has no legislation in the works to provide *sui generis* protection but is considering the WIPO proposals, the courts having rejected the "sweat of the brow" justification for copyright of databases.   The U.S. Congress recently considered the *Collections of Information Antipiracy Act*, which has passed in the House and went before the Senate before being derailed by the Clinton impeachment scandal. This bill provided *sui generis* protection for databases, with some revisions to include limited fair use provisions. While this particular bill has not passed the legislature, it is clear that proponents of this legislation are capable of exerting strong pressure to get its provisions into law, and the issue is unlikely to go away.

Article 2B of the UCC is undergoing re-drafting prior to being put forward for adoption by Commissioners from the National Conference of Commissioners on Uniform State Laws (NCCUSL) and Representatives from the American Law Institute (ALI).   The current schedule is for finalization of the article by February 1999, with voting occurring in the summer of 1999.   Once finalized, it will be up to individual states to enact the legislation.

3.6   Conclusion: IP and Copyright in the Digital Age

The evolution of information technology and the growth of the Internet have undoubtedly raised new challenges and opportunities for providers of intellectual content.   Several key points were argued above.   While existing legislation already covers digital "content" or intellectual property, largely through copyright, there are grounds for seeking a clarification of legislation to sensibly address new technology.   Likewise, there is a need for international agreement on IP protection standards and harmonization of legislation. While recognizing these concerns, it is also clear this new technology provides producers and publishers of digital works with a range of technological and business strategy means by which to protect content. Ongoing technological efforts may provide a universal standard for the protection of digital content in the form of a persistent cryptographic wrapper. There also appear to be reasonable grounds for concern that recently proposed or enacted legislation both overprotects IP and sets dangerous precedents. Proposals to provide new *sui generis* database protection may protect the database owner's proprietary interest at the cost of making individual facts copyrightable, circumventing the doctrine of first sale, taking facts out of the public domain, and unduly restricting (or raising the price) of access to information. Overly restrictive licensing agreements may be socially as well as privately costly, as scientists, educators, and the media lose the types of access they have enjoyed in the past.

The need for new forms of IP protection for digital content has not been convincingly demonstrated. There is no clear evidence of market failure in the provision of digital content, information, or databases. Given the dangers of hastily enacting new forms of IP protection, the most prudent course, at least in the short run, may be to refrain from protection implementing radically new IP legislation. Instead, efforts could be directed toward more vigorous enforcement of existing provisions, in combination with clarification and international harmonization. These efforts should serve to adequately protect and reward the producers of IP while also respecting the rights of consumers.

4. MAKING INTELLECTUAL PROPERTY POLICY IN THE INFORMATION AGE

IPRs are critical infrastructure for the information age, not only because they define the nature and ownership of information goods, but because they also determine the economic performance of markets in which knowledge and information are important inputs and outputs to production. In these circumstances, policy choices by governments can clearly have very significant implications for future growth and prosperity. From this perspective, two general questions about the existing framework of IPRs need to be answered: first, does the framework provide adequate incentives for producers of knowledge, and second, does the framework allow for efficient distribution of knowledge? The preceding discussion suggests that these questions are particularly difficult to answer in markets driven by information-dense technologies.

Economic analysis of IPRs and incentives to innovate is a complex subject, ably surveyed elsewhere.[23] The central tension between incentives to innovate versus allocative efficiency continues to present challenges to researchers. On the one hand, IPRs address the market failure caused by the public goods nature of knowledge: since knowledge is largely non-rival and non-exclusive in consumption, incentives to create and distribute knowledge are weakened. On the other hand, the excludability conferred by IPRs may result in market failure to due imperfect competition. Debate on the economic properties of various IPR frameworks is far from settled, and in this context a number of results derived from both theoretical and empirical work are worth discussing.

Theoretical analysis of IPRs and incentives to innovate has identified a number of issues which germane to any policy debate. One recent stream in the literature has emphasized the cumulative nature of innovation and of the patent system, and highlights the consequences of patent scope and duration for incentives to innovate when future inventors can obtain patents on improvements to existing inventions. Another important proposition raised by models of R&D races is the possibility that strong IPRs may induce wasteful overinvestment in research as competitors try to be "first past the post." There are important interfaces between IPRs and competition policy, not considered here. Finally we note that theoretical analysis of alternative incentive mechanisms to induce innovation, such as prizes[24] or patent buy-outs,[25] suggests that these may be superior to patents along a number of dimensions.

Are current incentives to innovate provided by IPRs adequate? Arguably, yes. Counterfactuals are difficult to evaluate, but a number of pieces of evidence support this view. First, we note that efforts to calibrate the standard model of optimal patent duration typically suggest shorter, i.e., weaker, patent protection for many technologies.[26] Second, it is easy to find examples of highly innovative industries with no, or very weak, patent protection. Financial services, and software before the mid-1980s spring to mind. In both these cases, rapid and successful innovation took place without strong patents. Looking across countries, there is some weak evidence for positive correlations between economic growth (or R&D expenditures) and the strength of IPRs,[27] but it is also the case that some countries have achieved great economic success without adopting or enforcing the "WIPO model." Third, the available empirical evidence suggests that patents and other formal IPRs are ranked well below other appropriability mechanisms in all but a few industries. With the exception of pharmaceuticals, instruments, and specialty chemicals, R&D executives identify factors such as time to market, learning curve cost advantages, and possession of complementary capabilities such as superior marketing as being more effective means of securing returns to innovation. Among various means used to keep knowledge proprietary, trade secrets are consistently rated more highly than patents.[28]

The case of "digital content" discussed above is illustrative. While "fixing" some aspects of copyright law is clearly important, from a business perspective, relying on a reconfiguration of IPRs is a very poor solution. Instead businesses have created effective alternative appropriability mechanisms such as encryption, digital watermarking, and related technologies for proprietary distribution. It is also clear that much of the value of information goods, whether supplied via the Internet or not, derives from factors such as authenticity, timeliness, and complementarities with other products. In these circumstances reputation, brand names, and first-mover advantage may be far more economically important than "ownership" of information. Consider the case of current stock market prices, once available only by being physically proximate to the transaction, or by paying quite substantial fees to owners of proprietary distribution channels. Stock prices can be obtained free from many hundreds of sources on the Internet, but are rendered largely valueless to many potential customers by 20-minute delayed delivery, and uncertainty about reliability and future availability. Bloomberg, Reuters, and similar companies can continue to make money from supplying financial data precisely because they can address these concerns. Their positions are protected by existing common law on trade marks, contracts, and the "tort of misappropriation" which was successfully used in the early part of this century by telegraph news services which saw their "content" being captured and retransmitted by rivals.[29]

Turning to the question of whether knowledge is efficiently distributed under the current framework of IPRs, it is less easy to be sanguine. Modern theories of economic growth highlight the importance of "spillovers" of knowledge across firms and industries. Clearly, the extent to which agents in an economy effectively transmit and receive knowledge is a vital aspect of the growth process, and disclosure of knowledge is a vital part of the patent system. While there is considerable agreement among economists that positive externalities in the form of spillovers are present and are significant, precise measurements are difficult to perform. It is also worth noting that theoretical treatment of incentives to innovate in the presence of spillovers between firms produces ambiguous results. Again, the cases discussed above are instructive. In biotechnology, the patenting of gene sequences, while controversial, at least places the information in the public domain. Denying inventors these rights, for what may be perfectly good other reasons, may reduce incentives to identify genes, but will certainly result in many discoveries being kept secret. The likely results of secrecy are wasteful duplication by immediate competitors and decreased efficiency in research in other areas.

Absent viable metrics for measuring the efficiency of information distribution, it is difficult to take a position on the merits of alternative IPR frameworks. What is clear, however, is that careful attention should be paid to the disclosure and "fair use" provisions of IP law. Lobbying by producer groups for strengthened or expanded protection may be very costly, not just for immediate consumers, but for the economy as a whole. In debates driven by concerns over outright theft of intellectual property or over distribution of surplus between producers and consumers, it is easy to lose sight of the long-term consequences of overprotection: fewer and slower knowledge spillovers. As argued above, "keeping the Internet safe for Hollywood" may have unanticipated long-term adverse effects on education (i.e., accumulation of human capital) and research activity elsewhere in the economy.

5.   POLICY CONSTRAINTS, TOOLS, AND OPTIONS

5.1   Policy Constraints

Before considering the range of policy tools available to address the challenges presented by new technologies, it is worth reflecting on some of the constraints imposed by economic and political realities. IP policy is difficult to disentangle from a variety of other economic and non-economic issues, which may limit the scope of potential reforms.

The first, and perhaps most important, point to note is that IPR policy may best be understood as one component of a national innovation system, which consists of a distinct "bundle" of related policy choices about government support of R&D through procurement, taxes, grants, or "direction" of state enterprises, about education policy, about competition policy, and about the role of planning versus markets.[30] From this perspective, it may be counter-productive to design IP policy piecemeal.

Another important reality for a country like Canada is that it may be difficult for small, open economies to run an independent IP policy. Countries like Canada can, and do, make independent choices about IPRs for a variety of economic and non-economic reasons, but these can result in significant economic costs in the form of lost investment, or transfer of surplus from domestic consumers to foreign producers. Consider again the "Harvard Mouse" case. Canada may choose to exclude higher life forms from patentable subject matter as a matter of non-economic principle, but will then likely have to accept the economic consequences if the biotechnology industry reacts by relocating some investment elsewhere. The actual amount of investment involved is difficult to assess, and may indeed be small, but it is worth noting that these high-profile decisions can exert a disproportionate "chilling" effect. While Canada may not be a large producer of transgenic higher organisms, it is certainly the case that the patent covers a very important research tool, and that U.S. patent law allows for action by U.S. patent holders against imports which have been produced in violation of a valid U.S. patent. A common feature of knowledge-intensive industries is that their principal assets (highly skilled people) are globally mobile, and these industries are therefore likely to be unusually sensitive to "small" changes in IP policy which affect perceived returns to innovation.

As another example, consider Canada's position as a net "importer" of patented technology. (Research on international patenting indicates that foreign entities obtain more than three times as many patents in Canada as Canadian entities obtain in foreign jurisdictions, and, concomitantly, the value of Canadian patent rights held by foreigners is 300% greater than the value of foreign patent rights held by Canadians.[31]) Policy decisions or precedent-setting cases which have the effect of strengthening the position of patent holders, for example by lowering the standard of obviousness,[32] may well induce additional innovative effort by domestic inventors, but these benefits may be swamped by the costs incurred by domestic consumers whose position has been worsened *vis-à-vis* foreign producers of patented products.

Another set of constraints reflects social and political concerns about information and intellectual property. Vocal critics of the "WIPO model" allege that it is simply inappropriate for the knowledge-based economy. It may be difficult to agree with John Perry Barlow that "everything you know about intellectual property is wrong"[33] but statements such as "information is a life form," "information wants to be free", and "information is perishable" reflect a set of influential beliefs among people who play an increasingly significant role in producing, trading, and consuming information goods. In this vein, IP policies designed on purely economic grounds can come into serious conflict with civil liberties, interacting in subtle ways with privacy, freedom of speech, and other ethical and political issues. Legitimate concerns about cultural sovereignty are also connected with the positions taken by aboriginal peoples who have argued, with some cogency, that the "author-centric" conception of creativity and invention underlying Western notions of intellectual property systematically undervalues or overrides collectively held knowledge. Extension of IPRs into new domains of knowledge as well as new countries may not exactly amount to a "land grab" by powerful interest groups[34] but it certainly brings IP policy into conflict with strongly held values and beliefs.

5.2 Policy Tools

In addressing the challenges presented by new technologies to the traditional framework of IPRs, policy-makers have a fairly wide choice of levers to push upon.

Consider first the law and procedure for granting patents. One set of policy choices relates to the scope of patentable subject matter, which could be broadened or narrowed. Economics offers little guidance here: while it is widely accepted that some ideas should not be patentable (laws of nature), traditionally excluded technologies largely reflect historical policy choices rather than economic analysis of costs and benefits. The USPTO has been pushing at the frontier of "methods of doing business" by issuing a variety of patents on electronic commerce, and by logical extension we may yet see patent protection significantly expanded into the service sector.[35] Another set of choices relates to the scope of protected material and the length of time protection lasts. A wide range of tinkering with the duration, "breadth," and "height" of patents is possible in principle, but should be approached with caution. Economics certainly speaks to these issues, but conflicting theoretical results have been obtained on, for example, the desirability of infinitely-long-but-narrow versus short-and-broad patents. One persistent theme in the literature is that "one size may not fit all" in the sense that the optimal patent regime is a function of parameters which vary across technologies and markets. Yet in practice, it may be formidably difficult to gather appropriate data required to make optimal choices, and rather than open the door to endless and costly debate by special interests, most jurisdictions have settled on a single lifetime for patents across all technologies, with the glaring exception of pharmaceuticals, for which patent lifetimes have been lengthened and shortened through compulsory licensing or awarding additional market exclusivity to compensate for delays in regulatory approval.[36] Other tools for modifying patent protection include instituting "prior user rights" which allow inventors who have used a technology in secret to continue to do so in the face of a subsequently issued patent, or reform of the examination process. Some countries allow pre-grant opposition or operate a registration system where the validity of a patent has to be established *ex post* by a court before it can be asserted, with quite different consequences for the quality of issued patents.

Copyright presents some of the same difficulties, but the strength and nature of protection can be easily adjusted only by changing duration. The scope of copyright is so deeply embedded in case law that changing the definition of "originality" may require significant legislative reform. One suggested remedy for the challenges to copyright presented by digital media is to replace the right to control physical copying with a more general "exclusive right of exploitation" for the products of creative activity.

As mentioned above, governments can also create incentives for innovation through alternative mechanisms such as prizes. These mechanisms may be less distortionary than traditional IPRs and have been used historically with great success.[37] Difficulties in establishing how much to offer, and the question of who should pay for innovations which may benefit all mankind, are among the factors limiting the use of prizes. There would seem to be considerable scope for increased activity by governments on this front. Consider the case of malaria and other tropical diseases, where low incomes, poor medical infrastructure, and the historical absence of IPRs in the countries where these diseases are most prevalent have severely depressed incentives to develop vaccines or treatments. Here, a significant prize offered by some national or supranational authority could be very effective in generating innovation.[38]

A final set of policy options concern steps to enhance the enforceability of IPRs. The incentive effects of IPRs are limited by the costs and feasibility of enforcing them. Timely and consistent treatment of patent cases by the courts is clearly an important aspect of a functional IPR framework.

5.3   Policy Options

Formulating and implementing an optimal IP policy is a formidable task, and given our tight economic ties to the U.S., as a practical matter Canada's freedom of choice in this respect may be rather limited. There are, however, a number of simple and relatively inexpensive steps which could be taken to respond to the imperatives of the knowledge-based economy. Some of these concern funding and administration of the CIPO. In our view, treating the CIPO as a revenue generator makes little sense. Government should be building infrastructure for the knowledge-based economy, not charging tolls on existing facilities. Increased resources for the CIPO could be used productively in speeding up examination of patents, and in increased efforts to educate and assist Canadians in developing and managing IP assets. Enhanced legislative scrutiny of IP issues and court decisions may also be warranted.

A "steady as she goes" policy is probably the safest option for Canada. Given treaty obligations and economic ties with major trading partners, Canada probably cannot stray too far from the "WIPO model," and should therefore continue to respond promptly to harmonization proposals. The unfortunate experience with compulsory licensing of pharmaceuticals suggests that Canada should be quite careful about attempting to "go it alone" on issues like the Harvard Mouse patent.

Nonetheless, it may be worth considering more radical options. One such (unpalatable) choice would be to abandon efforts to emulate the innovation system of the U.S. and to make IP policy choices consistent with a "drafting" strategy which free-rides on other nations' production of knowledge. Becoming such a "fast follower" would require significant reallocation of resources to build the "absorptive capacity" required to identify and assimilate knowledge generated elsewhere. It would entail "unenthusiastic" enforcement of "WIPO model" IPRs, and use of a variety of regulatory tools, compulsory licensing provisions and the like to reduce the effective lifetime of IPRs. It would certainly mean accepting that many knowledge-intensive industries might leave Canada, and would likely invite significant retaliatory action from major trading partners.

Another radical option would be to maintain an innovation-oriented national innovation system, but to abandon independent patent examination. It is unclear how much Canada gains economically from examining and issuing its own patents. Domestic registration and honouring of patents issued by the EPO, the USPTO, or some future incarnation of the WIPO would free up resources at the cost of surrendering sovereignty over some aspects of technological development. Freed-up resources could be productively invested in supporting education and enforcement, or used to enhance the efficiency of knowledge flows in the economy.

6. CONCLUSION

One conclusion to be drawn from this paper is that formulating an optimal IP policy is a formidable task, complicated by the challenges presented to the existing framework of IPRs by the new technologies and methods of doing business which are driving the transition to the knowledge-based economy. It is clear, however, that IPRs will continue to be an important policy issue in an environment characterized by accelerating technological change and economic transformation. While the private sector seems to be successfully looking after itself in some key respects inventing and implementing a variety of solutions to IP problems, these issues will likely need to be revisited frequently by policy-makers and government bodies. To better inform these debates, more and better empirical research will be required on the incentive and efficiency properties of IPRs, and it is therefore encouraging to see an upswell of interest in these issues in the academic community.

NOTES

[1] See, Griliches (1990).

[2] See Kortum, and Lerner (1997).

[3] The term "moral rights" refers to the rights of authors of a copyrighted work to assert authorship or require their names to be associated with it, to object to or restrain uses of or associations with a work, or any distortion, mutilation, or modification of a work to the prejudice of their reputation. These rights are independent of actual ownership of the copyright.

[4] In most countries, law and practice exclude a number of technologies or types of invention from "patentable subject matter." In Canada these include: plants, animals, and seeds; surgical methods; processes based on interpretative or judgmental reasoning, or artistic or personal skill; methods of doing business; rules for playing games; and scientific principles or abstract theorems.

[5] 447 US 303, 308-09.

[6] U.S. Patent no. 4,736,866 Leder et al. "Transgenic non-human mammals." The Oncomouse™ is a mouse bred from a strain whose genome has been permanently altered in such a way that they have a high incidence of cancer which, though disastrous for the mice, makes them a very valuable research tool.

[7] As one eminent ethicist put it, following the Chakrabarty decision, "What is the principled limit to this extension of the domain of private ownership and dominion over living nature? Is it not clear, if life is a continuum, that there are no visible or clear limits once we admit living species under the principle of ownership? The principle used in Chakrabarty says that there is nothing in the nature of a being, no, not even in the human patentor himself, that makes him immune to being patented" (Kass, 1981).

[8] See the survey results reported by Wagner and contributors (1997) or the debate reported at *http://www.britcoun.org/france/intro.html.*

[9] See Eisenberg (1994).

[10] 450 U.S. 175, 185 (1981).

[11] As of December 1997, Nielsen Media Research estimated that some 58 million adults in the U.S. and Canada use the Internet. The Internet is predicted to grow to one billion users globally by 2005.

[12] Figures are from the International Intellectual Property Alliance, and are available at: *http://www.IIPA.com/html/pr_05071998.html.*

[13] 499 U.S. 340 (1991). In Canada, a similar decision was arrived at in *Tele-Direct v. American Business Information,* leaving originality (in selection and presentation) as the only basis for copyright protection for databases.

[14] Press release from the Software Publishers Association, Washington, D.C., June 16, 1998.

[15] A comprehensive introduction to public key cryptography is available from RSA Laboratories at: *http://www.rsa.com/rsalabs/newfaq/.*

[16] Modern public key cryptography techniques are based on mathematical approaches, specifically "one-way trapdoor functions." Any content so encrypted can, eventually, be decrypted by breaking the code: a time-consuming and numerically intensive process. Depending on the value of the content, a key of sufficient length can be chosen to make decryption an economically infeasible alternative to purchasing the content.

[17] Trade names for cryptographic wrappers include "Cryptolope," "RightsWrapper," and "Digibox."

[18] A disposable DVD allows a user to watch the content on the disk, usually a film, for 24 hours upon purchase. To access the disk again, the user must purchase an access code (by telephone) which again grants 24-hour access.

[19] Ideally, each version of streamed content (even from the same cryptographic wrapper) should be encoded with a unique watermark, allowing for exact identification of copyright violators. While real-time watermarking is currently infeasible due to processing constraints, it is unlikely to remain so.

[20] ABA Resolution 458-3.

[21] This example is taken from, Mann (1998).

[22] See, Samuelson (1998).

[23] See, McFetridge (1995).

[24] See, Wright (1983).

[25] See, Kremer (1998).

[26] See, McFetridge and Raffiquzzaman (1986).

[27] See, Thompson and Rushing (1996).

[28] See Levin, et al. (1987); Cohen, Nelson and Walsh (1997); Baldwin (1997).

[29] *International News Service v. Associated Press* 248 U.S. 215 (1918).

[30] See, Nelson (1993).

[31] See, Putnam (1996).

[32] Canadian jurisprudence has instituted a significantly lower standard of obviousness compared to the U.S., by using the fiction of an "unimaginative skilled technician" rather than a "person ordinarily skilled in the art" to decide some cases.

[33] See Barlow (1994).

[34] See, Boyle (1996).

[35] A recent decision upholding a patent on a method for "hub and spoke" administration of mutual fund portfolios has worried some observers. See, Ellis and Chatterjee (1998). See *State Street Bank and Trust Co. v. Signature Financial Group, Inc.* (July 1998).

[36] Patent holders can, to some extent, adjust patent lifetimes endogenously by failing to pay renewal fees.

[37] A famous historical case is that of the prize offered by the British Admiralty in the 18th century for a solution to the problem of determining longitude at sea. See Sobel (1995).

[38] See, Lanjouw and Cockburn (1999).

REFERENCES

Baldwin, J., "Innovation and Intellectual Property." Statistics Canada Occasional Paper Catalogue No.88-515-XPE, March 1997.

Barlow, J. P., "The Economy of Ideas: A Framework for Rethinking Patents and Copyrights in the Digital Age (Everything You Know About Intellectual Property Is Wrong)." *Wired,* March 1994, 85.

Boyle, J. S., *Shamans, Software and Spleens: Law and the Construction of the Information Society.* Cambridge, MA: Harvard University Press, 1996.

British Council, *http://www.britcoun.org/france/intro.htm*

Cohen, W., R. Nelson and J. Walsh, "Appropriability Conditions and Why Firms Patent and Why They Do Not in the American Manufacturing Sector," Mimeo, Carnegie Mellon University, 1997.

Eisenberg, R., "A Technology Policy Perspective on the NIH Gene Patenting Controversy." *University of Pittsburgh Law Review*, 55, 1994, 633-652.

Ellis, W. and A. Chatterjee, "Shakeout on State Street: A Seismic Federal Circuit Precedent Makes Patents a Potent Financial Services Weapon." *IP Magazine,* 1998.

Griliches, Z., "Patent Statistics as Economic Indicators: A Survey." *Journal of Economic Literature,* 28(4), 1990, 1661-1707.

International Intellectual property Alliance, *http://www.IIPA.com/html/pr_05071998.html*

International News Service v. Associated Press 248 U.S. 215 (1918).

Kass, L., "Patenting Life." *Commentary,* 72(6), December 1981, 45-57.

Kortum, S. and J. Lerner, "Stronger Protection or Technological Revolution: What Is Behind the Recent Surge in Patenting?" NBER Working Paper No. 6204, September 1997.

Kremer, M., "Patent Buyouts: A Mechanism for Encouraging Innovation." *Quarterly Journal of Economics*, 113(4), 1998, 1137-1167.

Lanjouw, J. and I. Cockburn, "Do Patents Matter? Empirical Evidence after GATT." Paper presented at the "Patent System and Innovation" Conference of The Industry and Technology Project of the National Bureau of Economic Research, Santa Barbara, CA, January 8-9, 1999.

Levin, R., R.C. Levin, A.K. Klevorick, R.R. Nelson and S.G. Winter, "Appropriating the Returns From Industrial R&D." *Brookings Papers on Economic Activity*, 3, 1987, 783-820.

Mann, C. C., "Who Will Own Your Next Good Idea?" *The Atlantic Monthly,* September 1998.

McFetridge, D., "Science and Technology: Perspectives for Public Policy." Industry Canada Occasional Paper No. 9, July 1995.

McFetridge, D. and M. Raffiquzzaman, "The Scope and Duration of the Patent Right and the Nature of Research Rivalry" in J. Palmer (ed.) *The Economics of Patents and Copyrights.* Research in Law and Economics series, 8, JAI Press, 1986.

Nelson, R. (ed.), *National Innovation Systems.* Oxford: Oxford University Press, 1993.

Putnam, J., Unpublished Ph.D. dissertation, Yale University, May 1996.

RSA Laboratories, *http://www.rsa.com/rsalabs/newfaq/*

Samuelson, P., "Does Information Really Have to be Licensed?" *Communications of the ACM,* 41(9), 1998, 15.

Sobel, D., *Longitude: The True Story of a Lone Genius Who Solved the Greatest Scientific Problem of His Time.* New York: Walker, 1995.

State Street Bank and Trust Co. v. Signature Financial Group, Inc., United States Court of Appeals for the Federal Circuit, Appeal No. 96-1327, Decided: July 23, 1998.

Thompson, M. and F. Rushing, "An Empirical Analysis of the Impact of Patent Protection on Economic Growth." *Journal of Economic Development,* 21(2), 1996, 61-79.

Wagner, W., and contributors "Europe Ambivalent on Biotechnology." *Nature,* 387, issues 6636, June 1997, 845-847.

Wright, B., "The Economics of Invention Incentives: Patents, Prizes, and Research Contracts." *American Economic Review,* 73(4), 1983, 691-707.

13. INDUSTRIAL RESTRUCTURING IN THE KNOWLEDGE-BASED ECONOMY

Marcel Boyer
Stephen A. Jarislowsky Professor of Technology
And International Competition. Ecole Polytechnique de Montréal;
Professor of Economics, Université de Montréal & CIRANO

Jacques Robert
Département de sciences économiques and
CRDE, Université de Montréal & CIRANO

Hugues Santerre
Research Professional, CIRANO

1. INTRODUCTION

Restructuring a company is something common in today's competitive global markets. Companies sometimes need reforms of their management practice to keep their competitive edge. They may even proceed to a transformation of their entire operating structure to stay in business.

Over the last 10 years, with the wave of deregulation, trade globalization and new information technologies, we have witnessed a number of restructurings involving not only single companies, but groups of companies and entire industries. Needless to say, the latter reforms involve more details than cases involving single companies. Industries are made of several decision centres, notably the companies themselves. But companies do not really act as a single identity, they are also divided into interest groups. So any attempt to reform must coordinate a large group of individuals.

This paper considers the particular difficulties and challenges faced by potential reformers. We draw both from the economic literature and from accounts of actual industrial reforms. We state a number of principles, illustrated by case studies. We surveyed restructuring efforts in the electric power industry in the U.K., New Zealand, Argentina, the U.S. and Canada; in the gas industry in the U.K. and the U.S.; and in the telecommunications industry in Chile, New Zealand, Guatemala, Japan, the U.K. and the U.S. We also examined the cases of Alex in Canada and Minitel in France, as well as Quebec's Pork Electronic Exchange. Alex was a terminal resembling the French Minitel that was launched by Bell Canada in the early 1990s but never took off. From this survey, we then identified factors common to a successful restructuring and distinguished elements that lagged, endangered or caused other reforms to fail.

The analysis of inertia in broadly defined organizational contexts is relevant to our understanding of the difference between adopting a new technology and successfully implementing it in a firm or in an industry. We consider here a whole set of factors of organizational inertia such as: the dynamic adjustment costs in investment theory; the sticky routines and procedures which are, almost by definition, difficult to change; the presence of multi-principals in organizational structures, which discipline agents and principals but at the same time prevent smooth adjustments to a changing environment; the rational suppression of potentially valuable information in the contexts of arm's-length relationships, of the separation of ownership and control and of the existence of strict chains of command in corporations, which potentially boosts short-term efficiency but at the same time introduces impediments to change; the information cascades that promote social cohesion and imitation but also make it difficult to trigger or start a movement for change; the incentive mechanisms, usually based on successful completion of tasks, that may prevent agents from coming forward with bad news about an impending problem; and finally the optimal dynamic incentive schemes in contexts of specific investments and asymmetric information.

The data show that literally billions and billions of dollars will be spent, a good part of it unsuccessfully, in trying to implement technological and organizational changes in firms. Much remains to be done to reach a good understanding of the difficulties organizations and firms face in successfully implementing new technologies they have chosen to adopt. A research program aimed at uncovering the real rather than the superficial roots of those difficulties, many of them implied or created by the firm's own rational policies, must be of interest to public agencies. Since the new trade agreements make it more and more difficult for governments to subsidize local industries, it becomes necessary to rethink national industrial policies. We will show that a properly defined public agency could be quite useful to industries in need of restructuring.

2. PRINCIPLES OF ORGANIZATIONAL CHANGE

Principle 1: Organizational Inertia Is Endogenous.

Boyer and Robert (1998) have shown how the "optimal" probability of adopting a change of action (project, technology, organization, etc.), when such a change would be implemented for sure if full information were available, will optimally depend on the parameter structure of the problem at hand and, in particular, on the relative informational rents of the different participants. Their objectives were "to better understand the unavoidable trade-off between incentives and flexibility in dynamic contexts of asymmetric information, and second to determine the appropriate organizational response to this trade-off." They showed that decision and power structures which have negative effects on the flexibility[1] to implement change in an organization may nevertheless be necessary to maximize the organization's overall performance.

Restated in the context of technology adoption and implementation, their results suggest that more flexibility in adopting and successfully implementing a new technology, which may become necessary because of a changing environment or new information, may come at the expense of efforts exerted up front to make the organization more successful. They identified a clear trade-off in such contexts between *ex ante* efforts and *ex post* flexibility of adaptation. They also characterize the optimal contract between the principal and the agent, expressed in terms of payment profiles and of the relative power of the principal and the agent to recommend and initiate change.

In a related context, Levitt and Snyder (1996) consider an organization composed of a principal and an agent where the agent has access to early warnings about impending problems in the organization. They consider a situation where the agent has private information not only on his own efforts to make the firm (or, more precisely, the project) more profitable but also on the likelihood of success of the current project. They show that the principal can entice the agent to truthfully reveal his private signal by making explicit in the incentive scheme the existence of rewards for coming forward with bad news. For instance, the principal must reduce punishment for those who admit failure early rather than follow the crowd in trying to hide bad news through some form of tacit collusion or information cascade. Levitt and Snyder show that, if the information revealed by the agent can be used by the principal to make adjustment decisions (for instance, to abandon the project), the principal weakens in so doing, that is, in using the information, the link between the agent's initial effort and the project's outcome. Reducing this direct linkage between effort and outcome reduces the agent's incentives to exert great efforts. To induce a great effort from the agent nevertheless, the principal will have to offer a larger expected wage and also credibly commit, if possible, not to cancel some projects with *ex post* negative expected payoffs, a clear form of inertia. This striking result is due to the fact that the *ex post* cost of continuing the projects is smaller than the beneficial impact of inducing higher effort *ex ante*.

Those results suggest that the challenge of successfully implementing a new technology may have deeper rational roots in the organization. The factors which are responsible for a firm's *ex ante* level of profitability may be the same factors that reduce *ex post* its flexibility to adopt and successfully implement a new technology.

The theoretical foundations and empirical grounds for dynamic adjustment costs in investment theory have been a concern of both theorists and practitioners at least since the seminal contributions of Lucas (1967a, 1967b) and Rothchild (1971). Ito (1996) provides us with an institutional perspective on the economic understanding of those costs. He conducts an empirical investigation of investment adjustment costs in mainframe computer investments and shows that those costs are rooted in micro-level dynamics and institutional characteristics of adjustment activities. He derives significant non-convexities in those adjustment costs and finds that they vary with the presence of "on-line business transaction applications" (order-processing, inventory, accounts payable rules and procedures). New investments in mainframe computing hardware are likely to involve complementary changes in work routines and incentive (information) structures. More interestingly, Ito shows that adjustment costs in mainframe computer investments are not significantly affected by the absence or presence of engineering and programming resources. He claims that those resources may possibly be generally available on external competitive markets and therefore do not constitute a constraint on change. On the other hand, internal organizational routines and business practices impose serious impediments to change and are the sources of significant levels of inertia.

It is important to realize that routines and procedures are rationally chosen and implemented by efficiency-seeking firms. Gabel and Sinclair-Desgagné (1996) claim that routines and procedures offer a good compromise between achieving efficiency as consistently as possible and economizing on managerial time spent in repeatedly making decisions.[2] They insist on the ambivalent role of routines inside the firm: "The routines which undoubtedly increase an organization's efficiency also reduce its adaptability to changing circumstances." The fact that many such organizational routines and procedures in different sectors and at different levels of the organization must be interrelated and coordinated through organizational compatibility standards, will generate a significant level of inertia; changing any one of those routines will be difficult because of the coordination process involved. Indeed, casual observation indicates that those changes are typically infrequent, disruptive and costly.

Dewatripont and Tirole (1996) provide a different perspective on the endogenous sources of organizational resistance to change. They consider the pervasive nature of multi-principal structures in different organizational contexts. These structures can be rationalized as discipline devices in two particularly important contexts: the soft budget constraint context and the public project cost overrun syndrome. Dewatripont and Tirole observe that a commitment to *ex post* inefficiency, in the form here of "multiple partisan actors," may be required to obtain efficiency *ex ante* in an organization. They interpret their results as supporting the usefulness of the *ex post* inefficient multiplicity of shareholders (investors) in firms and the complementary roles of different government departments (Finance and Treasury, together with spending departments such as Education, Health, Transport) as an *ex post* inefficient supervising mechanism insofar as those government entities are given objectives and missions that "differ from social welfare maximization and furthermore are at odds with each other." Interpreted in the context of adapting to change, these results suggest that the *ex ante* maximization of the firm's performance may trigger conflicting interests *ex post* and undermine the successful implementation of a newly adopted technology. The multi-principal structure may appear *ex ante* as the optimal organizational structure, but it will make the necessary coordination of the different principals or interest groups more difficult to achieve if a new technology is to be implemented across the organization.

A major source of organizational inertia in a corporation takes the form of a rational suppression of potentially valuable information. In this context, Crémer (1995) considers the possibility for a principal of monitoring an agent's activities by acquiring information on the conditions which may explain the agent's performance. He shows that a lower cost of monitoring may in fact hurt the principal because it reduces his commitment to high-powered incentives given to the agent. Such situations are quite prevalent in corporations: the principal will then typically make efforts to credibly convey to the agent that there will be no such monitoring *ex post* and no acquisition of information about the conditions which may explain *ex post* his poor performance. Crémer compares two monitoring technologies, a first (efficient) technology which allows the principal to observe, at some cost, whether the agent is truly good or bad, and a second (inefficient) technology which allows him to observe only the output level realized by the agent, a random function of the agent's quality. With the former monitoring technology, the agent is fired if and only if he is found to be bad by the principal. With the latter technology, the agent is fired if and only if his output is low. A reduction in the cost of the first monitoring technology has mixed effects on the principal's welfare: the better information about the quality of the agent must be traded off against the loss of power of the incentives. It is quite likely that new technologies have effects on the relative costs of monitoring technologies. Insofar as a new production technology reduces the cost of the above "efficient" monitoring technology, the implementation stage may clearly suffer from the principal's less credible commitment to the new technology.[3]

In a related framework, Burkart, Gromb and Panunzi (1996) consider the agency problem that the separation of ownership and control in modern corporations creates. Tight control of managers by shareholders may be *ex post* efficient but represents a form of expropriation threat that may reduce not only managerial initiatives but also non-contractible investments and thus may reduce the profitability of the firm. They show that monitoring and performance-based incentive schemes may have opposite effects on performance.

Along the same lines, Friebel and Raith (1996) consider the chains of command in organizations. If middle managers compete with lower managers for higher management positions, the former may be induced to hire lower-quality junior managers in order to secure their promotion to higher positions. The net effect of more competition, which should raise the incentives for superior performance, combined with lower-quality recruiting, which is detrimental to the overall performance of the corporation, may be negative. To prevent this damaging negative impact of low-quality recruiting, firms have put in place strict chains of command and promotion. Although such strict chains of command may be a significant source of organizational inertia, they may induce middle managers to hire the best available lower managers and therefore improve the firm's performance. By restricting its use of potentially useful *ex post* information (competition in promotion), a firm can increase its *ex ante* probability of higher performance through better-quality recruiting.

It has been known for some time that tenure has potentially ambiguous effects on the quality of universities. Once tenured, the faculty may not feel the same pressure to perform in teaching and research. But tenure has also positive effects on the quality of junior faculty recruiting because it protects the tenured (older) faculty against the threat newcomers may represent. The tenured faculty, usually in control of recruiting, are then more likely to recruit the best possible candidates in order to improve the quality of their department and university.

The delegation of authority, that is, the separation of ownership and control in modern corporations, due in part to the opposite effects of monitoring and performance-based incentive schemes, together with the existence of strict chains of command, and in part to the negative effects a freer flow of information may have on recruiting and long-term profitability, may increase the implementation problems of new technologies by reducing the flow of information from lower-level managers to the principal and general decreasing the organization's adaptability to the new technology imperatives.[4]

These results may be considered as illustrations of Rumelt's (1995) paradoxical assertion that successful change may require the promise of future inertia, as evidence of Dewatripont and Tirole's (1996) claim that *ex ante* efficiency may require a commitment to *ex post* inefficiency, and as illustrative cases of Boyer and Robert's (1998) trade-off between flexibility and incentives in dynamic asymmetric information contexts.

The first principle states that adopting a new technology and successfully implementing it through a suitable organizational change may be made more difficult and uncertain because of the very factors which the firm put in place earlier to ensure its profitability and survival.

Principle 2: Adopting a New Technology Does Not Mean Successfully Implementing It.

American corporations are expected to spend some US $ 50 billion per year during the latter part of the '1990s on reengineering projects, with 80% of that amount going into information systems. More than two-thirds of those efforts are likely to end up in failure, according to the prominent reengineering guru Michael Hammer.[5] According to a survey by Arthur D. Little Inc.,[1] only 16% of executives say that they are fully satisfied with the results of their reengineering efforts while 39% say they are totally dissatisfied. Finally, according to a survey of 400 Canadian and American firms by Deloitte and Touche,[1] the main reasons for reengineering failures seem to be the significant resistance to change and the lack of consensus and commitment among senior executives. This state of affairs has led many industry consultants, both individuals and firms, to propose new buzzwords and reengineering procedures such as "organizational agility" and "value engineering," focusing more on growth potential than on cutting costs through different downsizing variants.[6]

These developments suggest that a fundamental difference exists between adopting a new technology and successfully implementing it. They stress vividly the significant risks and uncertainties in the transformation process from one technology to another. Clearly, inventions and innovations are quite unpredictable and, once available, their adoption and implementation are even more intrinsically risky. The fact that many economists consider the processes of selecting, adopting and implementing inventions and innovations, both technological and organizational, as the main engines of economic growth, makes the above observations even more interesting, though troublesome.

Numerous examples abound to illustrate the difficulty of recognizing the value of inventions. Consider, for example, the case of the laser which, besides its uses in measurement, navigation, chemistry, music, surgery and printing, is revolutionizing, together with fibre optics, the telecommunications industry. Yet, after its invention at Bell Labs, it was not at first considered (by lawyers!) to be valuable enough for the telephone industry to warrant even a patent application. Similar stories exist for other major inventions such as the telephone, the radio and the transistor. Western Union turned down the possibility of buying Bell's 1876 telephone patent cheap, considering that its long-term interest was to concentrate on the cheap market for telegraphy, its core activity. Marconi thought that his invention of the radio would be useful only where wire communication was impossible, as in ship-to-ship or ship-to-shore communications (a journalist even suggested that its main, and possibly only, use would be to transmit Sunday sermons). IBM considered leaving the computer business in 1949 because it estimated that the world market for computers would level off at around 15 units. The inventor of the transistor thought that his invention might possibly be useful in improving hearing aids. And many other examples exist. There is an even larger number of examples where the difficulties in implementing a previously chosen invention, innovation or, more generally, a previously chosen technology have been misunderstood or miscalculated. All of the above examples are in some sense examples of the difficulty of predicting future technological progress, an umbrella concept which must be understood as covering both the adoption (or diffusion) and the implementation of both inventions and innovations in both techniques and organizations.

Remarkably, relatively few efforts have been made to foster our understanding of the (strategic) differences between adopting and implementing a new technology and of the theoretical and practical implications of these differences. The risks and uncertainties involved in the transformation process from one technology to another are different from and add onto the output uncertainty that economists have studied.

Building on a model first proposed by Stenbacka and Tombak (1994), Boyer and Clamens (1998) showed that a reduction in the (investment) cost of adopting a new technology for the market leader increases the difference in adoption timing, with the leader adopting earlier and followers adopting later; there is a possibility that the mean adoption time in the industry will increase. A reduction in the (investment) cost of adopting the new technology for the market followers reduces the difference in adoption timing, with the leader adopting later and the followers adopting earlier, resulting again in the possibility of a postponement in the mean adoption time in the industry. These results suggest that subsidizing the adoption of new technologies in first-mover firms or second-mover firms may have negative impacts on the mean adoption time (diffusion) in an industry. Such situations are not pathological but likely to be quite common. Boyer and Clamens also show that a more efficient implementation program in the leader firm induces the follower firms to postpone the adoption of a new technology but, more surprisingly, that it may also induce the market leader firm to postpone the adoption of that technology because of the followers' behaviour: this striking result would be obtained if, for instance, the market discount rate is relatively high. Those results indicate that unstructured (non-analytical) discussions of industrial restructuring in strategic contexts are likely to mislead policy- makers. Unfortunately, such discussions are more the rule than the exception in too many public policy circles.

Some authors have also advocated that cultural differences, and in particular human-machine or human-technology relationships, are another possible source of problems at the implementation stage. Because of deep-rooted unobservable differences in human perceptions, values and related attitudes across societies, populations and organizations, it may be difficult to predict how a new technology will be accepted in any given organization. Indeed, a new technology or organizational form may very well be successfully implemented (or accepted) in some but not all sectors, plants or national subsidiaries of a given global firm. We will not cover this third group of factors that may influence the fundamental distinction we make here between adopting and successfully implementing a new technology. Suffice it to mention that they may be part of the answer to the questions we raise here.

Principle 3: Time Is Information (Waiting Has Value and Cost)

Adapting to change involves real option values. Waiting to adopt and implement new technologies may be beneficial insofar as new information will become available over time and the best practice technology is likely to evolve. This new information may allow a better decision regarding the adoption of a new technology. This situation is analogous to real call and put options, and the importance and value of those options will dictate whether advancing or postponing the adoption of the technology is warranted.

Weiss (1994) derived some interesting conclusions on a firm's decision to postpone adoption of the current best technology to replace its incumbent technology or to suspend the adoption decision process when improvements are expected in the currently available best practice technology. He provided empirical evidence from the printed circuit board industry, where in 1993 the incumbent technology was the Through-Hole Process (THP) and the best practice technology was Surface-Mount Technology (SMT): some 90% of firms in 1993 were using the incumbent technology. From a purely theoretical point of view, uncertainty concerning future improvements may favour or inhibit the adoption of the current best practice. Weiss concluded in particular that the expectation of future improvements in the technology does not necessarily slow down the adoption decision: an expected faster pace of improvements led firms to slow down or suspend the adoption process but had no significant effect on the decision whether or not to adopt. Firms which had more certain expectations of improvements were more prone to adopting but also to suspending the adoption process. Finally, more stringent product market competition led firms to pursue the adoption process more vigorously but had no significant effect on the decision to adopt.

Parente (1994) considers an economy-wide growth model with technology adoption and learning-by-doing in using technologies. At each instant of time, a firm chooses whether to continue to use its current technology or to adopt a more advanced one. The firm gains expertise over time in the use of a technology. Hence, learning-by-doing is specific to the technology and cannot be (fully) transferred to a new technology. So the firm faces a trade-off in its choice of technologies because the more advanced the new technology is relative to the current technology, the greater its productive potential but the lower the firm's starting level of expertise in that technology. Parente found that the firm's optimal decision is to continue to use its current technology until it has accumulated a threshold level of expertise in that technology and then switch to a new one, starting a new round of learning-by-doing. Because the firm's production level will be lumpy in such a context, he found that the technology adoption timing decisions of firms and the growth rate of per capita output depended significantly on the efficiency of capital markets.

The above analyses dealt with firm-level considerations. Similar lessons can be derived from the analysis of industry-level adoption of changes in technology: waiting has value insofar as information from others' experience may prevent the reformer from making costly errors. The U.K. was the first industrialized country to liberalize its electric power industry (1988-1990). The U.K. served as a laboratory for the other industrialized countries which enacted similar reforms. The British government had in turn followed its own experience in railways (1987), telecommunications (1988), gas (1986), and steel (1988) (Armstrong, Cowan and Vickers, 1994). Through a learning process, New Zealand, Australia and the Nordic countries benefited from the U.K. experience and their success in reforming their electricity industries was supported by the case of England and Wales. Argentina based its reform on the Chilean experience, but without making the costly mistakes of its neighbour. In the U.S., the current electricity sector reform is based on the gas industry restructuring that took place during the late 1980s and several documents have set our the parallels between both industries.

3.   PRINCIPLES OF INDUSTRY-LEVEL RESTRUCTURING

In the previous section, we described the difficulties and challenges faced by the reformer of an organization. In this section, we extend this discussion to the transformation of entire industries.

A priori, it may seem more difficult to change an industry than to change a single organization, as the former requires that many different organizations change in the same direction. But a closer look may lead to a different conclusion. Each individual firm within an industry need not change for the industry itself to be transformed. The constant creation of new firms and destruction of existing ones may suffice to transform the industry. Competition provides an impetus for change within an industry that does not necessarily exist within a single organization. For example, IBM failed to restructure itself, for a long time, while the computing industry experienced radical transformations.

As a general rule, industries are in continuous mutation through a natural selection process. Changes in consumers' moods and needs, technological innovations, etc., induce firms to adapt, and those that do not are replaced by new ones. In this section, we wish to go beyond this natural process of industrial evolution to look at cases where an industry must be changed in a coordinated way, where the rules specifying how firms interact must be changed. In these cases, "industrial" restructuring is a real challenge.

Principle 4: Implement Incremental Evolution Rather Than Revolution.

Revolutions are rare (and often failures) while evolution is an ongoing process (and often successful). Industries are changing every day. The so-called invisible hand acts as a natural agent of change. Firms disappear and are replaced by others; they are forced to change in order to adapt to market pressures. Standards also change and new technologies are implemented. Each of these simple transformations or innovations can together transform an entire industry in ways that are unpredictable and quite often initially perceived as impossible.

A reformer must understand that there are good reasons for this. Evolution is obtained though the process of individual (decentralized) decision-making. Each participant responds to incentives and adapts its behaviour accordingly. A smart reformer must typically engineer evolution or at least a sequence of small incremental changes rather than a grand revolution. More precisely, the reformer should structure the industrial environment in such a way that the industry by itself will evolve towards adopting the proper changes.

As a direct corollary, a reform is unlikely to be successful if it does not move in line with the natural evolution of things. It is difficult to drive reforms in any direction except towards more modern forms of increased efficiency. Therefore, a reform is likely to succeed only if there are significant inefficiencies in the historical development of the industry (Brunsson, 1993). What is optimal nowadays will be suboptimal tomorrow. In this context, the role of the reformer is to identify the market failures that prevent or slow down the natural evolution of the industry, make the necessary corrections, and let the participants in the market identify the path for better organizational forms.

Recent and ongoing restructuring programs in the electric power and gas industries aimed at bringing the system towards more rational forms of organization. The setup of trading pools and electronic auction bidding, and the standardization of rules through national and supranational guidelines, codes and protocols have created more efficient environments for investments and trade. One example of the effect of rationalization is the price arbitrage produced by the restructuring of the U.S. gas industry, where regional disparities have almost disappeared (De Vany and Walls, 1995). Systems of pools are making their way in the U.S. electricity sector and transforming the industry into a more rational market where the laws of supply and demand will eventually optimize the price and the allocation of each kilowatt-hour to its best use.

Throughout the world, reforms have been carried out over long periods and reformers have introduced changes with phase-in approaches. Nonetheless, the complexity of these reforms required periods of adjustment. In the case of the U.K., the governance structure allowed a rapid phase-in approach. The reform took about two years to complete, although the industry is still in a period of adjustment more than ten years after the completion of the restructuring. In the case of the U.S., the phase-in approach is again being used, but the governance structure and the extent of the changes called for many more steps. It appears that the phase-in approach is a sum of smaller phase-in steps followed by periods of adjustment. The importance of the network industries is such that even the most aggressive reformers (the U.K., Alberta and the state of Victoria in Australia) have not attempted snapshot and spontaneous reforms.

Principle 5: Congruence of Interests Is a Blessing, but Expect Opposition.

Any reformer would like to have a general consensus in favour of change. This consensus would allow the implementation of changes without much opposition. That is unfortunately a utopian world.

It is hard to identify a change that is actually a Pareto improvement or a nearly Pareto improvement. Most transformations negatively affect at least some individual agents. A policy seeking to eliminate transaction costs is certainly advantageous to both sellers and customers, but not to the intermediaries. We should not forget that some people make their living out of exploiting market inefficiencies: the best way to make money is to be efficient in an inefficient market.

If the benefits of change are spread out in favour of a large number of agents while the costs are imposed on a smaller group of agents, the latter will be willing and able to organize themselves more efficiently to block change. Many industrial transformations of the last decade were related to deregulation and lower trade barriers. Economists have long argued that more competition leads to greater efficiencies and long-term prosperity, but it is hard to say this to the stakeholders of the suffering industries. The political authorities are sometimes sufficiently sensitive to these interest groups to delay or block change.

As a general rule, the best way to understand or predict agents' behaviour is to analyze their incentives. The incentives of agents within a firm or within an industry are not perfectly aligned and are often directly opposed. In a zero-sum game, what benefits some must necessary hurt others. Quite often, restructurings are not zero-sum games but rather increase total welfare; however, participants may perceive a given proposal as a zero-sum change.

Incentives are often based on some form of benchmarking, where the performance of workers is compared with that of others. It is, then, not how well they do that matters but rather how well they do relative to others. Arguing that a change will increase industry efficiency is not much of a comfort. Those that perform relatively well in one structure may be reluctant to accept a change in their environment if they are not guaranteed that their comparative advantage will persist.

Vested interests are often mentioned as a barrier to change. Those who perform well in one context often do so because they have invested in specific assets. In knowledge-based industries, vested interests most likely take the form of human capital, and no idea is more threatening than the idea that one's savoir-faire may become obsolete. Unless the reformer is able to take proper account of those vested interests, any attempt at reforming the industry is likely to fail.

In the cases of gas and electricity, the incumbents had invested in infrastructures prior to the restructuring. These investments are sunk and may be a stranded liability when new rules make them uneconomical. Compromises, such as sharing and managing the stranded costs, have to be worked out to accommodate the transition from the old industrial structure to the new one (Brennan and Boyd, 1997; Baxter, Hadley and Hirst, 1996; Hirst, Baxter and Hadley, 1997)). One would suggest a write-off to settle the problem of the stranded costs. But customers who avoid paying historical costs simply shift the costs to the utilities; shareholders or to other customers (such as small businesses and residential customers). In addition, a write-off might yield higher interest rates for future construction (the extra margin would cover the risk of another write-off decree). Stranded costs can take other forms in other cases. Whatever their names and their forms, it is important to address these issues in a fair way, guaranteeing a successful restructuring without damaging the industry's future needs.

In the presence of a divergence of interests, the reformer must choose between three courses of action: first, it could attempt to build a consensus, which may delay action substantially. Second, the reformer may decide to proceed despite opposition. Of course, this approach may be infeasible if a large critical mass is necessary and if the set of supporters is initially small. The reformer then needs to downscale its project to make it viable for a small group of participants. If the second path is available, this is the simplest route to take. Finally, the reformer can force opponents to change despite their resistance. The last approach requires that the reformer hold coercive and legal powers. This applies when it is a public regulator. We consider public policy issues in section four.

Principle 6: Look for Design Characteristics and Network Externalities.

More and more industries are built around common standards or networks. A significant benefit of standardized education is to provide a common standard of communication so that knowledge or information can be shared and commercially exploited. Reading and writing are useless if there is no one to read from or write to and a new technology is useless if it is too advanced for anyone to exploit it.

The really challenging cases of industrial restructuring are related to the presence of network externalities. When there are such network externalities, such as in knowledge-based industries, change may require a form of coordination among firms. The privatization and deregulation of utilities in various countries required the creation of new interaction rules between firms within the industry: rules that specify how the prices are fixed, what the standards of quality are, etc.

Standards naturally evolve over time. They too benefit from the natural selection process. This is certainly the case of humans' dearest standards: languages. However, some standards are inherently inflexible and cannot be changed through sequences of individual decisions. Farrell and Saloner (1985) argue that standards can exhibit *excess inertia*. If no one benefits from using the new standard alone, each participant may rationally stick to the old, inefficient standard. This will be the natural course of action if everyone believes (correctly) that others will also use the old standard. In game-theoretical terms, the persistence of a Pareto-dominated situation can be a strategic (Nash) equilibrium. Hence, it is possible that a commonly advantageous change will not take place, and that an inferior standard will persist in a non-cooperative, uncoordinated environment.

The literature on fads, customs, fashions and cultural change can also explain how rational behavior may lead to the suppression of valuable information and hence to inertia. These fads, customs, fashions and, in general, cultural factors of inertia appear as examples of imitation strategies or informational cascades. Those informational cascades, characterized by Bikhchandani, Hirshleifer and Welch (1992), occur when imitation is the best reply function of an individual to the actions of those "ahead" of him. In such contexts, an individual finds it optimal to hide his own private information and instead follows the behaviour of the others, his predecessors, hence generating observed localized conformity. Informational cascades are examples of social learning, that is, of dynamic social inertia. More generally, one cannot expect that competitive markets will systematically lead to the selection of the best standards or common rules of interaction.

One example often cited as an illustration of persistent inferior standards is the persistence of the QWERTY standard for typewriters and computer keyboards.[7] The layout of the early typewriters was alphabetic. As a result, some close keys ended up being typed in short sequence, hitting each other and getting stuck. In order to solve this problem, the QWERTY keyboard was patented in 1878. As the typewriters improved, the mechanical constraints that justified the QWERTY layout no longer existed and alternative keyboard layouts were proposed. August Dvorak patented an alternative design where the most often used letters were aligned on the home (central) desk. Dvorak claimed that the new layout increased typing speed but his attempts to replace the old standard failed. This is an example of market failure to replace old standards by better ones. However, Liebowitz and Margolis (1990) argue that the performance of a typewriter depends less on the layout of the keyboard and more on the abilities and training of the typist: the QWERTY design may not be the best design available, but no alternative design justifies the costly retraining of professionals.

Computer programmers often mention Microsoft's Windows as a ill-designed operating system. The domination of Microsoft's operating system relies less on its quality and more on the network externalities it allows. Whether the customers would be better off with an alternative system remains an open question, but there is no doubt that changing the system appears to be an unprofitable, if not impossible, task.

Among the threats to Windows (besides the U.S. Justice Department) are Sun's JAVA and LINUX. JAVA is a programming language designed to be interpreted on every possible platform. A JAVA program can be downloaded from the Internet and executed on any machine. Sun hopes to replace Windows-based personal computers by cheaper JAVA-based network computers. In the near future, the Windows-based computers are likely to dominate, but JAVA is growing as a programming standard and undermining the (network) benefit of sharing a common operating system. LINUX is a hacker-developed operating system. It has become one of the most advanced operating systems by relying on a web of "volunteer" contributors. All hackers are free to propose modifications and improvements, and the new code is freely downloadable for users to try and test, so the code evolves through natural selection. LINUX and JAVA have common features: the code has been distributed freely and developers around the world are adding to it.

This is a rather common feature of the new network economy. Kelly (1998) argues that, contrary to the common wisdom that scarcity creates value, value is derived from plenitude in a network economy as it explodes exponentially with the number of users. When copies are cheap to make, they should be distributed widely and freely. This creates a critical mass and initiates a virtuous circle where more users lead to more value which leads to more users. Standards should then thrive in open spaces and should strengthen the network rather than set boundaries around it. Standards should provide a common base so that a large web of contributors can build on it and help create constant innovation through a decentralized evolutionary process.[8]

The transformation or restructuring of industries, and in particular knowledge-based industries, must rely on these key ideas. There are ways to change old and obsolete standards for new ones. But the reformer should take care not to try to replace the old standard with a restrictive and narrow standard that will quickly become obsolete itself. The reformer must foster open architectures that allow for evolutionary improvements. The most important task of the reformer should be to create a critical mass. The importance of critical mass is illustrated by the experiences of Minitel, France Telecom's electronic catalogue system, and its Canadian equivalent, Alex. Minitel was a major success; it is now widely used. The Alex system proposed by Bell Canada was a total failure. The main difference was that Minitel reached the necessary critical mass early. France Telecom pulled out the phone books and offered the Minitel terminals for free, and the implementation of Minitel was supported by the French political authorities. In addition, Minitel was introduced all over France under the supervision of a centralized authority. The major drawback of Minitel is its inflexibility and, with the introduction of the Internet protocol, Minitel is rapidly becoming obsolete. For Alex, Bell Canada could not pull out the phone book and on its own create enough value for using the system. It was also too costly for the proposed services. The Alex project never reached the tipping point, estimated at 20,000 users, to generate the virtuous circle.

There are many other examples where proper coordination must be achieved in a network industry. In the case of the U.S. electricity market, coordination must be achieved on a local level by a supra-regional body. The U.S. Federal Energy Regulatory agency FERC issued guidelines to be adopted by state commissions to ensure that the new-created open industry in state A will resemble the industry in state B even though they might not evolve at the same pace. The FERC is moving towards supra-regional integration. The regional power councils and state industries are progressively being pulled together under the same guidelines and standards. The second model is the British model, where there is no supra-regional coordination because the national industry is restructured as a whole. This model was used by Alberta, the Nordic countries and New Zealand. In both cases, the standard brought in by the reformers of the gas and electricity industries was the Poolcos, power and gas exchange and electronic auction bidding systems replacing or being added to bilateral contracts (Stalon, 1997).

4. PRINCIPLES OF PUBLIC POLICY

Public policies can affect the decision of firms and industries regarding the adoption of new technologies, and in particular new transaction technologies, in the emerging knowledge-based economy. They do so by changing the relative costs and benefits of such changes as perceived by the different individual agents in the industry. On the other hand, this role of public policies must be embedded in a formal political economy analysis of government organizations or bureaucracies rather than being simply based on an assumption that the government entity responsible for designing policies and implementing them is a benevolent social welfare maximizer. This question is crucial in a context where asymmetric information structures, and therefore informational rents, are most likely going to be important and pervasive.

Principle 7: Provide Information.

As we mentioned in the introduction to this section, information asymmetries are a major contextual element of the adoption process. Moreover, the costs and benefits of adoption are directly affected by public policies.

Wozniak (1993) studied the relationship between the innovation adoption decision and the complementary decision to acquire information on the new technology. He considered the joint decision whether or not to adopt a new technology and invest in technical knowledge to "facilitate faster learning about innovations." Although the acquisition of information is observed before the adoption per se in Wozniak's model, both decisions are made jointly. Innovations are initially unfamiliar and hence characterized by subjective uncertainty. By learning about the new technology, potential users are able to form better expectations of the profitability of adopting. Explicitly considering the existence of different sources of information (one of them being public information) and the strategic positioning of the firm (early adopters versus late adopters), Wozniak conducted an empirical analysis on a sample of Iowa farmers. Two innovations are considered: growth hormone implants and feed additive monensin sodium. Four information sources are considered: talking with personnel from or attending demonstrations or meetings sponsored by either a public or a private information provider. He found that managers with more education were more likely to adopt new technologies and to contact the *public* source of information than less educated operators. Furthermore, more educated adopters were more likely to make contact with the public information source than with the information officers of private agricultural firms. More generally, he found that the adoption and technical information acquisition decisions are made jointly and that the relative influences of the factors explaining those decisions differ with the timing of adoption and the channel of information dissemination.

In an influential paper, Saha, Love and Schwart (1994) stressed the fundamental role played by the quality of information on the decision whether to adopt or not and on the intensity of adoption of a new technology. Recognizing that producers' adoption intensity is conditional on their knowledge of the new technology and on their decision to adopt, they found that larger and more educated operators are likely to adopt more intensively. They modelled an individual producer's decision to adopt a divisible technology in the presence of risk. They looked at factors that could affect adoption and intensity of adoption, and considered the concept of incomplete information dissemination among potential adopters. Their objective was to understand the analytical and empirical implications of incomplete information in the adoption process. They specifically studied the adoption of BST (bovine somatotropin, a yield-enhancing growth hormone). The approval of this technology by the FDA in November 1993 made milk the first genetically engineered food allowed by the U.S. government and, for many observers, this decision opened the gates of the biotechnology age. Saha, Love and Schwart stressed that the role of information gathering and learning-by-doing was particularly important in the adoption of new or emerging technologies. They developed a three-phase model explaining first the acquisition of information on the existence of the technology, second the decision whether to adopt or not, and third the intensity of adoption. They used a data set from the Texas dairy industry obtained through a telephone survey, conducted a year before the FDA decision, in which the respondents were asked first whether they had heard about BST. If they had, they were asked whether they would adopt it or not if and when the FDA approved it and, if so, what percentage of their herd they would expose to BST. About 84% of respondents were aware of BST and 52% of them said they would adopt it; these adopters (44% of the sample) said on average that they would expose 43% of their herd to BST. Saha, Love and Schwart found, using a maximum likelihood dichotomous-continuous estimation framework, that education and herd size had a positive and generally significant effect in all three phases (although education had only a marginally significant impact in phase 2, the adoption phase); that the decision whether or not to adopt was determined only by the producer's perception of BST-induced yield and adoption costs; and that risk attitude and perceptions had no influence on the adoption decision, while risk factors did influence the intensity of adoption once the producer had decided to adopt. Finally, plans to expand dairy operations and prior adoption experience (of dairy innovations in the past) had a positive and significant influence on adoption intensity. The diffusion of information on a new technology and the different measures that affect that diffusion could, according to the authors, have a positive effect on adoption intensity by reducing the uncertainty associated with the new technology. Hence the potential role of public policies.

Principle 8: Create Proper Incentives.

Creating proper incentives is crucial and we can offer three significant examples. The *British Electricity Act* of 1983 provides a case where the pricing regime thwarted a reform. The authorities wanted to attract entrants in the generation sector but low rates of return were kept to prevent the CEGB (the Central Electricity Generating Board) from making too much profit.   However, these two measures were contradictory and the strict pricing regime prevented entry (Armstrong, Cowan and Vickers, 1994).   A second example comes from Chile.   The Chilean authorities adopted measures to attract foreign investors in an electricity industry that needed fresh capital to be revamped and modernized.   Among these measures, a premium was designed to attract investments in far-away regions or distribution centres.   This measure distorted investment decisions (misallocated the resources) since Gencos (generators) chose locations near far-away Distcos (distributors) to obtain the premium and underinvested in the transmission segment.   This resulted in a reduction in transmission capacity and a significant economic loss since transmission costs are shared among grid users (fewer users implied higher costs per user and transmission lines were not fully used network effect).   The investment scheme which had been designed to cover sunk costs and attract private investments resulted in the misallocation of the facilities, the distortion of consumption below optimal levels and the giving of market power to Gencos.   A third example can also be offered.   The Argentine and U.S. state governments learned their lessons from the two cases above.   In the U.S. for instance, some states permitted non-utility producers to sell their production to the most profitable sectors of the economy, allowing them to penetrate the market without being bumped out by predatory pricing by the incumbent.   This way, the new entrants had a chance to settle down and eventually become powerful enough to compete with the incumbent.   Argentina adopted measures where Distcos would contract with Gencos in advance (pay-in-advance contracts) in order to promote private investment, but without adopting investment schemes as in Chile that would lead to economic loss.   The Argentine network was also decentralized to enable measures and policies specific to each of its four regions.

Restructuring allowed the introduction of new techniques to improve the acquisition and verification of information.   Information and data are easier to gather with management systems that guarantee transparency.   For example, any firm that wants to access new competitive power markets in the U.S. must gain the FERC's approval.   Firms that do not position themselves to penetrate the new environment will soon be pushed out of business or bought out by their competitors.   For this reason, firms have an incentive to enter the newly competitive electricity market.   The FERC's approval is only gained if the firm in question respects certain standards and requirements.   For instance, the FERC demands the accounting and financial unbundling of any utility's activities. Breaking up firm operations and shedding some light on accounting practices prevent cross-subsidies between the segments and other obscure behaviour. It is a simple way to control the quality of information and prevent opportunistic tactics.

Common carriers, Poolcos and auction bidding are systems preventing obscure bilateral contracting between traders. These exchange systems are profitable to power suppliers and power demanders, but they also shed light on the activities of the electricity sector. Nonetheless, the most innovative changes have been introduced by the U.K. with price caps. In other industries, the U.K. has introduced yardstick regulation, where the size of the subsidy to an innovative agent is inversely correlated with the difference between the agent's cost and the industry average. With mechanisms restraining collusion, an agent will likely have an incentive to innovate and distance itself from the average to maximize its gains in terms of subsidies.

These light-hand regulatory methods not only are less expensive and simpler to manage, but they are efficient in controlling the quality of information and promoting innovation. One good example comes from a heavily regulated sector: air emissions and water effluents. The Ontario Environmental Regulator uses a system of fines and subsidies to induce paper-makers to divulge truthful information about their pollution levels (voluntary disclosure). The focus is put on the quality of the information rather than on the respect of environmental standards. By controlling the quality of information, the regulator has a clear picture of the industry and can subsequently assist heavy polluters unable to comply with environmental standards. Otherwise, the regulator could be subsidizing the wrong companies because of asymmetric information. Down the line, this kind of approach may make more economic sense in terms of costs and efficiency than more coercive approaches (such as command-and-control approaches). As a result, the Ontario paper-making industry has the greatest level of compliance and is the cleanest in Canada (Livernois and McKenna, forthcoming).

In the U.S., the 1978 PURPA (the *Public Utility Regulatory Policy Act*) changed the expectations of the U.S. electricity industry. The PURPA only focused on the generating segment of that industry. Nonetheless, the PURPA set out new priorities for the industry as a whole and led to subsidized research that prompted new developments in electricity generation. Subsidizing alternative power sources and guaranteeing access to independent producers had the effect of reducing the industry's inertia. Following the PURPA, other changes could readily come into effect.

Similarly, the U.K.'s 1983 *Electricity Act* was enacted to increase the number of independent producers in Britain and bring about more competition in the production segment of the CEGB (quite like the PURPA). However, promoting entry by removing barriers could not by itself create a sizable independent power sector since the regulator kept implementing low rates of return for the electricity producers and therefore discouraged new entrants. The move was unsuccessful in reforming the industry, but may have been useful in changing the industry's expectations. The 1983 attempt prepared the ground for the 1989 *Electricity Act* which enabled the restructuring of the CEGB.

In Alberta, Ontario and many U.S. states, the local authorities supported their reforms with public hearings and consultations. Were these hearings useful to the restructuring? The nuts and bolts of restructuring an electric power industry were known and the project had already been tested elsewhere. Nonetheless, these public hearings certainly helped the psychological restructuring and changed the industry's expectations.

Principle 9: Commitment Is Crucial and Easier if Goals Are Coherent.

This principle is a crucial element of strategic thinking. The ability to credibly commit allows one to change others' behaviour in a desirable way. Opponents to a reform project will behave quite differently if the change is perceived as irreversible. Opponents to change will resist until they understand that change is bound to happen and that it is in their best interest to adapt to it or be part of it. Commitment may come in diverse forms. International trade treaties are a useful commitment device. If the stakeholders of a protected industry believe that the government will maintain trade protection if sufficiently pressured to, they will exert pressure in order to block trade reforms. By signing international trade treaties, local governments commit themselves to trade liberalization. Implementing new laws is another powerful commitment device.

Reforms in the electric power industries have been based on clear goals: providing solutions to the energy crises of the 1970s and the public finance crises of the 1980s. In the U.S., the federal government undertook the restructuring of its electricity industry in the late 1970s, following the first oil embargo. The first bill adopted by the Congress was the PURPA in 1978. The *Energy Policy Act* (EPA) of 1992 extended PURPA. In both federal laws, the goals of the electric power section were succinct: encourage competition through new market structures to curb the costly inefficiencies of the old system. Introducing competition and pooling the utilities also appeared to be the panacea for price disparities between U.S. states. Australia was dealing with monetary restraints and debt pressures in the early 1980s. Budget constraints called for a better use of government resources for economic performance. The national government believed that bringing competition to the Australian electric power industry was the best alternative to the costly system in place. The national government adopted measures to foster competition by setting out national guidelines to be followed by all states of the Commonwealth of Australia. The goals of the reform consisted in giving large customers, such as plants or municipalities, a choice of suppliers (wholesale competition). Competition was also clearly promoted though the opening of the industry to foreign entrants and investments. The reformers, in both the U.S. and Australia, followed the guidelines clearly established by their national governments' legislation. The success of these reforms is in part due to the coherence of the authorities' intentions.

In the U.S., the FERC received extensive power from the EPA. The FERC has the power to set guidelines for the gas and electricity sectors. This legal power has been supported by the U.S. Supreme Court on many occasions. In addition, the FERC possesses extensive physical and human resources which give it the power, the expertise and the authority to intervene within its jurisdiction. The British Office of Energy Regulation (OFFER), the Australian National Electricity Code Administrator (NECA) and National Electric Market Management Corporation (NEMMCO), and the Argentine CAMMENA all have similar powers, know-how and moral authority. Their discretionary power and independence also make them efficient governance structures.

Commitment can first be increased by past or parallel experiences. The U.S. reform of the electricity sector is based in part on its experience in reforming the gas industry. To an outside observer, if the reformer has been able to stick to its commitments in the gas industry, chances are that it will stick to its commitments in the electricity sector. Second, commitment can be increased also by a code of conduct, a sort of constitution or a social contract. The Australian government set out a Code for the electricity industry defining the terms and the parameters of the future industry. One of the Australian government's goals was to attract foreign investments, and the Code explicitly addresses the framework of investment and rate-of-return issues. The Code is not likely to be altered by political interventions since it is administered by NECA and NEMMCO, which are independent from the national government. Third, concepts like the "common carrier" have been developed for newly deregulated electricity industries. A common carrier ensures, for example, that new entrants are penalized in terms of market access. These credentials are essential to success in reforming, in particular when the reform needs foreign investments.

Principle 10: Perfect Governments Do Not Exist.

The purpose of this section, based on Boyer and Laffont (1999), is to provide some preliminary thoughts on the construction of a formal political economy of public regulation or policy regarding the emergence (adoption and implementation) of new transactional technologies, and more specifically on the choice of instruments in public policy. Economists' general preference for sophisticated incentive mechanisms is reconsidered in a political economy approach based on two main features: private information of economic agents, which explains the rents accruing to them as functions of policy choices, and the incomplete contract nature of constitutions, which explains the need for public policy and for politicians as residual decision-makers.

Incomplete information is by now well understood as a major obstacle to efficient public policy. In the context of regulation (clearly a special but quite important case of public policy), it is now common to model regulation as a principal-agent problem. In such a framework, the requirement for incentive compatibility puts constraints on the public policy actions that can be implemented.

This framework has been extensively used for environmental economics[9] and can be used to analyze public policies concerning industrial restructuring. A revelation mechanism can be viewed as a command-and-control instrument but nevertheless is clearly optimal here. In such a framework, the question of instrument choice in public policy is empty. This question often arose in the literature because authors were not careful enough in defining their instruments.

Two types of meaningful comparisons of public policy instruments are then possible. Either one considers constraints on instruments (the analysis should explain the origin of these constraints) and various constrained instruments can be compared, or one considers imperfections somewhere in the economy that cannot be corrected by public policies (in which case a good explanation of this inability must be given). This is often the case when subsidies, for instance, are not allowed.

As stated by Boyer and Laffont, a systematic analysis of the choice of public policy instruments "should then be conducted in well defined second best frameworks, which are all methodological shortcuts of an incomplete contract analysis. [Public policy] constraints such as limited commitment, renegotiation-proof commitment, collusion, favoritism, multi-principal structures should be considered. Political economy constraints can be viewed also as a special case of this methodology." It is the lack of finely tuned social control of the public policy authorities, who may have private agendas (an incomplete contract feature), that introduces inefficiencies in the restructuring decision process. It may become desirable to impose constraints on public policy instruments and indeed restrict the use of direct sophisticated public policy instruments in favour of cruder ones.

The asymmetric information about the new transaction technology to be implemented, for instance, implies that a rent will have to be given up to those who have stakes in the firms. The choice of a public policy regarding restructuring affects this rent. In a formal political economy context analogous to that of Boyer and Laffont (1998), the majorities have different stakes in the informational rent of the firms and the delegation of public policy to politicians may enable them to pursue their private agendas, that is, here, to favour the agents who belong to their majority. As majorities change, this induces a suboptimal excessive fluctuation of policies. Restricting the instruments used in restructuring policy becomes a way to restrict this excessive fluctuation, at the cost possibly of a lack of flexibility. More specifically, one must compare the policy consisting in the choice of a given restructuring profile, a typical command-and-control policy, with the policy consisting in the choice of a menu of restructuring-transfer pairs, a typical incentive policy. We must then determine the conditions under which the greater discretion associated with the second policy is compensated by its greater efficiency potential.

We cannot here explore in detail the foundation of the delegation of industrial restructuring policy to public policy officials. But let us mention that restricting public policy choices and interventions to general, all-inclusive instruments necessarily has little flexibility. On the contrary, public officials could use their current detailed knowledge of the economy to choose more specific policies, but in so doing will likely pursue their private agendas. We can and must characterize the conditions under which the public policy conducted by changing authorities is superior to a social-welfare-maximizing but inflexible public policy imposed by the "constitution" in contexts where different types of interest groups, stakeholders in the firm and consumers, for instance, may benefit from the capture of the public policy officials. Analyzing the distortions due to the political process as well as the impact of the dynamics of re-election, based on campaign contributions, on the comparison of instruments for environmental policies, Boyer and Laffont (1998) found that the competition of interest groups may kill otherwise desirable reforms targeting more sophisticated environmental regulation by raising the stakes of political conflict, a kind of negative rent-seeking effect. Similar effects are likely present in the choice of public policy instruments for industrial restructuring.

Sophisticated industry restructuring policies are dependent on non-verifiable variables which cannot be contracted upon to limit public policy interventions. Consequently, it must be delegated to public officials, creating an incentive problem when those officials' motivations do not include maximizing social welfare.

State reforms in the U.S. have experienced lags because of the nature of the public reformers. The state commissions may be seen as utilitarian reformers taking into account different agents' concerns. The U.S. reform may certainly be rightful in terms of fairness, but the restructuring itself is less effective because the transformation is subject to lobbying forces. On the other hand, if the reforms were piloted by factions, such as boards or political parties with vested interests, they might be conducted more efficiently and rapidly. The best example is the Thatcher government's aggressive reform of the CEGB, which was prompted by conservative and pro-business motives.

Other examples are found in the water industry, where municipalities delegate the management of their water and sewage systems to private firms through open bidding. Municipal governments have formal authority over their water and sewage systems since water is a municipal jurisdiction guaranteed by legal agreements (a social contract or a constitution for example). However, municipal governments may be impaired because of the terms of their electoral mandate. A four-year government may not have the moral authority to carry out an infrastructure change when it may be defeated in a coming election. The fact that political majorities are changing weakens long-term responsibility for their decisions. So, in the case of municipal employees, their contracts are shorter than the duration of a water and sewage system and their removability does not make them liable for the long-term decisions they take. Therefore, delegating the management of the water resources to a private firm, which depends on its international reputation to continue doing business abroad, can guarantee moral authority to the reformer.

5. CONCLUSION

The specific purpose of this paper was to analyze the adoption of major changes such as technological adoptions and implementations, industrial restructuring, deregulation or business reengineering in a selected number of industries. We observed and derived ten principles we consider to be common to a successful organizational change. The challenge of policy-makers is to consider, combine and apply these ten principles when designing policies and instruments to achieve an organizational change.

We grouped the principles in three sets. First, those related to organizational and technological change in general: Organizational Inertia Is Endogenous; Adopting A New Technology Does Not Mean Successfully Implementing It; Time Is Information (Waiting Has Value And Cost). Second, Those Related To Industry-Level Restructuring: Implement Incremental Evolution Rather Than Revolution; Congruence Of Interests Is A Blessing, But Expect Opposition; Look For Design Characteristics And Network Externalities. Finally, Those Related To Public Policy: Provide Information; Create Proper Incentives; Commitment Is Crucial And Easier If Goals Are Coherent; Perfect Governments Do Not Exist.

Knowing the long-term potential pay-off, but short-term risk of losses, an organization is a priori unwilling to change since the internal routines which guarantee its success also act as impediments to change. Being outsiders to an organization, policy-makers are in a position to introduce some flexibility into the organization. However, policy-makers should make use of the Principle 1 in parallel with Principle 9 to obtain the proper level of flexibility and commitment in implementing public policy. In the omnipresent context of asymmetric information, policy-makers should induce agents to come forward with the truth regarding the real costs of change. However, rewarding truth-telling rather than success curbs the agents' efforts to achieve the change. So, policy-makers must compensate with higher present pay-offs (higher wages, for example) and increase the level of commitment.

Policy-makers should ford the river rather than attempt to leap over it. Major organizational changes are costly and risky. Hence, real option evaluation should be an important concern of policy-makers and several periods of phase-in implementation followed by adjustment periods may allow the efficient use of upcoming information. Policy-makers should provide incentives to create a consensus about the change: a project will take off only when it reaches a certain critical point or threshold level and policy-makers should be aware and make use of design characteristics and network externalities to build credible support for an organizational change.

Agents' attitudes towards organizational change are based on their knowledge of the project. Policy-makers' main role in developing a positive state of mind may be the provision of objective and credible information regarding the relative costs and benefits of an organizational change. Policy-makers should create proper incentives to foster the adoption of organizational change throughout the economy: changing regulation, fine-tuning the corporate tax rules, holding public hearings, introducing investment schemes or implementing a new procurement and market framework are powerful sources of incentives. Commitment to these rules is crucial and should be established in form of a social contract, for example, if the reputation of the policy-makers allows for it. Finally, policy-makers should have the moral authority to lead an organizational change. A powerful policy-maker must be above political manipulation, lobbying and rent-seeking from vested interest groups that attempt to distort a would-be beneficial reform to their advantage. But that is easier said than done.

ENDNOTES

[1] For a discussion of the different definitions of flexibility in the economic and management literature, see Boyer and Moreaux (1989).

[2] Boyer and Robert (1998) suggest that those routines may in fact be rooted in the firm's best response to internal informational asymmetries.

[3] See also Atallah and Boyer (1998) on the related subject of competition, technological progress and outsourcing.

[4] See also Boyer and Laffont (1998) for a theory of constrained delegation of legislative power to the government in matters related to environmental policy-making.

[5] *Information Week* (1994). The figure (for 1997) is a prediction made at that time (1994) by Computer Economics Inc. and published in its newsletter *Systems Reengineering Economics*.

[6] *Wall Street Journal* (1996).

[7] The QWERTY story below is well known, but some analysts consider it to be a myth. We present it here as an example, either real or fictional.

[8] See also Shapiro and Varian (1998) for a competitive analysis of these "new" information industries.

[9] See Baron (1985a), Laffont (1994), Lewis (1997) and Boyer and Laffont (1996, 1997).

REFERENCES

Armstrong, M., M. Cowan, and J. Vickers, *Regulatory Reform: Economic Analysis and British Experience.* Cambridge, MA: MIT Press, 1994

Atallah, G. and M. Boyer, "Concurrence, changements technologiques et intégration verticale," in M. Poitevin (ed.) *Impartition: fondements et analyses.* Montreal CIRANO, PUL, 1998.

Baron, D., "Regulation of Prices and Pollution under Incomplete Information." *Journal of Public Economics,* 28, 1985a, 211-231.

Baxter, L., S. Hadley and E. Hirst, "Assessing Transition-Cost Strategies: A Case Study." Energy Studies Review, 8 (1), 1996, 27-43.

Bikhchandani, S., D. Hirshleifer and I. Welch, "A Theory of Fads, Fashion, Custom, and Cultural Change as Informational Cascades." *Journal of Political Economy,* 100, 1992, 992-1026.

Boyer, M. and S. Clamens, "Strategic Adoption of a New Technology under Uncertain Implementation." Mimeo, CIRANO, Université de Montréal, 1998.

Boyer, M. and J-J. Laffont, "Environmental Protection, Producer Insolvency and Lender Liability," in A. Xepapadeas (ed.) *Economic Policy for the Environment and Natural Resources.* Edward Elgar, 1996.

Boyer, M. and J-J. Laffont, "Environmental Risks and Bank Liability." *European Economic Review,* 41, 1997, 1427-1459.

Boyer, M. and J-J. Laffont, "Toward a Political Theory of the Emergence of Environmental Incentive Regulation." *Rand Journal of Economics,* 30, 1998, 137-157.

Boyer, M. and J-J. Laffont, "Toward a Political Theory of the Emergence of Environmental Incentive Regulation." *Rand Journal of Economics,* 30 (1), Spring 1999, 137-157.

Boyer, M. and M. Moreaux, "Uncertainty, Capacity and Flexibility: The Monopoly Case." *Annales d'Économie et de Statistique,* 15/16, 1989, 291-313.

Boyer, M. and M. Moreaux, "Capacity Commitment versus Flexibility." *Journal of Economics and Management Strategy,* 6, 1997, 347-376.

Boyer, M. and J. Robert, "Organizational Inertia and Dynamic Incentives." Mimeo, CIRANO, Université de Montréal, 1998.

Brennan, T. J.and J. Boyd, "Stranded Costs, Takings, and the Law and Economics of Implicit Constracts." Journal of Regulatory Economics, 11 (1), January 1997, 41-54.

Brunsson, N. and J.P. Olsen, "The reforming organization." London and New York: Routledge, 1993, vi, 216.

Burkart, M., D. Gromb and F. Panunzi, "Large Shareholders, Monitoring and the Value of the Firm." Mimeo, Stockholm School of Economics, Sloan School of Management and Universita di Pavia, 1996.

Crémer, J., "Arm's Length Relationships." *Quarterly Journal of Economics*, CX, 1995, 275-295.

De Vany, A.S. and W.D. Walls, "The emerging new order in natural gas: Markets versus regulation." Westport, Conn. and London: Greenwood, Quorum Books, 1995, xii, 136.

Dewatripont, M. and J. Tirole, "Biased Principals as a Discipline Device." *Japan and the World Economy,* 8, 1996, 195-206.

Farrell, J. and G. Saloner, "Standardization, Compatability, and Innovation." Rand Journal of Economics, 16 (1), Spring 1985, 70-83.

Friebel, G. and M. Raith, "Strategic Recruiting and the Chain of Command." Mimeo, Université Libre de Bruxelles, 1996.

Gabel, L. and B. Sinclair-Desgagné, "The Firm, Its Routines and the Environment," in *The International Yearbook of Environmental and Resource Economics: A Survey of Current Issues,* 1996.

Hirst, E., L. Baxter and S. Hadley, "Transition Costs: Estimation, Sensitivities and Recovery." Resource and Energy Economics, 19 (1-2), March 1997, 29-46.

Kelly, K., *New Rules for the New Economy.* Viking Penguin, 1998.

Laffont, J-J., "Regulation of Pollution with Asymmetric Information," in C. Dosi and T. Tomasi (eds.) *Nonpoint Source Pollution Regulation: Issues and Analysis.* Dordrecht: Kluwer Academic publishers, 1994.

Levitt, S. D. and C. M. Snyder, "Is No News Bad News? Information Transmission and the Role of 'Early Warning' in the Principal-Agent Model." Mimeo, Harvard University and George Washington University, 1996.

Lewis, T., "Protecting the Environment When Costs and Benefits are Privately Known." *Rand Journal of Economics*, 27, 1997, 819-847.

Liebowitz, S.J. and S.E. Margolis, "The Fable of the Keys." Journal of Law and Economics, 33 (1), April 1990, 1-25.

Livernois, J. and C.J. McKenna, "Truth or Consequences: Enforcing Pollution Standards with Self-Reporting." *Journal of Public Economics,* forthcoming.

Lucas, R. E. Jr., "Adjustment Costs and the Theory of Supply." *Journal of Political Economy* 75, 1967a, 321-343.

Lucas, R. E. Jr., "Optimal Investment Policy and the Flexible Accelerator." *International Economic Review* 8, 1967b, 78-85.

Parente, S.L., "Technology Adoption, Learning-by-Doing and Economic Growth." *Journal of Economic Theory* 63, 1994, 346-369.

Rothchild, M., "On the Cost of Adjustment." *Quarterly Journal of Economics,* 85, 1971, 605-622.

Rumelt, R. P., "Inertia and Transformation," in Cynthia A. Montgomery (ed.) *Resources in an Evolutionary Perspective: Towards a Synthesis of Evolutionary and Resource-Based Approaches to Strategy.* Norwell, MA: Kluwer Academic Publishers, 1995.

Saha, A., H.A. Love and R. Schwart, "Adoption of Emerging Technologies Under Output Uncertainty." *American Journal of Agricultural Economics,* 76, 1994, 836-846.

Shapiro, C. and H. Varian, *Information Rules,* 1998.

Stalon, C.G., "Electric Industry Governance: Reconciling Competitive power Markets and the Physics of Complex Transmission Interconnctions." Resource and Energy Economics, 19 (1-2), March 1997, 47-83.

Stenbacka, R. and M.M. Tombak, "Strategic Timing of Adoption of New Technologies Under Uncertainty." *International Journal of Industrial Organization,* 12, 1994, 387-411.

Weiss, A.M., "The Effects of Expectations on Technology Adoption: Some Empirical Evidence." *The Journal of Industrial Economics,* XLII, 1994, 341-360.

Wozniak, G.D., "Firm Information Acquisition and New Technology Adoption: Late Versus Early Adoption." *Review of Economics and Statistics*, 1993, 438-445.

14. CANADIAN PUBLIC POLICY IN A KNOWLEDGE-BASED ECONOMY

Randall Morck
University of Alberta

Bernard Yeung
University of Michigan

1. GOOD GOVERNMENT IN A KNOWLEDGE-BASED ECONOMY

The basis of Canadian freedom is the right to "peace, order and good government." In an information-based economy, "good government" is a more tightly defined concept than what many Canadians are used to. Since the 1970s, the federal government has justified an activist and interventionist public role in the economy as a way of fostering a unique Canadian identity, equalizing incomes across the country, and differentiating Canada from the United States. In this paper, we argue that these undertakings seriously compromise Canadians' economic security in a knowledge-based economy, and are therefore no longer "good government" by any definition.

This does not mean that good government in a knowledge-based economy must be small government. Rather, a good government is a "competitive" government. A competitive government delivers only the public goods and services people want and at prices they are willing to pay. A competitive government is also an innovative government, always searching for ways to bring down costs to taxpayers and for new public goods or services they might be willing to pay for.

Canada's government hardly fits the description of a competitive enterprise. While the real costs of airline travel, computer power, and many other goods have declined markedly with a succession of innovations, the cost of Canada's government has risen. While quality and consumer satisfaction have risen with each innovation in car making, music distributing, and telecommunications, Canada's government delivers more or less the same public goods and services it delivered 20 years ago to an increasingly unappreciative public. While many other governments are little more competitive than Canada's, accidents of geography and history make the United States Canada's primary competitor for capital and talent. Therefore, it is by that economy that we must gauge our government's performance.

The U.S. economy illustrates the sorts of trade-offs that are feasible in the public sector. States like Massachusetts, Minnesota, and California have relatively large public sectors and high taxes. Others, like Arkansas, Oklahoma and Texas, have small public sectors and low taxes. Yet entrepreneurs, skilled workers, and savings do not drain from Minnesota to Arkansas. Enough people think that life in the higher-tax state is worth the price. An even larger public sector could be competitive if it provided public goods and services people want at prices they are willing to pay, though we suspect that most Canadians are coming to prefer a less intrusive government.

As Canada becomes a more thoroughgoing knowledge-based economy, the need for competitive government will grow more pressing. Many traditional activities of government will have to be discarded if their costs, including the capital investment, knowledgeable workers, and entrepreneurs they discourage or drive out, fail to justify their benefits to Canadians, who are growing accustomed to continually improving and expanding consumer choice. We argue that economic nationalism already falls into this category for the average Canadian, let alone the highly skilled and talented Canadians we most need to retain and motivate. Good government must offer the public goods and services *these* people view as valuable at a lower cost than they would have to pay elsewhere.

2.   CANADA'S NATIONAL ECONOMIC SECURITY AND NATIONAL IDENTITY

Canada is not guaranteed a leadership role, or even a comfortable supporting role, in the global knowledge-based economy. Our stage fright stems from some deep, underlying insecurities that we seem unable to exorcise. We believe that two problems in our national psychology cause the greatest dysfunction.

First, Canadian nationalists have sought to build a national identity around a web of redistributional social programs. Many of these are both deeply dysfunctional in today's economic environment and ineffective in their stated goals of eliminating gross inequality. For example, our high income taxes prod our brightest young people to flee, while our aboriginal people live in third-world squalor and fill our jails. The result is a lack of new domestic competition for Canada's established wealth and a rising gap between tax revenue and demands for more social spending.

The idea that Canada's uniqueness lies in an egalitarian tradition is a very recent notion. Twentieth-century Quebec was, in many ways and until recent decades, an appendix of prerevolutionary France, and British North America was founded by United Empire Loyalists – Tory refugees from an egalitarian republic. It is also delusive, for Canada is not now, and never was, an egalitarian society. Old and wealthy families control the Canadian economy in a way that is the envy of U.S. billionaires, using mazes of intercorporate ownership unknown in the republic to the south. Rather, our egalitarian rhetoric conceals an unwholesome fear of change. Economic nationalists demand that foreign capital be kept out of this country, perhaps unwittingly defending the power and status of our old wealth. In return, they insist that the nobility recognize their feudal duty to employ their workers, regardless of changes in supply and demand. The fact that this deeply conservative philosophy is most strongly ensconced on the left of the formal political spectrum makes it both tenacious and virulent.

Second, Canadians are unable to appreciate the consequences of Canada's being a small economy. The essence of a knowledge-based economy is that competition is, first and foremost, competition to innovate. The profit from an innovation depends on the size of the market into which it is sold. To justify the cost of conceiving, developing and commercializing new products, their markets must often become very large very fast. Modern science requires huge amounts of capital, and people who have front-line knowledge are scarce and able to command high pay throughout the developed world. The costs of innovation are similarly high in modern finance, auto making, tourism, and virtually every other industry at the beginning of the 21st century.

Innovation and globalization are therefore inextricably intertwined. To know whether it was innovation or globalization that harmed this industry or benefited that one is to know the sound of one hand clapping. In a small economy like Canada's, nothing happens unless both are present. This means that Canada's prospects hinge on Canadian firms' access to foreign markets, and most especially the American market. It is therefore no surprise that Canadian nationalism is also deeply protectionist, or cryptoprotectionist in arguing for more diversified trade. Without innovative goods and services, Canadian business cannot draw European and Asian consumers, and without a huge market to sell into, innovation is financially perilous. This inescapable logic motivated many Canadian businesses, politicians and academics to support Free Trade in the 1980s. It must continue to dictate Canadian public policy if future generations of Canadians are to be protected from penury.

Canadian public policy must shed its dysfunctional attachment to the *status quo*. The attempt to create a national identity around income redistribution to preserve that *status quo* has become a clear danger to Canada's national economic security in the era of the global knowledge-based economy. Inward-looking policies may preserve the *status quo* for a while, but only by denying Canadians both the new jobs an internationally competitive economy would generate and the income to buy the new goods and services it would produce. Genuinely liberal social policies must supplant our cryptoconservative nationalism and protectionism. Canada's national identity should be as a vibrant microcosm of the new century's global civilization, not an echo of defunct doctrines like socialism, nor of even older fables of *noblesse oblige*. These conclusions follow from mundane econometric studies, yet they bring within our grasp a meaning of "Being Canadian" that transcends ideology and political fashion.

3. THE REPUBLIC TO THE SOUTH OF US SHALL SOUTH OF US REMAIN

A political slogan in the 1844 U.S. presidential election, "Fifty-Four Forty or Fight", epitomized many Americans' dissatisfaction with the border at the 49th parallel, and prompted the title to this section as a subsequent election slogan in Canada. This refrain equally nicely encapsulates many Canadians' feelings. Canadians seek a free and just society without the violence, extremism, and dogmatism they associate, rightly or wrongly, with the United States. The fact that the United States has become the world's leading information-based economic powerhouse consequently creates an unpleasant psychological tension in the Canadian identity. This tension has had unfortunate influences on Canadian public policy.

The key to a healthy Canadian identity is a healthy psychological distance from the United States. When a sequel to the war of 1812 never came, and the 49th parallel seemed secure, nationalists saw a secret economic conquest happening all around us. These cherished delusions prevent us from looking at modern America objectively. The United States is the foremost knowledge-based economy in the world. Why?

The idea that Americans are more entrepreneurial and more enterprising than Canadians is both offensive and empirically wrong. Canadians and Americans show broadly similar approval ratings for various aspects of entrepreneurship, and roughly equal proportions of the populations of the two countries are owner/managers.[1]

Canadian public policy need not match U.S. policy law for law. Rather, we must give careful thought to which aspects of U.S. public policy have been most important in fostering knowledge-based economic activity. We will first identify these policies and then explain why they matter.

First, the United States has, except for a brief period in the 1960s and 1970s, avoided high personal income taxes.[2] These policies most likely reflect lobbying by the wealthy, but their accidental consequence is that U.S. entrepreneurs can start out poor and become rich. This possibility induces creative people to gather information, create knowledge and commercialize innovations. Consequently, the U.S. economy sustains a higher level of creative destruction than most other economies.[3] The continual destruction of old firms by dynamic new upstarts prevents an ossified economic elite from forming as easily as it otherwise would. In contrast, Canada's relatively high income taxes prevent innovators from becoming rich, and therefore from out-competing old money.[4] The result is a hereditary family compact that governs corporate Canada more or less unchallenged.

Second, Americans have long been suspicious of concentrated economic power. This fear is manifest in a series of powerful antimonopoly laws beginning in the first decade of the 20th century. These laws may or may not have discouraged monopoly pricing. Their critical unintended consequence was to break the link between family fortunes and massive corporate control. There was no point in breaking up Standard Oil in 1911 if all the resulting pieces were still owned by John D. Rockefeller or his heirs. Antitrust rulings also necessitated divestiture orders. This created large, widelyheld firms. While widelyheld firms are subject to well-known governance problems, we have shown elsewhere that the governance problems that accompany extremely concentrated wealth are probably worse.[5] American antitrust law thus, entirely by accident, led to a better system of corporate governance. In Canada, inherited family firms preserve 19th century U.S. corporate governance problems.

Third, the United States, since the 1930s, has borne a number of populist banking laws that stifled the development of its banking system. These laws were most likely due to lobbying by borrowers, who feared powerful lenders. As recently as the early 1980s, the largest U.S. banks were barely comparable to Canada's large chartered banks, despite the tenfold larger size of the U.S. economy. Ill-conceived legislation cosseted U.S. banks from competition and laws against branch banking created a multitude of small and inefficient local banks. The unintended consequence of this sickly banking system was a set of alternative financing channels that have proven more amicable to knowledge-based ventures. Stock markets, junk bond markets, venture capital funds, and all the other components of the U.S. financial system grew to take the place of its weakling banks.[6] In Canada, the big chartered banks have always been the central pillar of the financial system, and now control most aspects of the finance industry. Their reliance on collateral-based lending has probably starved Canadian innovators of funds.

Fourth, the United States is a large market. This is the result of a series of territorial purchases and wars of conquest driven by coarse jingoism. Their unintended consequence is a market large enough that entrepreneurs can recoup their costs by selling their innovations to many buyers. American businesses did not need access to a global economy to make money from innovating. Their domestic market was big enough.

Fifth, the United States has maintained a set of elite private universities, which compete vigorously with each other. Their origin was most likely the illiberal desire of the elite to let their children socialize only with their peers. These elite universities built up huge endowments, but depend on continued private support. They now compete globally for the best professors and the most brilliant students to develop unmatched reputations as centres of knowledge creation. Many of these students became innovators, and some became very wealthy. The unintended consequence of the elite U.S. universities was thus unprecedented class mobility and increased creative destruction. In contrast, Canadian universities are all state-run. They are sound but unexceptional institutions that educate our middle classes well and sporadically produce good research in isolated departments. But our best universities are only slightly better than our worst ones. Many brilliant Canadians look south for professional fulfillment, and Canada can retain them only with great difficulty.

Finally, the United States, almost alone among liberal democracies, has limited the growth of social programs, and thus the size of the government. This is perhaps due to its legacy of slavery and the racism that continues to plague U.S. society. In other liberal democracies, social programs, though often proposed originally by well-meaning idealists to benefit the poor, were ultimately sold to median voters as transfers of wealth to them from the rich. In the U.S., however, social programs have been successfully portrayed as wealth transfers to a parasitic and violent underclass. The unintended consequence is that the U.S. public sector is, proportionately, unusually small. Since governance problems in the public sector have been shown to be generally worse than in the private sector, this has benefited the U.S. economy.[7]

These public policies, almost wholly accidentally, created an environment uniquely conducive to creative destruction, and consequently to a knowledge-based economy. This in no way suggests that brilliant American economists were unaware of the likely effects of these policies. Many understood perfectly their probable consequences, and supported them fervently. Our point is only that equally fervent arguments along the same lines elsewhere fell on deaf ears. The political economy of the United States, by fortuitous circumstance, was uniquely receptive to them, and might well have followed the same policies even in the absence of support from academia.

Nor should these arguments suggest that U.S. voters and politicians are more self-interested than voters and politicians in other countries, or than other people in general. Modern economic theory assumes that the average person is both self-interested and altruistic. Empirical economics largely confirms this. It should surprise no one that public policy partially reflects the perceived self-interest of voters and politicians.

The United States, by historical accident more than mindful design, established the institutional underpinnings that make a knowledge-based economy work. By geographic accident, the Unites States is both the measure by which Canadians assess their own economy and the sanctuary to which Canadian savings, talent, and resources can most readily flee. By mindful design, Canada is a free society and will not forbid such flight, though it surely could not in any case. The Canadian economy and government must therefore be competitive with the U.S. over the longer term. Our challenge is to chart a path to that goal that Canadian voters will embrace.

4.   SOME SUGGESTIONS

We described earlier, in the chapter entitled "The Economic Underpinnings of a Knowledge-Based Economy," the fact that knowledge-based economic growth happens through the process of creative destruction, the creation of new knowledge-based economic processes that render established firms obsolete – and so destroy them. Knowledge-based growth, because of the increasing returns to scale typically associated with it, can lift the economic fortunes of more people more rapidly than conventional growth through capital accumulation.[8] So far, in this paper, we have argued that certain properties of the Canadian economy impede creative destruction, while other properties of the U.S. economy nurture it.

This framework now allows us to consider specific public policy suggestions that might spur creative destruction in Canada.   These suggestions do not require that Canada ape U.S. policies, for that country's historical development shaped its economic institutions in ways that Canada cannot replicate.   Rather, we must consider the economic destination we want, a knowledge-based economy, and how best to get there from here. It is in this spirit that we propose some rough and preliminary policy suggestions.

4.1   Empowerment as Equality

English Canada was founded to preserve inequality. The United Empire Loyalists, who fled the thirteen colonies at the end of the War of the American Rebellion (1776-1783), included their wealthiest citizens. Called "Tories" by other colonists, they included the elite business class, especially of New York and Virginia Colonies. Some were rich because of class or political connections, but most were wealthy through hard work and ingenuity. Many Loyalists were Scots merchants, representing the great merchant houses of Glasgow, who lent money to colonial land-owning aristocrats, like the Washington and Jefferson families of Virginia. The local gentry apparently resented their economically dependent positions. Indeed, much of colonial politics involved unsuccessful ploys by landowners to gain power over their creditors. Unsurprisingly, these Loyalists distrusted the egalitarian and democratic rhetoric of the revolutionaries.

In all, about one-quarter of the population of the thirteen colonies were Loyalists. At the war's end, despite explicit clauses protecting Loyalists in the Treaty of Paris, their civil rights were curtailed, they were subjected to confiscatory taxes, and their homes, businesses and other assets were expropriated by self-appointed revolutionary tribunals. These seizures amounted to a vast transfer of wealth. Indeed, ambitious colonial politicians, like Isaac Sears of New York, may well have fanned the war, hoping to get rich quick by confiscating Tory property.[9]

Rather than accept their fates in the new republic, upwards of 100,000 Loyalists fled to Canada. Their absence played no small part in the new republic's depressed postwar economy. It would no doubt surprise these dispossessed pilgrims to learn that the essence of Canada's national identity is now supposed to be social programs that take money from people with higher than median incomes and give it, net of administrative costs, to everyone else. Canadian taxes are surely less crude than confiscation by revolutionary mobs, but there is still a disturbing resemblance. We forget the lesson of the United Empire Loyalists and, by degrees, relieve our own most ingenious citizens of burdensome wealth, or send them into exile.

In the "The Economic Underpinnings of a Knowledge-Based Economy," we argued that entrepreneurs in knowledge-based businesses must be able to accumulate great wealth quickly to cover their often large up-front costs and justify the great personal financial risks they take. High income taxes make this hard, and so prevent new wealth from displacing old wealth. High income taxes are "barriers to entry" around existing businesses and existing wealth. High income taxes discourage the creation of new knowledge-based businesses, and unnaturally preserve the lives of old, stagnant businesses.

Many Canadian politicians see unequal wealth as an injustice to be righted. This would not entice such popular support if it did not resonate with truth. Many wealthy families have dubious pedigrees, with slaving, opium, alcohol, weapons, smuggling, whaling, and pillage all counting heavily. Perhaps taking their wealth and their heirs' to help poor honest folk is wise and just. But we tax the heir to a 19th-century opium trading fortune and the star neurosurgeon by the same laws; and the neurosurgeon is perhaps less able to evade them.

Something seems amiss in our concept of equality. Perhaps not all income is equally fair game for redistribution, and perhaps not all income inequality is necessarily undesirable. We have argued that knowledge creation is different from other economic activity in that it stimulates broader, more self-sustaining growth. Ideally, we might want to tax incomes that arise from knowledge creation less heavily than those from labour or capital holdings. However, our political system is surely unable to launch or sustain such a system. How are the tax authorities to decide whose income fits which category? What happens if job characteristics evolve? Are auto mechanics and secretaries not knowledge workers in the 21st-century? Clearly, fine-tuning the income tax system to make it impede knowledge creation less would be an administrative, political and legal nightmare.

A simpler way of avoiding these problems is to define the equality we would see in terms other than income. One candidate, popular with right-leaning politicians, is "equality of opportunity." This is the argument that everyone should have the same opportunities, and the freedom to grasp them or shrink from them. Unfortunately, true equality of opportunity is a subtle and slippery concept. Everyone does not have the same opportunity to be born rich, strong, smart, attractive and healthy. The words "equality of opportunity" often disguise a smug satisfaction with the *status quo*. Children born to poverty, the physically and mentally disabled, the repulsive, and the infirm may simply lack the power to grasp the opportunities before them.

Such unequal access to life's opportunities is perhaps the deepest and most pernicious form of inequality. If we accept that remedying this is the proper goal of social policy, striving for greater income equality *per se* is once more questionable, for it leaves more fundamental inequality unaffected. Government action aimed explicitly at tempering such deep-set inequality is perhaps best called "empowerment." We believe that empowerment, rather than simple redistribution, can be a unifying and economically sensible theme for social programs in a knowledge-based economy.

Policy Implication: The purpose of social programs should be the empowerment of individuals. Government should open the greatest number of doors for the greatest number of people.

Thus, quality public education, laws and programs to assist the disabled, equal rights laws and basic health care all come within the legitimate sphere of good government. Indiscriminate income levelling does not. Universality for all social programs amounts to indiscriminate income levelling and so makes no economic sense.

4.2   How to Improve the Tax System and Replace the GST

The main mechanism for indiscriminate income levelling in Canada is the progressive personal income tax. If our aim is to empower people and to let knowledge creators keep the fruits of their work, such an income tax is unwise for it impedes creative destruction.

Policy Implication: New taxes should be vetted and old ones replaced according to how seriously they impede creative destruction. Progressive personal income taxes are arguably the worst by this standard, and should be transformed into low, flat taxes. If a progressive tax system is desired, it should tax luxury consumption, bequests, land holdings, or other aspects of personal inequality that are less related to knowledge creation and wealth creation.

In our view, a comprehensive reform of Canada's tax system is long overdue. Canada is steadily losing its most talented and best educated people to the U.S. Figure 1 shows the total tax bite the Canadian and U.S. government each takes out of their economies. The Canadian government has been growing steadily more expensive. Table 1 compares the net inflow of top scientists across countries. Canada is clearly losing talent at a hemorrhagic rate. Unfortunately, the outflow of talent in the sciences, economics, medicine, and law suggests that too many people have come to regard it as not worth the money. Although Canada is also attracting highly qualified immigrants from Asia and elsewhere, the U.S. is both keeping its own best people *and* attracting top people from everywhere else. Canada must do this too. Living in Canada has to become less of a financial sacrifice for high-income, professional knowledge workers.

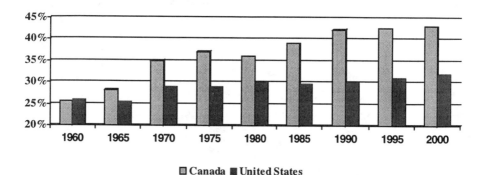

□ Canada ■ United States

Source: OECD Economic Outlook

Figure 1: Growth in the total tax burden (total government revenue over GDP) in Canada and the United States compared

Table 1: Net immigration of star genetic researchers as of 1990

Country	Net Migration Rate (%)
United Kingdom	32.3
Belgium	14.3
Japan	9.6
Germany	8.3
Australia	7.1
France	4.0
United States	2.9
Canada	-30.0
Switzerland	-40.0

Source: Zucker and Darby, (1996).

Highly skilled people like star geneticists can demand high salaries, for the worldwide demand for their skills currently outstrips the supply. High income taxes in Canada make it unnecessarily difficult to retain the best such people in this country. To give them after-tax salaries commensurate with those they could earn elsewhere, their before-tax salaries in Canada must be very high indeed. Since such people usually have access to prepaid health care and quality education for their children anyway, the costs of Canada's public sector usually outweigh its benefits to them. Consequently, corporations find it less costly to locate their knowledge creation operations elsewhere. The most attractive alternative location for these operations is, of course, the United States.

Policy Implication: Canada's personal income taxes should be adjusted from time to time to be competitive with those in the United States from the point of view of people with skills that are in high demand. We believe such an adjustment is critically needed now.

Since giving tax breaks to individuals in some professions, but not others, is probably not politically doable, the entire tax system must adjust to accommodate these sought-after people.

In recent years, tax experts have debated the viability of shifting from income taxes to consumption taxes, with consumption defined as income minus saving. The chief virtue of a consumption tax is that it encourages saving, which is essential to growth in a traditional economy. Savings finance investment in new plant and equipment, which produce more output. Since growth in a knowledge-based economy arises from innovation rather than capital accumulation, this argument is perhaps less urgent in our context. However, much commercialization of innovations does require capital expenditure, and this is more forthcoming if savings are not taxed. The argument for a consumption tax therefore remains valid in a knowledge-based economy.

A comprehensive consumption tax could be implemented either as an income tax that exempts savings or as a sales tax. They are equivalent, the only difference being whether the tax is calculated by consumers and remitted like a personal income tax or tacked onto each purchase and remitted by merchants.

Canada's provincial sales taxes (PST) and federal goods and services tax (GST) are examples of consumption taxes. The provincial sales taxes are uncontroversial and no less popular than any other tax. The GST was a federal move in this direction that was seriously flawed economically and badly bungled politically. The economic flaw is the long, growing and irrational list of exemptions. The political bungle was presenting it as a tax on goods and services.

The GST and corporate income tax should be scrapped and replaced with a single flat tax (SFT) on business revenue net of costs. A 7% tax of this sort would be algebraically identical to the GST. It could be extended to a broader base than the GST's because political populists cannot easily argue that Safeway should pay no corporate tax as they argued that food should not be taxed. An SFT could be implemented at a higher rate than 7% so that it would be revenue-neutral *vis-à-vis* all existing corporate taxes. Packaged in this way, a consumption tax could be sold as a way to make corporations pay "their fair share," though it would still logically be a tax on consumption. The SFT should be simpler and cheaper to administer than the GST because there would be no need to classify particular goods as taxable or exempt. This is because the SFT is a tax on businesses, not a tax on goods. Also, a flat tax with few or no deductions is more transparent and immune to wasteful lobbying by special interests.

Policy Implication: The GST and corporate income tax should be scrapped and replaced with a Single Flat Tax on business revenue minus costs.

The precise structure of the SFT can be altered in a number of dimensions. It should treat R&D as an expense, just as the current corporate income tax does. However, the treatment of depreciation could be similar to the current Capital Cost Allowance (CCA) system. More sorts of capital expenditure could be made expensable to spur business investment. Indeed, the logic of the consumption tax argument, pursued further, implies that all capital expenditures might be expensed in the year they are incurred. Again, the flat rate would have to be adjusted accordingly if the switch to the SFT were to be revenue-neutral.

4.3   That It Rise Again, the Sun Must Also Set

A knowledge-based economy is capable of sustained self-reinforcing growth through creative destruction. Innovative new firms continually displace existing firms, keeping the economy on the technological frontier. This economic effervescence is most vigorous in a highly flexible economy.

Knowledge creation, innovation, and commercializing innovations are costly high-risk activities that take concentrated effort. To see them through, people need to foresee very substantial rewards. Employees do not generally propose innovations unless they receive real compensation for them. Managers do not implement them unless they too have an economic stake in the winnings. Consumers cannot buy new products if their buying patterns are artificially restricted or distorted. Their purchases should be the signals that guide the direction of innovation.[10] In markets with better signals, the search for innovations is less costly and more fruitful. These are all calls for flexibility.

Regulatory and legal hurdles to new ventures should be minimized. Innovators must be free to enter the market, and consumers to choose goods and services they see as useful. The consequence is that a good innovation generates high demand and so high returns.

Labour market flexibility is equally important. Innovations often require that firms hire new workers with new qualifications, and these often displace existing workers. Or innovation can call for a restructuring, and the laying-off of workers in one location as more are hired in another. Creative destruction requires that divisions, firms, and industries with improving business prospects grow, raising wages and employment, while firms whose business prospects sour shrink. Workers must be freely able to relocate and switch jobs in response to wage changes. A flexible labour market allows all this, a rigid one does not.

Managers must support promising innovations, and not try to suppress them out of fear for their jobs. This is most often a problem in rigid hierarchical corporations built around "command-and-control" management. This is why innovators are often happier and more productive in smaller, more flexible firms.

It is therefore important that public policy not induce artificial rigidities into the economy, and enhance its pliancy whenever possible. Unfortunately, many well-intentioned public-sector initiatives induce cumbersome economic rigidity. Because government programs are mainly needed where free market incentives fail to function properly, they must use "command-and-control" management, which is inherently inflexible. They rely on laws, regulations, and administrative rulings enforced by police, courts and lawyers.

Moreover, such laws, regulations and rulings are usually not repealed when their *raison d'Être* fades. Our tax laws, industry regulations, and labour laws arguably gather anachronisms as the studies that justified their particulars gather dust. Many argue that whole government programs are no longer needed. Yet these public initiatives do not die gracefully. People to whom they are economically advantageous lobby for their continuation long after their original purposes are forgotten.

Canada currently has complex regulations about who can own radio and television stations, and about what percentages of the broadcast hours must be devoted to what sorts of offerings. As Internet television becomes increasingly available, viewers can point and click to watch whatever "Star Trek" episode or Jerry Lewis rerun they want whenever they want. It will be impossible to control what viewers watch without blockading the Internet, which will be impractical in a knowledge-based economy.

Canada also has Byzantine marketing boards that still attempt to administer markets for agricultural produce. These were designed to bail out desperate Depression-era farmers. By forcing all farmers to sell at the same price, the boards prevent efficient and innovative farmers from driving inefficient ones quickly out of business. The boards now amount to a tax on efficient sophisticated agribusinesses to subsidize old-fashioned dirt farms. This is not helpful in moving Canada towards a knowledge-based economy.

To loosen this legal tenacity, we must consider building flexibility into our laws, rules, and regulations.

Policy Implication: Laws, regulations and administrative rulings on economic issues should always include sunset clauses and should become void if not explicitly renewed. The main criteria for renewal should be the continued urgency of the problem they address, their efficacy in correcting it, their drag upon knowledge creation and implementation, and the absence of new approaches that lead to better trade-offs in these dimensions.

In general, our hope is that laws and regulations that limit business's actions would usually not be renewed, for the problems they address often fade from public concern. Laws and regulations that continue to be useful should be updated as they are renewed. Where possible, new approaches to correcting the original problems should be tried. Other laws and regulations should die in peace.

It is especially important in a knowledge-based economy to clear out legal overgrowth regularly. Laws, rules, and regulations that are not enforced, incomprehensible, or inconsistent complicate business dealings unnecessarily, especially for new, small and rapidly growing businesses. The result is that such legal quack grass protects the economic positions of large existing businesses and deters the new innovative businesses we need in a knowledge-based economy.

4.4   Economic Disestablishmentarianism

Creative destruction, the basic process of economic growth in a knowledge-based economy, requires that creative new firms continually rise to displace old stagnant ones.   Does this actually require the creation of entirely new firms?   Or can old firms become innovative and displace their former peers?

The answer appears to depend on what sort of innovation we are talking about.[11]   Radical innovations, the kind that start whole new industries, generally require brand new, upstart companies. Established firms appear better at the improvement and extension of existing ideas.

Examples of radically innovative start-ups in recent decades are Apple Computers, Microsoft, and Wal-Mart.   Earlier decades produced Ford, Standard Oil and International Harvester.   Each of these companies either sold a product that had never been sold before or did business in a way that was completely original in some important dimension.   These innovative businesses all grew by overthrowing the existing economic establishment.

Existing companies were either incapable of or uninterested in developing these innovations. Often, this was due to the hierarchical nature of large existing firms, but the way property rights were allocated to vested interests within firms also mattered.   In 1980, IBM had all the technology necessary to build PCs and dominate PC software.   Top management consciously decided not to, apparently because senior managers and technicians saw their careers as dependent on mainframe computers. Moving into PCs would have required giving new people key positions in IBM's hierarchy, possibly sidelining many current decision-makers.   Therefore, IBM missed the initial phase of the PC revolution.

Innovators also usually have little wish to work within large existing corporations.   When John D. Rockefeller came up with the idea of standardized oil products, he founded his own firm, Standard Oil, and became a billionaire.   Had he instead persuaded an existing oil company to implement his idea, he would have had a few years of salaried employment while the firm's owners got rich.

For an economy to become a spawning area for radical innovation, it must be conducive to the formation of new companies.   The main problem entrepreneurs usually face in setting up and expanding new companies is obtaining capital.   Investors are understandably leery of handing their life's savings over to unknown alleged geniuses.

Government can help here by giving entrepreneurs the privileges of being open to lawsuits, going bankrupt, and going to jail when they are dishonest. Honest entrepreneurs do see these as "privileges" because they keep rascals away from investors' money, raising trust in entrepreneurs and lowering costs of capital. The money that rascals steal, after all, should be reserved for bankrolling the ideas of honest entrepreneurs.

Public investors' rights should be firmly ensconced in law. They should have clear rights to sue nefarious insiders, to inspect meaningful financial accounts, and to invest in a climate of general law and order. Corporate insiders should be held to a higher standard than outside board members because they are the true decision-makers. Outside board members should be liable too, but should have a "due diligence" defence, for they can often be duped by corporate insiders. The stronger and more discriminating these laws are, the bigger the advantage honest entrepreneurs have over rascals. Of course, arbitrary, obtuse and onerous laws have just the opposite effect, as they are as likely to hamper honest entrepreneurs as dishonest ones.

For new firms to rise quickly, capital markets and institutions must work efficiently. This mainly means that it must be made as easy as possible to tell good investment opportunities from bad ones. Fortunately, corporate and securities laws can induce entrepreneurs to disclose this information themselves. This happens when these laws deliver swift and sure punishment to rascals who misuse investors' money.

Policy Implication: Laws that protect investors should deliver swift and substantial penalties against fraudulent, reckless and negligent disregard of public shareholders' trust.

These laws include effective shareholder rights laws, meaningful financial disclosure, and efficient courts capable of dealing with complex financial matters. Insiders who violate investors' trust must quickly become outsiders.

If punishment for financial misdeeds is certain, rascals will find other venues for their scams and leave capital markets to honest entrepreneurs. This is important because mistrust of the financial system harms overall economic growth and so hurts everyone, not just its direct victims.

Perverse laws and practices that let people control corporate assets they do not own invite abuse, even from the most saintly insiders. These situations, called "entrenchment," arise in Canada in three main ways.

The first is multiple classes of common stock. These typically give insiders many votes per share and outsiders few or no votes per share. The result is that the insiders control the firm though they own little of its stock, and decisions that cost the firm money have little financial effect on their own wealth.

The second is equity cross-holdings. These arise when a wealthy individual controls more than one firm and has these firms issue large amounts of stock to each other. Often, this is done so that net dividend payments between firms are zero, but this is not required. If the majority of each firm's stock is held by other firms, the initial insiders retain voting control of all their firms even though they may own little or no stock on their own accounts.

The third is control pyramids. These are perhaps the most common method of entrenchment. Insiders own 51% of one holding company, which owns 51% of another, which owns 51% of another, and so on. Ultimately, the final firm in this chain of holding companies owns firms with actual productive assets. The initial insiders control these assets because they control every firm in the chain. However, their actual ownership stake in the production companies is 51% of 51% of 51% of ... of their value. This usually works out to a very small number.

Equity cross-holdings and control pyramids both rely on corporations owning stock in other corporations. This is common in Canada and virtually unknown in the United States. The reason U.S. firms do not own shares in other publicly traded U.S. firms is that dividends paid by one firm to another are taxed. Canada, in contrast, taxes dividends paid by a firm to a person, but not dividends paid by one firm to another.

Policy Implication: Different classes of common stock with different voting rights should be banned. Dividends received by a corporation should be taxable as part of that corporation's income.

If any distinction is defensible between dividends paid to a corporation and dividends paid to people, it is that the former should be taxed (to deter cross-holdings and control pyramids) and the latter left untaxed (to avoid double taxation).

Innovative businesses, whether implementing radical new ideas or valuable incremental innovation, must be able to grab market share quickly.

They must be able to push non-innovative firms aside post-haste. Bankruptcy laws and merger laws are important here.

Policy Implication: Bankruptcy laws should force quick and clean transfers of control from the previous owners to new owners. Ownership should immediately pass to creditors, and they can then decide whether to liquidate the firm or restructure it. All credit contracts should contain clauses indicating how many shares the lender, supplier, or prepaid customer gets in the event of bankruptcy.

Bankruptcies can often happen for reasons that are beyond managers' control, but when this happens, the creditors can usually be convinced to give the managers a second chance. "Kind" bankruptcy laws that give incumbent management a court-mandated second chance are costly, for they also protect managers who frustrated or ignored innovation in their firms. Chapter 11 of the U.S. *Bankruptcy Reform Act* of 1978 allows for very kind and gentle bankruptcies, which may end up protecting inefficient operations.

The origins of debtor-friendly bankruptcy laws in the United States lie in the American Revolution itself. Virginia tobacco farmers faced a mounting debt crisis in the mid-1770s, as they had borrowed much more from British (mainly Scottish) creditors than they thought themselves able to repay. Had the American Revolution not occurred, many of the new republic's most famous founding fathers would have lost their farms. When Alexander Hamilton proposed that the tobacco growers should honour their debts, George Mason, in a letter to tobacco farmer Patrick Henry, quotes the planters as complaining, "If we are now to pay the debts due British Merchants, what have we been fighting for all this while?" Once freed from Westminster, the thirteen states immediately placed severe restrictions on creditors' remedies.[12] "Fresh start" bankruptcy laws have been intimately tied to American populism ever since.

This philosophy appears to have impeded economic growth in that country.[13] Chapter 11 should not be copied by other countries, least of all by Canada.

Another mechanism for dislodging established firms is corporate takeovers. Existing managers may be unable to cope with the changed market conditions that arise when a rival introduces an innovation. Bankruptcy is a costly and disruptive way to replace them. A less socially disruptive way of doing the same thing is for another firm, with more flexible and imaginative managers, to take the struggling firm over.

Policy Implication: Corporate takeovers are necessary and useful in a knowledge-based economy. Laws and regulations that restrict them, either directly or indirectly, are costly and should be avoided.

For example, Ontario's 20% takeover trigger rule indirectly makes takeovers less attractive by preventing control block trades. The 20% rule gives public shareholders a piece of the action in any takeover, but probably reduces the number of such takeovers. The legality of poison pills, poison puts and other anti-takeover devices is also highly problematic in a knowledge-based economy. So is the legitimacy of voting caps on privatized crown corporations and banks, for these are *de facto* poison pills.

Of course, some takeovers are poorly planned and ultimately destructive. To avoid such disasters, the directors of firms contemplating takeovers should ask hard questions about whether their firm really has the expertise needed to add value to the target. When the answer to this is negative, or unclear, the takeover should be stopped dead. Corporate insiders who waste shareholders' money on ill-conceived takeovers should be liable to legal action. Their defence to such action should be a clear and economically reasonable explanation of how the takeover should have added value.

Corporate takeovers can also create market power. When one or a few firms control most of a given market, they can raise prices to monopoly levels and extract whatever the market will bear for their output. In a knowledge-based economy, market concentration *per se* is not necessarily bad. A large market share that results from a successful innovation, whether achieved through greenfield expansion or acquisitions, is generally in the public interest. Also, market power in a globalized economy is not defined by percent sales in one single market. A firm occupying a large market share may still be threatened by foreign entrants. As long as barriers to entry are kept as low as possible and another innovator can enter and grab market share from the previous dominant firm, any monopoly power will be short-lived and will, in fact, spur innovation. In a knowledge-based economy, a series of temporary monopolies with constant turnover is expected. Only long-term monopolies protected by artificial entry barriers are clearly undesirable.

Policy Implication: In a knowledge-based economy, anti-combines powers should be triggered by artificial barriers to entry, not by market share.

In a knowledge-based economy, it is important that productive assets be transferred quickly from less to more able hands. A sentimental attachment to family control is often inconsistent with this. Intelligence is, at most, only partially hereditary. Entrepreneurial talent is certainly a dimension of intelligence, so most of the time, the child will be a less able entrepreneur than the parent. The transfer of control from one generation to the next in a family firm should therefore not be encouraged, and perhaps should be discouraged. The economy as a whole is often better off if the heirs are encouraged to sell out.

Policy Implication: A tax on inheritances makes sense in a knowledge-based economy.

This tax should be effective immediately. Devices like family trusts that postpone taxes due on death are inconsistent with the tax's goal of quickly getting productive assets into the most innovative hands. The idea is to create a tax liability large enough that the heir can only pay it by selling control.

Inheritance taxes are subject to evasion, but probably no more so than are income taxes. Certainly, gifts that look like evasions of the inheritance tax should be taxed as inheritances. Revenue Canada auditors would have to develop skills at assessing property values and at valuing private firms.

Since inheritances are clearly not the result of the recipient's knowledge creation, a tax on such income is minimally distortionary in a knowledge-based economy.[14] Inherited small family businesses, farms, and fishing boats should not be exempt. These assets too belong in the hands of those most able to use them in the most innovative way. An inheritance tax encourages heirs to sell out for cash, and so forces more productive assets onto the market. In this respect, an inheritance tax is more effective in a knowledge-based economy than a realization of capital gains on death, which (with some exceptions) is currently the law in Canada. The latter does nothing to encourage the sale of assets whose value has stagnated, as they have posted no capital gains, yet these are the assets we most want in other hands.

Implementing a strict and effective inheritance tax would allow a reduction in the income tax. An inheritance tax also gives entrepreneurs an incentive to endow concert halls, hospitals, and scholarships and otherwise provide for the public good in their wills, as such beneficence should be tax-exempt.

4.5   Globalization

In the long, or even medium, run a small open economy like Canada can control the pace of innovation no more than it can control the interest rate. Global forces set both. As a knowledge-based economy, Canada can either keep up or fall behind.

Our paper "The Economic Underpinnings of a Knowledge-Based Economy" argued that knowledge-based commercial activities frequently, indeed usually, have increasing returns to scale. Once created, productive knowledge can be applied over and over again, improving the way many businesses in many countries function. These increasing returns to scale are the reason a knowledge-based economy can sustain self-reinforcing growth. Since innovation is often difficult, expensive, and risky, these huge returns to scale are important incentives to innovators.

The domestic Canadian market is much smaller than the U.S. market or the European Union market. Consequently, the returns to Canadian innovators would be correspondingly low if innovators were restricted to their domestic markets. Global trade and capital liberalization are especially important to innovators in smaller economies, for these reforms effectively give them access to the same markets innovators in large countries can reach.

Policy Implication: Trade and capital flow liberalization are critically important to a small knowledge-based economy.

Paradoxically, many small knowledge-based firms in small countries can "go global" without exporting. This is because they sell their products to multinationals that operate in their countries. The multinationals then ship these goods to their worldwide operations, where they either use them as inputs in their own production processes or resell them. We have called this "intermediated globalization" in other writings.[15] The advantage to the small firm is that it retains control of its production process and keeps its technology at home, yet avoids the costs of running its own exporting operation.

Thus "export subsidies" and other government programs aimed at helping small domestic firms tap foreign markets on their own may not always be necessary. Intermediated globalization may be cheaper and more efficient in many cases. This is especially true if many multinationals are competing with each other to act as conduits to global markets for local producers. If only one multinational is present, it might try to extract monopoly prices for acting as a conduit. All multinationals, not just Canadian multinationals, can serve as conduits to global markets for small Canadian firms. To make global access as cheap as possible for small Canadian firms, Canada should welcome foreign multinationals.

Cross-fertilization in ideas encourages innovation. Multinationals, both Canadian and foreign-owned, not only serve as conduits by which small Canadian firms can reach global markets, they are also pipelines that bring knowledge of foreign innovations to Canada, and these often stimulate Canadian innovations. This two-way flow makes openness to multinationals important.[16]

Policy Implication: Canada should remain fully open to multinational firms. Local knowledge-based firms benefit from the presence of many competing multinationals, whether Canadian or foreign-controlled, and can use them as two-way conduits to world markets.

Free capital flow is as at least as important as free trade in goods and services. This is because initial investments in knowledge-based firms are risky and hard to value appropriately. Large U.S. venture capital funds retain specialized technical experts to evaluate requests for capital. Good experts are expensive. Also, since venture capital funds want to keep their discoveries secret from rival funds, outsourcing such expertise is undesirable. This means venture capital funds must be large enough to spread the cost of such expertise across many investments, or highly specialized so they can get by with a smaller number of technical specialists. Thus venture capital funding works best in a very large economy, like the United States, where such economies of scale and economies of specialization can be achieved. In a smaller country, like Canada, venture capital funds have difficulty flourishing.

To be economically viable in the long term, a Canadian-based venture capital fund should be able to invest much of its capital outside Canada. Similarly, Canadian entrepreneurs will have to rely on foreign venture capital funds. This cross-fertilization is the only way the necessary scale and specialization can be brought to bear on the Canadian economy.

Policy Implication: Capital, including venture capital, must be allowed to flow freely across national borders, especially if it is to be available to entrepreneurs in small economies.

The Canadian government's support of the Multilateral Agreement on Investment is therefore justified, and whatever successor treaty emerges from the World Trade Organization should be steered, if possible, towards national treatment for venture capital funds worldwide.

The current rules that limit tax-exempt investment funds, such as RRSPs and pension funds, to 20% foreign content are costly to Canada. They effectively prevent these institutional investors from fully entering the venture capital field by restricting the feasible scale and specialization of their venture capital operations. Canada just is not big enough to support such high-cost financing. Canadian entrepreneurs need access to globally competitive venture capital funds. Canadian savers should also be able to hold such funds in their RRSPs and pension funds.

Policy Implication: The 20% foreign content limit on pension and other tax-exempt investment should be eliminated.

Also, tax rules that discourage Canadians from investing abroad make no sense in a knowledge-based economy. Canadian investors should be able to hold many venture capital funds, not just funds based in Canada. Moreover, such arbitrary restrictions on savers' freedom to invest wherever they want risk discouraging private savings and encouraging dependence on government-run old age income support plans.

Policy Implication: Personal income from Canadian and foreign investments should be taxed identically.

Of course, if our earlier advice about switching to consumption taxes is heeded, this point is moot.

Finally, Canada needs technical expertise and entrepreneurial talent. Even if we provide first-class education for our children, the technical and entrepreneurial expertise we need to compete in the global knowledge-based economy will be too sparse in our aging population. The simplest solution is to quit exporting such people and to import more of them. We have already argued that lower personal income taxes are the way to dam the outflow of talent. Canada's immigration policy should manage the inflow.

Policy Implication: Canada's immigration policy should be fine-tuned to correct economic and demographic imbalances. Specifically, we should deliberately target young, educated people for rapid, hassle-free immigration.

To some extent, our current immigration policies do this. These aspects of immigration law should be held sacrosanct. Economically and demographically managed immigration should dominate other considerations in the future.

4.6   People First

Ultimately, new knowledge is created by people.   Corporations, universities, hospitals, communities, ethnic groups or geographic regions can either support innovative people or frustrate them. Encouraging innovation means, first and foremost, encouraging innovative people. This calls for a more "individual-oriented" political philosophy than many in Canada are comfortable with.

Education should be about empowering individuals to prosper in a knowledge-based economy. Recent experiments with free competition among public schools for students, and between public schools and charter schools, have been largely successful, despite some isolated cases of malfeasance and fraud. Alberta, where these programs began, has achieved considerable success, with its students recently ranking third in the world, behind only Singapore and Korea, in basic science competence.[17]   This competition has fostered a bounty of educational choices for students, ranging from foreign language immersion to Montessori public schools, to public schools focusing on music and fine arts. The costs, some narrow sectarian religious schools and a few instances of fraud, seem piddling.

Policy Implication: Institutions that provide education, including public schools and universities, should have to compete freely for students.

Municipalities and provinces should be encouraged to allow students to attend whatever school they want to attend, not the geographically nearest one. Schools should be paid by governments on a per-student basis. Schools that fail to attract enough students to be viable should be closed. Their physical premises should be turned over to successful schools as satellite campuses.

Universities, technical institutes, and colleges should also be forced to compete for students. Currently, institutions of higher learning charge out-of-province students high fees and subject them to quotas while offering steeply subsidized education to residents. This prevents competition between universities.[18] Canadian students, dismayed at the poor quality of their local universities, face much higher costs if they try to go elsewhere. Canadian universities have correctly come to regard local students as a captive market and government support as their entitlement. This removes any incentive to innovate or otherwise improve the quality of their teaching and research.

Each university should charge one flat fee for all students. Governments should subsidize people, by giving students scholarships valid at any approved university, rather than funding universities out of general revenues. Scholarships worth more could go to students with better academic records or greater need, simulating a sliding tuition scale. Provinces whose universities are inefficiently run or academically substandard would pay the price more visibly in an outflow of top high school graduates. The federal government's recently announced national scholarship programs are a welcome step in this direction.

Even elite private U.S. universities depend heavily on government funding, especially to support research. Large-scale targeted research projects like the space program, the war on cancer, and so on have provided political support for research and, since they have clearly defined goals, can be evaluated meaningfully. Other agencies, like the National Science Foundation, provide large grants to credible research leaders who then subdivide the funds among junior researchers. Canada's federal research granting agencies dole out relatively small amounts of money to many individual researchers, both senior and junior. To some extent this is necessary because Canada lacks sufficient credible senior researchers in many areas. However, Canadian granting agencies' arcane and complex application and evaluation procedures unnecessarily deter good people from serving on granting committees. This leads to apparently random funding decisions that, in turn, deter good junior researchers from applying.[19] The result is a system lacking in quality control and exposed to unnecessary academic politics. Not surprisingly, public support for increased research funding is tepid. These problems appear to affect the social sciences and humanities most severely, but are far from unknown in the natural and medical sciences.

Policy Implication: Research funding in Canada should be subject to better quality control. Simple, objective criteria, like the applicant's track record, should determine what gets funded and what does not. Researchers with world-class reputations, not academic bureaucrats skilled in "grantsmanship," should be in charge.

Attempts to move in this direction have been undermined in the past. For example, a few years ago the rules for one agency were changed so as to rank applications by established researchers two thirds on track record and one third on the granting agency committee's opinion of the research. Unfortunately, the agency imaginatively interpreted these rules as allowing its committees to decide which applications should get funded any way it wanted, and then to rank the approved applications in the required way. This method remains in use to our knowledge. This resistance to quality control underscores the critical lack of world-class researchers at most Canadian universities.

Weak universities are a serious problem in a knowledge-based economy. An increasingly persuasive line of empirical research in economics shows that knowledge-based firms in the United States are geographically clustered, mainly around elite universities.[20] Many Canadian universities neither foster frontier research nor deliver stimulating teaching. Rather, a sort of pseudoresearch dominates. Poorly paid, mediocre professors write scores of papers that are never read, financed by federal research grants that are given out by committees of the same sorts of professors. The role of peer review in Canada is to make sure too many of our universities never get any better.

If the government is serious about fostering a KBE, the universities should play a central role. That means they should pay higher salaries to attract and keep star professors. It also means that very large research grants should go to such people. This would be a big departure from the current flat salary structures and egalitarian (or perhaps progressive) distribution of research grants by the federal grant committees. Given these problems, Canadian universities are poorly equipped to lead Canadians into a knowledge-based economy. However, the situation is not beyond help.

Policy Implication: It may be necessary for the government to focus research funding on institutes that are only loosely affiliated with Canadian universities.

In the United States, institutions like the National Bureau of Economic Research, the National Institutes of Health, and the Woods Hole Oceanographic Institution are unrivaled centres of research activity. In Canada, such institutions could be used to attract top-quality people without initially breaking the salary norms of sleepy universities. Subsequently, the institutes might invigorate the neighboring universities. Alternatively, top researchers could have university positions with normal Canadian salaries and simultaneous appointments to research institutes to top up their salaries to internationally competitive levels.

A common characteristic of U.S. high-technology clusters is a core of competing, geographically proximate universities surrounded by a ring of research institutes and research-oriented firms. The centre of the Route 128 cluster in Massachusetts is Greater Boston, which contains MIT, Harvard, Boston University, Boston College, Northeastern University, the University of Massachusetts, Suffolk College, Brandeis University, Tufts University, Simmons College, Wellesley College, and many other advanced education institutions. The high-technology cluster in North Carolina is built around a "research triangle" encompassing Duke University, the University of North Carolina and North Carolina State University. That in northern California is centred on Stanford, but draws on several universities in the California state systems, most noticeably U.C. Berkeley.

The reasons for this clustering are not fully understood. The right mixture of competition and cooperation between these schools may be critical, or knowledge used in one firm may "spill over" to others, or a critical mass of skilled people may be the essential factor.

Certainly, it makes sense for knowledge-based firms to locate where a pool of skilled labour already exists. This reduces recruiting costs and competition between job applicants keeps salaries more under control. Similarly, risk-averse skilled workers are drawn to places where many potential employers are located first, because competition between employers drives wages up, and second, because high-technology ventures are often high-risk propositions. If one employer goes broke, or just fails to take off, this is certainly less traumatic with a multitude of other employment opportunities at hand.

Labour market flexibility can be increased or decreased by government policies. The allowable vesting rules for pension plans are one factor that appears to prevent workers from moving readily from one firm to another. If pensions are not portable, jobs at high-risk enterprises become relatively less attractive.[21] Excessive job security laws both deter companies from hiring people in the first place and lessen employees' incentives to keep their knowledge up to date.[22] Ironclad tenure no longer exists in many universities, including the University of Alberta, and is even eroding in the civil service. In a knowledge-based economy, with high bankruptcy rates and rapid turnover in the ranks of leading corporations, legally mandated job security is a costly anachronism.

Policy Implication: Labour laws should aim to reduce the pain of job changes rather than the frequency of them. The focus should be on "risk management," not risk elimination.

As we argued in the chapter on "Economic Underpinnings of a Knowledge-Based Economy," it makes more sense for government to help people manage the inevitable risks in their careers than to quixotically strive to eliminate those risks.

Many commentators on the knowledge-based economy express grave doubts about the prospects of low-skill workers. Canada's unskilled workers have done relatively well off industries like oil, mining and assembly-line manufacturing. Are their incomes now at risk? It is too early to tell, but we doubt it. At the turn of the century, the majority of jobs in Canada were in agriculture. Agriculture became more automated in the 1920s as companies like International Harvester came of age, and farm labour jobs largely disappeared. Entrepreneurs found other uses for these people they did not all become permanently unemployed. The wages of unskilled workers probably have to fall until a new knowledge-based industry finds uses for them. In the 1930s, it was hard to predict that GM would hire tens of thousands of unskilled workers in the 1950s.

We do not know who will hire unskilled workers in the 21st century, but unless governments make it impossible, someone will. Perhaps the only opportunities for the unskilled will be in fast food restaurants, but we doubt it. If emerging economies continue to exhibit high volatility and political instability, as Russia and Indonesia now do, companies in the developed world will be reluctant to move production facilities there merely to tap low-cost unskilled labour. If emerging economies stabilize and prosper, their wage costs will rise rapidly, as in Singapore, Korea and Japan, and again the advantage of relocating production there will disappear.

Government can help minimize the pain of the transition. Education opportunities for adults, laws that protect the mobility of pensions, guaranteed free movement of workers between provinces, and the removal of artificial barriers to entry around trades and professions all help. Universities and colleges can be encouraged to offer "fast-track" degree programs for adults.

4.7   Government in the Nordic Tradition

Canada's experiments with social democracy have borrowed heavily from the Nordic countries, especially Sweden. An old Nordic legend tells of the Viking high king, Canute the Great, Lord of Denmark, Norway, Sweden and England, who tired of his ministers' and courtiers' continual flattery and begging for favours. The king ordered his throne and court moved to the beach, and then decreed that the tide should not come in. He ordered the ministers and courtiers to stand by the throne as the tide nonetheless rose, drenching them all. The moral of this story is that there are some things totally beyond the power of government, even in an absolute monarchy like Canute's realm.

Canada needs to learn from the ancient wisdom of the Nordic countries what their own modern history forgot. The power of the state is limited, sometimes severely. Even if the goal of public policy is made more modest, like empowerment instead of equality, trade-offs still limit the possibilities. Trying to open every door for everyone would require exorbitant taxes that would quickly swing most doors shut. Opening the most doors for the most people implies accepting a trade-off.

In the past, economists regarded government as a power above the economy, an umpire that could regulate and direct it, but not part of the game. This model makes little sense in a knowledge-based economy, for its government is a key part of the economy. If a country's government is not competitive, the economy itself is also not competitive.

We have argued that a competitive government provides only the public goods people want and does so at the lowest possible price. A competitive government in a knowledge-based economy should also be innovative. It should always be searching for more efficient ways of producing existing public goods and for popular new public goods that might replace or supplement existing ones.

Policy Implication: Competitive government is innovative, cost-effective government. It need not be the smallest possible government.

People do want publicly provided goods and services. Skilled people and knowledge-based firms do not flee Massachusetts and California for Arkansas and Louisiana, even though this move would reduce their taxes. People and companies value the superior education systems, honest judicial systems, and smoothly paved highways their higher taxes make possible.

The issue is value for money, not the size of government *per se*. Innovators, skilled knowledge creators, and entrepreneurs will locate in jurisdictions that provide the most desirable public goods and services at the best price. The task of government in a knowledge-based economy is therefore to determine what public goods people want and then to find ways to deliver them more cheaply than other governments without compromising quality. Unsurprisingly, this is exactly how knowledge-based companies have to behave to retain their customers. Innovative, knowledge-based economies need innovative, knowledge-based governments.

An example of this is municipal government in Silicon Valley, California. In a typical municipality it can take weeks or months to procure the approvals, stamps and permits necessary to begin construction. Competition between municipalities there has recently come to a pinnacle with Santa Clara County's Internet-based building permit system. Contractors need not even go to city hall, they just have to point and click. Fussy Yuppie residents nonetheless safeguard neighbourhood characteristics and quality control by having these characteristics incorporated into the computerized system.

Many of Canada's regional governments appear, at first blush, rather uncompetitive. Canada's attempt to prevent internal migration by equalizing economic outcomes across provinces and regions with equalization transfers has the pernicious side-effect of propping up inefficient governments.

The uncomfortable, and rarely discussed, relationship between tax burden and economic performance across provinces is displayed in Table 2 and graphed in Figure 2. Poor provinces have high tax burdens and rich provinces have low tax burdens.

Table 2: Tax burdens across provinces and provincial economic performance

Province	Income tax on C$100,000 wages	PST and GST based on 10% savings rate	Total taxes	Pretax GDP per capita
British Columbia	$37,614	$7,861	$45,475	$27,478
Alberta	$35,029	$4,093	$39,122	$31,078
Saskatchewan	$39,572	$7,614	$47,186	$23,895
Manitoba	$38,654	$7,730	$46,384	$23,139
Ontario	$37,013	$8,503	$45,516	$28,376
Quebec	$40,603	$7,751	$48,354	$23,796
New Brunswick	$37,991	$8,371	$46,362	$20,824
Nova Scotia	$37,239	$8,473	$45,712	$19,996
Prince Edward Island	$37,967	$9,491	$47,458	$19,030
Newfoundland	$40,054	$8,093	$48,147	$17,299
Average	$38,174	$7,798	$45,972	$23,491

The income tax calculation uses the computer package Quick Tax and assumes a dependent spouse and two dependent children. The taxpayer's wages are the only source of income.
GDP per capita is from Statistics Canada, 1996 year-end figures.

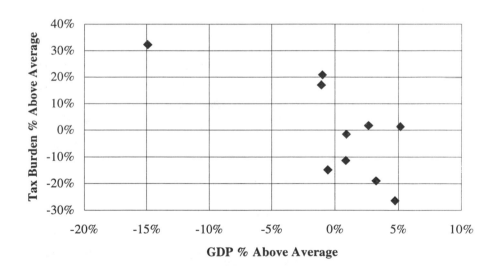

Source: Table 2

Figure 2: Above-average tax burden versus above-average income. Each observation corresponds to one province.

Figure 2 shows a clear negative relationship between tax burden and per capita GDP. Since all Canada's provinces provide roughly similar public goods and services, the vertical axis of Figure 2 can be thought of as the cost premium (or discount) different provinces give their citizens. Cheaper public goods and services accompany higher incomes.

This reasoning suggests that Canada's "have-not" provinces might be poor because their governments are uncompetitive. They cost more than governments in the "have" provinces, but produce public goods and services that are, at best, similar to those available in "have" provinces.

The implication is that interprovincial equalization payments penalize competitive provincial governments and subsidize uncompetitive provincial governments. They thus lower the overall quality of government in Canada.

Policy Implication: Interprovincial equalization transfer payments should be phased out.

Interprovincial equalization may have another unintended pernicious effect. It may block the natural formation of such local concentrations of innovative businesses and knowledge. This discourages innovative businesses that require such concentrated pools of talent. The shortage of such employers makes knowledge-based industry careers less attractive in Canada than they would otherwise be. Further market-driven centralization of Canada's economic activity may be desirable. Depressed regions of the country should ultimately benefit as emigration and business failures force their regional governments to provide better public services at lower cost.

4.8   No Special Deals

Governments that compete with each other to offer special subsidies and tax concessions to potential new businesses are not providing good government. Businesses that do business by haggling, like car dealers, are regarded with suspicion, even when they are giving the customer a good deal. Businesses long ago learned that fixed prices are an important signal of honesty and impartiality, and these perceptions are good for business. Governments need to absorb the same lessons.

Policy Implication: Do not provide special subsidies or tax breaks to chosen companies.

Aside from the public relations costs of such deals, governments have a very poor track record at picking winners. Even Japan's once lauded Ministry of International Trade and Industry (M.I.T.I.) has been humbled by careful econometric studies showing that it mainly propped up losers and certainly did not pick winners.[23] Firms that know they are winners do not need such special deals, and generally do not want them so as to avoid owing favours to politicians. Offering such subsidies and concessions therefore tends to attract only weak, uncompetitive firms.[24] Innovative firms flourish in a competitive environment with cost-effective government that provides sound legal and economic institutions.

When the public learns of multimillion-dollar subsidies to businesses, it is understandably upset.[25] (The feeling is much the same as learning that a neighbour bought the same car you did for $5,000 less). If the subsidized firm goes under anyway, politicians generally end up taking the blame for wasting taxpayers' money. Allegations of corruption usually follow.

To some extent, these popular misgivings are justified by the track record. The Alberta Treasury branch, a provincial bank founded to relieve Alberta farmers during the Depression, has recently become involved in bribery and corruption scandals.[26] In our view, the basic problem is that subsidies attract troubled businesses. Sound ventures neither need nor want them.

Government in a successful KBE must be especially deaf to lobbying by special interests. Creative destruction of necessity destroys non-innovative firms. Out of desperation, many of these turn to lobbying. Where the lobbying is clearly for special favours, it is relatively easy for politicians and civil servants to resist. Therefore, much corporate lobbying by non-innovative firms is for "level playing fields." Such demands should be viewed with suspicion. They are too often euphemisms that really conceal demands for special favours and subsidies. Studies have shown, using both theoretical arguments and empirical data, that "rent-seeking," or investing in lobbying to gain preferential legal or regulatory treatment, is seriously detrimental to economic growth.

Policy Implication: We need a treaty here.

Canada's concentrated capital ownership affects government-business relationships by altering the dynamics of political lobbying. Control pyramids, cross-holdings and restricted voting shares all let controlling shareholders lobby government with other people's money. These altered dynamics make political rent-seeking exceptionally menacing to Canada's success in the global KBE.

4.9 Regulating the Internet

On July 31, 1998, the Canadian Radio-Television and Telecommunications Commission (CRTC) asked Canadians to tell it whether to regulate Internet video and audio real-time services. The CRTC said regulation could be used to promote Canadian culture and to protect youngsters from pornography. While parents' groups reacted enthusiastically, the CRTC itself seemed more concerned about its role in promoting Canadian content than about policing smut on the Internet.[27] The CRTC statement said that its role is to "ensure the availability of high quality and diverse Canadian programming ..." and pointed out that the "substantial growth and development of new media, and their delivery over both global and domestic networks, have not altered this fundamental objective." The CRTC suggests that one way to do this is to force Internet access providers to contribute to a fund for developing Canadian content. This would essentially be a tax on Internet access.

Canada has hate laws and pornography laws that apply to the Internet as well as to any other media. If voters feel they are too weak, these laws can be strengthened. Special laws for Internet smut are probably unnecessary.

Canadian content regulations have become obsolete and no attempt should be made to revive them. The Canadian culture industry has been protected from foreign competition for a full generation now. It can no longer credibly claim to be an infant industry. Canadian cultural industries should now be weaned. They should be exposed to global competition. In our opinion, many Canadian cultural businesses will succeed in this forum. Canadian radio and television are now mature commercial businesses capable of holding their own.

Taxes on Internet access would unnecessarily discourage Canadians from using on-line businesses. This is bad for two reasons. First, access taxes are most likely to deter low-income families from gaining Internet access, widening the gap between their children and the computer-literate children of high-income families. Second, Internet commerce, entertainment, and information access are a potential boon to small, isolated Canadian towns and cities. Anything that artificially deters people from using the Internet only unnecessarily adds to their problems. A geographically dispersed country like Canada is where Internet services are likely to be most valuable.

Policy Implication: The Canadian government should not regulate or restrict Canadians' access to the Internet in any way. The rule in a knowledge-based economy is to facilitate rather than impede information flow.

The CRTC's old mandate, to promote Canadian content, is fulfilled. It is understandably anxious to move on. We suggest that the CRTC's mandate should be changed to one of ensuring that Canadians have the widest possible access to radio, television, and Internet access at the lowest possible price. It could be charged with investigating fraud claims against Internet businesses and with ensuring orderly Internet commerce. In this capacity, the CRTC might well come under the administrative umbrella of Industry Canada. Certainly, the transformation of the CRTC we are suggesting would be as abrupt and dramatic a change as the transformation of the Foreign Investment Review Agency into Investment Canada in the mid-1980s.

4.10 A Compassionate Society?

Canada has a self-image of being a "kinder, gentler" North American society. Canadians feel sorry for losers and envy winners. This is a costly philosophy. The hard-nosed approach of leaving the shareholders and managers of losing firms to swing in the wind probably works out well in the long run. The workers can find jobs if the economy is buoyant enough and shareholders and corporate managers are incongruous recipients of dole money. Unfortunately, the long run is often too long for many voters.

The problem is therefore to find social programs that deal compassionately with the economy's destructive side, but that do not undermine the essential process of creative destruction.

We admit that we do not know how to do this. Clearly, there must be welfare for the unemployable and the seriously ill. Clearly, welfare should not be available to able-bodied loafers. But who is in which category? What should be done with people who are neither loafers nor unemployable? Dealing with these problems will require innovative thinking.

Governments must find ways to deliver social assistance more effectively and at a lower cost. Paying private contractors to run social assistance programs for flat fees should encourage such innovation. Different provinces should be able to try workfare, retooling programs, and other promising innovations. Whistle-blowers who expose corruption or waste in the delivery of social assistance should be rewarded and protected from reprisals. Most importantly, different provinces should be free to try radically different approaches. This lets us try ten times as many alternatives as would be feasible under strict national standards.

Policy Implication: Adherence to national standards in social programs should not be an absolute requirement for provinces. Deviations should be legal if they might lead to innovative new approaches in the delivery of social programs.

5.   CONCLUSION

Canada is part of the global knowledge-based economy, whether we like it or not. We can either restructure our economy on our own terms, or delay change until our economic retardation becomes a crisis. Improving the competitiveness of our government is a key part of the required restructuring.

Economically essential people, and everyone's savings, can and do choose governments. Our government has to out-compete other governments to retain mobile people and capital. It must do this by providing better public goods and services at a lower cost. This is the same goal any other enterprise anywhere must strive for to out-compete its rivals.

In steering towards this goal, our public policy-makers must safeguard the essential features of a knowledge-based economy we sketched out in the chapter "The Economic Underpinnings of a Knowledge-Based Economy". These are individual empowerment, incentives, and continuous change. The basic idea is that empowered individuals should get rich when they come up with innovations that consumers value. This process of economic growth is called creative destruction, because creative new innovators are continually rising to destroy stagnant old firms.

Public policy should support these basic workings of a knowledge-based economy. In particular,

1. Public policy should promote and protect an institutional environment that empowers individuals, creates sensible incentives, and accommodates change. Creative destruction requires both the rise of new businesses and the fall of old ones.
2. Government should provide the public goods and services people want, and only those, at the lowest cost, measured in terms of both actual costs

(taxes, fees, the deficit, and the like) and hidden costs (perverse economic incentives, waste, delay, red tape, and the like).

3. Government should be innovative in the same way businesses in a knowledge-based economy must be innovative. It should constantly be searching for ways to deliver better public goods and services at a lower cost.

These points all require government to recognize that a knowledge-based economy is a people-oriented economy. Knowledge is stored in people more than in companies, ministries, universities, communities, or ethnic groups. It takes human effort to create and apply knowledge. Public policy must be based on how human beings actually behave, not how brainless robots follow instructions. Actual human beings respond to incentives – positive and negative – not government's wishes.

NOTES

[1] This is based on 1,000 interviews done in each of several countries on behalf of the London Business School and Babson College. Both North American countries score markedly better than Western European countries on these measures. Source: Global Entrepreneurship and Opportunity Index, P.L.C.

[2] For a concise introduction to the U.S. tax system and a comparison of the U.S. and OECD countries' tax burdens, see Ch. 2 in Slemrod and Bakija (1996).

[3] Empirical studies have failed to find a clear link over time between U.S. taxes and entrepreneurial activity. This does not refute the existence of such a relationship, as our measures of entrepreneurial data are very unsatisfactory and "expected future taxes" may matter as much as actual current taxes.

[4] The tax burden on "upper-middle-class" Canadian professionals is particularly high. That discourages both the accumulation of human capital, the cornerstone of knowledge-based activities, and innovation *per se*.

[5] See Morck, Stangeland and Yeung (1998).

[6] The allocation of capital through financial markets rather than through banks appears to allow a quicker shift of funds from non-innovative to innovative firms and industries.

[7] See Boycko, Shleifer and Vishny (1996).

[8] This is the basic thesis of the economic literature on "endogenous growth."

[9] See Beard (1915).

[10] See von Hayek (1945).

[11] See Acs, Morck, Shaver and Yeung (1997).

[12] See Beard (1915).

[13] See Bradley and Rosenzweig (1992). See also Buckley (1994a,b).

[14] Some tax experts have argued that founding a business dynasty is an important motive for many entrepreneurs. Other evidence suggests that people use bequests as a way to control the behaviour of their prospective heirs. Clearly, further research in this area is needed.

[15] See Acs, Morck, Shaver and Yeung (1997).

[16] See also Morck (1995).

[17] In the results of the *Third International Mathematics and Science Study*, released November 20, overall Grade 8 science students in Alberta tied for third place with Japan. In mathematics, Alberta Grade 8 students earned a spot in the top one-third of participating countries. The study was conducted between 1994 and 1996. In Alberta, over 2,240 students from 51 schools were tested in 1995. For details, see the ATA News (1996).

[18] This reflects universities' desire to raise more money and voters' desire for cheap education. High out-of-province tuition is a politically perfect tax. It is a tax on foreigners living abroad – or at least parents living out of province. Canadian universities can do this because many foreign students still see them as competitive with U.S. schools of similar quality.

[19] Even researchers need incentives. See Lazear, (1997).

[20] This idea was originally proposed by Marshall (1920). It has been taken up again by Krugman (1995). Empirical support is presented by Henderson, Jaffe, and Trajtenberg (1998) and Adams, and Jaffe (1996).

[21] See Lazear, (1990).

[22] Consider the high unemployment rate in Germany and the poor test results of teachers in public school systems who are required to be recertified.

[23] See Beason and Weinstein (1996).

[24] Conceivably, the negative relationship across provinces between above-average taxes and below-average per capita GDP shown in Figure 2 might reflect this attraction of weak firms to provinces with generous subsidies and correspondingly high taxes.

[25] The ongoing press coverage of subsidies to Montreal aerospace firms featured headlines like "Billions in Federal Loans Unpaid" (*Globe and Mail*, June 13, 1998) and "Ottawa May Hike Bombardier Subsidies" (*Globe and Mail*, September 8, 1998).

[26] See *Globe and Mail* (May 19, 1998).

[27] See *Globe and Mail* (August 1, 1998).

REFERENCES

Acs, Z., R. Morck, M. Shaver and B.Yeung, "The Internationalization of Small and Medium Size Firms: A Policy Perspective." *Small Business Economics*, 9(1), 1997, 7-20.

Adams, J. D. and A. B. Jaffe "Bounding the Effects of R&D: An Investigation Using Matched Establishment-Firm Data." *Rand Journal of Economics,* 27(4), 1996, 700-721.

ATA News, 31(8), November 26, 1996.

Beard, C.A., *Economic Origins of Jeffersonian Democracy.* pp. 270-72, 1915.

Beason, R. and D. Weinstein, "Growth, Economies of Scale, and Targeting in Japan (1955-1990)." *Review of Economics & Statistics,* 78(2), 1996. 286-295.

Boycko, Shleifer and Vishny, "A Theory of Privatization." *Economic Journal,* 106(435), 1996, 309-319.

Bradley, M. and M. Rosenzweig "It's Time to Scrap Chapter 11." *Business Credit,* 94(8), 1992, 40.

Buckley, F. H., "The American Stay," *Law &,* 3(3), 1994a, 738-779.

Buckley, F. H., "The American Fresh Start". *Law &,* 4(1), 1994b, 67-97.

Globe and Mail, "A Black Mark for Alberta." May 19, 1998.

Globe and Mail, "Billions in Federal Loans Unpaid." June 13, 1998.

Globe and Mail, "CRTC Asks if It Should Regulate the Internet." August 1, 1998.

Globe and Mail, "Ottawa May Hike Bombardier Subsidies." September 8, 1998.

von Hayek, F. A., "The Use of Knowledge in Society." *American Economic Review*, 35, 1945, 519-530.

Henderson, R., A.B. Jaffe and M. Trajtenberg "Universities as a Source of Commercial Technology: A Detailed Analysis of University Patenting, 1965-1988." *Review of Economics & Statistics,* 80CD, 1998, 119-112.

Krugman, P. R., *Development, Geography, and Economic Theory.* Cambridge, MA: MIT Press, 1995.

Lazear, E. P., "Pensions and Deferred Benefits as Strategic Compensation." *Industrial Relations* 29(2), 1990, 263-280.

Lazear, E. P., "Incentives in Basic Research." *Journal of Labor Economics*, 15(1) (Part 2), 1997, S167-S197.

Marshall, A. "Industrial Organization, Continued - The Concentration of Specialized Industries in Particular Localities," Chapter X in Book IV (The Agents of Production, Land, Labour, Capital and Organization) of the *Principles of Economics*, 8th edition. Philadelphia, PA: Porcupine Press, 1920.

Morck, R., "The Corporate Governance of Multinationals," in R. Daniels and R. Morck (eds.) *Corporate Decision Making and Governance in Canada*. Ottawa: Industry Canada, Canadian Government Printing Office, 1995.

Morck, R., D. Stangeland and B. Yeung, "Inherited Wealth, Corporate Control and Economic Growth: The Canadian Disease." NBER working paper, 1998.

Slemrod, J. and J. Bakija, *Taxing Ourselves: A Citizen's Guide to the Great Debate Over Tax Reform*. Cambridge, MA: MIT Press, 1996.

Zucker, L. G. and M. R. Darby, "Star Scientists and Institutional transformation: Patterns of Invention and Innovation in the Formation of the Biotechnology Industry." *Proceedings of the National Academy of Sciences*, 93, 1996, 12709-12716.

15. BRINGING IT TOGETHER: SOME POLICY CHALLENGES

Élisabeth Lefebvre
École Polytechnique & CIRANO

Louis A. Lefebvre
École Polytechnique & CIRANO

Pierre Mohnen
Université du Québec à Montréal & CIRANO

This book has addressed some complex and difficult issues facing individuals, organizations and governments doing business in a knowledge-based economy (KBE). In this last chapter, we will try to map out the major issues raised in the preceding chapters and examine some of the challenges for those involved in formulating microeconomic policies. Our objective here is not to substitute ourselves to what the authors have proposed in the different chapters or summarize their thoughts, but merely to draw together some of the threads of the arguments the authors have presented in this book.

1. MAJOR ISSUES

By first focusing on the major trends, we tried to understand some of the forces behind the KBE (Part 1). This in turn helped us understand how and why organizations, institutions and industries were restructuring and reorganizing to take these new imperatives into account (Part 2). Only then can governance issues be addressed to support the restructuring and reorganizing of the institutions, organizations, industries and markets (Part 3). In addition, all chapters devoted some attention to public policy. As it is impossible to do justice to all the individual contributions, some, but certainly not all, of the issues raised in this book are illustrated in the following figure.

Trends and forces shaping the new reality (Part 1)	Restructuring and reorganizing (Part 2)	Key governance Issues (Part 3)
Fast rate of technological change	High-tech firms vs high-tech industries	E-commerce and the shifting value chains
Global competition	Management of intellectual capital	Dilemma: invention protection vs the granting of monopoly power
Participation in international networks	Active learning and continuous improvement of skills	Need for a competitive government
Crucial role of knowledge in growth and competition	Organizational adaptation to new technologies	Intellectual property protection and international patent harmonization
The coming of the virtual enterprise and the emergence of the virtual/digital economy	"Infomediaries" reducing transaction costs	Risk management
Increased labour insecurity and income inequality	Strategic partnerships in knowledge creation between government, industry and academia	Mass customization of products and services
Importance of consumers		Compatibility of standards
Flexible production capabilities	Coordination in the presence of network externalities	Managing positive R&D externalities
Liberalization and deregulation		Creating proper incentives
Disappearance of low-value-added intermediaries	Cost of capital in knowledge-based firms	Promoting openness and transparency
Need for continuous innovation		
Growing markets that require constant innovation		

Figure 1: Some major issues raised in preceding chapters

2.   SOME POLICY CHALLENGES

One of the major contributions of this book has been to look at the KBE from many different perspectives. This was made possible by the fact that the authors came from very different backgrounds, as well as from different regions of the world. From this unique mix of papers, four sets of policy challenges seem to emerge. We will briefly outline these challenges in the following pages.

2.1   Searching for New Indicators – The Measurement Challenge

As chapter 1 demonstrates, a significant number of observable indicators are already available to assess some of the key features of a KBE: trade, foreign direct investment, R&D intensity, collaborative agreements, shift of activity towards services, use of information and communication technologies. However, additional indicators are needed to more adequately define the evolving characteristics of a KBE.

Deriving new indicators of a KBE is a challenging task. Knowledge is not an ordinary good from an economic perspective nor is it viewed as a conventional asset from an accounting perspective; neverthless like other goods, it can be produced, exchanged, stored and used, and it is subject to depreciation and obsolescence. Measuring knowledge is hard because it is intangible, partially codifiable but to a great extent tacit. Further, the measurement challenge lies partly in the lack of any precise definition of a KBE (chapter 1) and in the difficulty of deriving empirically valid, comparable and systematic measures for underlying concepts such as knowledge stocks and flows, intellectual assets, human capital, and the rate of obsolescence of knowledge. Chapter 4 examines measures for two key theoretical concepts, namely organizational learning and intellectual capital which are central forces behind the competitiveness of firms.

Because most of the concepts underlying the KBE are multidimensional, we need to combine multiple indicators. A case in point is detailed in chapter 7, which proposes a set of metrics for technological prowess: firms can be considered as high-tech in terms of innovation (coming up with new products or processes), technology use (purchasing and adapting new technologies), worker skills (developing human capital, training). A firm may be very good in one dimension without being proficient in all three. Industry rankings may differ depending on the criterion adopted. Low-tech industries can still have high-tech firms. Following the same line of thought, chapter 5 stressed that successful modernization within firms hinges not just on the extent but also on the specific mosaic of technologies adopted, and on the organizational innovations adopted in conjunction with the technological innovations. The more radical the technology departure, the more radical the required organizational change.

If chapters 1, 4, and 7 place a strong emphasis on metrics, all chapters taken together address the following measurement issues:

(i)   Improve existing indicators of knowledge inputs besides the standard measure of R&D activity, by including training, investments in market research and scanning activities, employees' know-how and competencies, entrepreneurialism and other intangible investments. In addition, it would be useful to collect more data on knowledge outputs besides patents, such as new product announcements or introductions on the market, new technologies developed and commercialized, and innovations of all sorts, including administrative ones.

(ii)   Trace knowledge flows, with a specific emphasis on strategic alliances and acquisitions that promote interactive innovation processes; track R&D externalities arising from the only partial appropriability of knowledge.

(iii)   Develop technometrics to determine the technological and economic performance of technologies (emerging and dominant designs, innovative streams, technology cycles, technological discontinuity standards, rate of obsolescence, general purpose or generic technologies, etc.).

(iv)   Keep track of the structural changes outlined in section 2.3 of this chapter, and in particular the emergence of the digital economy and electronic commerce. The digital economy seems to be growing at a pace we are still struggling to grasp. Broader indicators of Internet use than on-line sales, purchases and orders would be valuable. The economic weight of the so-called "Internet companies" could be assessed. We also need improved methods of measuring the volume and characteristics of business-to-business e-commerce.

(v)   Create cost of capital measures and ways to evaluate technologically intensive start-up firms largely based on intangible capital.

(vi)   Gain more information about changes under way within firms (small and large), with specific attention to knowledge-intensive services, and intensify the collection of quality measures of improved goods and services.

Canadian policy-makers already have access to a rich set of reliable indicators and many pioneering and proactive efforts are currently addressing some of the measurement challenges outlined above. Do we really need additional efforts to develop new indicators without proven records? We believe that the answer is yes. It is crucial for firms, since it allows them to gain the sectorial, national and international intelligence to conduct business in a highly competitive, dynamic environment. Governments need additional indicators to design more appropriate policy programs, to better target expenditures and recipients, to more effectively monitor and more accurately evaluate the impact of public policies on economic growth and employment. Comparable indicators within and across countries are essential for international comparison and benchmarking.

2.2   Knowledge as the Critical Resource – Optimal Frame Conditions

Abundant natural resources, access to labour, capital, and superior technologies were the traditional sources of competitive advantage. While knowledge has always been a factor in social and economic progress, it plays a greater role now than in the past because of the progress in information and telecommunication technologies, increased public education, greater capital mobility, intensified globalization, increased wealth and greater competition. In fact, knowledge is now embedded in commodities and raises their value for consumers; it is a crucial input in virtually every business (chapter 2). Corporations that do not or cannot follow the innovative trend tend to be absorbed or disappear: think of Pan Am, Jaguar, American Motors or Eaton. Knowledge breeds knowledge because ideas move around in search of different applications. Investing in knowledge becomes less risky, as innovation frees up resources and increases demand.

Designing and implementing the frame conditions in which knowledge and knowledge-based organizations can thrive represents a major policy challenge. Among the more important frame conditions, particular attention was paid here to the following: (i) regulatory intervention, especially as regards property rights and competition; (ii) empowerment and appropriability as incentives for knowledge-based innovative firms and individual innovators; (iii) supporting infrastructures for R&D, innovation, the emerging digital/virtual economy, virtual enterprises and e-commerce; and (iv) educational policies.

Regulatory intervention

Intellectual property rights (IPRs), along with the jurisprudence and institutions which administer and enforce them, represent critical frame conditions in a KBE (chapter 12). In fact, intellectual property rights such as patents, trademarks, registered designs, copyrights and legal recognition of trade secrets seem to be playing an increasingly important role. For instance, we are witnessing an increase in patent applications as well as a trend towards more sophisticated use of patents such as thicketing core technologies or accumulating patents for defensive reasons.

An optimal IP policy faces particularly acute problems and controversies (chapter 12). First, globalization is making it more difficult to have an independent IP policy. In particular, it increasingly requires an international patent harmonization with respect to the treatment of priorities, opposition procedures, duration of patents, standards of patentability, etc. Following the WIPO (World Intellectual Patent Office) model and abandoning independent patent examinations are among the policy options available. Second, the balancing act between the incentive and efficiency properties of IPRs is a difficult one: on one hand, underprotection results in insufficient incentives for innovation; on the other, overprotection hinders knowledge flows and the ability to innovate. In the case of R&D-intensive industries such as pharmaceuticals and biotechnology (chapter 9), underprotection has been shown to be related to low levels of innovative activities, R&D spending and foreign investment, suggesting that weak patent protection in knowledge-intensive industries may not be desirable. Third, new technologies create controversies. Biotechnologies and higher life forms, as well as some software inventions, are at the centre of patent controversies, while digital content and the Internet challenge the law of copyright. Acting too hastily to adapt IP protection to these new technologies may lead to an undesirable precedent; and once protection is granted, it is difficult to step back. Fourth, administration and enforcement of IPRs by institutions require adequate funding, timely responses and speedy procedures. For instance, CIPO (the Canadian Intellectual Patent Office), which has significantly less funding than its international counterparts, cannot fully respond to the needs of domestic innovators. Finally, modifications to the current IPR regime require a systemic perspective that integrates related policy choices. Designing an IP policy in a piecemeal fashion may indeed prove to be counterproductive.

Regulatory intervention in matters of competition, in particular the control of mergers and acquisitions (M&As), is another controversial policy issue. As noted in chapter 9, the new wave of mergers and acquisitions in the 1990s which has overwhelmed the wave of the 1980s, is more global in nature and mainly involves R&D firms. The pharmaceuticals and biotechnology industries provide useful insights into M&As between knowledge-intensive firms. Pressures to develop new products, imperatives to reduce costs due to the rise of generics that require less stringent drug testing requirements, the looming prospect of price controls, and the delay in drug approval and patent examinations are among the main reasons for M&As. Some pharmaceutical companies turned to the field of biotechnology and we have witnessed a predominance of acquisitions of U.S. biotech firms by European pharmaceuticals over the last year; the more favourable regulatory environment in the U.S. is one of the main reasons for this trend. In fact, promotion of M&As through reduced regulatory intervention creates synergies, enhances innovation and attracts foreign direct capital. Obviously, the other side of the coin is the danger of excessive market concentration. One point that can be made is that, in research-intensive industries, the potential excessive market power created by M&As is constantly eroded by rapid technological change, the introduction of new products and services, and followers that can exploit leapfrogging possibilities. Overprotection of local industries against M&As may thus prove to be a sub-optimal frame condition for knowledge-intensive firms. Instead, competitiveness should be promoted at the local, national and international levels.

Appropriability of returns and incentives

Empowerment and appropriability of returns are vital requirements in a KBE. It is argued in chapter 2 that:

(i)   given the basic characteristics of knowledge (rival and non-exclusive good), an innovative firm must grow very large very quickly. Hence, knowledge leads to and benefits from expansion, and all hindrances to globalization and access to foreign markets must be abolished;

(ii)   as knowledge-based firms grow, their earnings increase because of economies of scale and decreased dependence on local resources. The unequal distribution of corporate revenues between and within industries that results from this is another characteristic of a KBE;

(iii)   returns to people with specialized knowledge and skills increase and so does the risk of losing one's competitive edge.

The above three points clearly suggest that both firms and individuals should be able to reap the financial returns of their own efforts in knowledge creation and application. Financial incentives to corporate and individual innovators constitute a positive feedback process that enhances further knowledge production and development. Modifications to the tax system, in particular taxation levels and structure, represent one of the starting points for improving financial incentives. More specifically, the size of the overall tax burden in Canada, which is rather high compared to our southern neighbour, should be further reduced. However, increased financial returns should also lead to increased accountability, which requires a cultural shift from "income support" to "income risk management" (chapter 2). The relative emphasis on certain social safety nets may then become less relevant than in the past.

Innovation-supportive infrastructures

Access to capital becomes an overriding concern for knowledge-based enterprises, i.e., organizations that thrive on knowledge as their principal asset. Financing enterprises with little or no tangible assets can be a major challenge, especially before they are listed on a stock exchange (chapter 8). Furthermore, the high cost of capital and scarcity of funds seem to impede their development during the start-up phase.

Privately held, knowledge-based enterprises (especially virtual enterprises) in the start-up phase require special valuation methods and, above all, access to venture capital. In the U.S., where venture capital is rather accessible, it has been shown that a dollar spent on venture capital produces three to five times more patents than a dollar spent on corporate R&D (see work of Samuel Kortum and Josh Lemer). Fostering the formation of venture capital funds is a key challenge for Canadian public policy-makers.

Frame conditions for managing R&D successfully and collaboratively are critical. First, the need for collaboration between the private sector, government and universities, as illustrated in chapter 6, is greater than ever and is particularly effective in the case of NGT (Next Generation Technology) focused research. This type of research "strategically bridges the short-term technology focus of industry with the longer-term science focus of university and the generic technology focus of government." Precompetitive collaboration between firms, government and universities is also quite beneficial for all parties involved. In the U.S., the record of cooperative research and development agreements (CRADA), like the Low Emissions Paint Consortium (LEPC) and the National Center for Manufacturing Sciences (NCMS), appears to be quite positive (chapter 5).

Second, the public management of positive research externalities (chapter 11) is increasingly vital in a KBE. Not only is public intervention needed to encourage these externalities but public authorities, especially in the case of long-term scientific and basic research, must ensure intergroup equity (stimulating research favouring one group of citizens more than another) and intergenerational equity (providing knowledge useful for future generations).

The role of frame conditions in fostering other knowledge-creating activities besides R&D is also essential. The innovative activities arising from continuing interactions between engineering product development, manufacturing and marketing are key requirements for the business success of small and large companies. Building up innovation-supportive infrastructures including technology demonstration centres, networking forums, and organizations responsible for market intelligence, technological scanning and monitoring activities (for instance, emerging standards, dominant designs, etc.) is particularly critical for firms and industries.

Adequate connective physical infrastructures such as roads, railways, airports, and telecommunication networks represent important priorities. However, National Information Infrastructure (NII), which is the backbone of the virtual (or digital) economy (chapter 4), is increasingly becoming the top priority. Continuous improvements are being made and will continue to be made as a result of many technological advances in fibre optic systems, digital compression, storage capacity of computer systems, digital wireless systems and software. Major challenges also arise from non-technological issues, and increased consumer protection, privacy and security are also critical, as pointed out in chapters 3 and 10. Electronic commerce, which is intrinsically linked to the digital economy, is totally dependent on the above-mentioned improvements to the NII. While Canada has developed core competencies, as in telecommunications, we should also ensure a rapid growth in business and commercial applications which are software-driven. There is a real urgency to go beyond merely improving communications systems. An NII/GII without content, applications and services cannot and will not fulfill economic expectations. An additional challenge for policy-makers is to foster the development of e-commerce applications in Canada, considering the very strong presence of U.S.-based applications.

The very characteristics of NII, namely mobility (of knowledge, ideas, capital, etc.), simultaneity (everywhere at once) and pluralism (access to multiple centres of expertise, skills, competitiveness or cultures) strengthen the properties of a KBE. NII and, to an even greater extent, GII represent the most complex, powerful, important and multifaceted infrastructures created to date and will certainly constitute the most challenging innovation-supportive infrastructure of the 21st century (chapter 3).

Educational policies

As argued in chapter 14, knowledge resides in people's mind more than in firms, institutions, ministries, universities or communities: the KBE is essentially a "people-oriented economy." Chapter 4 also emphasizes that superior performance derives from intellectual capital. Education must therefore be a key priority.

Public education systems are already strongly committed to the reinforcement of basic skills. Should they align with the specific skills now urgently needed in the workplace, such as computer literacy, software development expertise, e-commerce competencies or, in broader terms, IT skills? Too much focus on one particular set of skills may result in freezing processes, thus becoming a competence trap. It may therefore be important to enhance a variety of skills in order to avoid the "lock-in phenomenon." The equilibrium between "supply-led" and "demand-led" public educational systems will demand new, innovative approaches and a thorough validation of the needed skills and competencies.

Besides providing public education, governments have a responsibility for supplying information, making firms aware of the need to develop a learning mentality, and establishing connections and incentives to reward success (chapter 4). Learning is subject to externalities and hence underfunding by the private sector. Furthermore, governments and employers are increasingly becoming equally responsible for creating and maintaining "good" jobs, preventing deskilling of the workforce and validating the required skills and competencies.

The KBE puts a real premium on educational policies. These policies should strongly enhance a culture of creativity and innovation and ultimately reinforce the ability of institutions, firms and individuals to continuously learn, adapt and change (i.e., what Douglas Nork calls "adaptive efficiency"). Moreover, heavily institutionalized public education systems and rather scarce employer-sponsored training programs are not adequate to promote life-long learning and will require further changes. Finally, individuals are increasingly responsible for acquiring and maintaining the required skills themselves: making the leap to life-long learning demands major individual efforts. From the perspective of governments, employers and individuals, aligning educational policies to the requirements of a KBE represents a formidable and challenging undertaking.

2.3   Inducing and Adjusting to Structural Changes

The structural changes in a KBE are a palpable reality and several chapters of this book emphasize the necessity for policy-makers to both induce these changes and encourage adjustments in order to facilitate a smooth adaptation for all parties involved. More specifically, the structural changes occur at three main levels: (i) markets, (ii) sectors and industries, and (iii) firms. All of these levels are interlinked.

Structural changes in markets

Markets for goods and services are highly competitive and are currently undergoing profound changes. First, the competitive focus is on the added-value delivered to the final customer. In a customer-centred world (chapters 3 and 14), markets are defined by patterns of consumption and the specific needs of customers and are not dictated by existing lines of production, internal managerial convenience or protective local regulations. Second, norms and standards are a battleground enforcing market dominance for high-tech products such as cellular phones, software or computers. Third, e-commerce is also leading to a reorganization of markets (chapter 10). It allows many gains in terms of cost reductions and broader markets, but the three basic conditions for markets to function well – excludability, rivalry and transparency – are not there, at least in the case of purely informational electronic goods. When access to intangible goods and services which can be digitized and made available very quickly is free, it "represents to some extent the new wealth of the 21st century" (chapter 10).

If markets for goods and services are being restructured, so are the markets for inputs. Capital markets are becoming more open, global and transparent. Many new forms of financing with various degrees of risk and liquidity are invented. Mergers and acquisitions are also taking place among financial institutions in order to broaden their activities, enlarge their markets and decreasing costs. It has argued by several authors that markets for labour need to become more flexible (especially chapters 3 and 14). Labour markets are characterized by increased part-time work, skill-biased demand for labour, and greater wage gaps between skilled and unskilled workers. We have already mentioned that rising labour insecurity is part of the KBE, and workers have to be ready to adjust and acquire new skills as demand for labour changes.

Structural changes in industries and sectors

The restructurating of industries and sectors can be traced to several factors. First, the once regulated industries such as electric power and gas or telecommunications are or are becoming deregulated (chapter 13). Although it is acknowledged that industries are experiencing continuous structural changes through natural selection (in particular due to new entering and exiting firms), deregulation has the potential to transform entire industries. Second, there is a redistribution of activities, revenues and jobs between sectors and industries, in particular from manufacturing to services. Most manufacturing industries already have a strong strategic focus on service activities since manufactured goods are increasingly considered as physical embodiments of knowledge- and intelligence-based activities. Consequently, the traditional distinction between manufacturing and services is becoming blurred. In addition, within the service industries, more attention is being paid to the knowledge-intensive services such as accounting, banking, law, design, marketing and engineering, which rely on highly skilled and mobile professionals. Third, new sectors of economic activity such as multimedia and Internet-providers are emerging. Finally, the digital economy and, more specifically, e-commerce applications, can provide numerous new alternatives to reach and serve customers: this may bypass low-value-added intermediaries (disintermediation) and create new distribution channels or new interfaces such as "infomediaries" (reintermediation). These structural changes can be seen most clearly in industries that are already heavy users of e-commerce applications such as the computer industry, travel services or financial services (including banking), but they will be also persuasive in other industries that are the next candidates for rapid migration towards e-commerce (chapters 3 and 10).

Structural changes in firms

Most firms are adapting to some extent to the structural changes occurring in markets and industries and some are actually causing them. Some firms are responding to and reinforcing the current trend towards accelerated and much fuller integration of global markets. Companies are becoming increasingly global. For instance, recent data reported by Standard and Poor's provide a significant insight into this phenomenon: between 1993 and 1998, the share of sales at GE coming from exports markets increased from 16.5% to 30.1%; corresponding figures for Wal-Mart are 0% vs 13.85%, for McDonald's 46.9% vs. 61.5%, and for Nokia, 85% vs. 97.6%. The rate of technological and non-technological innovation to support these large global markets must be extremely rapid. Hence, high-performing firms transform themselves into learning organizations, which implies both cognitive and behavioural changes (chapter 4). As discussed in chapter 3, they also reorganize their business processes around a product or service in order to better respond to the needs of increasingly demanding and widely dispersed customers: they therefore thrive on mass-customization and redefine their upstream and downstream relationships with their business partners. To supplement traditional cooperative agreements, alliances, mergers and acquisitions, co-opetition – i.e., firms cooperating and competing at the same time – is emerging as a new business paradigm. With respect to e-commerce, several well-known corporations like Dell and GE have developed internally innovative ways of conducting business over the Internet, creating new business models and sending strong signals to their direct competitors. Changes made by firms run deep, from organizational design (chapter 13) to coordination mechanisms (chapter 3). These changes modify not only their internal structures but their relationships with business partners, the latter being part of the on-going industrial restructurating. However, not all firms change in time: organizational lag (chapter 5), organizational inertia (chapter 13) and inadequate management of firm-specific assets, especially intellectual capital (chapter 4), are among the obstacles to change.

Inducing structural changes

Public policy can induce structural changes. For instance, deregulation fundamentally disrupts core industries such as telecommunications or electric power. In particular, it changes the basis of competition and usually provides end consumers with better quality products and services at lower prices. Deregulation does not, however, mean a divestment of public policy efforts. On the contrary, reforms impose their own set of challenges. These reforms must be desirable, feasible and credible which necessitates providing information, creating proper incentives, building commitment and avoiding political manipulation (chapter 13). The involvement of public policy-makers is therefore essential, in both the short and long term. For instance, policy-makers may inherit long-term responsibilities, such as ensuring universal access to essential services.

Public policy may also spur structural changes by assuming a strong leadership role, such as becoming "a pulling factor for Internet uptake and e-commerce" (chapter 10). In fact, Canadian public services are already moving in this direction, encouraging individuals, firms and institutions to interact electronically with the various governmental agencies and profoundly affecting their relationships with government. Despite its inherent difficulties, this major undertaking appears very worthwhile and should be extended to a wider range of government services and activities.

Adjustment to structural changes

Given the structural changes described above, there is a potential threat to exclude people from production and social participation in society, because their skills are no longer required, they are unable to work, live and socially interact in electronically mediated environments, or they are simply in wrong place at the wrong time. Strong resentment against "globalization" and supranational agencies such as the WTO seems to be growing as we have recently seen, although one can argue that it is rather difficult to assess the role and influence of some pressure groups. But these resentments are real, and clearer insights into the social impacts of these structural changes are therefore needed. Although some of the frame conditions proposed in section 2.2 may ease the difficulties related to the necessary adjustments, social cohesion in a KBE certainly constitutes a pressing priority, and poses real challenges for public policy.

Structural changes disrupt firms and industries unevenly. Some of the more traditional, less innovative and less proactive firms (and even industries) may not adjust as quickly as necessary. They may lag behind or even disappear. Should public policy-makers intervene? In certain areas, the answer is yes. For example, the coordination of national and international market policies, a rather thorny problem, falls in the realm of a much needed intervention. With almost 40% of its GNP coming from exports and a rather small domestic market, Canada cannot afford to lag behind. The transition to the digital economy and e-commerce may also be eased by certain public policy initiatives. Governments and supranational agencies are responsible for ensuring that e-commerce entails the same market optimality and social welfare as traditional physical commerce, a fundamental and extremely wide-ranging issue (chapter 10). In order to smooth the transition, serious attention should also be paid to the pattern and pace of migration from traditional to Internet distribution of goods and services, within and between the three basic entities – firms, government and consumers/individuals. Analysis of product value chains and industry value chains may also lead to the identification of the critical core competencies needed for this transition (chapter 3). In other areas, government intervention may not be desirable. For instance, chapters 2 and 14 stress that corporations that cannot follow innovative trends should not be protected, even in a mitigated form. Non-innovators or badly managed firms are replaced by better performing firms, a natural process of selection. In such cases, bankruptcy laws and corporate takeovers should be swift so that productive assets are transferred from less to more able hands. Creative destruction must go on in a KBE, although this may lead to greater labour uncertainty and some other undesirable social impacts in the short run. Nevertheless, in the long term, the overall impact of this creative destruction should be positive.

2.4   Role of Key Entities

The KBE is challenging the traditional role of governments, multinationals and supranational agencies. First, greater economic convergence is limiting the ability of sovereign states to ensure their economic well-being through protectionist measures and reduces both the scope and the effectiveness of national economic policies. Second, national economies are being subsumed into a global system through the dynamics generated by the multinationals' business activities. In fact, most of these multinationals are already transnationals (TNCs). TNCs collectively exert enormous power, and some observers even suggest that they wield excessive influence. Economic activity is greatly concentrated within their hands as they control large amounts of capital that is considered "footloose" and, to a great extent, determine technological paths internationally while imposing their own business models, norms and standards (chapter 3). Third, national governments are relying on a more coordinated and cooperative approach to regulation and working closely with supranational agencies such as the WTO, WIPO and ITU. All these points suggest that the conventional foundations of governance are being challenged.

The relative influence of governments, TNCs and supranational agencies is changing, but this does not mean that the role of national governments is more limited in a KBE. In fact "good" government is critical, (chapter 14) and sections 2.1, 2.2 and 2.3 of this chapter have outlined some proposed courses of action along with the challenges they raise. In some respects, the role of national government is similar to what it was: government-driven consumption of goods and services and government-led procurement of technology can make a substantial difference. When government acts as a catalyst and lead user of new digital electronic/e-commerce applications, its role remains essentially traditional, and only the technology (i.e., digital technology) has changed. In other respects, the new governance implies several important shifts: (i) public policy issues are increasingly both domestic and international in scope; (ii) they rely to a greater extent on "soft" standards and procedures as opposed to "hard" laws and regulations; (iii) they favour greater economic openness rather than protectionist measures; and (iv) they promote more decentralized, diversified, competitive and customer-oriented public services, where the customer is the citizen, the taxpayer, the corporation, etc. The changing role of national governments represents indeed a formidable challenge. Good government in a KBE mainly depends on the ability of its public policy-makers to mobilize resources, their commitment to continuously innovate and their long-term vision of socially and economically desirable outcomes. Thus, new governance in a KBE is highly knowledge-intensive.

3.   IN CONCLUSION

We have covered a lot of ground in this book and have favoured a truly multidisciplinary approach. Collectively, all the chapters provide a unique and refreshing vision of a KBE, raising some critical issues for public policy. In this concluding chapter, four sets of challenges were presented. They intertwine and interact to some extent but, for purposes of discussion, were presented individually. None of these challenges is or will be easy to meet, but we hope that they will stimulate discussion and ultimately be useful for the development of specific courses of action.

INDEX

A

Accounting services, ranking of, 230
Acquisitions
  biotechnology, 273-306
  pharmaceuticals, 273-306
ADARDS. *See* Australian ADARDS (Alzheimer's
  Disease and Related Disorders)
Advanced Networks and Services, 164
Advanced Research Projects Agency, 163
Advertising agencies, ranking, 230
Aerospace industry
  collaboration agreements, 8
  research and development, 276
Aeterna Laboratories, Inc., 259
Aircraft industry
  research and development, 36
  technology acquired from abroad, 23
Allelix Biopharmaceuticals, Inc., 259
Alphanet Telecom, Inc., 259
American Society for Training and Development,
  131
Amusement services
  knowldege workers in, 29
  ranking of, 230
Apparel industry
  research and development, 36
  share of information technology investment, 26
  technology acquired from abroad, 23
Applications for patent, pharmaceutical,
  biotechnology industries, 284-285
Architects, ranking, 230
ARPA. *See* Advanced Research Projects Agency
AUSTRALIA
  growth in importance of service production, 4
  share of labour force with post-secondary
    degree, 25
Australian ADARDS (Alzheimer's Disease and
  Related Disorders), 144
Austria, growth in importance of service
  production, 4
Austrian School of Economics, 60-63
Automotive industry
  collaboration agreements, 8
  industry classification of, 229
  ranking of, 230
  research and development, 36, 276
  services ranking, 230
  share of information technology investment, 26
  technology acquired from abroad, 23

B

Ballard Power Systems, Inc., 259
Banking, internet, effect on banks, 321
Battery Technologies, Inc., 259
Beanie Baby, knowledge-based marketing
  technique, 52
Behavior, change in, learning process and, 121

Belgium

Belgium
  growth in importance of service production, 4
  share of labour force with post-secondary
    degree, 25
Beverage industry
  industry classification of, 229
  research and development, 36
  services ranking, 230
  share of information technology investment, 26
  technology acquired from abroad, 23
Biomira, Inc., 259
Bioniche, Inc., 259
Biotechnology industry
  clustering, in United States, 292
  foreign investment, in United States, 290-291
  growth of, 286
  innovation policy, performance in, 294-296
  international competition, 273-306
  patent controversy, 358-360
  research and development, 288
Biovail Corporation International, 259
Blue-collar workers
  high-skilled, per country comparison, 5
  low-skilled, per country comparison, 5
Business platforms, access to, 108
Business sector, manufacturing
  Canadian labour productivity growth, 33
  productivity growth, Canada, 33
Business services industry
  ranking, 230
  research and development, 36
  share of information technology investment, 26

C

CAD. *See* Computer-aided design
CALS. *See* Continuous Acquisition and
  Life-Cycle Support
Canada
  biotechnology industry, regulation, innovation,
    295-296
  business sector, manufacturing, productivity
    growth, 33
  competitiveness ranking with United States, 32
  cost of capital, for knowledge-based
    enterprises, 239-272
  distribution of worker skills, 5
  economy, 21-32
  emerging knowledge economy in, 21-39
  empowerment, as equality, 433-435
  expenditure on research and development, as
    percentage of GDP, 35
  expenditures, research and development, 35
  Free Trade Agreement, 22
  gross domestic product, share of exports,
    imports, 22
  growth in importance of service production, 4
  GST, replacement of, 435-438